T0330724

BONDED LABOUR AND DEBT IN THE INDIAN OCEAN WORLD

Financial History

BONDED LABOUR AND DEBT IN THE INDIAN OCEAN WORLD

EDITED BY

Gwyn Campbell and Alessando Stanziani

Routledge
Taylor & Francis Group

LONDON AND NEW YORK

First published 2013 by Pickering & Chatto (Publishers) Limited

Published 2016 by Routledge
2 Park Square, Milton Park, Abingdon, Oxfordshire OX14 4RN
711 Third Avenue, New York, NY 10017, USA

First issued in paperback 2015

Routledge is an imprint of the Taylor & Francis Group, an informa business

© Taylor & Francis 2013
© Gwyn Campbell and Alessando Stanziani 2013

BRITISH LIBRARY CATALOGUING IN PUBLICATION DATA

Bonded labour and debt in the Indian Ocean world. – (Financial history)
1. Peonage – Indian Ocean Region – Case studies.
I. Series II. Campbell, Gwyn, 1952– editor of compilation. III. Stanziani, Alessandro editor of compilation.
306.3'63'091824-dc23

ISBN-13: 978-1-138-66471-5 (pbk)
ISBN-13: 978-1-8489-3378-1 (hbk)

Typeset by Pickering & Chatto (Publishers) Limited

CONTENTS

ACKNOWLEDGEMENTS

We would like to acknowledge the support of the Agence nationale de la recherche (ANR), France; the Fonds de recherche sur la société et la culture (FQRSC), Québec; and the Social Sciences and Humanities Research Council (SSHRC) of Canada. Many thanks also to Ruben Post for his editorial assistance.

LIST OF CONTRIBUTORS

Edward A. Alpers is Research Professor Emeritus of History at the University of California, Los Angeles. He has also taught at the Universities of Dar es Salaam, Tanzania (1966–8), and the Somali National University, Lafoole (1980). In 1994 he served as President of the African Studies Association (USA). Alpers has published widely on the history of East Africa and the Indian Ocean. His major publications include *Ivory and Slaves in East Central Africa* (1975); *Walter Rodney: Revolutionary and Scholar*, co-edited with Pierre-Michel Fontaine (1982); *Africa and the West: A Documentary History from the Slave Trade to Independence*, with William H. Worger and Nancy Clark (2001; 2nd edn 2010); *History, Memory and Identity*, co-edited with Vijayalakshmi Teelock (2001); *Sidis and Scholars: Essays on African Indians*, co-edited with Amy Catlin-Jairazbhoy (2004); *Slavery and Resistance in Africa and Asia*, co-edited with Gwyn Campbell and Michael Salman (2005); *Slave Routes and Oral Tradition in Southeastern Africa*, co-edited with Benigna Zimba and Allen F. Isaacman (2005); *Resisting Bondage in Indian Ocean Africa and Asia*, co-edited with Gwyn Campbell and Michael Salman (2007); *Cross-Currents and Community Networks: The History of the Indian Ocean World*, co-edited with Himanshu Prabha Ray (2007); *East Africa and the Indian Ocean* (2009); and *The Indian Ocean in World History* (2013). Professor Alpers has served as chair for fifty-nine PhD dissertations.

Gwyn Campbell is Canada Research Chair in Indian Ocean World History and Director of the Indian Ocean World Centre at McGill University. Author of *An Economic History of Imperial Madagascar, 1750–1895* (2005) and *David Griffiths and the Missionary 'History of Madagascar'* (2012), he is currently completing *Africa and the Indian Ocean World from Early Times to 1900* to appear in the new Cambridge Economic History of Africa series. He is also editor or co-editor of a number of studies of slavery, including *Abolition and its Aftermath in Indian Ocean Africa and Asia* (2005); *The Structure of Slavery in Indian Ocean Africa and Asia* (2004); *Children and Slavery*, 2 vols (2009 and 2010); *Women and Slavery*, 2 vols (2007 and 2008); and *Resisting Bondage in Indian Ocean Africa and Asia* (2007).

William Gervase Clarence-Smith is Professor of the Economic History of Asia and Africa, at the School of Oriental and African Studies (SOAS), University of London. He has written *Islam and the Abolition of Slavery* (2006), and also edited *The Economics of the Indian Ocean Slave Trade in the Nineteenth Century* (1989). He has written more widely on colonialism, diasporas, sexuality, transport, agriculture and livestock.

Isabelle Guérin is Senior Research Fellow at the Institute of Research Development/Paris I Sorbonne University (Research Unit 'Development and Societies'), and a research associate at the French Institute of Pondicherry and CERMi. Her academic interest spans from the political and moral economy of money, debt and labour to the social economy, NGOs interventions, empowerment programmes and linkages with public policies. She coordinates the research programme 'Labour, finance and social dynamics' at the French Institute of Pondicherry. She is also leading the RUME project (rural employment and microfinance, www.rume-rural-microfinance.org) and the Microfinance in Crisis project (www.microfinance-in-crisis.org).

Matthew S. Hopper is Associate Professor in the History Department at California Polytechnic State University, San Luis Obispo. He completed his PhD in History at UCLA in 2006, and was a postdoctoral fellow at the Gilder Lehrman Center at Yale University in 2009. His writing has recently appeared in *Annales*, *Itinerario* and the *Journal of African Development*. His book on the history of the African Diaspora in Eastern Arabia will be published by Yale University Press in 2014.

Bok-rae Kim is professor of European Culture and Tourism at the Andong National University, South Korea. She received her PhD in history from the University of Paris I Panthéon-Sorbonne. Since 2003, she has published several articles on Korean *nobis* in comparative perspective. She is particularly interested in a comparative history among China, Korea and Japan.

Yoko Matsui is Professor at the Section for Overseas Materials of the Historiographical Institute, University of Tokyo, specialized in the relationships between Japan and foreign countries in the early modern period (Edo/Tokugawa period), namely the relationship with the Dutch and engaged in compiling and translating the diaries kept by the heads of the Dutch factory in Japan. Matsui's recent research focuses on the people who had direct contact with the foreigners in the port city of Nagasaki, such as interpreters, suppliers and prostitutes.

Ei Murakami is Associate Professor of Institute for Research in Humanities, Kyoto University, Japan. He obtained his PhD from the University of Tokyo in

2012. His main academic interests are socio-economic history of modern China and maritime history of East and South China Sea. He is the author of *Umi no Kindai Chugoku: Fukkenjin no katsudo to Shincho* (Maritime History of Modern China: Local Fujian Actors and British and Chinese Empires) (2013).

Susan Newton-King is an associate professor at the University of the Western Cape. She completed her undergraduate studies at the University of Cape Town and received her PhD from the University of London in 1993. Her doctoral dissertation was published by Cambridge University Press under the title *Masters and Servants on the Cape Eastern Frontier, 1760–1806* (1999). Her present research concerns the formation of social identities in eighteenth-century Cape Town and the interconnections between Cape Town and the Indian Ocean world.

Michael Salman is an associate professor of history at the University of California, Los Angeles. He is the author of *The Embarrassment of Slavery: Controversies over Bondage and Nationalism in the American Colonial Philippines* (2003) and other publications.

Alessandro Stanziani is Professor of Economic and Global History at the EHESS and at the CNRS (Paris). He has worked on the history of competition, markets and food in France and Europe (eighteenth to twentieth centuries) and bondage and forced labour in Central Asia, Russia and the Indian Ocean (sixteenth to twentieth centuries). He is the author of *L'économie en révolution, le cas russe* (1998); *Histoire de la qualité alimentaire* (2005); *Rules of Exchange. French Capitalism in Comparative Perspective* (2012), *Labour, Coercion and Growth in Eurasia* (2012) and *Bâtisseurs d'Empires. Russie, Inde et Chine* (2012).

James Francis Warren is Professor of Southeast Asian Modern History at Murdoch University. He has held teaching and research positions at the Australian National University, Yale University, McGill University, National University of Singapore and Kyoto University. His current research focuses on slavery and the creation of trans-cultural identities and aspects of the environmental history of Southeast Asia. Warren's more recent publications include *The Sulu Zone, the World Capitalist Economy and the Historical Imagination* (1998) and *Pirates, Prositutes and Pullers Explorations in the Ethno – and Social History of Southeast Asia* (2008). In 2003, he was awarded the Centenary Medal of Australia for service to Australian society and the Humanities in the study of Ethnohistory, and in 2013, the Grant Goodman Prize in Historical Studies. He lives in Perth, Western Australia with his wife Carol, an anthropologist, and daughter Kristin, a wildlife medicine veterinarian and conservationist.

INTRODUCTION

Gwyn Campbell and Alessandro Stanziani

Context

This volume examines the relationship between debt and human bondage in the Indian Ocean world (IOW). The IOW refers to a vast macro region, running from Africa to the Far East, where agricultural production, in which the vast bulk of the population were engaged, and long-distance commercial exchange, notably but not exclusively maritime trade, were largely shaped by the monsoon system. The 'wet' (rice) and 'dry' (wheat) cultivation regions of Asia were largely dictated by the reach of the monsoon rains, while the monsoon winds (from the south-west during the northern hemisphere summer and from the north-east during its winter), dictated trans-oceanic exchange to the north and to approximately twelve degrees south of the equator. Moreover, terrestrial long-distance trade in regions affected by the monsoons and/or a cyclone season was also largely seasonal, restricted chiefly to the drier winter season.

Human trafficking in the IOW has taken place since at least 2000 BC and experienced three major periods of demand-led acceleration corresponding to sustained bursts of economic growth: from about 200 BC to AD 200, from the ninth to thirteenth centuries, and again from the nineteenth century. In the intervening periods, which were generally characterized by economic stagnation or decline, the slave trade was dominated by supply factors.[1] Systems of bondage existed throughout the IOW but varied greatly according to time and place. Slavery was limited amongst hunter-gatherer and pastoral peoples, but relatively widespread in sedentary agricultural societies. Few resembled the brutal regime of chattel slavery that dominates the popular image of slavery based on the transatlantic slave trade and American slavery, which in the IOW was largely confined to a few European-supervised plantation economies, such as those developed on the Mascarene islands in the late eighteenth and early nineteenth centuries. Chattel slavery represented one extreme of a wide spectrum of systems of bondage in which, occasionally, as in some agrestic societies in India, slaves could be sold only with the land they lived on, and sometimes, as in the case of concubines in Muslim societies who had borne their master a child, could not be sold. Most of those subject to IOW bondage systems were accorded rights; some rose to positions of influence and wealth superior to that of nominally free peasants, and a few even became sovereigns and founded dynasties. They comprised people of all ethnic and cultural backgrounds. Overall, black Africans formed a minority of slaves in the IOW, constituting a majority only in Africa and, at certain periods, in other lands littoral to the Western Indian Ocean. Moreover, most of those enslaved and trafficked in the IOW were women and children.[2]

It is impossible in a brief volume to evaluate the historical relationship between debt and bondage in all IOW societies, from early times to the present. The contributions here concentrate on the period from the mid-eighteenth century. However, what they clearly demonstrate is that there was considerable continuity, as well as change, in the transition from older forms of debt-related bondage to the new ones that emerged with the forces accompanying the international economy that developed in the long nineteenth century, namely European colonialism and the more recent process of globalization.

Debt and Enslavement

Indebtedness was central to both the process of enslavement and to slavery. Slavery first developed as a significant social institution in the centralized hierarchical polities of the Middle East, South Asia and the Far East. These were at the core of the Neolithic Revolution that enabled the production of agricultural surpluses sufficient to maintain the ruling elite, and eventually a specialized artisanal sector as well as a merchant class that traded agricultural and craft products. Agricultural surpluses and the imposition of forced labour permitted the formation of standing armies used by the elite to expand its frontiers. When successful, these armies generally killed male opponents and enslaved their women and children. The chief reason adult male opponents were killed was because they would be more likely to resist and revolt, and thus required heavy surveillance and, whenever necessary, physical restraint.[3] They were also less amenable than women and children to adapt to, and adopt, the mores of the victor society. Moreover, as the labour for agricultural production and public works was generally satisfied by the existing subject population,[4] the costs of transport and supervision usually outweighed the benefits of enslaving adult males. All enslaved captives owed their lives to their captors, to whom they were thus totally indebted. Slave-raiding early became a major motive of such campaigns, and a class of specialist slave-raiders emerged.[5]

Army commanders and traders marched enslaved women and child captives back to the imperial centre to be distributed as prizes by members of the court and army generals, or sold to those who could afford them. This is, for example, the reputed origin of bondage as a significant institution in Mesopotamia in the third millennia BC[6] – records from the reign of Zimrilim, king of Mari (r. *c.* 1775–61 BC) indicate that probably some two-thirds of bondspeople in Babylonia were female.[7] As servile non-slave subjects provided most menial productive labour, the majority of the enslaved were absorbed into court or elite households. As their numbers grew, the bulk of the enslaved in elite households became used as objects of conspicuous consumption both in private and in public reflecting the wealth and power of the owner. In all cases, however, they represented indebted bodies.

A second form of early enslavement occurred when conquering armies overran settled agricultural communities without meeting resistance. Military commanders then executed possibly few if any male leaders and maintained the captive communities, whose members were also indebted to their captors for preserving their lives, *in situ* in a form of bondage that tied them to the land. The conquered land was distributed by the court to leading supporters, who thus also owned the bondspeople on it as well as the products of their labour. This is most clearly seen in agrestic forms of servitude that developed in South India. However, it is also reflected in forms of bondage, such as developed after the Persian conquest of Babylonia in 539 BC, when Persians forced non-slave but conquered Babylonians to help construct the palace of Darius I (r. 521–486 BC) in Susa;[8] and in Imerina (Madagascar) in the late eighteenth century, when warlords who emerged victorious in civil wars tied newly subjected peoples – who owed their lives to the new sovereign (described as 'god') – to the land and organized them into 100 to 1,000-strong territorially-based units that they employed in unremunerated forced labour (*fanompoana*) for public works.[9]

Nevertheless, the greatest supply of slaves and other forms of servile labour in the IOW over the *longue durée* was probably more a result of non-violent, local, even intimate forces. Some people were sold into slavery by their families or larger kinship groups. Others voluntarily entered slavery, such as, for instance, certain Filipino girls who chose to become concubines of high status Sulu males.[10] Possibly the majority of people enslaved through non-violent means in the IOW did so as a result of debt. Indebtedness is a universal phenomenon that directly imposes obligations upon the debtor to the creditor which, when formally witnessed and agreed to, have the sanction of customary law, even where this differs from statutory law.[11] Traditionally, enslavement was legally enforced for debtors and their relatives in many IOW regions. In Imperial Madagascar, for instance, creditors could through the application of law enslave a debtor, his wife and children.[12] This was also the customary practice in Thailand and Malaya.[13]

High legal interest rates – such as the rate of 50 per cent or more normal in late Chosun Korea (1392–1910) – caused many debtors to default on debts.[14] Indeed, because interest rates were so exorbitant, those seeking debts often knew that the likely outcome of their action would be enslavement – to the extent that for some it was tantamount to voluntary entry into bondage.[15] In addition, the punishment for certain crimes was exacted in fines, which often led to indebtedness and subsequent enslavement;[16] such enslaved debtors could, however, regain non-slave status if they managed to pay off their debts. In the same vein, in the nineteenth-century Sulu Sultanate, acts of sexual impropriety, notably adultery, were punished by fines so heavy that many of those convicted became so indebted that they were forced to enter debt bondage – which could become permanent.[17] As Bok-rae Kim points out in her chapter, enslavement of people due to debt removed the enslaved from the proportion of the population subject to taxation by the state. In that sense, the deliberate use by individuals of extortionate interest rates and other mechanisms to induce debt and the subsequent enslavement of others could be viewed as an economic challenge to the authorities. In this context, it is interesting that certain states of the IOW introduced measures forbidding the enslavement of free subjects for debt. This was the case in all Muslim societies governed by sharia law, but also occurred elsewhere, as in Korea under the Chosun dynasty in 1392.[18]

Although those falling into debt were overwhelmingly adult males, the majority of those enslaved as a result of male indebtedness were, generally by choice of the male debtor, women and children.[19] This was because the latter were often both the most vulnerable members of a household, extended family or community and the most in demand as slaves. Indebtedness was normally expressed in monetary terms, although it was often incurred in non-cash forms such as food or tools. If the debt was paid off, an enslaved debtor could regain non-slave status.[20] In some regions, such as Korea, enslavement of local people for debt ensured for them a permanent, heritable slave status, whereas in others, such as Imerina (Madagascar), enslaved Merina subjects (but not non-Merina) could be redeemed or redeem themselves.[21]

However, as Michael Salman reminds us in his analysis of Maria Henson's *Comfort Woman*, indebtedness could arise not just from financial debt, but also from any one of an array of obligations owed by servile people to those who dominated them that could not be satisfied by monetary payments. Indeed, such indebtedness often could never be eradicated, and could thus endure through the generations. However, possibly more than in cases of monetary debt, non-financial indebtedness established relationships that for the person indebted could offer 'the potential to manipulate intimacy, shame and reciprocal need for the purposes of survival, protection and even resistance'.[22]

Debt Bondage

It is necessary in approaching the topic of debt and slavery to distinguish between slavery and debt bondage (though the two could overlap). Enslavement for indebtedness was involuntary, whereas most people entered debt bondage voluntarily as a credit securing strategy. Mortgaging a child, or wife, to raise a loan was a common practice in the IOW from early times,[23] and one that even persisted into the twentieth century; in such cases men often used 'adultery' as a pretext for mortgaging wives or concubines.[24] Certainly by the nineteenth century, debt bondage embraced a vast range of people in the IOW, from farmers mortgaging future harvests and potential grooms borrowing a bride price to small traders living off the credit of larger merchants, the ubiquitous rural gamblers of Southeast and East Asia and opium addicts in nineteenth-century China.[25] During catastrophes, people often entered debt bondage or slavery as a survival strategy, either voluntarily, as was the case of many *dvija* caste members in India, or propelled by their kin group.[26] They did so whether they lived in regions of relatively low population density, such as Cambodia, Laos and Indonesia, the Middle East and Africa, or of relatively high population density, such as Bengal, Vietnam, Korea, South China and Japan.[27] Moreover, most victims appear to have been pushed into debt bondage as children – in early twentieth-century Thailand, for instance, they were rarely more than ten years of age.[28]

In some IOW societies, those subject to debt bondage outnumbered slaves. For example, the former were possibly the most numerous social category in Majapahit, Java, while they formed up to 50 per cent of the total population in central Thailand in the eighteenth and nineteenth centuries. Again, in Burma in the mid-nineteenth century, when debt bondage was far more widespread than hereditary slavery, male heads of impoverished households frequently sold their wives and children to pay taxes.[29] Debt bondspeople could sometimes be exchanged, as could other servile people, as part of a marriage dowry or a monastery donation.[30] The servitude to which those in debt bondage were subject was generally taken as paying off interest on the loan they had contracted, to which was added the cost of lodging, feeding and clothing the debtor. Consequently, the debt in most cases increased, eventually making servitude permanent, even hereditary, at which point there was little to distinguish debt bondage from slavery.[31] Indeed, in nineteenth-century Thailand, where up to 50 per cent of the population of the central provinces were trapped in debt bondage, if the interest owed by a debt bondsman grew to a level exceeding the original loan, the master deemed the debtor a bad investment and customarily sold him – albeit on unfavourable terms.[32]

Pawnship

Debt-related pawnship was widespread throughout the IOW. In Ancient Meso-potamia, a man in debt could either sell his dependents (preferably female slaves, concubines, wife or daughter) as slaves in order to pay off the debt, or pawn them. In the latter case, should the debt not be repaid within a stipulated time, the pawns generally became the slaves of their new master.[33] In medieval Japan, creditors were legally permitted to seize the children of debtors until such time as the debt had been paid off; if the debt were not to be paid in full, creditors then had recourse to local authorities who could transform their pawns into per-manent slaves.[34] The general term appears to have been ten years.[35] Pawnship was also common in East Africa, where a girl was frequently given as security for a loan. The creditor could use the girl for labour until her family paid off the debt, but he did not normally have the right to sell the pawn. However, in cases where an inordinate amount of time passed with little or no sign of repayment, the creditor's ownership of the pawn became established.[36] From the late eighteenth century, as noted by Edward Alpers in his contribution to this volume, a rapidly growing slave export trade substantially altered the mechanisms of pawnship in East Africa, ultimately transforming it into an institution for the creation of slaves. Thus, the links between debt, pawnship and enslavement were strongest along the littoral and the main trade routes into the interior. However, supply factors, notably famine, also played a significant role in inducing household heads to 'sell' kin, chiefly girls and women, into pawnship.[37] This marked East Africa apart from sub-Saharan West Africa, where pawns could not be reduced to slave status – although if a female pawn gave birth to a child by her 'mas-ter', that child was considered to be his slave, while on the Muslim–non-Muslim commercial frontier, cultural 'misunderstandings' often led to pawns being car-ried as slaves into Muslim markets.[38]

Enslavement as a Credit-Raising Strategy

Human beings were also sold outright to raise credit. In late imperial China, a major category of those enslaved comprised women and young girls sold by their impoverished parents. They thus became indebted to their 'enslaver', who sub-sequently re-sold them as concubines, wives and prostitutes.[39] In some societies, such as in the Far East and Imerina, wives were sold – in the case of Imerina in special wife markets.[40] Throughout the IOW, parents also let their children out for adoption in exchange for money.[41] In other cases, girls were 'apprenticed' out in return for payment to their parents. In her paper in this volume, Yoko Matsui considers the case of girls who, in return for payment, were apprenticed by their parents to brothels, where they were obliged to work as prostitutes to pay off the debt incurred. Invariably, the girl thus enslaved considered it her filial duty to obey her parents and submit to her new owner. Again, in 1899 John Foreman commented of the traditional practice in many *kasama* (tenant farmers) communities in the Philippines:

> Under the pretext of guaranteeing a loan, parents readily sell their children (male or female) into bondage; the child is handed over to work until the loan is repaid, but as the day of restitution of the advance never arrives, neither does the liberty of the youthful victim. Among themselves it is the law, and is still a practiced custom, for the debts of the parents to pass on to the children, and ... debts are never repudiated by them.[42]

In particularly dire times, sons were also sold, although in China and Korea every attempt was made to spare the eldest son in order that he might perform the ancestral rites and offer a hope for the family line to continue.[43]

The Muslim IOW

Here, however, a distinction needs to be drawn between Muslim and non-Muslim societies. This is of immense significance in the IOW, where between the seventh and thirteenth centuries Islam spread from its Middle Eastern heartland (*Dar al-Islam*), southwards down the East African littoral, and eastwards through South to Southeast Asia. Initially, as William G. Clarence-Smith points out in Chapter 1, a *hadith* (tradition) relating the sale of a debtor by the Prophet was used to justify enslaving insolvent debtors, but given its uncertain legitimacy, the *hadith* was from *c.* AD 800 declared invalid. As freeborn people, according to sharia law, could legally neither be pawned nor enslaved for debt, this generally also held true in practice in the Islamic heartland of the Middle East.[44] However, the distinction between indebtedness, debt-bondage and slavery was often blurred – a notable example being in the Gulf pearl diving industry of the late nineteenth and early twentieth century that forms the subject of Matthew Hopper's chapter. There, the lines between different types of bondage, and often between bondage and freedom, became increasingly blurred due to the generalized and growing indebtedness of workers in an industry highly vulnerable to the pressures of global capitalism – a phenomenon that, from the emergence in the nineteenth century of a truly international economy onwards, precisely because it was global in nature, increasingly affected all IOW societies, irrespective of either their religious or political affiliations. Alessandro Stanziani in his contribution notes a similar blurring of distinctions between apprenticeship and forced labour in the latter part of the nineteenth century.[45] Boys were trained for military and domestic services, while adult men and less attractive women were assigned more menial tasks. Slaves were employed in all sectors, from domestic service to urban activities, agricultural labour and the army. The utilization of servile labour was common on medium and even small properties, and slaves were widely employed in irrigation, pastoralism, mining, transport, public works, proto-industry and construction. Slave status in Muslim societies was also hereditary in cases where both parents were slaves, but children of a servile mother by a free man were free in Shi'I Islam polities – although not in societies governed by Sunni Islam.[46]

In addition, slaves in Muslim societies could be bought and sold, and thus pawned. However, there were important exceptions. Sharia prohibited, for instance, the sale of a slave woman who bore the child of her master, and the children of such a sexual union acquired free status – as did their mother, should she outlive her master (a common occurrence given that slave owners commonly took much younger women as concubines). The extent of pawning in Islamic societies was also limited by the religious enjoinment to Muslim slave owners eventually to manumit their slaves. Indeed, such a significant proportion of slaves were manumitted and absorbed into the slave-owning society that slave populations failed to become, as in the American South, self-propagating – thus fuelling constant demand for slave imports.[47]

Enslavement for debt was also barred among *dhimmi*, that is, Jews, Christians and Zoroastrians, who as 'people of the book' (possessing scriptural traditions similar to the Quran) were granted protected status under Muslim rulers. However, Muslim societies were highly commercial and inevitably produced debtors who in many instances, because of gaps in the law, or in Muslim societies outside the Middle East where elements of pre-Islamic customary law were upheld, were often ensnared in forms of debt bondage and slavery. There was also no firm legal ruling on the purchase of people enslaved for debt outside Muslim and *dhimmi* communities.[48]

The Rise of the International Economy, Debt and Bondage

In the nineteenth century, the rise and development of the international economy resulted in acute manpower shortages in the IOW. Pre-industrial economies were heavily labour intensive. With the growth of the international economy there was greater recourse to capital-intensive means of production, notably in the northern United States and Germany. However, in other industrial regions, and in non-industrial zones, production continued to be labour intensive. In the IOW, as elsewhere, the enhanced commercial opportunities offered by the creation of an international economy greatly increased demand for labour, which was required, for instance, for the clearing of vegetation and cultivation of cash crops (such as cloves, coffee, cocoa, tea, sugar), collection of forest (like wax, rubber, exotic hardwoods), animal (ivory, rhino horn, oil, skins, feathers) and marine (pearls, turtle shell, whale oil, ambergris) products and exploitation of minerals (gold, tin), porterage, storage, loading and offloading vessels and manning ships. Indigenous and

European powers simultaneously engaged in state – or empire-building projects that involved large numbers of soldiers, administrators and workers, not least in indigenous industrial experiments, such as occurred in nineteenth-century Egypt, Madagascar and China.[49]

However, this placed great structural strain on the labour market, as growth on the demand side failed to result in a growth in the supply of labour for two main reasons: uneven demographic growth and the prevalence of systems of bonded labour. Before the eighteenth century, Asia possessed a greater population than any other continent, but while Europe's population more than doubled in the nineteenth century, from 190 million to 423 million (that of Britain, Germany and the United States increased almost fivefold in the hundred years prior to 1914), it took almost 200 years for the population of Asia to double, from about 415 million to 970 million between 1700 and 1900. Thus, whereas in 1750 Asia possessed 64 per cent of the global population, Europe 21 per cent and Africa 13 per cent, by 1900 Asia's share of the global population had fallen to 57 per cent and Africa's to 8 per cent, while Europe had increased its share to 25 per cent, and the Americas to 10 per cent. In addition, population growth within the IOW was uneven. China's population increased rapidly during the eighteenth century to reach about 300 million in 1795, and it climbed further to reach 420 million by 1850. However, the rate of growth then slowed, the total population reaching only approximately 480 million by 1900.[50] Sumit Guha has estimated that the Indian population increased by 44 million between 1600 and 1800, when it reached 161 million, followed by a further 76 per cent increase to reach 283.4 million by 1901.[51] However, while the populations of these regions of Asia increased dramatically from 1700 onwards, population growth rates in Africa, for example, expanded significantly only from the 1920s.[52]

The conventional view is that demographic stagnation in Africa was a result of instability, petty warfare and especially the slave trade.[53] The impact of slave exports, which may by mid-century have bled sub-Saharan Africa of half of its potential population of 100 million, were compounded from the late 1880s, at least in eastern Africa, by the impact of European conquest, human and animal diseases and droughts.[54] However, it is now clear that demographic stagnation in Madagascar – conventionally attributed to French colonial policies from 1895 – was evident from the early 1830s and resulted from both man-made (warfare, slave raiding, economic mismanagement, labour exploitation) and natural (climatic variations, disease, cyclones) causes. Many of these factors also affected the neighbouring African continent, which in addition suffered acutely from rinderpest and other cattle diseases, notably from the 1880s. It is therefore likely that the same mixture of forces as were active in moulding demographic trends in Madagascar were present in the rest of Eastern and Southern Africa from the early nineteenth century.[55]

Climatic Factors

In the long nineteenth century, as global warming set in after the Little Ice Age, climatic fluctuations also critically influenced harvests and disease, and thus indirectly impoverishment, indebtedness and bondage. The process was uneven, however. In the northern hemisphere, temperatures fell from 1770, the period 1805–20 being the coldest on record in Europe, North America and Japan. From 1825, temperatures started to increase, but the Far East was affected by low temperatures from 1870 to 1900, exceptionally cold weather hitting South China from 1876 to 1895.[56] Moreover, between 1830 and 1900 the southern hemisphere was in the grip of a colder climate, with an advance north in the rain zone.[57] Longer-term climatic change was complicated by shorter-term factors. Strong 'Southern Oscillation' or 'El-Niño' ('ENSO') effects, associated with severe droughts followed in consecutive years by unusually heavy rain, were experienced in 1844–6, 1876–8 and 1899–1900. Again, high volcanic dust veils marked the periods 1783–8, 1832–8 and 1884. Both the ENSO effect and high dust veil indexes correlate with crop failures, food shortages and disease.[58]

Those whose livelihoods were undermined by the ravages of disease, drought or other natural catastrophes, warfare and famine, were often pushed into slavery or irredeemable debt, the ultimate consequence of which was bondage. Throughout the region, impoverishment forced families into debt which was normally expressed in monetary terms, although it was often incurred in non-cash forms such as food or tools. Commonly household heads attempted to meet debt payments through the sale or mortgage of a household member, notably a girl, but, if they were in dire straits, also boys and wives. This was a common pattern across the IOW, from East Africa to the Far East, where, in Korea alone, the percentage of the slave population that entered slavery voluntarily as a consequence of destitution rose from under 1 per cent to almost 50 per cent during the nineteenth century.[59]

Disease

The incidence of disease also increased from 1700 to 1900, at least in some regions of the IOW, often reducing entire communities to poverty. For instance, two decades of drought and diminished harvests experienced by most of Eastern Africa from *c.* 1820 to 1840, and a generally significantly warmer and wetter period from *c.* 1850 to 1880, created an environment more conducive to disease vectors. Similarly, the expansion of irrigation and construction projects in the more disease-friendly tropics created pools of stagnant water (ideal breeding ground for disease vectors of, for example, bilharzias and malaria). Large troop, population and cattle movements, and hugely increased transport facilities, resulted in increased diffusion across the IOW of diseases, including those, like cholera (of Ganges Delta origin), that had before been regionally contained. Among the major diseases to spread widely were malaria, which proved a greater killer than any other disease or famine, cholera (an epidemic of which in 1834–5 killed an estimated third of the Egyptian population), the plague and smallpox. Human diseases took a particularly heavy toll on forced labour as well as malnourished and displaced peoples, who all possessed lower physiological resistance. By the same token, cattle diseases, such as the 1863–4 rinderpest outbreak in Egypt which killed an estimated 700,000 animals, and the great rinderpest plague of 1889–97 which caused an 85 per cent mortality rate among unprotected cattle in Eastern and Southern Africa, inflicted significant socio-economic damage.

Moreover, increased trade and migration and improvements in transport and communications associated with the rise of the international economy helped diseases to break out of old disease-tolerant environments and spread to hitherto protected environments, with devastating consequences. For example, from 1817 cholera, endemic in Bengal, was carried by British troops to Nepal and Afghanistan, and by British ships from 1820 to 1822 to Sri Lanka, Southeast Asia, China and Japan, as well as to Muscat, from whence it travelled to the Persian Gulf and East Africa. By 1831, cholera was established in Mecca; between 1831 and 1912, it broke out forty times during the *Hadj*, pilgrims carrying it to every part of the Muslim world, from Indonesia to East and West Africa.[60] A similar pattern developed with other killer diseases, such as smallpox and malaria. Venereal disease, which was rarely as dramatic but severely affected health and fertility, also spread rapidly throughout the IOW. Only from the mid-twentieth century did the spread of modern medicines and effective treatment counter this pattern in some IOW regions.[61]

The spread of virulent diseases had considerable demographic impact in the IOW. Cholera killed approximately 13 per cent of Cairo's population in the 1831 outbreak, and almost 30 million Indians in epidemics that swept through India in the second half of the century. In China, a combination of epidemics, experienced in thirty-six of the sixty-one years from 1811 to 1872, and almost constant warfare from 1850 to 1878, left vast tracts of the centre and north depopulated; in the T'ai-p'ing and Nien uprisings alone, some twenty-five million people died. In the famine of 1877–9, a further ten million perished in Northern China. By 1900, the Chinese population stood at only 450 million.[62]

The State

In all, the commercialization associated with the rise of a truly international economy and imperial expansion, as well as climate change and disease resulted in increased demand for labour. Indebtedness also increased in the nineteenth century due a growth in the power and reach of the state, both indigenous and colonial, and thus increased impositions of taxation both in money and kind.

In the late nineteenth-century imperialist surge in the IOW, abolition formed a central justification for the imposition of European colonial rule. In part, this reflected abolitionist pressure in the West; this was mainly due, however, to the fact that colonial officials in the IOW quickly realized that 'liberated' slaves were a potentially vital source of both taxation and labour in a region characterized by a lack of capital and manpower and colonial regimes governed by precepts of self-financing. A colonial priority was thus to transform the local working population into a free wage labour force. In this context, early abolitionist pressure, which was concentrated principally on the Atlantic, had an initially muted influence in the IOW except in the Cape where, well before the 1834 abolition of slavery, the 1826 removal of measures protecting wine had diverted investment into the far less labour intensive wool-producing sector – a measure that effectively undermined slavery.[63] Elsewhere, however, the labour intensive nature of the economy and lack of free wage labour rendered academic any arguments that slave labour might be inefficient.[64]

Indeed, the nineteenth century witnessed the apogee of indigenous IOW slave trades. Because of the conventional focus on black slaves, the only IOW region with concentrated estimates for the slave export trade is Eastern Africa, for which estimates range from between 800,000 to over two million, and Madagascar, for which estimates again vary from between about 72,000 and double that figure.[65] However, the greatest IOW slave traffic was overland, notably within Africa, Hindu India and the Confucian Far East.[66]

Moreover, until the abolition of slavery in European territory, in British colonies in 1833, in French colonies in 1848 and in the Dutch East Indies in 1860, the inhabitants of European-held territory in the IOW initially depended largely on slaves to meet their labour demands. For instance, Robert Farquhar, the first British governor of Mauritius, delayed anti-slave import measures in acknowledgement of the cheap labour requirements of local sugar planters.[67] In India, where government by the East India Company formed the pretext for the lack of rigorous application of abolition in 1833, there were an estimated eight to nine million indigenous slaves in 1841[68] – double the number of black slaves in the United States on the eve of abolition in 1865. Again, European powers often declared newly conquered territories to be 'protectorates', and thus avoided enforcing some abolitionist measures compulsory in colonies. Complete bans on slavery in European-controlled territories occurred fitfully well into the twentieth century. In Africa, the internal slave traffic remained buoyant for some fifty years after the abolition of the external slave trade. In Somalia, the colonial regime initially permitted European settler farmers access to slave labour, and even returned fugitive slaves to their owners,[69] while in the Sudan effective measures to curtail slavery were taken only in the late 1920s.[70] On the eastern side of the IOW, the French first seriously applied anti-slavery measures in Indochina in 1897, while the British abolished slavery in Hulsawng valley in eastern Burma only in 1926. Slavery was outlawed in the Netherlands Indies in 1860, but the Dutch then possessed only one quarter of the Indonesian territory that was to pass under their control by 1910 – in much of which they tolerated slavery. Slavery endured in remoter regions of French Indochina and the Dutch Indies into the 1940s. In the Middle East, drawn into the British informal empire after the First World War, abolitionist pressure remained muted until after 1945. Indeed, in the IOW generally, there were few swift and effective abolition measures taken by European powers.[71]

Also, while using the suppression of slavery as a pretext for the imposition of colonial rule, European authorities in the region needed to retain the goodwill of local slave-owning elites. Thus, while increasingly hindering the maritime slave trade in Africans in the western IOW, colonial authorities neglected both the maritime slave trade in non-Africans and most human trafficking overland, notably of females and children. They also proved reluctant to attack indigenous institutions of slavery lest such measures sparked revolt, as occurred in the Muslim province of the Southern Philippines after abolition was enforced in 1904.[72] Moreover, even when emancipated, former slaves proved remarkably reluctant to work on European-run concerns.

Furthermore, Europeans encountered the problem that indigenous states and authorities claimed the labour of all 'free' subjects. Indeed, in the eighteenth and nineteenth centuries, some IOW states, such as Korea and Imerina, purposefully applied selective measures of abolition without compensation to former masters in order to 'free' slaves formerly tied up in the private sector and make them available for state use. In Korea, the state abolished the public *nobi* system of hereditary enslavement in 1801 – a measure which undermined slavery (finally abolished in 1894),[73] and in Thailand successive state decrees ensured slavery had largely disappeared by the end of the nineteenth century;[74] both these measures increased state access to forced labour. Again, in Madagascar in June 1877, the Merina court 'emancipated' all African slaves imported since 1865. No compensation was paid to their former owners, depriving the private sector at a stroke of an estimated 150,000 slaves, a considerable portion of its labour reserve, whom the imperial court immediately classified as *Tsierondahy*, a category of the *Mainty* (traditional hereditary slave) caste. A few such *Masombika* in and around Antananarivo were genuinely liberated, generally finding employment in the construction sector or porterage. However, most were grouped into distinct forced labour units – hence constituting 'simply the appropriation on the part of the Government of so much private though stolen property'.[75]

There are also striking incidences in the nineteenth century of indigenous states imposing such heavy impositions on the 'free' population that it drove many to destitution, indebtedness and forms of bondage, including slavery.

Egypt under Muhammed Ali and Imperial Madagascar under Radama I and Ranavalona I are major examples.[76] Such a process was also promoted by the imposition by indigenous states of high legal interest rates – up to 100 per cent in nineteenth-century Madagascar. Consequently, it was common for individuals to default on their debts.[77] However, European colonial regimes, through the imposition of monetary taxes, the promotion of commercialization and the enforcement of credit contracts, facilitated a growth in indebtedness. At the same time, colonial authorities both maintained tight budgetary regimes that avoided funding public welfare programmes and distinguished debt bonds-people from 'true' slaves, whose condition they attributed solely to violent capture. As a result, debt bondage and enslavement through debt expanded considerably, affecting a wide range of people in the IOW, from farmers mortgaging future harvests and potential grooms borrowing a bride price to small traders living off the credit of larger merchants, opium addicts in nineteenth-century China and Gulf pearl divers.[78] India is another prime example. In a century characterized by rising taxation and years of famine, 'freedom' for members of the former slave castes, who had deliberately been kept destitute and debarred from land ownership, translated into the liberty to starve. Some adopted sharecropping, but with two thirds of the crop paid to the landlord, the risk of failure was high. In order to survive, many entered debt bondage that was from 1859 reinforced by the Breach of Contract Act. In some areas of India, members of the most oppressed castes formed the overwhelming bulk of those in debt bondage. The situation closely resembled slavery in that bondage could be inherited and the vast majority of bonded people had their geographical mobility restricted.[79]

Emancipation and Debt

Thus, in the lead-up to, and in the wake of, abolition, European authorities in the IOW required access to non-slave labour, forms of which were frequently so coercive that they have often been described as akin to slavery. Often central to their coercive nature was indebtedness. Emancipated slaves were rarely compensated for their enslavement, with the result that many slaves, whether individually manumitted prior to abolition or emancipated en masse following abolition, were destitute and fell into debt and thus forms of debt-bondage, as described by Susan Newton-King in her fascinating case study of Arnoldus Koevoet in the Cape in the early eighteenth century.[80] In Madagascar, the stark brutality of the 'free' labour market under the French colonial regime following abolition in 1896 persuaded many former slaves to remain in slave-like relationships with their former masters.[81]

Ransom and indebtedness were also closely related. The ransoming of kidnap victims or war captives was a well-established practice in many traditional

IOW societies, as in the Mediterranean – in both regions applying chiefly to adult males.[82] In the nineteenth century, with increasing Western abolitionist pressure and rising demand for servile labour, ransoming, often in its new guise of redemption, assumed new proportions and was extended to children. Ironically, the rationale for ransoming stemmed from the widespread belief in Enlightenment Europe that members of 'primitive' pagan societies required 'domestication', and that slavery was the protected status best suited to that end. From the Enlightenment era, religious leaders propounded parallel concerns for the moral progress of 'children' that was translated into the provision of Christian ministry to 'childlike' slaves. Ransomers, like slave-owners, needed to discipline their undeveloped wards into accepting the physical and moral discipline and training necessary for the attainment of civilized virtues – which alone could justify 'freedom' in the sense of political participation or economic autonomy.[83] This provided the rationale for some missionary groups in Africa who redeemed slaves into mission villages, where they worked off their redemption in situations of virtual bondage.[84] Another example, from the eastern IOW, was that of Christian Filipinos who in the nineteenth century and into the early twentieth century, in return for a small payment to their parents or guardians, 'adopted' children of the Aeta, a non-Christian Negrito group, traditionally hunter-gatherers, from the isolated mountains of Luzon. Filipino masters justified such purchases as being a means of Christianizing pagans.[85]

Moreover, as James Warren graphically describes for the Sulu zone, Westerners involved in redeeming slaves frequently passed the cost of redemption on to the 'liberated' slave, whom they subsequently considered indebted to themselves. Consequently, the liberated slave was obliged to work off the cost of the ransom and passage to a place of refuge – in the process often becoming more indebted to the new 'master'. In some cases this was the act of private traders, such as William Wyndham, cited in Warren's chapter, who incorporated many ransomed slaves into his own private workforce. Warren notes similar practices for slaves who escaped to Spanish warships or otherwise sought refuge in Spanish-held ports in the Sulu Archipelago.[86] Subject to criticism were the practices of British anti-slave trade naval patrols that landed 'Prize Negroes' – African human cargoes aboard captured slaving ships – at British-controlled ports in the western IOW. Over 2,000 such 'emancipated' slaves were landed at Cape Town in the decade 1806–16, for example. Prize Negroes were treated as 'confiscated' property and transferred to the British government. As such they were placed at the disposition of local British officials, who took some to serve in the military, but allotted most as indentured labour to satisfy the private manpower needs of prominent local whites.[87] Prize Negroes granted to Mauritian planters were 'leased' back to the government for four days a year to perform public works.[88]

European regimes in the IOW also widely used convicts, who were a traditional source of bonded labour. Prior to the nineteenth century, the British shipped tens of thousands of indigenous convicts, predominantly male, to their settlements across the IOW,[89] and indigenous convicts were sent from Goa to Mozambique by the Portuguese and by the Dutch from Batavia to the Cape.[90] This practice increased in the transition years of abolition as slave labour progressively dwindled. For example, during the early nineteenth century the English East India Company dispatched Indian convicts to Singapore, Malacca, Mauritius and Burma. Clare Anderson presents a case study of some of the 1,500 Bengali convicts shipped to Mauritius between 1815 and 1836 (the migrant convict labour system there lasted until 1851), ostensibly for public works, but sometimes assigned, in return for payment, to private planters, who often treated them as slaves.[91] Penal labour was also widely used by indigenous authorities for the harshest types of work. For instance, the Merina regime in Madagascar used convicts in road construction, mining and foundry work.[92]

However, indentured labour constituted the major form of non-slave labour in the wake of abolition. Although this has conventionally been portrayed as a phenomenon that arose in the nineteenth century, indentured labour was an old institution in the IOW where, as demonstrated by Alessandro Stanziani in his chapter, there were clear and often overlapping relations with European forms of indentureship and the concept of the 'servant'.[93] For instance, indentureship was a feature of eighteenth-century Cape Society, in which it was either formalized by contracts or imposed ad hoc, as with Khoi and San boys captured by Dutch farmers in the interior. Such captives were forced to work until the age of twenty-five, by which time they were often married with sons who were subject to similar obligations. Many parents refused to abandon their children, and so remained tied to the farm for life. Following abolition of the slave trade in 1807, the Caledon Code of 1809 formalized indenture in the Cape through a 'pass' system, which restricted San and Khoi to farms in a system of 'virtual slavery'. Thus, Nigel Worden argues, the first effective formal abolition in the Cape was not official abolition in 1834, but the 1828 repeal of the Caledon Code.[94] Upon abolition in the Cape and Mauritius, ex-slaves, who received no financial assistance, were declared 'apprentices' and obliged to continue working for a fixed period for their old masters. In the Cape, where the system ended in 1838 (in Mauritius it continued until mid-century), many apprentices fell into debt bondage to their old employers or chose to continue working for them in order to remain with their children.[95]

The failure of the 1834 and 1848 abolitionist measures to transform ex-slaves into pliant wage labourers resulted in the creation of a modified indenture system. Generally involving five-year contracts, it channelled manpower resources to enterprises both within and without the IOW, such as the sugar plantations of the Fiji Islands. Recruits comprised essentially poverty-stricken Indians, Chinese and, for the French islands, Africans. By the end of the nineteenth century, approximately one million Indian indentured labourers were employed in India; two million were also shipped to overseas plantations between 1834 and 1920. Contemporary observers and subsequent historians have underlined that the recruitment, transport and living and working conditions of indentured labourers were often similar to those of slaves.[96]

Attention on indentured labour in the IOW has often been focused on European plantation agriculture[97] and mining – including that which emerged in Australia from the discovery of gold there in 1851 – but recent research has revealed forms of indigenous indentureship. European sources indicate that by the mid-1840s an estimated 15,000 Chinese workers were being carried in Chinese junks to Bangkok every year.[98] However, Chinese sources suggest that the number of Chinese migrants involved in forms of indentured labour schemes was far greater than previous estimates based on European language sources. They indicate that some 7.7 million people emigrated from South China from 1851 to 1901, of whom some 87 per cent travelled to Southeast Asia. Moreover, most of this migration met indigenous IOW rather than European demand for labour. Adam McKeown has posited that only about 4 per cent of such emigrants constituted 'indentured' labour on European estates, and that even these 'were still often bound to other Chinese through a variety of debt and contract schemes with widely varying levels of obligation'.[99]

Throughout, indebtedness was a central feature of indentureship. Debt was central to the recruitment system, as advances were made from the chief broker to lesser brokers, who in turn often made advances to the heads of households of enlisted workers or local agents through whom they were recruited. Recruits were then obliged to remit sums to their home regions to ensure that such advances were repaid. Others were already in debt and signed up to indenture schemes in order to earn the money to repay debts. As Ei Murakami points out in his chapter on the export of Chinese indentured labour through the port of Amoy, workers were often also obliged to repay the capital and interest on the cost of transport to their place of employment.[100]

Sex Slaves

As a result of changed conditions of demand, indebtedness also led to the rise of an unprecedented trans-IOW traffic in impoverished females to serve as sex slaves – a traffic that, like forms of debt-bonded labour, is still vibrant today. The trade in females for sexual purposes was an age-old phenomenon. However, in the pre-1800 era it was chiefly confined to elite markets, and the women involved were generally highly valued and enjoyed a lifestyle superior to that of peasant women. This was particularly the case with concubines, courtesans and singing girls, but might also have been true of the majority of slave prostitutes. The sex trafficking that arose in the 1800s was of a different order. Nineteenth-century demand emanated chiefly from the emergence of permanent and concentrated masses of poor contract workers and soldiers. For example, the migration of millions of Chinese male labourers to IOW centres such as Singapore led to a huge demand for females for sexual purposes that was met by a traffic in mostly involuntary prostitutes notably from impoverished rural communities in Japan and China. Large concentrations of soldiers led to a similar demand. While the intermediaries were often women, frequently ex-prostitutes, who generally hoodwinked parents and girls into thinking that they would be offered a legitimate job in a distant city, European authorities, eager to minimize tension among men on work sites and in army camps, often colluded in the trade. Thus, British authorities in Hong Kong facilitated the flow of Chinese and Japanese girls to Singapore to serve as prostitutes, and British army officials did likewise for girls from the Himalayas to service the sexual needs of soldiers in India. In many cases, 'advances' were given to the girl's parents, the capital and interest on which, along with the cost of travel, lodging, clothing and food, were deducted from the girl's earnings – to the extent that she was often permanently in debt.[101]

Twentieth-Century and Contemporary Forms of Bondage

Colonial powers across the IOW considered debt bondage to be a benign form of private welfare, and generally condoned its continuation well into the twentieth century.[102] In some areas, such as Thailand, Burma and Indochina, this encouraged a revival of covert slave raiding.[103] In Africa, where debt bondage was represented by the 'pawnship' of a person, usually a young girl, to a creditor in return for a loan, the system weakened only during the post-Second World War boom.[104] In all cases, the debtor had a clear market value, expressed in more monetized Asian economies in terms of cash, and in less monetized economies, as in most of Africa, in terms of 'human' wealth. In 1930 in Hijaz, slaves were said to make up 10 per cent of the population of Mecca, but they were also widely used in the countryside. The British believed that there was no social stigma attached to bonded people and slaves and that in Hijaz they were often better off than the free poor.[105] Pilgrimage was an important source of supply: Persians, Iraqis, Egyptians, Syrians and Africans might pay for their journey by selling off a woman or child on the way or in Hijaz itself.

In India in the late colonial period, the authorities declared themselves avid supporters of free labour. The belief, so strong in the past, that colonial rulers should adapt to local customs was undermined by a growing awareness that paying landless people a non-living wage forced them to accept advances for expenses that exceeded their daily earnings. The resulting bondage enabled land-owners to maintain wages at minimum levels. Thus, in July 1923 the government of Gujarat declared forced indentureship to be illegal by proclamation.[106] After independence, Indian planners established both minimum and maximum limits for landownership, and thus envisaged an agrarian society of self-cultivating owners. They called for the state to ban various forms of debt-based bonded labour; for instance, they demanded that bonded labourers be released from debts incurred more than five years previously and be allocated uncultivated lands. Unfortunately, the promise was not fulfilled; only half of the land worked by tenant farmers changed owners, usually to the benefit of high caste farmers.[107]

Forms of debt-bonded labour, wherein freedom of choice, wages and bargaining power are 'significantly restricted', are still central features of work regimes throughout the IOW, although often hidden from the eyes of authorities, and thus missing from official statistics. In her chapter, Isabelle Guérin analyses such cases in Tamil Nadu, where, despite the 1976 Abolition of Bonded Labour Act, impoverished villagers often fall into debt bondage.[108] Lured by wage advances, thousands of peasants migrate to work in distant brickworks and rice and sugar cane plantations where, however, the rates of pay are so low that most return home still impoverished or indebted, although some fall into even greater debt that obliges them to work for their hirer, bonded to their workplace as virtual slaves. Guérin argues that the process is not accidental and that employers, while fully subscribing to the tenets of classical economics, which in theory rejects bonded labour, in practice use whichever form of labour most maximizes profits. In the case of the three industries she studies in Tamil Nadu, local capitalists encourage debt bondage because it helps them to cheapen, discipline and control local manpower. There are deep connections to traditional forms of exploitation, for upper castes dominate ownership while Paraiyar, ex-untouchables (in the brick and sugar cane industries) and Irulars, a 'tribal' group (in rice drying) – historically the bulwark of local servile labour – form the majority of the workforce. In these industries, the workforce often comprises entire families – men, women and children alike. Moreover, it can be argued that with globalization exploitation of these traditionally servile groups has increased, rather than diminished. The processes of mechanization and vertical integration in an increasingly competitive global market have, in creating business structures that survive through cost-cutting, left certain sectors highly dependent on cheap servile labour.

Conclusion

Any discussion of forms of servitude and the labour market needs to be framed within a discussion of the wider economy. There is growing consensus that the history of servitude in the IOW can no longer be limited to that of the East African slave trade and the African diaspora. Rather, issues of servitude and labour relations need to be considered within the context of the global IOW economy that had emerged by at least the tenth century, linking the entire region from China to Africa and all points in between in a sophisticated and durable system of maritime exchange. Moreover, this system of exchange remained vital during the nineteenth century, when the growth of a truly international economy created an unprecedented commercial boom in the IOW that established a large and growing demand for menial labour. There was difficulty meeting that demand, however, for two main reasons: comparatively low and uneven demographic growth, and the tying up of the potential workforce in largely indigenous systems of bonded labour. Western abolitionists focused far more on the Atlantic slave system than on forms of bondage in the IOW. Moreover, European officials in the IOW were reluctant to attack systems of indigenous servitude that most regional elites held dear, and they therefore perpetuated some traditional forms of bondage while also introducing new ones. And although abolition formed a central justification for the imposition of colonial rule at the end of the nineteenth century, colonial regimes likewise resisted outright attack on many forms of bonded labour, and borrowed from pre-colonial regimes in introducing varieties of *corvée* labour. Increased commercialization also gave rise to an unprecedented traffic in young debt-bonded girls as sex 'slaves' in particular – one that, like many other forms of IOW debt-bonded labour is still vibrant. For example, India outlawed debt bondage in 1976 and Pakistan followed suit in 1992, but this practice, which affects chiefly the illiterate and landless rural poor, is still entrenched in both countries. In Muslim Pakistan, charging interest is illegal, but it can be disguised as an advance in pay. Once bonded, labourers lose all freedom of movement, and have to work for their creditors. The creditors are usually landlords – sometimes the very officials charged by the government with ending debt-bondage. In Southeast Asia, as in Pakistan and India, creditors can keep debtors in bondage in two main ways – either through levying illegal fines or through charging for food, tool, fertilizers and other essentials, while keeping wages too low for the debts ever to be repaid.[109] In Nepal, by 2000 whole families could be passed from one creditor to another through this system. The problem is that the only way to keep former bondsmen out of debt and prevent new persons from falling into it is to provide those at risk with land or good wages as well as access to credit and education – solutions that require strong political and financial support, neither of which has yet materialized.

1 DEBT AND THE COERCION OF LABOUR IN THE ISLAMIC LEGAL TRADITION

William G. Clarence-Smith

Introduction: Enslavement and Debt in Islam

Enslavement was the only acceptable form of coercion of labour in the Islamic legal tradition, and this held to a considerable degree in practice. Chattel servitude was permitted and regulated by the Qur'an, *hadith* (tradition), Prophetic biographies, and the huge body of exegetical legal texts. The religious legitimacy of slavery was only gradually challenged from the 1870s, as Islamic abolitionism began to develop.[1] At the same time, the *ulama* consistently taught that there was no sanction in the holy texts for bonded or coerced labour of any type other than slavery.[2]

This religious view of the matter did not always prevail, especially under powerful rulers, who might pay little heed to the law of God. Thus, the Mamluk sultans of Egypt and Syria, who wore their religion rather lightly, employed much forced labour for construction and other purposes.[3] Similarly, the Ottoman sultans press-ganged or conscripted men to supplement slave rowers on Mediterranean galleys, together with some convicts.[4] Muhammad 'Alî was notorious for the extent to which he imposed *corvée* labour across Egypt in the early nineteenth century.[5] However, Egyptians denounced this kind of forced labour (*sukhra*) as illegitimate 'tyranny'.[6]

Religious syncretism might result in forms of labour mobilization other than slavery. The Circassians of the north-western Caucasus were famed alike for their superficial Islam and for their harsh system of serfdom, which coexisted with slavery proper.[7] Baluchistan, straddling modern Iran and Pakistan, exhibited similar traits.[8] In South India, a type of serfdom, reinforced by caste, prevailed among Hindu populations. Muslims were noted as being lords of such communities, even if Hyder Ali, the reforming late eighteenth-century ruler of Mysore, tried to turn pariahs into free Muslim cultivators.[9] In Islamic West Africa, slaves typically became more akin to serfs from the second generation, and thus subject to less oppression, but also less likely ever to be manumitted fully.[10]

Despite such exceptions, the general dearth of forms of coercion intermediate between slavery and free labour meant that there was little social space for the emergence of types of debt bondage that did not lead to chattel slavery. Only in areas where the sharia was particularly weak did substantial non-slave forms of control through debt emerge. For most Muslims, the crucial question was whether unredeemed debt could legitimately result in enslavement as a chattel, both for the debtor and for members of the debtor's family.

The Religious Prohibition of Enslavement for Debt

A *hadith* told of the Prophet selling a debtor by the name of Surraq, and this was used by early Muslims to justify enslaving insolvent debtors. However, the Surraq Hadith was classed as a 'weak' tradition, for its chain of transmission was uncertain, and it was eventually excluded from all the canonical collections. As the era of the early caliphs passed, and as the jurists of the schools of law hammered out a compromise position on slavery by around AD 800, a consensus arose that the Surraq Hadith was spurious. From then on, it was decided, no believer was to be enslaved for debt.[11] Believers could sell neither themselves nor their children into slavery, whether to redeem an obligation or for any other purpose.[12] Not only was this formally prohibited for Muslims, but the infidel 'people of the book' (*dhimmî*), living peacefully under Islamic rule, also had to forbear from reducing debtors to slavery.[13]

The assertion that Islam was hostile to debt itself because of a ban on the lending of money at interest (*ribâ*) can only be accepted as a possible factor in lessening the overall burden of debt on Islamic societies.[14] As Sidi al-'Arabi Burdalah put it pithily in a fatwa issued in Fez (Morocco) around 1708: 'Allah hath permitted trade and forbidden usury'.[15] However, this prohibition could be side-stepped, and, even if applied, it did not eliminate debt as such.[16] As a highly commercial and monetized civilization, Islam certainly created many possibilities for debt.[17]

That Islamic lands continued to be home to many people reduced to chattel slavery as a result of debt can be attributed to different factors, including the sinfulness of the faithful. Many owners of debt slaves believed themselves to be good and pious Muslims, however, and it is argued here that there were more structural causes for the existence of debt slavery. Loopholes in the law left a place for this practice, especially when the loss of freedom occurred beyond the frontiers of the faith.

Enslavement for Debt Beyond the Frontiers of Islam

Justification for the methods of enslavement employed by non-believers beyond the frontiers of Islam became an issue after the time of the rightly-guided caliphs, from the late seventh century onwards. The Umayyad dynasty permitted non-

Muslims to supply slaves to believers, as trade goods, gifts or tribute, even though the theological and legal underpinnings for this decision were extremely weak. In turn, this raised the problem of whether methods of enslavement employed by unbelievers in the abode of war (*dâr al-harb*) should be of any concern to believers. There existed a long-standing tension among the *ulama*, with some seeing sharia precepts as valid only for Muslims and *dhimmî*, whereas others considered that they were more widely applicable to all the 'sons of Adam' (and, by implication, the 'daughters of Eve').

Whether those enslaved for debt in the abode of war might legitimately be purchased by Muslims was examined in an influential fatwa. Taqî al-Dîn Ahmad ibn Taymiyya (1263–1328) was a noted jurist of Damascus, whose opinions are revered by Wahhâbî and other 'fundamentalist' strands of Islam to our own day. He was once asked whether a Muslim, finding himself in lands beyond the abode of Islam (*dâr al-Islâm*), could legitimately buy debtors who had sold themselves; whether he could buy children who had been sold to discharge a debt; and whether the believer could bring such slaves back to the lands of Islam and sell them there. Ibn Taymiyya replied that if the said Muslim was in a land of infidels who had a pact or treaty (*amân*) with Muslims, then some great jurists allowed such a transaction, but others did not. The Hanafî school of law (*madhhab*) thought it permissible, but not the Shâfi'î school. As for the Mâlikî *madhhab*, it was divided down the middle on the issue. Curiously, Ibn Taymiyya seems not to have revealed the views of his own Hanbalî school. In any event, Muslims in lands where infidels had no covenant with Islamic states could, with a clear conscience, purchase debt slaves for re-sale at home.[18]

This opinion was contested. While jurists for a long time turned a blind eye to what went on beyond the borders of Islamdom, Western critiques in the nineteenth century encouraged the *ulama* to look again at the issue. Increasing numbers of Muslim scholars suggested that the rules regarding enslavement in the *dâr al-Islâm* should also be applied in the *dâr al-harb*, even in lands that had no pact with believers. This effectively reduced legitimate slaves to those nonbelievers either born into slavery or captured in 'just war', a concept which was hard to define for lands with other religions and laws.[19]

In the hands of a Moroccan scholar from Sale, Ahmad b. Khâlid al-Nâsirî (1834–97), such arguments turned into quasi-abolitionism. He wrote his attack on slavery in 1881, as part of a history of the Maghrib, and his opinions were more widely disseminated through a posthumous publication in Paris in 1906. Al-Nâsirî not only denounced unacceptable conditions of enslavement in the lands of unbelief, but also rejected the justification of slavery in terms of the 'curse of Ham'. As he additionally affirmed that no wars after the time of the Prophet and his companions could be called holy wars, he effectively challenged the status of all existing slaves in Islamic lands.[20]

Enslavement for Debt within the Frontiers of Islam

More shocking to the pious and sharia-minded was the persistence of enslavement for debt within the *dâr al-Islâm* itself, imposed on Muslims and *dhimmî* alike, in part because the sharia coexisted with other types of law. Firstly, rulers were allowed to promulgate decrees, known as *qânûn*, or statute law. Secondly, the *ulama* recognized a subordinate place for custom, *'âda* or *'urf*, terms that covered everything from unwritten local lore to the elaborate and ancient codes of conquered peoples. In theory, these bodies of subordinate law were only tolerated as long as they did not override the law of God. In practice, relations between the sharia and other laws were often conflictual.

The *ulama* generally upheld the primacy of the sharia, but local communities were not necessarily of the same opinion, especially in regions where conversion to Islam had been peaceful, recent and gradual.[21] A Kazakh *qâdî* in Inner Asia dispensed a bewildering amalgam of Turkic custom, Mongol law, Russian codes and the sharia, and this mix was only codified in the 1820s.[22] A proverb from Aceh, North Sumatra, held that holy law and custom were 'like the pupil and the white of the eye', both emanating from God.[23] Christiaan Snouck Hurgronje, the great Dutch scholar of Islam, commented acidly that *adat* was really the 'mistress' and sharia 'her obedient slave'.[24] This was even a problem in the heart of Islamdom, for Bedouin 'customary law could be as distant in Arabia itself from the Shari'ah law of the books as in the remotest corner of the hemisphere'.[25]

That said, statute law rarely played a role in enslavement for debt, for rulers tended to follow the sharia in this matter. At worst, practical considerations at times led to the toleration of the enslavement of debtors. Making slaves of criminals and debtors was a convenient alternative to putting them in prison, and was even a humane alternative under certain conditions of incarceration. Similarly, self-enslavement and the sale of children in times of want parried the nefarious effects of natural disasters and social crises, which often gave rise to unredeemable debt.

Customary law, in contrast, frequently decreed enslavement as a penalty for crime and debt, and sanctioned the sale of oneself or one's dependents for the repayment of debt. The practice was allowed in Roman law, common throughout much of the early Christian world, which formed the *'âda* of many of the western lands of Islam.[26] Slavery in Hinduism could originate in a similar manner, although debt gave rise to a wider variety of possible statuses.[27] Buddhism inherited slavery for debt from Hinduism,[28] though Theravada Buddhist kingdoms were dominated by a variety of serfdom, and numerous unredeemed debtors blended into this wider serf population.[29] Muslim reformists targeted debt slavery within the lands of Islam as something requiring rapid elimination, for the *ulama* believed that it conflicted blatantly with sharia precepts. Adding insult to injury, the immoral charging of interest on loans was frequently the root cause of the problem. Secular and colonial officials, worried by the social implications of debt, thus made common cause with the *ulama*, seeking to eradicate both debt and enslavement.

Southeast Asia

In all the Islamic world, enslavement through debt was said to be most widespread in Southeast Asia.[30] The laws of Melaka allowed unredeemed debtors to be reduced to slavery in the fifteenth century, albeit with exceptions for victims of natural disasters, and this famous code served as a model for centuries in the 'Malay World'.[31] The eighteenth-century Luwaran code, from the southern Philippines, enshrined the principle of servitude as the penalty for debt, allowing for either self-enslavement or the sale of children by parents.[32] Unredeemed debtors quite quickly became chattels, so that unpaid debts were generally 'the most common origin for the heritable slaves found in many societies'.[33] There is general agreement that selling such debtors, and treating their descendants as chattels, was commonplace.[34] High levels of indebtedness were made worse by usurious interest rates, themselves an overt breach of sharia principles. Among the Maranao of Mindanao, in the southern Philippines, a loan could allegedly double in size in as little as ten days.[35] Malays recognized that the sharia only allowed the seizure of debtors' property, not their person, but they appealed to the authority of Malay custom (*adat*) for the enslavement of unredeemed debtors, and regularly presented children as collateral for loans.[36]

Rather unexpectedly, some colonial officials thus became the agents of sharia-minded reform. Hoesein Djajadiningrat, a West Javanese administrator working for the Dutch, argued that replacing customary law with the sharia would be the best way to eradicate persistent servitude in South Sumatra.[37] However, the Dutch in other ways reinforced debt bondage, paradoxically as a means to eradicate slavery proper. As late as 1909, the Dutch turned South Sulawesi's numerous slaves into debtors, obliged to repay owners in cash or labour services. The period of payment was set at a short two years, but it is far from clear how well this was enforced.[38] In British Malaya, Richard Winstedt roundly denounced enslavement for debt as an 'unauthorized and illegal innovation' in terms of Islamic law.[39] In seeking to resolve the widespread social problem of indebtedness, British officials, such as William Maxwell, stressed to the Malay elite that the Qur'ân urged the remission of debts.[40] One Malay response to growing colonial criticism was to insist that debtors were technically free, being merely under an obligation to repay the sum owed.[41] Loopholes of this kind permitted forms of debt bondage, falling short of slavery proper, to persist under the British flag.[42]

Java was unusual in Southeast Asia in that any transition from the status of a debtor to that of a chattel slave was deemed to be unacceptable in terms of Javanese legal principles, and no Javanese was permitted to be made a slave.[43] Javanese customary law was a mixture of Indian codes and local lore, but as Hindu legal principles did allow debt slavery, these prohibitions were a Javanese peculiarity.[44] The Javanese case formed a significant exception to the wider Southeast Asian pattern, given that a clear majority of Southeast Asian Muslims lived in this densely populated island.[45] Nonetheless, Java's indebted peons were worked hard in industries such as Cirebon's textile-weaving workshops around 1800.[46]

Sub-Saharan Africa

With respect to debt slavery, Islamic Sub-Saharan Africa was akin to Southeast Asia, in that rules on slavery were subject to customary law and included the possibility of enslavement for debt.[47] Thus, in around 1870 the sultan of Wadai did 'not delay in announcing clearly to the negligent debtor, whether a high official or a slave, "If you have not satisfied your creditor by such and such a date, you will go with him [across the Sahara] as a slave, as a substitute for the money you owe him".[48] Indeed, rulers might even pay off their own debts by seizing their people and handing them over to their creditors.[49] In West Africa, however, pawning was the most commonly accepted way of structuring credit relations, and legal barriers to the enslavement of pawns were substantial. Sharia law did not even recognize pawning, although some West African *ulama* justified it as a form of hiring. Muslims may have been among those who sometimes turned pawns into slaves, but this was seen as transgressing both local customary law and Islamic law. This helped to encourage the redemption of debtors threatened with enslavement in an Islamic context.[50] In Eastern Africa, it was also possible to pay off debts at any point to avoid enslavement. When Arab traders sought to buy Swahili people who had accumulated debts or failed to pay fines, relatives of these people might turn up at the last minute to pay off the sums owed, thereby saving their kin from being exported as slaves.[51] This may have reflected local cultures of debt, about which more needs to be known. For example, Swahili men were reported to be able to pawn their children or nephews, but not their wives.[52]

Sharia-minded reform at times led to the reduction or elimination of enslavement for debt. In Futa Jalon, in West Africa, a regime born of holy war imposed more 'orthodox' Islamic norms on believers from the 1720s. One of the reforms implemented was the freeing of Muslims who had been reduced to debt slavery. However, it is not clear whether this extended to those originally enslaved for debt when they lived as non-believers in Animist societies. Moreover, defaulting Muslim debtors were instead to be beaten, a punishment that was not condoned in the Mâlikî version of the sharia that was in force in West Africa.[53]

Inner Asia and China

The Inner and East Asian marches of Islamdom shared many characteristics with Southeast Asia and Sub-Saharan Africa, and the awkward relationship between indebtedness and bondage surfaced there as well. There is no apparent evidence for debates about the acceptability of enslavement for debt, or control of people in other ways as a result of indebtedness. However, this may simply reflect the limited nature of research on Islamic slavery in Central Asia and China.

In Central Asia, the expanding Russians sought to stamp out servitude. They obliged Amir 'Abd al-Ahad of Bukhara to abolish slavery in 1885, but it 'lingered on in the form of debtors' bondage'.[54] Indeed, as late as 1914, a Russian veterinary surgeon witnessed a man selling his daughter for 400 roubles to pay a debt.[55] An ambiguous example of the Islamic use of debt to bond labour came from China. Buying indebted people, and more especially their children, was deeply entrenched in Chinese society, and the practice was responsible for a large proportion of all slaves in the empire. To adhere to increasingly abolitionist Qing legislation, this process was frequently expressed as 'adoption'.[56] Hui Muslims became notorious in the eighteenth and nineteenth centuries for purchasing and 'adopting' large numbers of children from distressed Han compatriots, enlarging the Muslim community in the process. However, it remains unclear whether the Hui treated these 'adopted' children as slaves; rather, it seems that they looked upon them as junior lineages.[57]

South Asia

South Asian Muslims only partially converted subject societies, in which debt bondage was ancient and strongly rooted, and it is thus scarcely surprising that the practice persisted. Characteristically, however, South Asian Muslims turned debtors into slaves. Already in the fourteenth century, Ibn Battuta reported a trade in indebted women in the Maldive Islands, which were entirely Islamic by that time.[58] Under the Mughals, the sale of children by famished parents persisted, and the purchasers were often Muslims.[59] In the early nineteenth century, Muslims were reported to own, or in some way control, large numbers of indebted persons across the sub-continent.[60] Moreover, Muslim rulers in South Asia were prone to enslave tax-defaulters, whom one can define as debtors to the state. This was already noted in the time of the Delhi Sultanate, in the thirteenth century.[61] Akbar, the great Mughal emperor, tried to stop this practice in the sixteenth century, but with no more than partial success;[62] after his death, the enslavement of tax-defaulters resumed.[63] Nineteenth-century Afghan rulers also regularly reduced to slavery those who failed to pay their taxes.[64]

South Asian views of debt slavery differed from those found in other 'peripheral' areas of Islam, however, in that justifications of servitude as a penalty for debt relied partly on a controversial interpretation of the sharia. Sir Bartle Frere's rather surprising statement in 1873 that Islamic law authorized the enslavement of 'insolvent debtors' probably reflected his long experience in British India and his consequent familiarity with such arguments.[65] An influential South Asian Islamic text, the *Mohit-u-Surakhsi*, held that a free man hard pressed by his creditors could sell himself to pay off what he owed. The second element in the title of this work may refer to Surraq, who gave his name to the discredited *hadith* of the early years of Islam. Indeed, the *Mohit-u-Surakhsi* specified that a tradition of the Prophet gave legitimacy to the practice of debt servitude. According to this tradition, however, repayment of debt would result in freedom, so that this was not chattel slavery in the usual sharia sense. Adam stated that the *Mohit-u-Surakhsi* was a 'work of unquestionable authority', but numerous South Asian *ulama* contested such an interpretation. Moreover, justifications of slavery for debt did not appear in the *Fatawa Alamgiri*, a generally accepted authoritative collection of Mughal legal opinions.[66]

Prodded by the ardent abolitionist John Richardson, the East India Company's Calcutta muftis issued a fatwa on slavery in 1809. In it, they stated that it was only legal to enslave 'infidels fighting against the faith'. Sale of self or children was prohibited, as was slavery originating in debt. Specifically prohibited were the enslaving of 'distressed debtors' and selling children in times of famine. Indeed, the legal opinion also outlawed enslavement through kidnapping, fraud or life-long labour contracts, regardless of whether those involved were Indian or African.[67] A fatwa of 1841 authored by the muftis of the Madras Presidency echoed the findings of their Calcutta colleagues.[68] These legal opinions thus rejected both the importation of people reduced to servitude for debt in the lands of unbelievers and the enslavement of people for debt within India. However, the sale of people for debt, including Muslims, continued in practice. Thus, famine-afflicted Baluchi Muslims found a ready market in Persia and the Gulf well into the twentieth century.[69]

The British were more inclined to repress chattel slavery than debt bondage, for they saw the latter as too deeply embedded in the fabric of South Asian social life to be challenged directly. Chattel slavery ceased to be recognized in law in 1844, in terms of legislation from the previous year, and owning slaves or trading in them became illegal in the penal code drawn up in 1860, effective from 1862. However, debt bondage was not affected by these measures.[70] The newly autonomous state in British India cautiously initiated legislation against debt bondage in 1920. However, in 1934, the League of Nations denounced the survival of harsh forms of debt peonage in Hyderabad, the largest Muslim-ruled princely state in India, albeit probably referring to Hindu debtors.[71] Indeed, the practice continued till at least 1976, long after India's independence in 1947, as abolition met with tremendous problems of implementation.[72]

The Middle East

The enslavement of Muslims for debt persisted de facto in the Middle East, but the issue comes up more rarely in the literature than for other areas. One might be tempted to see this as proof of religious orthodoxy in the heartlands of Islam, but it should be recalled that, after the period of initial conquest, very few of the Middle East's numerous slaves originated from the area itself. As for the troops of slaves entering the Middle East from farther afield, it is impossible to estimate what proportion had been enslaved for debt in their homelands.

Not only was enslavement for debt unusual within the Middle East, but there is also no obvious indication that such behaviour was justified in terms of either holy or customary law. In early eighteenth-century Egypt, a man pawned an orphan boy as surety for a debt, but, when the sum was reimbursed, the boy was freed.[73] As late as the dawn of the twentieth century, villagers of north-eastern Iran sold their daughters into slavery in West Turkistan to pay their taxes. However, this was acknowledged as being morally and legally wrong, and was blamed on the rapaciousness of secular tax collectors.[74] A flow of Kurdish girls sold into Iran, reported in the mid-nineteenth century, may have had similar origins.[75]

The Persian Gulf witnessed the most extensive control of labour through debt, which was used at times to retain the services of manumitted slaves.[76] The most prevalent example of debt slavery in this region is that of pearl divers, comprising African slaves and poor and indebted local people, including freed Africans.[77] A British report from 1935 observed that Bahrayn's pearl divers were still poor, but that they were no longer in hereditary debt bondage to ships' captains as they had been some fifteen years earlier.[78] Debt bondage may have reflected the heavy involvement of South Asian merchants in financing the business and their importation of methods of labour control common in the sub-continent.

Conclusion

The relative scarcity of writings on debt peonage in Islam suggests that it was not a significant phenomenon. The formal bonding of labour through debt without actually enslaving workers only occurred on any scale in lands where religious syncretism was strong. Java presents a particularly good example of such a phenomenon. The question that most preoccupied the faithful was whether unredeemed debt could result in chattel slavery, which was the 'default mode' of the coercion of labour in Islam. The 'men of the pen' soon forbad this type of enslavement, but three main factors conspired to blunt the effectiveness of this reform, especially in the 'peripheral lands' of Islam. Firstly, the invention of a distinction between the abode of Islam and the abode of war, which is not present in the Qur'ân, enabled the faithful to evade what was arguably the spirit of the holy law by importing slaves who owed their status as chattels to debts incurred in the abode of war.

Secondly, the space granted to secular and customary law within Islamic societies created a conflict of laws, which at times also permitted the enslavement of
debtors in the abode of Islam. Finally, the authoritarian nature of political power
meant that some rulers and social elites simply rode rough-shod over the holy law,
enslaving or otherwise exploiting debtors despite objections of the *ulama*.

While the general outline seems fairly clear, much still needs to be discovered
about the relationship between debt and labour in Islamic societies. Whether
the prohibition on lending at interest affected overall levels of debt is one significant question. Another is the balance between enslavement for debt and other
responses to indebtedness, and how this reflected the conflict of laws prevalent
in particular Islamic societies. In terms of available sources, a potentially fruitful
avenue for future research might be to investigate more fully the ways in which
sharia-minded reformers in all ages sought to stamp out what they considered to
be an abuse of the holy law.

2 DEBT, PAWNSHIP AND SLAVERY IN NINETEENTH-CENTURY EAST AFRICA

Edward A. Alpers

In recent years, the study of slavery and the slave trade has developed much more sophisticated and comprehensive quantitative data than were previously available, while at the same time re-focusing attention on the experiences of enslaved Africans. One aspect of this latter effort has been to identify sources that give voice to those Africans caught up by the slave trade and to draw upon them to humanize our understanding of this terrible traffic. In approaching the topic of this chapter, I adopt this methodology and seek to place these African voices in the wider context of the extant historiography on slavery in East Africa.

One of these voices was that of Swema, a young Yao girl from northern Mozambique who was born in about 1855, a time when the demand for slaves in Zanzibar was approaching its height and Kilwa Kivinje had emerged as the principal slave-trading port in eastern Africa. The death of her father in a hunting accident and the absence of any matrilineal kinsmen to protect Swema and her mother left these two women in an especially vulnerable position. Forced to borrow millet seed (*mtama*) to consume and sow from a neighbour in the village to which they relocated, Swema's mother found herself unable to repay her debt at the end of a poor season. After several delayed attempts to collect his debt, the neighbour decided to redeem his investment by selling Swema to a coastal slave caravan. According to the record of Swema's own story, 'Creditors profit from circumstance to extract the payment of debts. When the debtors are unable to pay, one seizes their slaves or their children. Often it happens that they are reduced to selling themselves into slavery'.[1] The point is then driven home in Swema's reported account of what followed this decision by her mother's creditor:

> Without asking permission, he entered our hut and said with severity to my mother: 'Mother of Swema, you haven't anything to pay in return for my two sacks of *mtama*: for that reason I am seizing your child.
>
> 'You are my witnesses', he said to the elders [of the village in which Swema and her mother resided]. Then turning towards the Arab, he said to him: 'Well, Sir, it's settled, six *coudées* [about three meters] of American cloth [*merikani*] for this little girl'.[2]

As Mary Douglas first argued in a pioneering article in the 1960s, pawnship was an important feature of the matrilineal societies of Central Africa from the Atlantic to the Indian Ocean.[3] However, according to Douglas, pawnship – a term she seems to have coined to describe the institution of blood-debt that she first encountered while conducting fieldwork among the Lele of Kasai in today's Democratic Republic of the Congo – 'was the system of transferring the rights over persons as compensation for offences and settlement of debts.'[4] She considered that 'Rights as owners of pawns are transmitted matrilineally through the generations, so that an enduring heritable property is created by the system, which gives stability and strength to the owning clan section'. She argued further, 'I should emphasize that a pawn is in no way a slave', ending her definition by observing that 'since everyone is liable to be pawned at any time, and since pawns can be owners of other pawns, it is not a humiliating condition.'[5] With her focus squarely on the way in which pawnship modified matrilineal kinship, Douglas emphasized the following point: 'Let me make it clear at this point that what I am interested in is not any transfer of persons in payment of debts, but a transfer which creates an enduring property by building up a pawn lineage belonging to an owning descent group.'[6] In attempting 'to isolate pawnship from slavery', however, as Marcia Wright has pointed out,[7] it is clear that Douglas did not appreciate the way in which the historical contingency of the nineteenth-century slave trade subverted the ideal system of pawnship that she so carefully reconstructed from the transformations wrought by the imposition of colonial rule.

In this chapter I explore the wider existence of pawnship in nineteenth-century East Africa, moving beyond the constraints of Douglas's matrilineal context, as it relates to the problem of debt, slavery and the slave trade. In undertaking this survey it is important to pay attention to the changing character of the slave trade during this century, rather than reducing it to an unchanging phenomenon. If we condemn Reginald Coupland for propagating the unsustainable claim that the slave trade ran through the history of East Africa 'like a scarlet thread' for two millennia, then we must equally beware of flattening out the changing contours of the slave trade during the century when this traffic was at its height.[8] Specifically, we need to appreciate that while the demand for slaves in East Africa was driven by various external forces in the Mascarene Islands, Madagascar and Arabia, it was the internal demand from the nineteenth-century development of a plantation economy on Zanzibar, Pemba and the coastal strip which, as Abdul Sheriff has demonstrated, constituted the primary market for enslaved labour in East Africa.[9] Similarly, although the export markets for East African captives tended to emphasize males over females, Frederick Cooper's fundamental study of slavery on Zanzibar suggests that there was a large market for both men and women.[10] My reason for making this broad chronological distinction is to establish a historical context for the gendered nature of the slave trade as it might have affected – if at all – the relationship between debt, pawnship and slavery.

At the same time, we need to bear in mind the wide range of differences across the hundreds of different societies and polities that constituted nineteenth-century East Africa. While debt is a universal phenomenon, individual societies had different resources available to them with which to repay debt and fashion forms of servitude. Thus, for example, in pre-dynastic seventeenth-century Rwanda, debt and clientage were focused on the loaning of cattle to poor individuals, as in the institution of *ubugabire*, a contract that 'created a relation of inequality, but its duration was not unlimited and either party could end it, particularly after the death of the first cow that had been given'. Under Ruganzu Ndori, founder of the Nyiginya kingdom, this kind of debt-relationship transformed into a more permanent and more onerous relationship called *ubuhake*, binding the client to the king in a hereditary relationship.[11] In the eighteenth and nineteenth centuries, the military expansion of the kingdom produced booty in the form of cattle, women and children, some of the latter being adopted. During what Jan Vansina calls the 'nightmare' reign of Rwabugiri (1867–97), this process was accelerated, and eventually a trade in slaves based on captive women and children emerged as African traders connected to the central Tanzanian caravan route reached the borders of the kingdom.[12] My point here is that by the end of the nineteenth century Rwanda had developed a highly coercive state with an elaborate system of debt-based clientage as well as both internal slavery and an external slave trade, yet because of the significance of clientage and the competition for accumulating clients within the Nyiginya kingdom, there is no evidence that debt was exploited to produce victims for the slave trade.

To take a completely different example, in one of two contributions about East Africa in Paul Lovejoy and Toyin Falola's seminal collection of essays on pawnship and slavery in Africa, Fred Morton begins his chapter with the unambiguous statement that 'In the nineteenth century, Miji Kenda children who had been pawned were, as a rule, sold as slaves'.[13] Located in the immediate hinterland of Mombasa and consisting of a loose grouping of corporate units, the Mijikenda could not be farther away from the Nyiginya kingdom of Rwanda both geographically and politically. Morton argues that thousands of Mijikenda children disappeared into slavery as 'pawnship was subsumed within slavery as one mechanism that generated new slaves for the expanding economy' of plantations on the coast or export to Arabia.[14] Like cattle clientage in Rwanda, pawning among the Mijikenda reflected important differences in wealth within the coastal region, where those groups and individuals connected to the Busaidi sultanate at Zanzibar had resources unavailable to poor Mijikenda farmers.[15] Morton makes several important points in his discussion of pawning and slavery. First, he sees 'no firm evidence of pawning on the Kenya coast before the growth of the East African slave trade'. Secondly, he clearly links pawning and slavery to the ravages of famine, beginning with a famine recorded by Church Missionary Society stalwart J. L. Krapf in 1837, the very year in which Seyyid Said b. Sultan coincidentally defeated the Mazrui and incorporated Mombasa into his emerging East African empire. The availability of cheap labour in a market with a growing demand for labour, Morton continues, argued against 'the notion that pawns were not saleable property', which was, in fact, 'ignored by the major creditors'. He adds further that even 'where pawns were held rather than exported, redemption was rare', as the cost of slave labour against which the pawn's value was assessed (rather than the cost of whatever food was exchanged originally for the pawn) made it virtually impossible for their Mijikenda kin to afford the price of redemption.[16]

Justin Willis is somewhat less certain than Morton about the complete novelty of Mijikenda pawns being sold into slavery, but he also quotes Krapf to emphasize the role of famine in driving desperate Mijikenda into slavery at Mombasa: 'During the great famine she [a Swahili woman] had provided a Mnika mother and her child with 20 pishis or measures of Turkish corn [*mtama*], then to the value of 4 or 5 dollars ... in consequence of this act she considered the persons she had maintained to be her slaves'.[17] A different perspective on the basis for Mijikenda selling their children into slavery comes from the testimony of Kaje wa Mwenye Matano, a freeborn elderly woman born in about 1890 and interviewed by Margaret Strobel in the early 1970s, on slavery in her family household in Mombasa.

> Among those people, the Digo [a Mijikenda group] – if you hear about Digo-style slavery – it's not that a person comes and sells his or her child. No. Say you have a brother. Now your brother goes and steals somebody's child. He takes the child, and they want compensation. Now you are poor, you have no money. You tell your brother, 'Take your nephew, when you get somewhere, sell him, get some money and repay the people's money'. This is the origin of the Nyikas' slavery, all the people from around here, those people from our part of Africa, all of them. This is the only way they were sold. He has taken someone's child, he has no money. They catch him and will imprison him. His sister gives her child and tells him to sell him and get money from that master ... That is why their children were enslaved. To save yourself, that's the origin of the Nyika slaves, the Digo.[18]

Here we are closer to the link between debt, pawnship and slavery that marks the story of Swema. Thus, based on Bi Kaje's testimony, we can see that there may have been more than one element among the Mijikenda that explains the history of this set of relationships. Bi Kaje, whose household included thirty slaves, twelve of whom were Mijikenda, also provides an example of a Mijikenda male pawn named Majaliwa who became a slave and was eventually redeemed by his father. 'Majaliwa was Saidi's slave ... Majaliwa's father came and gave Saidi money. He returned the money and said, "Here is your money, Saidi. My child is not your slave"'.[19]

Further evidence of the various ways in which individuals could become enslaved through debt or famine in coastal society is found in the *Desturi za Waswahili* of Mtoro b. Mwinyi Bakari, a man of mixed Swahili–Zaramo parentage from Bagamoyo who eventually served as a lecturer at the Seminar für Orientalische Sprachen in Berlin. Mtoro begins his chapter on slavery by identifying 'some disaster such as war' as the first cause of enslavement, but he follows that immediately by stating:

> Or slavery may arise from a debt of blood money. If somebody has killed another and his family is poor and he has no money, he is liable for blood money; but if he cannot pay, he is taken and sold, or he goes as a slave to the creditor. If he has killed a freeman, the blood money is a large sum, and if he has a brother or an uncle, he may also accompany him into slavery ... Or if an adulterer has lain with another man's wife, he has to pay compensation. If he cannot, he becomes a slave. Compensation for adultery used to be paid inland and on the coast, even among the Swahili. Or in time of famine people would sell themselves to each other. Or a person may pledge a child or a brother-in-law, and when he has not the money to redeem him, he becomes a slave.
>
> To return to consideration of the inland country: prisoners of war, pawns, and persons taken in adultery whose families cannot redeem them become slaves. Arab and other traders go inland and buy them and bring them to the coast and sell them to others. This is the origin of slavery.[20]

In this lengthy passage we can see that debt could be incurred in several different ways in coastal society and, according to Mtoro, these same situations obtained upcountry. Furthermore, although the translation of Mtoro's text uses the word 'pledge' and 'pawn', the Swahili text more explicitly makes the link between the two concepts by writing *kuweka rahani* and *rahani*.[21] The new wrinkle that he adds to the mix of famine and blood-debt is adultery. Writing about the far interior of East Central Africa along the Nyasa-Tanganyika Corridor, Marcia Wright also notes that adultery was sometimes punished by compensating the aggrieved party with the payment of a pawn, something also noted among the Zaramo, the Luguru and the Bena of southern Tanzania.[22]

At the coast slave owners could also use their slaves as pawns for their own debts. 'Any debtor', Mtoro tells us,

> can send his slave as security, whether the slave likes it or not, if security is required of the master. Such a slave is allowed one day to go and visit his master and to return on the next day. A married slave can be used as security and his wife too, and they have to do the same work as they did for their master. If they are idle, he can send them back and demand his money.[23]

Writing about Indian merchants at Pangani, on the Mrima between Bagamoyo and Mombasa, Jonathan Glassman also records the settling of debts with slaves.[24] Indeed, as coastal caravans pushed the ivory and slave frontier farther into the interior of East Africa, such arrangements travelled with them. During one of his trading ventures deep into the heart of Central Africa, Hamed b. Muhammad el Murjebi, the notorious Tippu Tip, records the following transaction:

> Throughout this trip I had four slaves, which I had bought from Abdessalam, himself the slave of dhow-captain Hilal. At that time slaves were cheap. Abdessalam had advertised them to Khamis wad Mtaa, saying, 'What about buying these slaves, they're Yao, elephant hunters. I wouldn't have offered them but I'm in debt; I want 100 dollars for them (200/ – 500/-); 25 dollars each'. He had said he had no money and Khamis had brought them to me and suggested I buy them. I gave him the 100 dollars.[25]

Although Tippu Tip was not the debtor in this instance, Abdessalam, who was possibly a 'slave *fundi* – typically an *mzalia* who had been apprenticed to his craft in the town',[26] clearly was, so he was fortunate to be able to acquire the cash so as to be able to satisfy his debt by selling his slaves to Tippu Tip.

Mtoro also includes an account of the consequence of famine in Zaramo country, which lay in the immediate hinterland of Bagamoyo. For most of the nineteenth century, Zaramo political leaders extracted a form of tribute from the town; this changes in the mid-1870s, when the forces of Seyyid Barghash b. Said finally established the Sultan of Zanzibar's exclusive authority there. Accordingly, relations between the Zaramo and the inhabitants of Bagamoyo, those whom Steven Fabian calls the Wabagamoyo, were closely intertwined.[27] Mtoro writes:

> In the time of Sayyid Barghash there was a famine, and the Zaramo sold and pawned each other.[28] When the Zanzibar Arabs heard that slaves were easily obtained on the coast, they came to buy Zaramo slaves; but when they went to sleep at night, the Zaramo ran away and by morning was back at home. Once he was there it was hard to recover him. Those who were shipped to Zanzibar stayed for a month and then claimed not to be slaves but freemen and the courts were full of complaints. When Sayyid Barghash found out that the Arabs were going to the coast to buy Zaramo, he rebuked them, saying, 'Anybody who goes to the coast to buy Zaramo is throwing his money into the sea, and in addition I shall give him six months in fetters'. The reason for this was that they were not being bought; when people were going out of the town [Bagamoyo] into the country and they saw Zaramo women and children, they would seize them, gagging them so that they could not cry out, and bring them into the town to sell to the traders.[29]

Here we can see how one subterfuge, the enslavement of pawns given as security in exchange for food during a time of famine, had itself become a cover for kidnapping, which we know from many sources was an increasingly important means of enslaving people in the later nineteenth century. In view of Barghash's desire to establish his legitimacy as ruler over Bagamoyo and the Mrima coast (*mrima* means coast) and hinterland, it is not surprising that the Omani ruler of Zanzibar came down hard on these opportunistic Arabs.

For the Zaramo, we are fortunate to possess an autobiographical account by a youth who had been liberated by the British naval anti-slave trade patrol and sent to the Anglo-Catholic Universities' Mission to Central Africa at Zanzibar, where he was converted to Christianity and educated at Kiungani, the UMCA boys school. He begins his personal history with these words:

> At first I was living with my father and my mother. From the first my relations kept an eye upon me, I think. After my mother's death, I remained with my father perhaps four or five years. Well, my mother's father had borrowed six dollars from some people at Bagamoyo, who bargained that in six years they should come and receive their money. When the six years expired, they came. Now my mother, when she was alive, warned me, saying, 'When I die, your friends will make away with you'. I was but a little child, and I thought she was only talking nonsense, but she was quite right. The men from Bagamoyo said to my grandfather, 'Give us our money. If you do not, we will seize you, and take you to the governor to be put in prison'. 'Wait a bit', said he, 'and give me time to get your money together. As soon as I get it, I will give it to you'. 'No', they said, 'we cannot wait. Give it to us at once'. Now I was living with my father after my mother's death. My grandfather came to my father and said, 'Give me this child to give to my creditors, and let me ransom him when I get their money'. My father said, 'I cannot give him to you in that way. I will have nothing to do with it'. Afterwards my father said, 'Go and hide yourself, for your grandfather is keeping a sharp look-out for you'. Well, I thought it was all nonsense, and said, 'What? Am I to hide myself in the bushes?' And I said, 'I cannot stay in the bushes. It's no matter. If I am caught, I am caught'. That very day my grandfather came and took me in his arms and fondled me, till I consented and went. He said to his creditors, 'Do not get rid of him. I shall ransom him'. They said, 'Very good', and we started off the same day. And then I thought how my mother had warned me, and cried bitterly. They said to me, 'Don't cry. We will put you in a comfortable home and feed you, till your family ransom you'. So I stopped crying.[30]

Following a day of travel they reached Bagamoyo, where after he fell ill and was nursed back to health, he remained for two years. He was then sold to another Arab master at Pangani, where he remained for another six months. Finally, he was shipped to Pemba, but when the British naval patrol intercepted the dhow upon which he was travelling, fate landed him at Kiungani.[31] This account from the Zaramo conforms to the general picture of pawnship and matrilineal described by Douglas, since the boy's matrilineal grandfather was able to exercise his kinship rights over the clear objections of the boy's father. What is most interesting about this boy's transition from a pawn to a slave for the purposes of this paper, however, is his realization after a while that no one was going to come to redeem him, which – reading between the lines – his Bagamoyo master may have known to be the case all along.

Further evidence of the connection between famine and the sale of junior kin to acquire foodstuffs comes from the other matrilineal peoples – Luguru, Kami, Doe and Kwere – who inhabited the farther hinterland of the Tanzanian

Mrima. Interviews with a number of community elders in the early 1970s across the region leave no doubt that nephews were regularly pawned by their matrilineal elders both as compensation for debt and in exchange for food in times of famine, of which there were many during the late nineteenth century.[32] Even among the Yao, among whom enslaved labour was obtained primarily through raiding and warfare, we possess one example of the link between famine, pawning and slavery. According to testimony recorded by H.M. Consul at Zanzibar Christopher Rigby at the British Consular Court in September 1860 from an eighteen-year old Yao male named Toombo, he was enslaved 'about ten months ago':

> There was a fight at my village which is called 'Kitondo' and is situated about 20 days from the sea coast. I was seized by my own elder brother and taken to Quali [Kwale] on the sea Coast and sold by my brother to my present master, the prisoner before the court [Ragoojee Namia, a Banian]. I do not know what he paid for me. When I say that my own elder brother sold me I mean that he was my half brother by the same father but different mothers. My mother was also sold with me by my half brother. The reason he sold us was because there was a famine in our country and we could not procure any food.[33]

Turning from the immediate coastal hinterland to the interior of central Kenya, we can see some of the same principles of blood-debt, famine and slavery at play in the nineteenth century. As Charles Ambler points out, although some female labour was acquired by raiding, 'The transfer of women was usually accomplished, however, through pawning agreements. Pawning was the basic customary instrument of the circulation of dependent labor within the region, and pawning arrangements were commonplace, particularly when food shortages occurred'. He goes on to explain that the

> extension of external trade into the regional exchange system forced a rapid commercialization of the transfer of female labor. Traders both from communities in central Kenya and from the coast manipulated the convention of pawning to obtain women – generally refugees – who it was understood could be reclaimed. In other words, the buyers were acquiring rights over the women themselves, not simply their labor. The women – now in effect slaves – were then resold, usually to farmers within the region. Few were transported beyond central Kenya.[34]

At the end of the century central Kenya was struck by a terrible famine that, exacerbating a decade of rinderpest and smallpox, virtually wiped out the region's cattle and weakened its human populations. Maasai and Kamba who would have previously exchanged their cattle for food were now forced to pawn themselves and, especially, their women and children into agricultural communities that were able to receive them. Ambler particularly emphasizes the commodification of women that accompanied this process during these famine years.[35] According to tradition collected among the Embu and related agricultural peoples of the central Kenyan mountains four decades ago, famine figured significantly in the collective memory. Not surprisingly, indigenous memories avoid the kind of analysis proposed by Ambler, but they do refer to the fact that many 'famine refugees' never returned to their natal homes and were absorbed into these societies. One consequence of this process, however one characterizes it, is that there remained a residue of resentment between those who could not recover their women and children and those who absorbed them as wives and children.[36]

A similar situation seems to have obtained among the Nyamwezi, the dominant traders along the central Tanzanian route for most of the nineteenth century.[37] As Jan-Georg Deutsch indicates very clearly, 'debt settlement could lead to enslavement, especially when a member of the family had already been given away as security for a loan ... In the event that the debtor or his family eventually failed to honour the debt, the creditor had the right to recoup the loan by enslavement and subsequent sale of the pawn'.[38] Deutsch also notes the frequency with which famine was the cause of being pawned into slavery in Unyamwezi. Furthermore, although he suggests that pawning a family member was usually done reluctantly as a last resort to provide sustenance for those members of the kinship group who remained, 'pawning was often a means of disguising the outright sale of a person by his or her family since the latter was regarded as an exceedingly dishonourable act'.[39]

Two other stories from Kiungani boys shed some further light on debt, pawnship and slavery among the matrilineal peoples of East Central Africa whom Douglas initially analysed. The first concerns a young Bisa who had lived a long time in Yaoland and did not remember the circumstances of how he left his homeland. He claims that he was well treated by his master, who 'was always fond of me':

> One year he said to me, 'Let us go to the coast and see the Arabs and Europeans and Hindis and Banyans', I said, 'Yes, let us'. So we travelled till we came to Kilwa, where a friend of his lived, one of the coast people. He took me and gave me to his friend, and said, 'I give you this slave, but do not sell him. I will come and redeem him, but' (speaking to me) 'I happen to have nothing to give my friend this time. Keep the boy till I return myself', Then my master went away to Yaoland to fetch things with which to redeem me. What did his friend do but carry me off and take me to live with his own master? And there I remained a very long time.[40]

Eventually he ran away, but he was soon kidnapped 'by some other Arabs'. After a few days, 'a man came searching for me. He saw me, and said, "How did you get here? Your old master has come back, and is going to ransom you". I was delighted when I heard he had come back. The Arabs who had kidnapped me said, "Come to-morrow morning, and we will hand over your slave". But as soon as it was night they packed up their things, all in the night, and woke us up, 'Come along, let us set off to-night'. The Arabs marched the captives of which he was one up the coast until they reached Bagamoyo. Finally, they walked to another place where 'We were seized on the land, not on the sea.'[41]

Two aspects of this story deserve comment. First, although the Bisa boy did not say so directly, the circumstances of his Yao master's handing him over to his friend at the coast and his promise to redeem the boy signal that the master was indebted to the Kilwan, perhaps because he was unable to repay trade goods that he had received on credit, and that the Bisa boy was his pawn. Secondly, although he had been 'liberated' by Europeans (presumably British) and entrusted to the UMCA, from his perspective his liberation was simply the latest in a series of seizures that had marked his young life.

The last testimony from Kiungani was recorded by a Makua boy from the coastal hinterland of northern Mozambique. His tale is a classic account of a younger child being pawned as payment for a blood-debt incurred by another member of his family and then sold into slavery.

> At my home where I was born, I belonged to a family of twelve, and there I lived with them a long time. Then one of my brothers trespassed, and his trespass was this: he was married, and his wife was a bad one, and a drunkard, too, and so, indeed, was her husband. Well, one day my brother went out at night and went to another person's house and knocked at the door. Inside there was a woman, and he went in and stayed with her. This woman had lost her husband, so he said to her, 'I will come and marry you'. And the woman consented. While it was still night my brother rose up and went away. In the morning the woman told her family, and said, 'Kinsmen, I was asleep last night, and so-and-so came and knocked at the door, and I opened it, and he came in and said, 'I want to marry you''. Her kinsmen said to her, 'We do not want to have you married. We want to have compensation'. So my brother was seized. All my family were grown except me; I was still a child. Well, they went on keeping my brother in confinement, till at last my family took me, and gave me in payment to his captors. The payment was made and ended, before my mother knew that I had been taken away. And my mother cried bitterly, but the others made her be quiet. The people who carried me off sold me to some other people, and then my brothers told my mother that I was really gone for good.[42]

After passing through the hands of several masters over a period of years, the child was eventually sent in bondage to the island of Mwali in the Comoro archipelago before his liberation by the British and redirection to Zanzibar and the care of the UMCA. Although his reference to what his brothers allegedly told his mother after he had been removed from the family suggests more about his powers of invention than his veracity, there is no reason to doubt the truth of his serving as a pawn for his miscreant elder brother. His story reveals, once again, the particular vulnerability of children within the power structures of kin groups and the probability of their being disposed of as chattel during the height of the slave trade in East Africa.

Based on research in the Nyasa-Tanganyika Corridor area of East Central Africa, Wright demonstrates vividly that women were as vulnerable as children. Her presentation of the life histories of the women whom she studies leave no doubt that at the end of the nineteenth century pawning was regularly resorted to by men to settle their debts. The most poignant example she provides concerns the granddaughter of a woman named Narwimba who 'was regarded by [Chief Mwachitete] as an appropriate pawn to compensate villagers who had been attacked because of a dispute between himself and [Chief] Mkoma.'[43]

Perhaps no better example of the vulnerability of children, women and the poor and weak more generally in the particular context of the slave trade exists than the history of the rise of a young and headstrong man named Chilangwe, later to be known as Litete, who eventually assumed the name of Mtalika, 'he who is known afar', a powerful Yao slave trading chief of south-eastern Tanzania whom Livingstone met in 1866.[44] According to the account of Canon Robin Lamburn, who indicates that his main source was Edward Kalale, a Makua teacher who conducted research in the 1940s and was adopted into the Mtalika clan in Tunduru District,[45] Chilangwe grew up around the south end of Lake Nyasa. Lamburn writes that he was

> a violent, obstinate, and obstreperous youth. There was constant trouble with him, for his violent temper and actions led to continuous rows with his neighbours. At last there came a big case. Probably Chilangwe had killed a man in a neighbouring village, for the demand of the offended village was that Chilangwe should become their slave'

Although Chilangwe had grown up in his father's village, he was a member of his mother's lineage (*mbumba* in Yao), so the father indicated that he would not give up Chilangwe to slavery unless his maternal uncle [who was named Chikweo] ... had heard the matter and given his consent too'. On the trip to the maternal uncle's village – a distance of two or three days' march – they rested at the village of a close friend of the uncle, a man named Akulukoloma. 'He called the plaintiffs and offered to pay them – presumably in slaves – to drop the case. They consented to take a slave or slaves in place of Chilangwe himself, and went home without ever seeing Chikweo'. In an interesting twist to this story of the child of a prominent Yao lineage being relieved of a blood-debt by payment of one or more slaves, Chilangwe was required to remain with Akulukoloma 'and help him with his work.'[46]

The example of Chilangwe/Litete/Mtalika, like that of the Kiungani Zaramo boy previously discussed, complements and modifies James Giblin's very reasonable argument, based on his research among the matrilineal Zigua of Handeni District in north-eastern Tanzania, that 'kinship and descent did not always take precedence over political relations in precolonial societies and hence were not necessarily the basis for decisions relating to pawning.'[47] In this last case from another matrilineal people who were deeply involved in the slave trade, it would seem that kinship and political influence, if not power, probably combined to determine the decision and the ability to substitute a slave as a pawn for the volatile Chilangwe.

In an essay on 'The Gospel and the Muslim in East Africa', Lamburn enters into a discussion of slavery and the role of Arabs in what he describes as modern slavery in the production of sugar in the Rufiji District of Tanzania in the years immediately following the end of the Second World War.

> These Arabs had a very simple way of getting new slaves. They would go on *safari* to any part of the country where they heard that there was a shortage of food. When the hungry men came and begged for assistance from these rich Arabs, they were given food; their relations were given food; but all on the condition that they should come with the Arab party and help with the baggage. When they reached Mohoro [the main town in Rufiji District] and home, the men asked for their pay and leave to return to their homes, but were told: 'No, you cannot leave till you have paid the debt for all the food that you and your relations have consumed; till then, you are our slaves'; and so they stayed and worked for a release that never came.[48]

Even allowing for Lamburn's anti-Arab and anti-Muslim bias, and the fact that he does not indicate his source for this passage, his description is reminiscent of Mtoro b. Mwinyi Bakari's account of Arab petty traders travelling to Bagamoyo to purchase famished Zaramo during a period of famine in the late nineteenth century.

The last area explored here is the Great Lakes region, where the history of slavery has recently received new attention.[49] One important result of this work is the evidence provided by David Schoenbrun's analysis of the language evidence for the existence of pawnship and slavery before the eighteenth century, both of which carried forward right into the early twentieth century.[50] In nineteenth-century Buganda, for example, slaves were not infrequently substituted for the sons of important families to serve as pages at the royal court.[51] What is most interesting in the two major kingdoms of Uganda in the nineteenth century – the great rival states of Buganda and Bunyoro – is that although pawnship was a well established institution for the settlement of debt in both societies, it seems not to have been a pathway to internal slavery or a significant vehicle for producing bodies for the export slave trade, although Michael Tuck gives one isolated example of how a woman who was pawned was subsequently transferred from one owner to another over the course of her lifetime. As Tuck's analysis of a group of fifty-five freed female slaves who came to the Roman Catholic Mill Hill Mission in Buganda at the end of our period shows, only one of them became enslaved because she had been given as a pawn in payment of a debt.[52] For the most part, in the Great Lakes region slaves were the product of warfare, as the story of a Nyoro boy at Kiungani makes clear.[53]

This survey suggests several conclusions and poses at least one important question for further research. First, it seems without question that throughout nineteenth-century East Africa there was a wide range of institutions for the settlement of debts that involved pawnship. Secondly, it is equally clear that during the heyday of the slave trade this connection regularly ended in the pawn being enslaved and, in many instances, sold. Thirdly, it appears that the closer to the coast and to the main trade routes connecting the coast to the interior, the stronger was the nexus between debt, pawnship and slavery. Fourthly, famine was probably the most frequent driver of this system, although violent crime and adultery also fed it. Finally, at the other end of the spectrum would seem to be the kingdoms of the Great Lakes region, where deeply embedded institutions of pawnage existed, but were apparently not linked to the slave trade. This contrast with the other East African societies I have discussed in this chapter suggests that the existence of powerful states was a more significant factor in determining the relationship between debt, pawnship and slavery than were descent systems. Proving or disproving this thesis will depend on further research into the important connection between debt and slavery in this broad region of nineteenth-century East Africa.

3 DEBT AND SLAVERY IN IMPERIAL MADAGASCAR, 1790–1861

Gwyn Campbell

Introduction

The relationship between indebtedness and bondage is complex. Debt – social, political and economic – is widespread in all societies, plunging the debtor into a position of obligation towards the creditor concomitant with his or her degree of indebtedness. The rules governing these obligations and their relationship to the debt may be oral rather than written, but when formally witnessed and agreed to, they have the sanction of customary law, even where this differs from statutory law. This was the case in Imerina, in central highland Madagascar, where regulations governing debt became codified in the imperial Merina era (*c.* 1785–1895). However, the creditor–debtor relationship became increasingly more complex as a result of the adoption of autarky from the mid-1820s, and the policies intrinsic to it, such as military expansionism and the growth of *fanompoana* – unremunerated forced labour for the state. This contribution first sets the historical context, then discusses the causes and consequences of the main changes in the creditor–debtor relationship in Imperial Madagascar, and subsequently compares and contrasts debt servitude to other forms of bondage.

Background

In the 1790s, Andrianampoinimerina (r. *c.* 1787–1810) emerged triumphant from a period of internecine wars to claim sovereignty over the four provinces of Ankova (the core region of the area that in expanded form became known as Imerina). He established two legal principles: first, that the traditional practice of the destitute becoming the slaves of those who offered them subsistence should be abolished; and secondly, that all those who became indebted, through gambling or borrowing goods and/or money, and were unable to pay off their debt were liable to be sold as slaves. Moreover, if the sale of the debtor did not raise sufficient funds to repay the loan, members of the debtor's immediate family (spouse and children) could also be sold as slaves.[1] Upon this basis, the person of the debtor and his/her family members stood as collateral for all debts contracted, whether in money or in kind. Andrianampoinimerina nominated judges to whom creditors could present claims for unpaid debt, and who, if the case was proven, could condemn the insolvent debtor and his family members to enslavement. In general, it would appear that from the proceeds of the sale of the debtor, the creditor was repaid, the judge compensated for his work and the government received a percentage of the total as a tax for regulating the affair.

Indebtedness in Imerina grew substantially from the end of Andrianampoin-imerina's reign as external forces perturbed the Merina economy. From the late eighteenth century, the burgeoning plantations of the neighbouring Mascarene Islands of Réunion and Mauritius had become increasingly dependent upon the supply of slaves and provisions from Madagascar, for which they exchanged money, armaments and cloth.[2] However, an estimated 80 per cent of revenue from east coast exports flowed to Indian and Swahili traders in payment for west coast imports,[3] while much of the remainder was hoarded, in caches either buried underground or placed in tombs. Moreover, from *c.* 1800, at the time of the Napoleonic Wars, notably during and following the 1809–11 British blockade and occupation of the Mascarenes, Imerina experienced a drop in revenue from east coast exports from approximately $200,000 in 1810 and $22,500 in 1817 to a low of $1,500 by 1820. From 1810, this resulted in sharp falls both in the domestic money supply and in the average price of a slave in domestic markets from $90 to $3 by 1820.[4] The problem was accentuated by the Merina custom of adulterating coinage.[5]

The Britanno-Merina treaty of 1820 banned slave exports, but hoped to compensate this directly through payments by the government of Mauritius to the Merina crown, and indirectly by promoting 'legitimate' trade. However, the slave export ban generally reduced incomes, the money supply and demand for imports, as no Merina slave dealer other than the king received compensation for loss of slave export earnings – which over the period 1820–6 would probably have totalled about $2.5 million[6] – while slaves, who constituted some 33 per cent of the total population by 1830, had little purchasing power. Moreover, the anticipated increase in revenue to the crown failed to materialize,[7] and in 1825–6 King Radama I (r. 1810–28) moved decisively towards autarky.

Autarky

The major policies adopted under autarky were the raising of customs duties and curtailment of foreign investment, import substitution through the exploitation of resources from within the island and labour-intensive investment. From 1826, the Merina Crown raised customs duties[8] and negotiated monopolistic export agreements with selected foreign trading partners that angered both the British, who from 1820 to 1825 had enjoyed minimal duties, and most French traders excluded from monopolistic accords. These measures, as well as a ban on the recruitment of Malagasy labour at a time of increasing anti-slavery pressure leading to abolition on Mauritius in 1835 and Réunion in 1848, united Mascarene planters and traders behind calls for armed intervention. However, the abortive 1829 French and 1845 Franco-British assaults on Merina-held positions on the north-east coast only resulted in the closure of imperial Merina ports to European trade from 1845. Imperial ports reopened in November 1853, after Mauritian merchants and planters paid an indemnity to Ranavalona I (r. 1828–61), but foreign commerce did not recover until Radama II's reign (1861–3).[9]

Central to autarky was a policy of economic modernization through import substitution. From the late 1820s, the Merina court established centres of industrial production on the high plateau, in and around the Merina capital of Antananarivo, and at Mantasoa, about 50 km to the east. These concentrated on the production of armaments, notably gunpowder, musket balls, cannon and swords, and of military equipment, including boots and uniforms.[10] The Merina crown sought to supply these centres with raw materials from within the island, and to this effect launched from the mid-1820s to 1853 an almost ceaseless series of dry-season military expeditions aimed at the conquest and subsequent exploitation of the human and natural resources of all regions of Madagascar.[11]

Tax, Debt and Slavery

In this context, indebtedness and enslavement for debt increased markedly. One of the main causes of indebtedness was government taxation, which was imposed in three basic forms: kind, money and labour:

Tax in Kind

Tax in kind appears to have been the most traditional. It assumed a number of forms, the most widespread of which was taxation of agricultural production. One such imposition comprised the *voalohany* or 'first fruits'.[12] The most common form of this was the *santa-bary*, comprising the first yield of rice,[13] the payment of which was mandatory from the time of Andriamasinavalona (*c.* 1675–1710).[14] Andrianampoinimerina also imposed an annual *isampangady* (lit. 'every spade'), a tax he appears to have combined with similar annual taxes on cultivated land to form a uniform land tax of a half-measure of rice (valued at about $0.008) per rice field, and which could be paid in money. It was rendered to the crown or, if the subject lived on a *menakely* (an estate granted to a vassal), to the lord of that estate.[15] Other taxes in kind included the *vodihena*, a rump of

beef, offered to the sovereign whenever a bullock was butchered, as in ritual sac-
rifices performed, for instance, on the occasion of a circumcision,[16] or an ox, goat
or sheep (depending on the wealth of the supplicant's family) upon the public
lifting of a taboo.[17] Half of this was, under Ranavalona I, distributed to clients of
the crown, royal slaves and those the crown designated as in need.[18]

Taxes traditionally collected in kind proved sufficient to build up considerable grain stocks and grant the Merina aristocracy a life of leisure. However, they
increased sharply with the adoption of autarky: Radama I raised the land tax to
a *fahafolo*, or 'one-tenth', of all agricultural produce, purportedly to help finance
military expansion, and extended it to artisanal production.[19]

Tax in Money

Traditionally, there also existed a number of regular and irregular taxes payable
in money. An annual poll tax of a *varairaventy* ($0.00139) was due a fortnight
before the *Fandroana*, or royal bath ritual, which marked the beginning of the
traditional Merina year.[20] Andrianampoinimerina also imposed annual taxes
specifically to pay for arms imports: a *kirobo latsaka valovaloventy* ($0.24) per
slave owned for slave-owners, and a *roavoamena latsaka variteloventy* ($0.08) per
non-slave-owning subject.[21] In addition, domestic commerce was taxed, comprising for Merina traders 20 per cent of declared profits, $4 per slave sold, and
2 per cent of the price of goods purchased from Indian and Swahili merchants.[22]
While these were nominally declared on the traders' cash profits, generally only
export duties were payable in cash. Import duties were largely levied in kind[23] – a
policy that accentuated the lack of coinage.[24]

Irregular taxes in money were also rendered to the crown on other important
occasions: for instance, a *hasina*, a tribute of $1, that had traditionally been paid
in kind, was offered to the sovereign on ritual occasions, as on visiting the court.
It was also payable by all subjects when the sovereign returned from a trip.[25] The
hasina became a substantial and regular source of cash revenue when extended to
the private porterage system, as each *maromita* (porter) upon entering the imperial capital paid a $1 *hasina*. For example, from July to October 1817, at the height
of the commercial season, 1,000 porter loads reached Antananarivo from the
east coast. Representing to foreign hirers a wage cost of $12,000, this would have
entailed for the crown a net gain of $1,000 from *hasina*.[26] From the late 1860s, this
raised an estimated annual minimum of $120,000 for the royal treasury.[27]

Other occasional monetary levies imposed from the late eighteenth century
included a *varifitoventy* ($0.104) payable upon the death of the sovereign,[28] a
sikajy ($0.125), due from a father on the occasion of his son's circumcision[29]
and a *volatsivaky* (lit. 'uncut coin' – a $1 piece or a piastre) whenever the head
of a household either adopted or repudiated a child.[30] Taxes were also payable

by plaintiffs and the accused to the crown upon every legal procedure, generally $0.04 to $0.06 when affairs were judged at *fokonolona* (community-level) hearings, and $1 at the start and completion of every procedure heard before *andriambaventy*, or high judges.[31]

While Radama I appears to have imposed higher monetary taxes chiefly on foreign traders, Ranavalona defrayed a significant proportion of industrial costs, including the salaries paid to foreign artisans, through extraordinary taxation. For example, in 1835, a minimum of $23,500 was thus raised to pay the salaries of LMS artisan missionaries George Chick (1797–1866), John Canham (1798–1881) and James Cameron (1800–75) and French craftsmen Droit (d. *c.* 1836) and Jean Laborde (1805–78),[32] all of whom were engaged in crown contracts. Again, in 1837, two levies were imposed: $1 on every slave owned, earmarked for the $31,800 owed to Napoléon de Lastelle (1802–56), a French trader and entrepreneur, for imported European muskets; and a poll tax of $0.25, which raised $70,000. This prompted the crown to impose a second extraordinary levy which yielded the $100,000 required to finance the construction by Laborde of the Mantasoa (Isoatsimanampiovana) cannon foundry in 1837–9.[33] It appears that, at another juncture, Ranavalona imposed a further extraordinary tax of $1.04 for every slave owned in order to pay for arms imports.[34] Other taxes introduced, possibly under Ranavalona I, were the *isantrano*, an annual tax of one *sikajy* ($0.125) on every house, and a tax imposed on each slave owner of one-fifth of the value of each child born to one of his slaves.[35]

Tax in Labour

However, the major form of taxation during the imperial Merina era was *fanompoana*. The crown claimed *fanompoana*, an unremunerated labour service, on the grounds that all subjects were, in principle, 'property' of the crown.[36] Traditionally, *fanompoana* was limited to a few high-status groups who performed honourific, largely ritual, labour prestations for the monarch. However, under Andriamasinavalona, such prestations were extended to the provision by freemen of labour for state construction projects, notably – following two major famines in *c.* 1708–16 and *c.* 1747–70 – the creation and maintenance of river dykes and irrigated rice fields.[37] The entire Merina male population was divided into caste-based units and mobilized for the construction of the Ikopa dyke. Andriamasinavalona then applied *fanompoana* to drain marshes over much of central Imerina.[38] The enforcement of such prestations was made the *fanompoana* of the *mpanantatra*, a group who were also responsible for collecting 'first fruit' taxes.[39] In addition, *fanompoana* units were used to build defences around towns containing strategic stores of grain. These granary towns attracted ordinary cultivators seeking both protection and, in times of dearth, provisions. The subsequent concentration of population facilitated the imposition by rulers of further limits on the geographical mobility of the population in order to control their labour for *fanompoana* purposes.[40]

Andrianampoinimerina further extended and formalized *fanompoana*. He incorporated the territorially-restricted population groups, or *foko*, into larger regional units called *toko*, six of which formed greater Imerina: Avaradrano, Marovatana, Ambodirano, Vakinisisaony, Vonizongo and Vakinankaratra. The inherently passive nature of the caste structure facilitated the transmission of royal orders concerning *fanompoana*, through the *mpanantatra* to the people via the *fokonolona* (local community) councils. The king claimed the labour of every male subject for six days each season (a total of twenty-four days a year) for 'public works', notably in agriculture. The application of *fanompoana* augmented food production by expanding rice cultivation from one to two crops annually, thereby guaranteeing a regular agricultural surplus for the first time in Imerina's history.[41]

It was upon this basis that Radama I built. In the absence of domestic capital accumulation and the refusal to accept external investment, the Merina court resorted to labour-intensive means of conquest and of production. It did this through transforming *fanompoana* into a universal, permanent obligation imposed upon all subjects: *borizany*, who performed civilian *corvée*, and *sorodany*, who undertook military service. In the early 1820s, Radama I conducted a population census with the express purpose of forming *borizany fanompoana* units, each comprising between ten and 1,000 men, on a territorial caste rather than clan basis.[42] To enforce participation, a royal edict of January 1823 obliged anyone who claimed to be ill upon recovery to spend a time corresponding to the length of their illness in public works *fanompoana*.[43] The new *fanompoana* underpinned attempted industrialization in the period 1820–61. Some industrial forced labour units had formed prior to 1820, notably for the manufacture of military goods. Also, in December 1824, most foreign artisans (at least half were LMS agents) signed royal contracts to promote craft production. Merina 'apprentices' to missionary artisans subsequently formed specialist craft *fanompoana* units.[44] The attempt to forge an industrial revolution following the adoption of autarky in the mid-1820s greatly expanded *fanompoana*. It functioned on both a permanent and an intermittent basis, utilizing a new core of factory workers, traditional artisans and general *fanompoana* to extract and supply raw materials. The concentration of labour was considerable. Cameron had a permanent *fanompoana* of 700 men in his Analakely factory in the imperial capital of Antananarivo,[45] while the Mantasoa industrial complex, built by a *fanompoana* of 20,000 workers – equivalent to about 5 per cent of the adult Merina male population – possessed a permanent 5,000-man *fanompoana* workforce called *zazamadinika* ('little children') by Laborde.[46]

The crown also adopted and adapted European methods to recruit and organize notably military *fanompoana*, which included both men to act as soldiers and craftsmen to maintain weaponry and build roads, bridges and forts. The demand for labour of the military alone was such that Radama I could not contemplate acquiescing to the request from Mascarene planters for Malagasy contract workers, even though such migrants would have earned badly needed foreign exchange, and helped stem the shift in foreign trade to the independent west coast.[47]

In 1823, Radama I established direct control over the LMS mission, transforming it into a machine for the recruitment of forced labour that, until most missionaries left in 1835, gave Merina youth basic literacy before channelling them into the imperial army or administration.[48] It is estimated that a minimum of 15,000 youths passed through the mission schools by 1835.[49] Military recruitment was steadily accelerated in the 1820s. The number of soldiers in the imperial Merina army reached 30,000 by 1830, 45,000 by 1835 and 100,000 by 1852, after which military expeditions were radically curtailed.[50] However, military mortality rates were high. An estimated 25 to 50 per cent of Merina soldiers in lowland provinces died each year, mostly of malaria, as did about 160,000 Merina soldiers – close to the estimate given by Raombana (1809–55) of 150,000 for the years 1820–53 – in imperial campaigns from 1816 to 1853, giving an average of about 4,500 soldier deaths a year (possibly 0.8 to 4.5 per cent of the Merina population).[51] Such mortality meant that the army had to be replenished constantly, the number of new draftees averaging 19,000 per annum between 1828 and 1830 (years for which there appear reliable recruitment statistics).[52]

Consequences of Taxation

Small farmers, who required cash primarily to meet taxes, competed fiercely to be the first to market their crop whilst the money supply was, at the beginning of the harvest and trading season, still relatively plentiful. As Wenceslas Bojer (1795–1856), a visiting naturalist, noted, this practice had disastrous consequences for the quality of produce for:

> [the cultivator] rarely waits until the products of the soil have reached maturity; they pick their vegetables and their fruit well before the proper harvest time and carry them to market, in order to secure a few petty pieces of silver.[53]

Those with insufficient cash were forced to borrow in order to pay taxes, which increased steadily during the autarkic era, and to meet other financial commitments, notably the construction of their family tombs and other funeral costs. Thus W. Ellis commented:

> many persons, endeavouring to make a display of respect for deceased relatives, often contracted debts in purchasing valuable clothes and ornaments to throw into the graves of the departed, agreeably to ancient usage; and several instances occurred,

where individuals had been reduced to slavery on account of their inability to discharge the debts thus created. Thus the dead had been enveloped in rich clothing,
covered with ornaments, and surrounded with silver, whilst the nearest living relatives were by these means reduced to the lowest state of degradation.[54]

In early 1823, Radama I attempted to outlaw debts incurred for funeral expenses,[55]
but as with similar legislation aimed to limit indebtedness, this remained largely
a dead letter. As a result, large numbers of small farmers found themselves mortgaging their crop before it had even been sown.[56] Their plight increased with the
imposition of extraordinary taxes for industry, imposed in the late 1830s, when
many subjects were forced to borrow at an exorbitant interest rate from, or sell
cattle to, members of the court whose monopoly on cattle exports enabled them
to dictate a purchase price of only $0.071 a bullock – which they resold to for-
eign merchants on the coast for $15.[57]

The pervasive nature of *fanompoana* in Imperial Madagascar helps explain
the equally ubiquitous system of bribery, in kind or cash, which constituted a
further prevalent form of clandestine taxation, and thus a contributory factor to
indebtedness. For example, Merina customs officers and port governors – who
invariably obtained their posts through some form of bribery, and who were per-
forming *fanompoana* labour and were thus unsalaried – permitted to pass through
customs free of official duty two-thirds or more of imported commodities upon
payment of a considerable bribe – generally 25 per cent of potential tax revenue.[58]
Bribery was ubiquitous, a requisite for obtaining any post or favour. Many had to
borrow to pay the bribe, sometimes from the benefactor of the favour demanded.

The creation of a standing army also greatly expanded indebtedness. All officers and ordinary conscripts were subject to *fanompoana*. The crown compensated
the officers by letting them keep much of the one-third of campaign booty, in the
form of cattle and slaves, normally reserved for the crown.[59] However, officers
also took advantage of the subsistence needs of unsalaried recruits. During military expeditions, court officers had their slaves carry provisions (traditional taxes
raised in kind) which they sold to conscripts at prices that soared as campaigns
progressed and individual soldiers' own stocks became depleted.[60] In order to
survive, many of those campaigning had to borrow money at extortionate rates
of interest from the very officers to whom they immediately returned these loans
in payment for exorbitantly priced rice and meat. If upon their return they could
not raise the money to repay their debts, these soldiers were sold as slaves, often
alongside their wives and children, in order that their creditors might be repaid.[61]
In addition, many officers blackmailed ordinary soldiers to extort money from
them.[62] This resulted in a considerable flow of cash from ordinary soldiers to
the crown and court elite. It was a vicious circle in which soldiers were drawn
from the small farmer class, who also paid a special tax to support the army,
yet, whilst serving under imperial colours, these men remained unsalaried. As

recruitment intensified, from approximately 6,000 soldiers per annum in 1822 to 14,250 in 1824, and 8,750 a year thereafter, the number of cultivators dwindled. Those excluded from the military draft were increasingly the older and less able-bodied. Consequently, farmers first channelled slave labour into subsistence agriculture – instead of into cash crop cultivation, as had been envisaged at the time of the 1820 treaty. However, as their impoverishment grew, cultivators were obliged to sell their slaves, who were thus increasingly transferred into the hands of the court elite.[63]

The widening gap between rich and poor, and the dwindling money supply, resulted in an increasing transgression of the taboo against robbing tombs. This probably explains why Ranavalona I started instead to store funds in earthenware jars buried in secret locations.[64] However, as impoverishment spread, so the numbers turning to moneylenders grew. From the start of the imperial era, an inadequate money supply resulted in high interest rates that enticed those with stocks of money into usury. By at least 1810, a group of professional moneylenders, called *mpanana* (i.e. 'rich'), had emerged in Imerina. James Hastie (1786–1825), British Agent at the Merina court from 1820, noted in 1817 that 'money is lent at interest and the interest calculated with a scrupulous nicety'.[65] They were joined from the onset of autarky by members of the Merina elite who accumulated large cash reserves from the sale of campaign booty and from commercial monopolies. The wealthier usurers also benefited by at least mid-century from access to credit facilities extended by Indian traders, agents of Indian financial houses in Zanzibar, whose monthly interest on loans stood in 1851 at only 12.1 per cent, and was reduced in 1853 to 0.75 per cent at which level it hovered, never falling below 0.625 per cent until 1890.[66] Despite this, Merina moneylenders only made their capital available as 'usurious consumption credit', rather than for commercial or industrial investment. Extortionate interest rates were intended to push debtors into bankruptcy, and thus enable creditors to seize their assets.

Indebtedness and Slavery

A debtor failing to clear his debt within the stipulated period was obliged to pay his creditor double the capital, plus an additional one-third of the capital in exceptional cases where no interest had been specified. However, there was no law stipulating the terms on which capital might be borrowed. All loan agreements were in essence private agreements, although once signed by the contracting parties they carried the force of law.[67] In the first two decades of the nineteenth century, interest rates were high, generally ranging from 100 to 150 per cent – regardless of government attempts to enforce a rate of 66 per cent.[68]

The Merina elite were backed by the domestic judicial system. Almost inevitably, debtors failed to meet repayment conditions, their property was seized, and they and their family could be sold into slavery to pay off the debt, as could their guarantors, should they possess any.[69] Ironically, the 1820 slave trade treaty may have increased the number so enslaved, for Radama I immediately afterwards 'published an edict, that if any of his subjects were indebted to the slave-traders, they must without delay pay them in money'.[70] As Hastie commented in 1824:

> if the money lender risques [*sic*] a portion of his treasure it must be under the expecta-
> tion of receiving exorbitant interest, and when the usurious covenant is not fulfilled,
> he does not hesitate to sell the person of his debtor.[71]

Ellis estimated that some who had initially borrowed only $1 ended up being sold as slaves.[72] An estimated 50 per cent of the slave population of Imerina (possibly totalling 300,000 by 1830) comprised Merina bankrupts and members of their families – a figure that excludes the many Betsileo kidnapped by Merina debtors and brought illegally into Imerina to be sold as slaves in order that the kidnap-pers might pay off their debts. Radama I attempted to ameliorate the effects of indebtedness by halving officially-prescribed interest rates to 33 per cent in the early 1820s and, in 1823, declaring void all debts contracted to pay for funerals or tombs. However, this measure had limited effect and only endured until 1828 (the year of Radama's death). Interest rates in the 1830s varied, but often reached 100 per cent.[73] Nevertheless, the system of squeezing the poor brought dimin-ishing returns to the court elite,[74] who from the 1840s started to turn upon the wealthy of other factions, often using trumped-up charges of sorcery to attack them and deprive them of their wealth, notably in slaves, 'which were only sold in the last extremity, for such a sale is somewhat humiliating for the master'.[75]

Merina enslaved for debt nevertheless enjoyed a relatively high slave sta-tus. The *mainty* (lit. black), or slaves, were ordered in a hierarchy of three endogamous groups. Those of lowest status termed 'Mozambiques' or 'Makua' comprised recently imported African slaves. Ranked above them were the *andevo*, non-Merina Malagasy peoples enslaved in Merina slave raids or battle. The highest-ranking group, from which the monarch drew to fulfil important ritual tasks, were the *zazahova* (lit. 'children of the *hova*' – the lower of the two free Merina castes). They were divided into two groups: *olomainty* (lit. 'black people'), hereditary slaves – possibly descendants of slaves imported to the island by the first settlers – who, like Mozambiques, could not purchase liberty; and Merina enslaved mainly for indebtedness or crime. Of these, those enslaved for debt could purchase their liberty, or be redeemed, normally by a family mem-ber. Nevertheless, the horrors of *fanompoana*, from which slaves were exempt, were such that some slaves who had almost paid their redemption price refused to complete payment, preferring to remain slaves than to again become vulner-able to forced labour.[76]

Postscript

The Merina regime faltered in its bid for autarky: attempted industrialization failed, in part because of revolt by the *fanompoana* labour involved, as did the attempted conquest of the entire island of Madagascar, due to high troop mortality and armed resistance, notably by the Bara and Sakalava in the south and west of the island. Following the ascension of Radama II (r. 1861–3), restrictions on foreign investment were largely lifted, and there followed a decade of relative free trade and economic prosperity. However, the international recession from the late 1870s onwards, coupled with the conflict with France (1883–5) resulted in a shrinkage of foreign investment and in the money supply. Consequently, the Merina regime resorted again to increased domestic taxation, notably *fanompoana*, which was implemented on a massive scale, and interest rates rose. Article 161 of the Code of 1881 stipulated a maximum rate of interest on a loan of 2 per cent per month. However, this was ignored in practice by major Merina trading houses, which for large respectable loans usually charged 5 per cent a month and insisted on major collateral, such as rice fields, houses and slaves.[77] Those with insufficient collateral were obliged to borrow from one of a myriad of smaller Merina usurers who demanded a guaranty two to three times the value of the loan at between 8 and 25 per cent interest per month – although such loans were often contracted on a weekly basis. Moreover, any failure to repay by the stipulated date usually incurred a doubling of the interest, which continued every day thereafter that the debt remained until such time as the debtor declared an inability to repay and was jailed pending repayment. In the countryside, interest was normally charged in rice, at a rate of 100 per cent.[78]

While the enslavement of debtors appears to have been banned from the time of Radama II, insolvent borrowers could still be imprisoned and their assets seized. From the 1880s, the reaction of many ordinary subjects was to flee taxation (primarily *fanompoana*) and prosecution for debt, and instead to become bandits. These individuals, ironically, survived in large part by raiding highland villages, seizing cattle and enslaving people, notably women and children, whom they either kept or sold to slave traders on the west coast.[79]

4 CREDIT AND DEBT IN THE LIVES OF FREED SLAVES AT THE CAPE OF GOOD HOPE: THE CASE OF ARNOLDUS KOEVOET, 1697–1735

Susan Newton-King

Debt slavery was common in the societies of Southeast Asia and the Indian subcontinent where the Dutch East India Company (Vereenigde Oost Indische Compagnie, or VOC) first entrenched itself, often in territories captured from the Portuguese. But at the Cape of Good Hope, where the Dutch established a refreshment station for their ships in 1652, debt bondage was apparently unknown.[1] Indigenous pastoralists (the Khoekhoe) and agro-pastoralists (the Xhosa) had long operated a system of stock-loans, whereby persons without livestock would herd the sheep and cattle of those who had more than they could manage in return for milk and a share of the offspring of the livestock. However, to the best of my knowledge, this system, generally described as a 'symbiotic relationship' or a mutually beneficial form of clientage by historians, did not evolve into permanent and heritable bondage.[2]

The small Dutch colonial society that emerged at the Cape after 1652 had no banks, but money lending was widespread and most loans were recorded.[3] Where large sums of money were involved, the debt was normally recorded before commissioned members of the Council of Justice, or the secretary of the Council of Policy. In such cases, the borrower would normally offer landed property as security for the loan. He would usually also pledge 'his person, and further all the goods he presently owns or might come to own, movable and immovable, none exempted'.[4] However, to the best of my knowledge, despite the formulaic reference to the 'person' of the debtor, no individual was ever forced into service as a consequence of default.[5] Lenders were permitted to charge interest at a maximum rate of 6 per cent per annum. Loans sometimes remained outstanding for years before they were called in, often upon the death of either the creditor or the debtor; but the more formal contracts (known as *scheepenkennissen*, *obligatien* or *schuldbrieven*) usually specified that a borrower should repay the full sum upon three months' notice, or 'at first warning'. Legal proceedings were sometimes initiated against recalcitrant debtors, and those who could not or would not pay within the period determined by the court faced the court-ordered seizure and sale of their assets. Moreover, an inability to honour one's debts was regarded as shameful. As in the Netherlands, credit-worthiness was highly valued. Bankrupts suffered a loss of honour and social status, though perhaps less so in the colonies than the motherland.[6]

Nonetheless, while unpaid debt could lead to shame and destitution, debtors at the Cape were seldom imprisoned and were never obliged to provide labour to their creditors or to the authorities in lieu of money owed.[7] The destitute were not enslaved, nor could they be forced to bond their labour or that of their children for an indefinite period in exchange for material support. Fixed term contracts of service were common, of course, and children were sometimes placed as 'apprentices' with a local artisan or farmer, to work for a specified number of years in exchange for board and lodging and the acquisition of a trade. The Orphan Chamber and the Church Poor Fund (the *diaconij*) frequently arranged such placements for the children in their care. But such contracts could not be extended indefinitely, nor were they (at least on the face of it) concluded in exchange for support provided by the employer to the family of the apprentice. The Church Poor Fund might also send out the children of paupers to board with local residents in exchange for a monthly fee. Such children were sometimes abused and exploited, but their circumstances were periodically reviewed by the Church Council, which had the ability to remove them from situations considered unacceptable.[8] Moreover, they could expect to be released automatically from foster care when they married or reached the age of majority, whichever came first.

In sum, there was no debt bondage as it is traditionally understood in the colonial society of the Cape of Good Hope. There are two reasons, however, why debt bondage is relevant to the history of this region. First, approximately half of the slaves imported to the Cape in the eighteenth century were brought there from Southeast Asia or the Indian subcontinent. Some may have been newly captured, but many must have been born into slavery in Asia, descended from persons already enslaved there, perhaps through the operation of one or another form of debt bondage. Second, as I began to investigate the life histories of freed slaves in Cape Town in the early 1700s (research undertaken as part of a team project entitled 'social identities in eighteenth-century Cape Town'),[9] it struck me that debt played a necessary and, in many ways, positive role in their lives, as they battled to construct dignified and satisfactory lives in freedom, with little or no capital and often quite late in life. In rare cases, usually when manumission followed the death of an owner, freed slaves received a sum of money or capital goods such as livestock, a wagon or fish-nets, with which to begin life in freedom, but most were obliged to start out with nothing but the skills they had acquired during their lives as slaves. Those who could often chose to borrow money, sometimes quite large sums, in order to make up for lost time, as it were. In so doing, they drew on social capital: their ties with a former owner and his or her circle of friends; their bonds with one another; and their connection (if any) to the Dutch Reformed Church, which supported the 'deserving' poor and lent money from the Church Poor Fund to individuals deemed worthy of credit.[10] Sometimes they over-reached themselves, like Louis of Bengal, whose creditors first claimed his house in Cape Town with all its contents and then, in 1711, his garden land in Table Valley.[11] Sometimes they died too soon, like Arnoldus Koevoet, the subject of this paper, and their brave and spirited efforts to carve out an autonomous space for themselves in the polyglot community of the free were sabotaged by death and the ensuing settling of accounts. And sometimes, however rarely, they survived and prospered, becoming substantial landowners, farmers and moneylenders in their turn, standing surety for the manumission of their friends and relations and extending credit to other members of the 'free black' community.[12] A detailed exposition of the role of credit and debt in the lives of free blacks at the Cape must await further research, but it seems to me nonetheless that it might be helpful to make some preliminary observations here, if only as a footnote to the other chapters in this volume.

This paper is largely based on my research into the life and social relationships of one individual: Arnoldus Koevoet of Cape Town. He was not among the most prosperous of the free blacks in Cape Town in the first third of the eighteenth century; nor was he among the poorest. He was freed relatively late in life, at the age of thirty-four or thirty-five, apparently through his own efforts. There is reason to believe that he had served a single master (probably a senior Company servant) prior to his manumission, but he was owned by the Company and he was obliged to pay a stiff price for his own freedom.[13] Like all slaves manumitted by the Company in this period, he had been baptized in infancy and spoke Dutch 'perfectly well'.[14] He was skilled, probably a carpenter and builder,[15] and in the view of his masters he was capable of 'earning his bread here alongside the other inhabitants'.[16] He also had sufficient backing from men of substance (and perhaps also from his wife, the freed slave Anna Rebecca of Bengal) to enable him to borrow money from the *diaconij* and, as we shall see, from the Governor himself. Yet he had little or no capital of own and, as his liabilities mounted, his position became more precarious. Just weeks before his death, one of his creditors obtained a judgement against him.[17] After his death, the outstanding debts of his estate ate into the inheritance of his daughter Diana. When the debts run up by Diana's new husband (perhaps in expectation of her soon-to-be-paid inheritance) were added to those of her father, Diana was left penniless.[18] In this, therefore – the vulnerability of his financial position and the precarious underpinnings of his self-sufficiency – Arnoldus Koevoet was probably fairly typical of his free black contemporaries. His story can stand for that of many at the Cape who embarked upon a new life of freedom full of energy and hope, but were chastened by the harsh realities of survival in an unforgiving economic environment. The most successful among his fellow freed slaves, men such as Robbert Schot of Bengal, Christiaan Wijnantsz of the Coromandel Coast and Jacobus Hendriksz, all of whom became substantial property owners in the 1720s and 1730s, were probably exceptional. Yet few of these men, whose landholdings were on a par with those of many middling freeburghers and whose deceased estates were far from insolvent, succeeded in passing on the fruits of their success to their direct descendants.[19]

I did not choose Arnoldus Koevoet as a subject of research primarily on the grounds of his representivity, however; rather, I was drawn to him initially by a unique and very special collection of letters which has been preserved among the papers of his deceased estate.[20] There are thirty-two of these letters, all incoming, written over a period of six years, from 1728 to 1733, that is, both before and after Koevoet's emancipation in May 1731. Fifteen of these letters were sent from Batavia by a man who addressed Koevoet as '*mijn waarde broer*' (my dear brother) or '*lieve broeder*' (dear brother), and signed himself '*UEd:es d:w: dienaer en broer tot der dood*' (your Honour's willing servant and brother unto death), 'Johannes Morgh *van de Caap*'. Though it seemed at first that *broeder* should not be interpreted literally, and that it meant 'brother in Christ', since the author of these letters was clearly a Christian, it now seems that the author was indeed Koevoet's brother, or rather his half-brother, Johannes, who was set free by the Council of Policy in Cape Town in September 1727.[21] Johannes (Jan) Morgh's letters are vivid and animated: they tell of his joy at his brother's emancipation and subsequent marriage, his hopes for his own career as coachman to the high and mighty in Batavia and his desire for the products of the Cape: red wine, harders, apples, raisins, crayfish, quince jam and sauerkraut. They are also full of concern and longing for family and friends in Cape Town: in 1729, while his brother Koevoet was still a slave, he wrote, '*broer gelieft de moeijte te doen om onse koitie hier te sture bij mijn want de jonge die kaan daar bij de boere geen goed leerin*' (brother, please take the trouble to send our *koitie* here to me, because the boy can learn nothing good there among the farmers). And again, in 1733: '*ook hebbe met groot verlangen naar neeff Kootje gewagt want hier komt geen een schip off ik vraag en verlang naar hen*' (I have also been waiting with great longing for nephew Kootje because not a single ship arrives here without my asking after him and missing him). Jan Morgh's letters also speak of his keen interest in the affairs of his employers and other members of the Company elite in Batavia, to whom his own fortunes were tied.

The remaining letters are equally revealing of the subjectivity of their authors and of the affection and respect which the correspondents showed one another. Twelve of the letters were addressed to Koevoet's wife, Anna Rebecca: six from a certain Anna Maria van Thiel of Amsterdam, who signed herself '*UE: genegenen Nonje*' (Your Honour's well-disposed missie/young mistress), three from Anna Maria's brother, Pieter van Thiel, apparently the black sheep of the family,[22] whose letters were more perfunctory and self-interested than those of the couple's other correspondents and three from a certain R:l Coijmans of Colombo, with whom Anna Rebecca regularly exchanged gifts '*tot een recompens en onderhoudinge onse vrindschap*' (as a reward and support for our friendship). Finally, the collection contains five affectionate and devoutly religious letters addressed to '*seer waarde broeder*' (Arnoldus Koevoet) from a woman who identified herself as Maria Magdalena Langenberg of the Cape. Now living in Batavia, she described herself as 'Maria Magdalena, *inboorling van Van den Brink*' (born in the house of Van den Brink) and said she was christened by '*mijn heer* Kalde' (Pieter Kalden, Dutch Reformed minister in Cape Town from 1695 to 1708).[23] It is not clear when she left the Cape for Batavia, but she seems to have been acquainted with Koevoet's daughter Diana (who was born in the Company's slave lodge and baptized in Cape Town in 1722) and several other members of the Cape Town community, both slave and free. She sends effusive greetings as well as presents to Diana, to Koevoet's wife, Anna Rebecca, and to '*mijn nonje Belletie*' (my young mistress Belletie). The nature of her relationship with Koevoet's half-brother, Jan Morgh is also unclear. She seems to have been close to him, sometimes relaying messages on his behalf and taking a keen interest in his affairs; but she was apparently neither his wife nor his lover, for she professed disappointment when his plans to marry a certain Urelia, a 'good-natured' woman who had 'her own house and two or three slaves', were scuppered by malicious gossip.[24] '*Ik ben tot deeser uure nog bij hem*' (I am up to this hour still with him), she wrote in June 1732, '*wij woonen over malkanders duur bij gevolg nog meer occatie om bij den anderen te sijn*' (we live above one another's doors and consequently we have even more opportunity to be with one another). The most likely explanation is that she and Jan worked for the same employer, or were in service with closely connected members of the Company's senior staff in Batavia.

The outgoing letters of Arnoldus Koevoet and Anna Rebecca of Bengal may never come to light; it is likely that they no longer exist. Many questions will therefore remain unanswered: for example, what was the accident that killed Koevoet's small daughter Christina in May 1731? What provoked Maria Magdalena Langenberg to express her 'dismay' at the contents of Koevoet's '*bejegende briefe*' (accusatory letter) of 3 July 1731? Nevertheless, the small bundle of incoming letters preserved among the annexures to Koevoet's liquidation account leaves the reader in no doubt that Arnoldus Koevoet and his wife Anna Rebecca were conscious of belonging to a complex network of social relations which linked slave and free, kin and non-kin, master and servant, patron and client in a web of friendship, affection and patronage which extended far beyond

Cape Town, to Ceylon, Batavia and even to Amsterdam. It is clear that they worked hard to cultivate and maintain these ties, regularly sending letters and presents abroad with the crew of VOC ships, exchanging trade goods, passing on messages and (in Koevoet's case) perhaps even planning to travel in person to Batavia. My research into the identity of their correspondents and those named in their letters is still far from complete. However, my ability to reconstruct the life of Arnoldus Koevoet and to explain his financial dealings has been greatly enhanced by the insights into his aspirations, his character and his motives afforded by these letters.

Arnoldus Koevoet was born in Cape Town in 1697, or thereabouts, probably in the Company's slave lodge at the top end of the Heerengracht (present-day Adderley Street), adjoining the Company's garden. His mother was Christijn Pietersz, or Christijn van de Caab, a Company slave.[25] She bore seven children for the Company, four of whom died in slavery and three of whom were manumitted.[26] Christijn Pietersz's eldest child, Anna, was manumitted at her own request in 1715.[27] She 'had been a slave for twenty-eight years at the Cape', she wrote, and was baptized. In exchange for herself she offered the Company a healthy male slave, named Alexander of Malabar.[28] Her request was approved and, as Anna of the Cape, also called Anna van der Heyde, she married the burgher Jan Jans van Böllen on 26 November 1719.[29] Before achieving burgher status in the year of his marriage to Anna, Van Böllen had been employed by the Company, first as a stable-boy and later as a coachman.[30] It seems reasonable to surmise that in these capacities he would have worked alongside Arnoldus Koevoet's younger brother Johannes Morgh, for as the latter's letters show, Morgh, like Van Böllen, was a skilled coachman and horse-trainer. It is likely, I think, that Jacobus, the eldest son of Anna van de Caab and Jan Jans van Böllen (baptized in 1716) was '*onse Koitie*' (our Koitie), 'our Coetie van bele' or '*neeff Kootje*' (nephew Kootje), of whom Johannes Morgh wrote so fondly from Batavia. In 1724, Anna van de Caab, wife of Jan Jansz van Beulen, requested the Council of Policy to free her nine-year-old daughter Anna, 'still a slave in the Company's Lodge ... that she might try to raise her in a better way of life', offering in her place a 'sturdy and healthy' male slave named January of Malabar.[31] The Council acceded to her request, together with a similar request from the free black woman Grisilla van de Caab, on the grounds that 'the Honourable Company would get far more service from good male slaves than from such children'.[32]

By the early eighteenth century it had become standard practice that any person requesting the manumission of a Company slave (including the slave himself or herself) should provide a 'sturdy male slave' as a substitute.[33] This was considerably more costly than the compensation of 100 guilders suggested by High Commissioner Hendrik Adriaan van Reede tot Drakestein during his visit to the Cape in 1685.[34] Between 1715, when Anna van Christijn Pietersz was manumitted, and 1731, when her brother Arnoldus exchanged a male slave named Masinga van Rio de la Goa for himself,[35] the price of male slaves at the Cape averaged ninety-seven rix dollars, nearly three times the amount set by Van Reede tot Drakestein[36] and three times the annual wage of a common soldier or sailor in the Company's employ.[37] How did Anna and her two brothers, Arnoldus (baptized in 1697 and freed in 1731)[38] and Johannes (baptized in 1703 and freed in 1727)[39] raise these large sums of money? Their mother Christijn died a slave on Christmas day 1719;[40] their four brothers – Hendrik, Andries, Willem and Pieter – were never liberated. Hendrik died in 1723, at the age of twenty-two or thereabouts; Andries (almost certainly the '*broeder Andries*' or '*broer Andries Morgh*' of Johannes Morgh's letters) in 1750; and Willem in 1753, all still counted among the Company's assets.[41] What enabled Anna, Johannes and Arnoldus to free themselves from what Maria Langenberg described as '*die harde slavernij*' (that harsh slavery)? Were they perhaps more skilled than their siblings? Did they use their skills to earn money on their own account? We know from the letters that Johannes was a coachman and Arnoldus a carpenter and perhaps also a builder.[42] In February 1727, Johannes was enumerated among the 'mandoors', or overseers of the lodge.[43] Mandoors, usually Cape-born and of mixed (half-European) descent, were given separate accommodation in the lodge and were responsible for work discipline, roll-calls and the allocation of rations.[44] They themselves received double rations of food and clothing and, according to the visiting church minister, Francois Valentijn, 2 rix dollars '*vrygeld*' (per month?).[45] Was Johannes able to manipulate his position to his own advantage? His brothers Andries and Hendrik were also described as 'skilled' in the Company's records.[46] Why could they not have deployed their skills to the same end?

Historians of Cape slavery generally acknowledge that racial preference played a role in the Company's attitude towards the manumission of its slaves, and in the selection of young male slaves to be trained as artisans. High Commissioner Van Reede had made this explicit when he instructed the Council of Policy in 1685 to single out the children of Dutch fathers for artisanal training and to allow the boys to claim their freedom at the age of twenty-five and the girls at twenty-two. The children of Dutch fathers, he wrote, 'the Company can entertain no idea of keeping in slavery'.[47] Johannes Morgh was '*halfslag*' (half-breed), and the consistency with which he used his Dutch surname in his letters suggests that he was conscious of its effect in a society pervaded by colour prejudice. However, his brother Andries (referred to as Andries Morgh by Johannes) was also *halfslag*, and he was never freed. Arnoldus, by contrast, seems to have been *heelslag* (full-breed) and he *was* freed.[48] In sum, having a European father may have counted in one's favour, but it was no guarantee of manumission. According to Robert Shell, 'in the 170 years of the Company's existence, only 108 of its slaves obtained their freedom; not all were mulatto'.[49] Manumission, Shell concludes, was an extremely rare occurrence among Company slaves. Those who were Cape-born, especially those born of European fathers, stood a better chance of manumission than did imported slaves, but even Cape-born slaves had a statistically-tiny chance of achieving freedom. 'Although 4,213 slaves were born in the Lodge', writes Shell, 'only 103 locally born slaves ever obtained their freedom. Their probability of freedom was .005 per cent'.[50]

The tiny minority of Company slaves who successfully petitioned the Company to grant them their freedom and themselves raised the substantial sum of money required to buy a substitute must, Shell concludes, 'have been extraordinary individuals. Most of the other slaves required the help of a family member who was already outside the lodge'.[51]

Anna van de Caab may have assisted her brothers to escape their '*harde slavernij*', and she in turn may have been helped at an earlier stage by her future husband. That is possible. But there is another possibility which has largely been overlooked by historians, perhaps because the evidence to support it is so hard to find. That is the possibility that women such as Anna, and men such as Arnoldus Koevoet and Johannes Morgh, who were, undoubtedly, 'extraordinary individuals', had cultivated a personal connection with individuals who held senior positions in the local Dutch East India Company establishment and with their friends and families. In theory, Company slaves had no single master; they worked for the directors in the Netherlands and the many shareholders in the Company's six chambers. Yet in practice, certain slaves were seconded to the private households of senior *gequalificeerde* personnel to serve them as domestics, wet nurses, seamstresses, cooks, stewards, musicians, builders, craftsmen and of course (in the case of the most senior households) coachmen. Such service provided a welcome opportunity to escape the crowded Company slave lodge, with its dilapidated fittings, leaky roof, pervasive squalor and stench and its overwhelming lack of privacy.[52]

I think it very likely that both Arnoldus Koevoet and his brother Johannes were able to benefit from such secondments. There are a number of references in the letters of Johannes Morgh and Maria Magdalena Langenberg which suggest that both men had individual 'masters'. In December 1731, for example, Maria Langenberg wrote to Arnoldus Koevoet to express her joy at his manumission and his continuing good health. She has heard, she says, of '*die goedertierende weldadigheijd van die edeleer Fontein om u uijt die harde slavernij en soo een vrije staat te setten in de welke ik hoope u de almagtige God nooit sal verlaaten*' (that compassionate generosity of that gentleman Fontein to remove you from that harsh slavery and set you in a free condition, in which I hope the almighty God will never abandon you).[53] Jan de la Fontaine was Governor of the Cape in 1731 when Arnoldus Koevoet was freed. The Governor was head of the Council of Policy, which oversaw all manumissions; but it could be that Maria Langenberg refers here to a more personal connection.

More tellingly, in February 1732 Johannes Morgh wrote from Batavia to inform his brother that his letters, dated 24 October 1731, had been personally delivered to him by Koevoet's former master:

> *UE:e aangename letteren, van den 24 October des gepasseerde jaar 1731, is mij den 26 Januarij deses jaar, door UE:e geweesen meester in persoon behandigt en uijt deselve gesien, en van den brenger verstaan, UE:e en UE:e huijsvrouw goede gesondheijd, hoope en wensche dat het noch veele reex jaaren mogen continueeren*

> (Your Honour's pleasant letters of 24 October of last year, 1731, were handed to me in person on 26 January this year by your former master, and I saw in them and learnt from the bearer that you and your wife are in good health, and I hope that it may still continue for many years)[54]

Who was this 'former master' of Arnoldus Koevoet who personally delivered his letters to his brother Johannes in Batavia and communicated his news (including news of his recent marriage)? My guess is that he was a senior Company employee. In February 1729, Johannes Morgh had written to Arnoldus (then still a slave) with news of his life in Batavia. His '*heer*', he wrote, had been coughing up blood and could not preach on Sunday afternoon.[55] In another undated letter he writes that '*ik koesier ben van mijn heer Rouwennoft in dienst de EEd: kompt*' [I am coachman to my lord Rouwennoft in service with the Honourable Company]. It should be possible in time to identify Rouwennoft. The point, however, is that Jan Morgh was apparently in service with a senior Company employee in Batavia and that, if Koevoet's master was also a high official, which I believe he was, he would have had ready access to Morgh upon arrival in Batavia, which would explain why he delivered Koevoet's letters in person. It is perhaps no accident, then, that among the creditors of Arnoldus Koevoet were several well-connected individuals.

We should also ask how Jan Morgh got to Batavia. There is no indication that he worked his passage, and so he must have travelled as part of the personal retinue of a senior Company servant. On 29 September 1729, he informed his brother in Cape Town that he had sent him several presents:

> een stuckt gestreekt, tweed gekeeper bocke [rocke?], een voor Johanna een voor Stijntie [Koevoet's two daughters, still in the lodge] en drie stukke linne een daar voor broer Andries Morgh ik en kaan UE liedi niet meer sture want dat is wat slegt op Batavia UE sal ontfangen uijt hande van den oppersturman Jan Kraenenborgh E die is met ons is uijt gekomen op het schip de Elusabedt voor onder sturmaan

(one piece of striped cloth, two twill dresses, one for Johanna, one for Stijntie and three pieces of linen, one for brother Andries Morgh. I can't send you all more because that is quite bad in Batavia. Your Honour will receive it from the first mate Jan Krae-nenborgh who came out [to Batavia] with us on the ship Elisabeth as second mate)[56]

Again, it should be possible in time to identify the senior Company servants who sailed from Cape Town to Batavia on the *Elisabeth* in December 1727, less than three months after Johannes Morgh was freed (as Jan van Christijn Pietersz van de Caab).[57]

⁂

Arnoldus Koevoet (spelt Arnoldus Coevoet by the secretary of the Cape Council of Policy) was freed by the Governor in Council on 17 May 1731 together with another Company slave, Pieter van Helena Titus. It was recorded that both men spoke Dutch 'perfectly well' and had been baptized. Both were 'well behaved and capable of earning their bread here alongside other inhabitants'. Pieter van Helena Titus, moreover, was a confirmed member of the Cape congregation. Each man (as noted above) gave the Company a Mozambiquan slave in exchange for himself.[58]

Three and a half months later, on 2 September 1731, Arnoldus Koevoet married Anna Rebekka of Bengal in the Dutch Reformed Church in Cape Town.[59] His marriage seems to have come as a shock to his brother and others in Batavia who knew him well. Judging from a letter written by Maria Magdalena Langenberg in October 1731, in reply to his letter of 8 August, he had given them no prior warning. He had reported the tragic death of his four-year-old daughter Christina (Stijntie), born in the lodge to a slave named Maria van Diana van de Caab and named, perhaps, for Koevoet's mother Christijn.[60] Maria Langenberg expressed her condolences and then moved on to discuss the canaries which Koevoet had sent her from the Cape. 'I received three ... although you wrote to me of five', she complained, 'and they are all three female'.[61] She asked him to send her dried crayfish and pickled herring and enclosed a present for his surviving daughter Diana. Two days later Johannes Morgh wrote a brief note informing Koevoet of the gifts of cloth that he had sent to him and their brother Andries.[62] There is no suggestion that either correspondent knew of his impending marriage.

Only in October 1731 did Koevoet write to inform his brother that he had recently married. This was the letter of 24 October delivered by his 'former master'. *'Wat UE:e huwelijk aangaat'*, wrote Johannes in reply, *'wensche als dat den almogende God UEd:e wilde zeegen en met veele plaijsier en genoegen van UEd:e wilde toe schicken'* (Concerning Your Honour's marriage, I wish that the Almighty God will bless Your Honour and grant you much pleasure and satisfaction). Maria Langenberg was less restrained in her comments. She hoped that God would give His blessing to the marriage, writing, '*en geeve dat gij lange jaaren in voorspoed met malkanderen mogt leven*' (and allow you to live many years in prosperity with one another). However, she added that, if Koevoet would not take it amiss, she wished to inquire about his relations with Aurora of Batavia.

> Ik sal u de rede seggen Auroora na dat se verstaan heeft dat UE: aan de Caap getrouwt is heeft Jan soo weeten te vleijjen tot dat hij na mijn besluijt genegentheijd voor haar heeft gekregen daarom heeft hij haar gevraagt of se ook ooit met u te doen gehad heeft waar op sij geantwoord heeft van neen datse maar aan u is verlooft geweest

> (I will tell you why: when Aurora learnt that you had married at the Cape she made such a fuss of Jan that, in my opinion, he began to be attracted to her and therefore he asked her whether she had ever had sexual relations with you, to which she answered, No, that she had merely been engaged to you)[63]

Aurora of Batavia had, it seems, been engaged to marry Arnoldus Koevoet. How had they met? Perhaps Aurora and her parents (who are also mentioned in the letters) had, like Johannes Morgh, sailed from the Cape as servants of a senior Company official; perhaps they had been visitors at the Cape, as part of the retinue of such an official in transit.[64] In his earliest surviving letters, written in 1729, Johannes Morgh made frequent reference to Aurora – '*UE: lieste mijn Susie Aurora van Batavia*' (Your Honour's beloved, my Sister Aurora of Batavia) – relaying her greetings and her gratitude for the presents that Koevoet had sent her. He urged his brother to come to Batavia. He was a little worried about Aurora, he wrote, 'because the whole of Batavia is saying that you will come here. Wherever I go there are questioners who ask about it because they are inquisitive, whether they know you or not. My Lord Eleijas and his wife and my Lord Toerand and others known and unknown to you, so do your best to come here'. '*Ik bidde u:e*', he continued

> dat gij nog UE: best wil doen daar onttrindt want ik kaan dat niet altijd an hooren. Ik maag nergens koomen of zij lij vraag al daar na want daar is een juff:r of twee die haar de brijloef toe geseijd heeft als zaake is dat zij huer op Batavia trouwde en broer lief schrijft met den eersten of UE: op Batavia komt want haar moeder en haar fader die wil niet dat zij aan de Caab koomt. Zij seggen dat so lang als God de Heer haar liede de ooge ope laat sal zij niet van Batavia gaan, daarom schrijft tog met den eersten hoe of UE: voorneemen is. Alszij niet an de Caap kaan kommen of zij hier mogt trouwe met een an der, want ik kaan de schemppe niet altijd aan hooren die haar ouwers aan mijn doet ... doet dog UE: uijterst best om op Batavia t'koomen.

> (I pray Your Honour that you will do your best about it, because I can't keep hearing that. I can't go anywhere without them asking about it, because there is a lady or two who has promised to fund/arrange a wedding for her if matters should be such that she marries here in Batavia. And, brother dear, write at once whether or not you are

coming to Batavia because her mother and father don't want her to go to the Cape. They say that as long as God the Lord leaves their eyes open they will not leave Batavia; therefore please write as soon as possible what your Honour's intentions are. If she can't come to the Cape, should she marry another here? Because I can't put up with the sneering of her parents ... so please do your utmost best to come to Batavia.)[65]

Arnoldus Koevoet did not go to Batavia; he was still a slave in 1729 and the obstacles may have been insurmountable. We do not know whether or not Aurora married another. But in the light of this evidence it is hard to resist the conclusion that Koevoet's marriage to Anna Rebecca of Bengal was a marriage of convenience. Anna Rebecca was approximately forty-nine years old in 1731, whereas Koevoet was thirty-four.[66] She had no children, or no surviving children; in 1724 she made a will in which she declared that she had no parents or friends still alive who could inherit her estate. She nominated Christiaan Wijnantsz and Jacobus Hendricksz, both prominent members of the free black community, as her executors.[67] They agreed to stand surety for the manumission of her slave, April of Ceylon, who would be freed when she died, on condition that he remained for ten years under the direction of Wijnantsz and Hendricksz. After her death, her executors were empowered to enter her house, sell her goods, arrange a respectable burial, pay the costs and debts of her estate and divide the remaining money between themselves, in equal portions, '*uijt hoofde van 't welke zij deselve voorne: twee persoonen tot haare erfgenaamen is institueerende*' (by reason of which she established the aforementioned two persons as her heirs).[68]

Anna Rebecca was thus a woman alone, without kin at the Cape. Despite my best efforts, I have been unable to establish how she came to Cape Town. She may have arrived in 1720, for there is an entry in the register of church members for that year which reads: 'Accepted through confession of faith or affidavit: having shown her affidavit 24 June 1720 Anna Rebecca'.[69] It is clear that she was closely connected to the family of her chief correspondent, Anna Maria van Thiel of Amsterdam, who signed herself '*UE: van haarte genegene nonje*' (your sincerely well-disposed young mistress). Another correspondent, Jan Tercks, refers to Anna Maria's mother, *juffrouw* Van Thiel, as '*uijuffrouw*' (your mistress) in a letter addressed to Anna Rebecca in 1731. And he adds:

it happened one evening that *ijuffrouw* Muijs and I sat talking of *ijuffrouw* van Tiel when she *ijuffrouw* Muijs said "do you also know that one, her *mijt* [female slave], to whom I taught her catechism?", then *ijuffrouw* Muijs was overcome with such an affection for you that she said, "come let us send her a cake from us both".[70]

It seems, then, that Anna Rebecca had been a slave of *Juffrouw* Van Thiel and her late husband, Otto van Thiel, whom I have recently been able to identify as a former *equipagemeester* (harbour-master) in Batavia, dismissed in 1701 because of his involvement in private trade.[71] It is very clear from the letters that Anna

Maria van Thiel regarded Anna Rebecca as a trusted confidante. She communicates intimate details of her difficult life in Amsterdam, bitterly reproaching '*broer Pieter*' for his feckless lifestyle. '*Hij en wil niet na de Oost nog na de West Indie toe, want hij wil van syn hoer niet af*' (he won't go to the East nor to the West Indies because he won't leave his whore). When Pieter married in April 1733, his sister wrote to Anna Rebecca: '*Wij benne blij dat wij van hem verlost sijn. Hij heeft ons veel verdriet en hartseer aangedaan en alles op verteert dat wij hebbe, soo dat wij nu bij luijde binnes-huijs op kaamers woone*' (We are happy to be rid of him. He has caused us much sorrow and heartache and has consumed everything that we had, so that we now live with others in rented rooms). 'We are the living dead', she writes; 'mother is getting old and is very weak and we are very melancholy, but not without reason'.[72] As for '*broer Jacob*', she wrote, 'we have had no letter from him in five years; we shall have the books at East India House opened, so as to see whether he is alive or dead; that is the son who was going to take care of mother'.[73] At the time of her marriage to Arnoldus Koevoet, Anna Rebecca was a woman of some substance. She owned a slave, April of Ceylon, and his small daughter Johanna; she had gold and silver jewellery, which she bequeathed to Johanna, along with 100 rix dollars in cash and she was a confirmed member of the Cape church, a status achieved by few freed slaves at this time.[74] It is not clear that she owned landed property: her first will, made in 1722, referred only to her *woonhuijse* (residence).[75] Perhaps she lived in rented accommodation.

Anna Rebecca's marriage to Arnoldus Koevoet came as a great surprise to Anna Maria van Thiel, much as it had surprised Arnoldus's friends and relatives in Batavia. 'I received your letter of 30 January 1732', wrote Van Thiel, 'and read therein, to my great astonishment, that you are married. I wish you abundance and blessings in the married state and that you may end your days in rest and peace with one another ... Mother wishes you the best of luck in marriage', she added, 'and hopes that it will go better with you than it did with her'. 'You write that you did it for various reasons', she continues. 'I can well imagine what the reason is: so that you would have an heir'.[76] This was indeed the case. On 13 August 1731, one-and-a-half months before her marriage to Koevoet, Anna Rebecca of Bengal drew up her third and final will. In it she appointed '*den vrijswart arnoldus coevoet*' as her sole and universal heir and the executor of her estate. April of Ceylon and his daughter Johanna would be freed at her death and Johanna would get the jewellery which 'belonged to the body' of the deceased, plus 100 rix dollars. Everything else would go to Arnoldus Koevoet.

Before we conclude that Koevoet married for money, we should bear in mind that he did have other resources: he was a carpenter (this is evident from details in the papers of his deceased estate) and, in the shape of his 'former master' and his master's friends and relatives, he may have had some financial backing. He also had, or had had, an alternative sexual partner in Cape Town. Maria van

Diana van de Caab, a Company slave aged twenty-three or twenty-four in 1731, had borne him two children: Diana, baptized in 1722, and Christina, baptized in 1727 and killed in 1731. Perhaps it was for the sake of Diana, still in the Company's slave lodge, that Arnoldus chose to marry a respectable church-going spinster fifteen years his senior. In May 1735, some six months after the death of his wife, he at last found the wherewithal to free Diana. On 4 May, his petition was read before the Governor and Council: 'the freeblack Arnoldus Koevoet', it read, wished to free his twelve-year-old daughter Diana van Maria van Diana van de Caab from the Company's slave lodge, 'so as to teach her about a better way of life'. His request was granted on the condition that Salamat van Java, the slave he had purchased on credit as a substitute for Diana, met with the approval of the Company's senior surgeon.[77] Diana van Maria van Diana (later known as Johanna Koevoet) thus became eligible to inherit from her father. And, since he was heir to Anna Rebecca's deceased estate, Diana became heir to both. Anna Rebecca's long-held wish for an heir to whom she was connected by blood or marriage had now been fulfilled. The pity is that Arnoldus himself did not live long enough to build on the foundations they had established together. He died soon after, on 21 December 1735. The debts he had incurred, both small and large, many of which (especially the large ones) he had probably intended to repay over the span of years, were called in by the Orphan Masters and cut deeply into the inheritance of his daughter Diana.

In his first few months as a free man, Arnoldus Koevoet may not have incurred much debt. Among the bills still outstanding at his death was one for items purchased 'since June 1731'. He bought a number of items on credit: an iron brazier, black silk for the lining of his wedding coat, a cloak for Anna Rebecca, a pair of stockings, one pound of tobacco and a grammar book 'to study'. He also obtained a chest containing carpenter's tools.[78] His debts began to mount at the end of 1731, when he bought an *afdak* (lean-to) and plot of land in Church Street, adjoining the house of the seller, the burgher Willem Fransen. It seems he bought the *afdak* with the intention of breaking it down and building a separate dwelling on the plot, because the transfer deed places certain restrictions on the construction of a new house.[79] The price of the cottage and plot was 2,200 Cape guilders.[80] The title deed, dated 14 December 1731, indicates that this sum was paid in full on the date of transfer, but that seems unlikely, because it was not until 24 January 1732 that Koevoet signed a formal *scheepenkennis* (acknowledgment of debt) before commissioners of the Council of Justice. He borrowed exactly 2,200 guilders from the Church Poor Fund (*diaconij armenfonds*), a loan which may well have been facilitated by his recent marriage and his wife's status as a full member of the church. He promised to repay the full amount upon three months' notice (a standard clause in such contracts) plus interest at the rate of 6 per cent per annum. As collateral, he pledged his '*huisje en erf staande ende geleegen in deese tafelvalleij thans door hem bewoond werdende*' (little house and plot situated in Table Valley, presently occupied by him).[81] Two members of the Cape Town congregation – Hendrik de Vries and Noach Backer (both from Amsterdam and both former members of the Church Council) – stood surety for the loan.

In March 1732, Arnoldus borrowed 100 rix dollars (300 guilders) from Appolonia Bergh, widow of the late Junior Merchant and *winkelier* (storeman) Jan Aldersz, offering as security his person and 'all his goods, those he presently has and those he will yet acquire, movable and immovable, none excepted'. The rate of interest payable on the loan was again set at the standard (and maximum) rate of 6 per cent.[82] In 1733, he seems to have incurred no major debts. It was not until 6 January 1734 that he borrowed again, this time from the Governor Jan de la Fontaine himself, incurring a debt of 1,000 guilders, for which he offered as security (for a second time) his 'dwelling situated here in Table Valley'. Noach Backer again stood surety for the loan, along with a third Hollander, Anthonij Visser of Utrecht. On 17 September 1734 (shortly after the death of Anna Rebecca), Koevoet borrowed another thousand guilders from the Governor, explicitly '*tot het optimmeren* [construction] *van sijn woonhuijs*'. He mortgaged his residence for a third time (there seems to have been no limit to the number of times one could mortgage the same property), and Noach Backer again accepted co-responsibility for the debt.[83]

The support of Noach Backer and other members of the congregation and council of the Cape Town church was clearly integral to Arnoldus Koevoet's attempts to establish himself as a respectable independent resident of Cape Town. Backer had come to Cape Town as a sailor in 1712. In 1713, he was appointed sexton of the Cape Town church, and in 1724 he became a free burgher.[84] By 1733, he was a brandy *pachter* (someone licensed to retail brandy in the town).[85] He must have cared deeply for Arnoldus and Anna Rebecca, since he three times underwrote the purchase and renovation of their little house in Church Street. When Arnoldus died on 21 December 1735, it was Backer who managed the funeral, paying the fees of the grave-digger and the church, ordering a coffin, buying supplies for the funeral meal (almonds, raisins, olives, tea, sugar, biscuits, *krakelinge* and wine) and ensuring that Diana Koevoet had a new frock and coat to wear for the occasion. He spent a total of 56 rix dollars, 4 schellings and 3 stuivers, an amount which was promptly reimbursed by the Orphan Masters.[86]

In September 1734, Arnoldus was obliged to pay the costs of Anna Rebecca's funeral. He seems to have done so without incurring further debt, except perhaps a small outstanding sum for the clasp and handles of her coffin.[87] On 4 October 1734, he received a small interest-free loan from his fellow free black,

Robbert Schot of Bengal, and on 24 October he pawned ten silver spoons and six silver forks as surety for a loan of 50 rix dollars (150 guilders) from Maria Schriek, widow of Hendrik Willem Schriek of Amsterdam. On 30 October, he borrowed a further 100 guilders from Appolonia Bergh, the Widow Aldersz.

In 1735, these small debts continued to mount. On 29 April, he borrowed 100 rix dollars from a certain Pieter Andriesse, at an interest rate of 6 per cent. On 26 May, he bought the slave Salamat van Java from Johannes Cruijwagen for 100 rix dollars, repayable in six months' time. In August, he borrowed 23 rix dollars from Roselijn of Bengal (a slave belonging to the free black Jacobus Hendriksz)[88] and 38 rix dollars from Simon Petrus Bergh, brother of Appolonia; in September, he borrowed 22 rix dollars from Johan Michael Molvanger. It is possible that his health began to fail around this time, because by October 1735 he owed the free black Zamson van de Cust Coromandel several small sums for *meesterloon* (doctor's fees) and 'purges'. The very last debt he incurred (besides the quite substantial costs of winding up his estate) was in favour of Otto Ernst van Graan, who made him a pair of slippers on 8 December 1735, just two weeks before he died.[89]

The papers filed as annexures to the liquidation account of Arnoldus Koevoet's deceased estate do contain some pointers to the sources of his income. For example, we know that he delivered 6,500 baked bricks to Antoni Visser and that he was owed outstanding fees for the renovation of a *veeplaatse* (stock farm) belonging to the brothers Wijnand and Pieter Besuijdenhout.[90] In 1733, moreover, his brother Johannes Morgh wrote from Batavia to acknowledge his request for *eenen timmerjongen* (a slave carpenter). Such slaves were too expensive, wrote Johannes, but he would do what he could if the occasion arose. He was also unable to send the planks and beams which his brother had requested, because 'the people here all want to take two or three boxes of tea along [on homeward-bound VOC ships]'.[91]

But, in general, one must infer the nature of Koevoet's business from the list of possessions which were auctioned after his death and the liquidation and distribution account which was drawn up by the Orphan Masters. At the time of his death, he owned three carpenter's benches, a saw-horse, a chest with carpenter's tools, a *schulpzaag*, a crowbar and two sledge-hammers, as well as assorted timberwork and door and window frames. He was, we may conclude, what his contemporaries called a *huijstimmerman* – a house-carpenter. He may also have made bricks, but, if so, it is curious that he seems to have had no cart or wagon of his own. His domestic furnishings were modest, but comfortable: two four-poster beds, four ordinary beds, some curtains, a few cushions, four bedspreads, a desk, three books, four sconces, two copper candle-sticks, two small mirrors, eight small paintings, twelve chairs, two foot stools, two *rustbanken* (wooden settees), four square tables and one oval table. His kitchen was well equipped, with six iron pots, a frying pan and assorted copper utensils, cake pans, tart pans and fish kettles. He and Anna Rebecca owned fifty-five porcelain plates, eleven porcelain dishes, ten silver spoons and six silver forks (the same that he had pawned in exchange for a loan from Maria Schriek) and a basket containing drinking glasses. They also owned six slaves: three males, two females and a child (excluding April of Ceylon and his daughter Johanna).[92] Given the large number of dishes and plates in their possession, it seems possible that Anna Rebecca had run a café or restaurant from home.

In 1736, Arnoldus Koevoet's house and plot were sold for 6,000 guilders to Jan Georg Hauptfleisch of Breslau, a local 'surgeon' who had treated him in the last year of his life. The auction of his movable goods brought in 2,561 guilders and 6 schellings.[93] When the value of all his assets had been calculated, the sum was 8,675 guilders, 7 schellings and 8 stuivers. The liabilities of his estate, including monies owed to Jan de la Fontaine, the *diaconij* and various other creditors (including Johanna, daughter of April of Ceylon, who was still owed 100 rix dollars from Anna Rebecca's estate) amounted to 8,258 guilders, 7 schellings and 8 stuivers. Koevoet's daughter Diana thus stood to inherit just 417 guilders. However, since her new husband, Pieter van Heemert of Stavenisse, had already borrowed 1,000 guilders against the anticipated receipt of her future inheritance, she was left with nothing at all (except debt).[94] By 1737, van Heemert had disappeared, leaving his wife Diana destitute.[95] Confronted in court by her husband's creditors and ordered to pay his debts, she told the court '*dat zij niets besit, dat zij de cost met hare handen moet winnen en dat haar man voor dat weg ging alles op een clandestine wijse uijt den huijse heeft weg gebragt en vervolgens vercogt*' (that she owned nothing, that she had to earn her bread with her hands and that before her husband left he removed everything from the house in a clandestine manner and sold it).

And that is how the story comes to an end.

It may seem, then, that the efforts of the freed slave Arnoldus Koevoet to construct a dignified and self-sustaining life in freedom and to share it with his only surviving daughter had been in vain. His wife Anna Rebecca's fervent wish for an heir who would assume control of her estate and benefit from her accumulated savings after her death had likewise not materialized. Koevoet died too soon, before the investments he had made with borrowed money could yield an adequate return. And yet, although Diana was destitute, she *was* free from slavery, and her right to bear her father's name in freedom was acknowledged by the Orphan Masters and the courts. That, at least, was a monument to his tenacity.

5 DEBT, LABOUR AND BONDAGE: ENGLISH SERVANTS VERSUS INDENTURED IMMIGRANTS IN MAURITIUS, FROM THE LATE EIGHTEENTH TO EARLY TWENTIETH CENTURY

Alessandro Stanziani

This chapter argues that from the late eighteenth to early twentieth century, there existed a strong relationship between the institutions and practices of debt and labour in Britain and those in the colonial world. Thus, one cannot fully understand the origin and evolution of indentured labour in the Indian Ocean without taking into consideration the notions about labour, and labour practices, in Europe.

Conventionally, historians have interpreted the phenomenon of indentured labour in two main ways. The first interpretation, advanced by colonial elites in the nineteenth century and later renewed in 'subaltern studies', is that the indentured contract was a 'legal fiction', and that those indentured experienced conditions of forced labour or even slavery.[1] This approach essentially negates the historical significance of the abolition of slavery[2] and underestimates the efforts of indentured immigrants to fight for their own rights.[3] Also, legal scholars have demonstrated that indentureship was initially viewed as an expression of free will in contract, and can only be considered as an involuntary contract that reflected forced labour in the second half of the nineteenth century.[4] This in turn reflects recent debates in the history of emigration that also stress the shifting boundary between free and unfree emigration.[5] This second approach emphasizes the differences between the legal status and living conditions of indentured immigrants and slaves.[6]

Here the core arguments presented by legal scholars are accepted, but I add a further dimension by showing that until the late nineteenth century, in both European colonies and in Europe, labour was considered chiefly as a service and obligation that working people had to fulfil. The main justification for this was the debt working people owed to their masters for advances of wages, raw materials and food, and for apprenticeship. This is not to assert that British wage earners were 'unfree', or that their legal and social conditions were the same as those of indentured immigrants. In simply argue that it would be misleading to put these actors into distinct, opposing boxes: the indentured immigrant, close to the slave on the one hand, and the wage earner, an expression of 'free labour', on the other. Here it is argued that all these actors belonged to one and the same world, but that inequalities between the legal and economic entitlements of working people and those of their masters were far greater in the colonies than in Europe.

British colonial elites conceived of the indentured contract within the framework of their understanding of notions and practices of labour in Britain – albeit filtered through the colonial experience. At the same time, however, one might argue that local forms of debt bondage also influenced colonial practices. Many authors have evoked indentureship in India and pawnship in Africa as expressions of debt bondage.[7] However, indentureship, debt bondage and pawnship were distinct categories. There were two major differences between African pawnship and the indentured contract. In the case of pawnship, the collateral used as the basis for raising the loan (and thus incurring debt) was a child (generally a daughter), not the debtor himself.[8] This contrasts with indentureship where, even if the indentured immigrant was accompanied by his family, and children contributed to the repayment of transportation costs, they did not enter the debt relationship as the head of the family did not have the power to give his children into bondage. A second fundamental difference was that pawnship, unlike indentureship (and slavery), represented a form of inclusion in society. By contrast, the integration of indentured immigrants into local society was not guaranteed; it depended on the ethnic origin of the immigrant, as well as the place and period of immigration.

The focus on Mauritius also requires some justification. That so many scholars have focused on this small island is related, on the one hand, to the availability of sources (in France, England and Mauritius) and, on the other, to the fact that Mauritius developed a plantation economy. Imports to Mauritius, first of slaves, then indentured immigrants, were relatively important given the small size of the island: 160,000 slaves reached the Mascarene islands (Mauritius and Réunion) between 1670 and 1810,[9] and it is estimated that from 1810 to 1829 a further 50,000 slaves were illegally imported.[10] In addition, between the 1840s and 1910, 451,000 indentured immigrants entered Mauritius – representing almost a fifth of the two million indentured immigrants recorded worldwide during this period.[11] This traffic, first in slaves, and subsequently in indentured labour, has caused most scholars to make comparisons with the transatlantic slave trade. Certainly the Mauritian case cannot be taken as representative of labour practices and markets elsewhere in the IOW where Indians, Arabs and

Africans began trafficking humans as early as the seventh century.[12] Forms of IOW bondage were multiple and varied: there were palace slaves, soldier slaves, female and child slaves, and slave labourers in agriculture and manufacturing – all with diverse statuses.[13] Hence, bondage in the IOW cannot be studied on the basis of the usual transatlantic paradigm;[14] rather, one needs to consider the peculiar way local rules and practices governing labour interacted with those imported into the region by Europeans.

This essay firstly discusses notions and practices of labour and debt in England; secondly, examines how these rules and practices were transplanted to Mauritius and why they changed in the mid-nineteenth century; and concludes by reformulating the fundamental issues at play and relating them to the colonial and global history of labour.

Debt and Labour Constraints in England

Indentured contracts in Britain were directly related to its labour institutions. The Statute of Labourers (1350–1) was followed by a set of legal rules and laws gathered, together under the umbrella of the Masters and Servants Acts, which multiplied in the sixteenth century and accompanied the Statute of Artificers and Apprentices (1562).[15] These measures were coherent in that in all, apprentices, servants and any other type of wage earner had an inferior legal status to, and fewer rights than, their employers and masters. Any untimely breach of contract on the part of a servant was subject to prosecution; and the term 'fugitive' was employed for apprentices and servants who left without giving notice. Underlying these measures was the concept of the worker's 'debt'. This comprised frequent advances on wages, which gave special power to the master/employer/creditor; and 'advances' on raw materials,[16] particularly in centralized manufacturing units, for which 'servants' were held accountable, and hence under 'obligation' to the master-merchant who commissioned the work. Indeed, employers requested and received criminal legislation that designated any appropriation of these raw materials as theft.[17]

The so-called Industrial Revolution promoted rather than challenged such concepts, which meant that associated forms of debt, labour and coercion were perfectly compatible with market development and industrialization. Indeed, the Masters and Servants Acts grew stricter from the 1720s, when penalties against servants who broke their contracts were reinforced. Between 1720 and 1792, ten Acts of Parliament reiterated or increased terms of imprisonment for unilaterally quitting work, or for misbehaviour. Rather than attempting to maintain a pre-industrial model of household employment, these 'new' Masters and Servant Acts aimed to impose a more rigorous work discipline upon the growing numbers of labourers, artisans and outworkers employed in manufacturing, as well as to maintain control of the agricultural labour market at a time of considerable upheaval.[18] In addition, the Acts dealt with insubordination and failure to comply with workshop rules, both of which were considered an implicit, unilateral breach of contract.[19]

Tighter constraints were also applied to anyone who refused work,[20] which demonstrates the relationship between labour contracts and Poor Law provisions – the Masters and Servants Acts having been supplemented from the late seventeenth century by a larger set of laws directed against the disorderly poor. Penalties against workers were coupled with those against vagrancy and disorderly behaviour.[21] As R. H. Tawney noted, the Poor Law began where serfdom ended.[22] In eighteenth- and nineteenth-century Britain, freedom to choose one's employer did not imply the freedom to remain unemployed. Apprenticeships formed an integral part of the same approach to work and workers.[23] At the same time as employers sought to retain 'good' workers, local authorities encouraged workers to leave in order to lower social expenses in their district. The apprentice's debt was conceived, in the first case as compensation for his work, and in the second as leverage to force him to migrate.[24]

The persistent importance of debt in labour relations is corroborated by details kept in employer accounts of workers. Conventionally considered to have been characteristic of the French, such record books were also widespread in Britain. Testimonials (discharge certificates) were mandated by the Statute of Artificers, and in the eighteenth century were feared by workers as means of increasing their servitude.[25] Employers claimed that testimonials were legal in every sector, and as late as the 1860s still demanded 'clearance papers' from a worker's previous employer in order to protect themselves against both 'unfair competition' from other employers and strikes by workers.

Enforcement of Labour Legislation

When historians encountered criminal sanctions in late eighteenth- and early nineteenth-century Britain, they depicted them as anomalous in a modern market society with a large population of 'proletarians', and considered that they were rarely enforced. However, recent and detailed quantitative analyses on the rate of penalty enforcement in the courts of England, Britain as a whole and the colonies, clearly demonstrate that the infliction of harsh penalties on servants was extensive. Between 1750 and 1875 (when they were finally abolished), labour legislation was not only increasingly enforced, but covered a growing cross-section of labourers and working people.[26] County and police district records, which are available for the period 1857 to 1875, show that about 10,000 people were prosecuted each year for Masters and Servants offences. Of these, 7,000 were convicted, 1,700 served a sentence in a house of correction, 2,000 were fined and 3,300 received other kinds of punishment (abated wages and cost assessments). Whipping was extremely rare (it was applied to eleven people in 1857, two in 1858 and 1859, one in 1860 and another in 1866).[27] Overall, between 5 and 8 per cent of servants were prosecuted. However, as the percentage reached as high as 17 per cent in some areas, and 20 per cent in London in certain years, most conflicts were seemingly resolved out of court – indicating that masters generally wanted 'to set an example' and have their workers and servants return to work.[28]

In contrast, under the Masters and Servants legislation, masters and employers were not subject to penalties; the first rulings in this sense occurred in 1844, exactly at the time the Poor Law was eliminated. Until that moment, masters were never threatened with imprisonment for breach of contract.[29] It is unclear if, subsequently, official statistics included worker-initiated proceedings.[30]

Apprentices were governed by the general Masters and Servants Acts. Douglas Hay's data shows that for every apprentice who lodged a complaint for mistreatment or unpaid wages, three masters brought apprentices to court for violations of contract such as lack of respect and undue absence. Most of these offences were related to the apprentice's obligation and debt towards his/her master in exchange for training. No masters were punished, while the number and percentage of apprentices (all aged under eighteen) sent to prison increased in the 1830s and the 1840s: The percentage was around 30 per cent in London, 26 per cent in Gloucestershire and 39 per cent in Staffordshire. These figures fell only in the 1860s.[31]

Thus, the debt of the worker (including the apprentice), for wages, raw materials, tools or simply learning, was one of the master's/employer's major means of controlling his workforce. Rules became harsher for workers during the Industrial Revolution when the rate of prosecution also increased. However, whereas in the mid-nineteenth century, the rate of workers' prosecution under criminal rules was around 5–8 per cent in Britain, it was about 20 per cent in the colonies, reaching particularly high peaks in the plantation and mining sectors of Mauritius.[32] The next section will analyse the analogies, differences and mutual influence of labour rules and their enforcement in England and its colonies, notably Mauritius.

Indentureship and Apprenticeships

English legal language first began using the term 'indenture' in relation to the apprenticeship contracts to indicate the apprentice's obligation to the master.[33] The guardianship of minors, the apprenticeship contract and the limited rights of apprentices were therefore interconnected. Like slaves, children and apprentices had diminished legal capabilities, and it was upon this that the master's authority was based. It was no accident that changes in the legal rules governing apprenticeship and family law came about during the same period, and were interconnected. During the last quarter of the eighteenth century, when the status of the apprentice came under increasing criticism from guilds, workers and officials, the authority of the head of the family over his children, particularly with regard to corporal punishment and labour, was similarly called into question.[34]

The hierarchical relationship between children and apprentices, on the one hand, and fathers and masters, on the other, formed the ground upon which family and labour relationships were regulated in the British colonies. Thus, the way children of indentured servants were viewed in the North American colonies was significant. The prevailing practice, imported from England, of placing orphans in workhouses, in part reflected a desire to avoid the danger of gangs of children and adolescents developing and growing out of control. Non-working children and teens, like indentured fugitives and runaway slaves, were viewed as challenges to the social order. Hence, the municipalities set up forced apprenticeship systems, either with masters or in correctional institutions and workhouses.[35] The same system applied to the children of indebted indentured servants: placing children in apprenticeship helped to redeem the parents' debt. It was for this purpose that a system was established in the main cities on the east coast of North America of putting children up for auction as indentured servants. Between 1740 and 1800, for example, there existed an estimated 1,400 such child indenture contracts in Boston, and 6,700 in Baltimore.[36] Children and their labour were considered as collateral for the repayment of the monetary (and eventually criminal) debt of their parents. This practice, formally forbidden in England, was a derivative of the colonial context.

The legal status of children and apprentices then, played an important role not only in the evolution of indentured service but also of slavery. When slavery was abolished in 1832, the British authorities decided that a given period (usually six years – reproducing the timeframe of individual emancipation as well as of apprenticeship contracts) be stipulated during which the quasi-former slaves were given an apprenticeship status. There are two aspects of this system: firstly, the decision to implement it occurred after the reform of the apprenticeship system in 1814; secondly, the similarities between apprentices, children and slaves were brought out in debates, and later in legislation and case law, on the apprenticeship of slaves.[37] The prevalent view was that children and slaves did not enjoy full legal status inasmuch as they were not yet 'civilized'; children, slaves and apprentices were supposed to be trained for life in society. During this transitory training phase, the almost-ex-slave and apprentice needed to be trained to become responsible 'free' labour. The 'cost' of this effort to the state/master/employer, was passed on to the ex-slave who, in order to repay this 'debt', was obliged to provide unpaid labour to her/his former master and the colonial government for a period of between five and seven years.[38]

However, in order to avoid abuse of the system and ex-slave by the master, apprenticeship relations were entrusted to special magistrates. These 'protectors' of slaves were settled in all the main British colonies in the wake of abolition, and their reports constitute a major source for historians.[39] It appears that, during the transitional apprenticeship period, very few slaves succeeded in redeeming their freedom. Moreover, even when this phase officially ended – between 1838 and 1841 depending on the colony – the degree of social and economic integration of former slave apprentices varied greatly. For example, in Jamaica, Trinidad and British Guyana, most former apprentices ended up indebted to their former masters and found themselves back working on the plantations.[40] Even worse, former slaves had to face competition from new immigrants, now under indentured contracts.

Conventionally, historians consider the indenture contract to reflect a form of forced labour. However, this was not the case until the mid-nineteenth century. From the seventeenth century, indenture had been viewed as an expression of free contract; the individual bound by the contract was a servant whose travel expenses were paid in advance, and who committed himself for a longer period of time than a labourer but a shorter one than a domestic servant. Like the others, however, he owed the contractual time to his master, who could sell the indentured servant, along with any debts owed by the servant, to someone else. Masters, whether in Britain or the colonies, had the legal right to recover fugitive indentured servants. In both cases, the worker's debt played a central role. The indentured immigrant had to repay the cost of travel exactly as the English servant had to repay advances of wages and raw materials, and the ex-slave had to redeem freedom and pay back the costs of his 'apprenticeship'.

Over time, however, masters in the colonies obtained broader rights than their counterparts in Britain, including the right to exercise corporal punishment, and authorize the marriage of their indentured servants.[41] Here, we can distinguish two periods: the first, from the seventeenth century to the 1830s, when slavery was legal and the traffic in human beings, operated by European traders, concerned about 300,000 European indentured servants intended chiefly for tobacco plantations and to a lesser extent manufacturing in the colonies.

The second phase, from the 1830s, concerned 2.5 million indentured servants, mostly Chinese and Indians, but also Africans, Japanese and Pacific islanders, employed primarily in sugar plantations and in manufacturing. Unlike the first phase of indentured servitude, the post-1830s bonded labourers usually renewed their indenture contracts and seldom returned to the world of free labour.[42]

Debt and Bondage in Mauritius

In this context, Mauritius is of particular interest.[43] In the late eighteenth century, 40 per cent of free men of colour in Mauritius were of Indian extraction, whereas they formed only 15 per cent of the servile population.[44] The British administration that succeeded the French in 1810 encouraged the arrival of indentured servants from Madagascar, India and increasingly of Swahilis from East Africa.[45] In this process, there existed many intermediaries in India, Mozambique, Madagascar and West Africa, ranging from local sultans to village chiefs; Indian, Arab and Portuguese middlemen; and French and English landowners and traders.[46] Contracts varied widely in terms, and in numerous cases were imposed through force or fraud – although many Indians signed voluntarily.[47]

Between 1834, when slavery was abolished, and 1910, 450,000 indentured servants arrived in Mauritius, chiefly from India, but also from China, Africa and Madagascar. Numerous observers drew attention to the inhuman living conditions of these immigrants.[48] Nevertheless, two-thirds remained. As a result, the number of Indians grew substantially from 35 per cent of the total population in 1846 to 66 per cent in 1871.[49] To these must be added the influx of indentured servants from South Asia and Africa: 30,000 in 1851, and twice that number ten years later. These forms of immigration to Mauritius provoked protest from English landowners in India, and railway companies in India and East Africa, against what they considered to be unfair competition for labour orchestrated by Mauritian planters aided by the British administration.[50] Female immigration to Mauritius remained secondary[51] until the mid-nineteenth century when the state started encouraging the immigration of indentured servants with their families both to meet growing demand for domestic, urban and plantation labour, and to promote social stability and order.[52]

The conditions for workers varied not only according to the time period and their ethnic origin, but also the estates on which they worked. Small plantation owners were most concerned about fugitive, insubordinate and vagrant indentured servants.[53] Large plantation owners, who were concerned with the excessive costs of slave surveillance, sought rather to increase the inflow of 'free' contract labour to create a large labour market and thus cheapen the cost of hiring a workforce. They found support from humanitarian and anti-slavery associations by underscoring the benefits of free immigration (indenture) as opposed to slavery, and of migration as a means of escaping 'famine' in India and Africa.[54]

However, despite the efforts of the British abolitionists who were on the lookout for any form of disguised slavery, laws protecting immigrant workers proved difficult to enforce, and conditions for immigrants remained harsh. As previously noted, indenture contracts were governed by the provisions of the Masters and Servants Acts which, in the colonies,[55] were strongly inspired by practices in England. It was extremely difficult for workers to profit from the law; local magistrates were often corrupt and had close ties to plantation owners. Indeed, the law was largely invoked on the part of masters to sue immigrants. Any unjustified absence by a worker was subject to criminal prosecution. Between the abolition of slavery in 1835 and the 1870s, anti-vagrancy measures took on particular importance in Mauritius. where their adoption testifies to the same concerns that prompted legal rules limiting the mobility of workers and peasants in the rest of the British Empire: considerations of public order (monitoring movements, knowing the exact location of the immigrants and amount of their wages) converged with those involving employer competition for workers. In both cases, labourers were supposedly indebted both to the community and their original master. In particular, small landowners complained of runaway engagés (contract workers), as previously of fugitive slaves – a problem that also stemmed from lack of cooperation between large landowners. In the 1860s, about 70,000 complaints a year were filed by landowners and employers against Indian immigrants; in 80 per cent of the cases, they pertained to desertion or illegal absence, while the debt of the worker was systematically evoked in trials to justify the sentence.[56]

However, the number of cases brought by indentured servants against their masters rose sharply from mid-century. In the 1860s, about 10 per cent of the indentured servants sued their masters, almost always for non-payment of, or insufficient, wages; and they won in over 70 per cent of the cases.[57] Nevertheless, this result, which was partly due to pressure from the abolitionist movement in Britain, did not indicate that the 'march to equality' was under way. Indeed, the percentage of labour complaints concerning indenture contracts declined by 5 per cent at end of the 1870s, and dropped to a mere 0.3 per cent by 1895–9 when labourers won less than 40 per cent of cases.[58] This was because, in response to the rise of work grievance complaints in the 1860s, employers sought alternative labour agreements, notably oral contracts, against which labourers found it almost impossible to lodge complaints. This was facilitated by the 1867 legislation that endorsed oral contracts at the point of recruitment of indentured labour in India. Moreover, coolies' contracts were from 1867 drawn up with Indian middlemen instead of plantation owners, which shifted the responsibility for settling any contentious issues to the former.[59] Moreover, the indentured labourer became increasingly indebted to the planter. This process started with the necessity, often poorly explained at the time of recruitment, for the labourer to repay the cost of travel to Mauritius.[60] In addition, notably small planters enforced a range of penalties that increased the debt of indentured labourers thus increasing the likelihood that the labourer was obliged to renew his contract; the percentage of contract renewals rose from 40 per cent in 1861 to over 70 per cent in 1881.[61]

Such abuses drew protests from the anti-slavery movement in Great Britain, as well as from the Indian colonial authorities.[62] The Free Labour Association replied that landowners had the right to recover the travel expenses they had advanced and that the market price did not allow them to raise the wages of contract workers to the level of other wage earners.[63] The estate inspectors, who were introduced specifically to oversee these relationships, confirmed that abuses occurred.[64] Nevertheless, planters succeeded in convincing magistrates appointed by London in the early 1840s that the indentured servants had invented 'malicious' complaints against them and should be punished for it.[65] Thus, the courts seldom ruled in favour of the immigrants.

Moreover, many indentured labourers found the cost of the return trip to India to be prohibitively expensive. In 1876, only 2,572 of the 150,000 Indians in Mauritius returned to India.[66] Most planters, in particular small planters, did their utmost to oblige workers to renew their contracts, especially from the late 1860s as Indian immigration to Mauritius slowed. In 1871, for example, 28,172 newly arrived Indians signed contracts, whereas 47,713 established Indian workers renewed their expired contracts – to which figure must be added the increasing number of Indian workers who, once their initial contract had expired, entered into new informal contracts with Indian sub-contractors who then transferred the immigrants to the planters. All these had to obtain police passes – the number of which increased from 12,597 in 1871 to 17,730 in 1875.[67] At the same time, planters sought local creole workers; those entering engagements on plantations increased from 2,938 in 1869 to 5,501 in 1873 and 8,001 in 1876.[68]

Thus government authorities promoted short-term six-to-twelve-month contracts instead of the traditional three-to-five-year contracts, most planters followed their advice because they gave them more flexibility in dealing with, and greater control over, immigrant workers. In 1876, of a total of 60,555 contracts signed, 52,292 were short-term. Officials trusted that such contracts would facilitate the early return of migrant workers to India. In fact, the opposite occurred and contracts were usually renewed. This was chiefly due to planters claiming damages from immigrants and retaining most of their wages as compensation. This was done in several steps. First, from the start of the contractual system, planters kept most of the wages due by arguing both that immigrants were in debt to them, and that they would spend any money received on alcohol and other vices. However, such arguments were increasingly attacked by British officials and the antislavery movement and, from the mid-1860s, it was stipulated that wages be paid on a monthly basis. Despite this ruling, as late as 1875–6, most planters still delayed the payment of wages to workers by a minimum of three to four weeks. Moreover, masters claimed that workers were indebted to them for most of their wages. In 1874–5, out of a total of £1 million in wages nominally due, masters deducted in 1874 £229,225 for absenteeism and about

£91,000 for costs associated with illness,[69] and in 1875 £103,756 for sickness and £254,193 for illegal absence. Their calculation was simple: a worker lost one day in wages for each day of sickness and two days' wages for every day in prison as well as for every day of absenteeism.[70] Plantation accounting books also show that planters arbitrarily made other deductions for various offences, including alleged 'theft', go-slows and inefficiency – so that, on average, the final payment to the worker barely reached one quarter of the contractual wage.[71]

Testaments and successions also provide important sources for such investigations. From 1875, vacant estates were put under the administration of a curator named by the colonial state. The curator provided details for each worker, including name, declared profession, place of birth, last place of residence, type and duration of contract, wages, debts, wages and her/his accounting balance with the estate. This huge mass of data has yet to be analysed in order to compare worker contracts, wages and debts on estates of different sizes and degrees of capital investment. However, the fact that all plantation workers appear to have incurred debt suggests that all estates were in financial difficulty, and that planters considered their workers to be part both of the problem and of the solution. This is further reflected in curator and public magistrate reports on the resources to be distributed to estate heirs and creditors.

Nevertheless, indentured immigrants were sometimes able to save money. In 1875, for example, when leaving Mauritius to return to India, 2,576 former contract workers declared that they were carrying with them a total of 437,039 rupees worth of money; of which 101,223 was in gold, 201,541 in silver and 134,275 in drafts on British Emigration agents.[72] The bulk of this sum belonged to 1,938 men. However, around 1,000 of the returning labourers that year had less than 300 rupees each; and 400 had no savings at all.[73] In the following years, declared savings showed a generally downward trend, to 358,314 rupees in 1876, and 281,089 in 1877, rising to 386,963 in 1879, and dropping thereafter to reach 172,653 rupees in 1881. In part, this trend reflected fluctuations in the number of returnees.[74] However, it also reflected the fact that immigrant workers increasingly chose to directly remit their savings For example, in 1875 the Mauritius immigration office remitted on behalf of workers 146,555 rupees, 48.57 per cent of which was sent to Calcutta, 40.57 per cent to Madras and 10.87 per cent to Bombay.

This flow of money to India encouraged more Indians to migrate to Mauritius, as did the growing possibility for migrants to access property. From the late 1860s, competition from sugar-beet led to decreasing cane sugar prices. To counter this, wealthier planters introduced mechanized farming[75] while small planters, who lacked the capital resources to mechanize, tried to survive by squeezing their labour force – imposing both harsh work conditions and penalties that indebted labourers to them. However, such methods bought them little time and ultimately most small planters were obliged to sell their estates. After 1880, large estate own-ers also started selling off the most unprofitable portions of their land. Such sales gave Indian immigrant workers the opportunity, which they seized, to purchase small plots of land in Mauritius. The process had started in the late 1840s,[76] but became significant only after 1880 when large morcellement (parcelling estates) accelerated.[77] Most Indian land acquisitions comprised small plots of less than two arpents (approximately 6,800 m²).[78] According to bank and notarial archives, Indian immigrants who bought land did so with a mixture of their own savings and bank loans.[79] These small Indian landowners (at least on paper), used family labour to work their plots, growing sugar cane to sell to big sugar producers, and thus gain the means to pay off their bank loans and remaining debts to planta-tion owners. In other cases, Indian merchants bought land and recruited Indian labourers to work it, chiefly on a sharecropping basis.[80]

At the end of the nineteenth century, Indians comprised a tiny minority of land-owners (1.1 per cent in 1891)[81] most of whom were still obliged to work for most of the year as labourers for bigger landowners in order to pay off the debt incurred to buy their small parcels of land – most of which lay largely unculti-vated.[82] The same trend continued into the early twentieth century. The end of Indian immigration in 1916 led to a stabilization of social hierarchies on the island and facilitated the integration of former immigrants. By 1910, Indians owned one fifth of the total area of land on Mauritius devoted to sugar produc-tion.[83] By 1930, the average size of Indian holdings was 2.5 acres compared to 15.1 acres for non-Indians;[84] and many small owners continued to work most of the year as labourers on large estates. They and other small planters were hit hard by the Great Depression, the colonial government recording an increase in the number of 'destitute' Indians from 11.2 per thousand in 1929 to 27.6 in 1935.[85] By that time, the ILO convention of 1930 had forbidden private labour contracts that were not signed voluntarily by workers, and in which criminal penalties were imposed for non-performance of work. However, labour contracts for public works, which were excluded from the ILO provisions, continued to be significant in India and Africa.[86]

6 RANSOM, ESCAPE AND DEBT REPAYMENT IN THE SULU ZONE, 1750–1898

James Francis Warren

Introduction

In this essay, I examine the origin and relationship of debt and emancipation within the context of a flourishing captive exchange economy in the Sulu Zone. In the process of exchange and emancipation, former slaves or captives invariably accrued a level of indebtedness. This debt implied a shift in 'master' from the Sultanate to colonial officials, ships' captains or land owners who had arranged their redemption. In this context, Muslim and Spanish colonial traditions of servitude and forced labour meshed with the framework of emancipation as a direct consequence of either the act of ransom or escape. A system of transportation and de facto servitude was formed whereby the emancipated slave or former captive became part of a dependent colonial workforce. The indebted former slave then performed services for their new masters and produced material goods until the debt for the granting of their freedom and/or transportation was repaid. Slave trading and the acts of ransom and manumission provided labour resources, redistributed wealth and fostered kinship connections that helped to integrate seemingly antagonistic groups – despite these practices further encouraging cycles of violence and slave raiding. Set against this background, debt repayment, as a consequence of ransom, escape and/or transportation must be viewed as one of the corrosive effects of the slave trade on the inter-connected nature of Muslim and colonial societies in the Philippines.

In the late eighteenth and nineteenth centuries, the Sulu trading zone was situated on the margins of three colonial states: the Spanish Philippines, British Malaya and the evolving Dutch East Indies – each of which was involved in a sustained and profitable trade with China. The broad backdrop of the Sulu Zone and the slaving port of Jolo provide the setting within which to enquire into the linked patterns of consumption; trajectories of tastes and 'frontiers of desire' in Europe, China and Southeast Asia with particular entangled commodities; and cases of ransom, escape and debt repayment. A basic interpretation of the history of the Sulu Sultanate, the heart of the zone, must focus on the place of the slave, or 'acquired person',[1] in Taosug and Samal society and the decisive importance of slaves in the functioning of Sulu's economy. It must be noted that slavery and slave raiding were fundamental to the Sulu State, primarily as a consequence of the onset of trade with China, and never as a strictly Islamic enterprise.

Links to the China Trade – Historical Background

At the dawn of the nineteenth century, the Sulu Zone was a place where borders were becoming ever more porous, less bounded, less fixed and stimulated in large measure by global-regional flows of commodities, people and ideas. Jolo's ascendancy as a slaving port and regional entrepôt was linked to Europe's globalizing trade with China.[2] The maritime and jungle products to be found within the Sulu Zone and in the area of its trading partners – tripang, birds' nest, wax, camphor, mother of pearl and tortoise shell – were new products ideal for redressing the British East India Company's adverse trade balance with China. The insatiable demands of the Sultanate for labour to procure and process these exotic natural commodities reached a peak in the first half of the nineteenth century necessitating a steady influx of captives and slaves. In this context, the Sulu Sultanate became one of the most strategic cultural crossroads in which to conduct global-regional commerce in insular Southeast Asia.

At this time, the accumulation of wealth and the transmission of power and privilege in the Sulu Zone were facilitated by the ownership of slaves. The slave played a major role in the economy, both as a unit of production and as a medium of exchange. As such, slaving became the exclusive vocation of the Samal-speakers of Balangingi and other small sand and coral islets, who combined their activities with certain Iranun groups from the north coast of Jolo and Mindanao.

Before 1850, the size of the slave population was several times larger than that of the host society. *Banyaga* (slaves) were being incorporated into the population of the Sulu Sultanate, which included, perhaps, half a million people by mid-century.[3] In this milieu, thousands of people chose to abandon their original culture and become 'moros'. Manumitted slaves and their descendants were continually being redefined according to the ethnicity of their host communities. The slave testimonies as a historical source provide the fullest, most balanced view of the fate of Southeast Asians who were wrenched from their villages and transported to Sulu, and who then lived out their lives initially as *banyaga*, and then as assimilated Taosug or Samal in the first or subsequent generations following captivity. The importance of the institution of marriage for the process of assuming a new ethnicity, what the Spanish referred to as *cruzameintos* ('crossing over'), cannot be underestimated. Manuel de los Santos, an escaped slave, stated as early 1836 'that the captives who were already married to many women no longer wanted to escape'.[4]

However, not all captives were happy to assimilate, and this paper focuses on the experiences of those who sought manumission and freedom through ransom and escape. Many of the captive experiences drawn on in this paper were related by Filipinos from the Visayas and southern Luzon. However, there are two European men whose experiences repeatedly emerge in the source documents. The first is Dutch captain of the cutter *Petronella,* Cornelius Zacharias Pieters (who was captured in 1838), and the second is William Wyndham, a self-educated merchant adventurer, who ransomed captives and in turn benefitted from their labour.

Ransom: Determining the Price

In Sulu the ransom price of slaves or recently-arrived captives was apt to vary with sex, age, ethnicity and personal condition and be influenced by perceived stereotypical characteristics of their ethnic group. The Tagalogs, or 'Manila men', were reputed to have great powers of endurance; they were thought to have been good rowers, skilful helmsmen and boat builders, but were prone to escape. Visayans were unsurpassed as divers and considered superior to the Tagalogs as sailors. The courageous reputation of the Buginese as traders and soldiers, with a talent for learning the use of arms, made them favoured in the ransom trade. Visayan women were known to be superior weavers, while Tagalog women were desired for their business ability. As wives of *datus*, they were often entrusted with the management of accounts. Most esteemed for their beauty were mestiza Chinese women.[5]

There appears to have been a standard schedule of prices for various categories of slave, but the basic price level for ransom varied according to Sulu's political and economic situation. In 1726, the value of slaves was as follows: a man or woman in excellent health, 40 pesos; a man or woman with a weak constitution, 30 pesos; boys and girls, 20 pesos; and small children, 10 pesos.[6] By the beginning of the nineteenth century, due to ethnic and social transformations in the Sulu Zone, the price of female slaves was much higher than that of male slaves, indicating the important role women played, both biologically and socially, in reproduction and production processes. In general, the price of a male slave varied according to his age and qualifications from 20 to 50 pesos, while the price of a female slave ranged between 60 and 100 pesos and occasionally more, her ransom value more than doubling in some instances depending on her age and ability to work and bear children. Small children were estimated to be worth half the price of a man.[7]

In addition, by 1800 on the standard scale of ransom fees a friar was valued at about 2,000 pesos and a European at 300 pesos. Lascars taken from English ships were ransomed at 100 pesos each.[8] The heavy ransoms offered for friars meant that they were especially coveted by slave raiders:[9] in 1769, the governor of Zamboanga paid 2,200 *kangans* (bolts of cotton cloth) to ransom three Augustinian friars;[10] a priest from Marivales was ransomed for 1,000 pesos in 1770;[11] the *cura* (curate) of Casiguran, Tayabas, was captured in 1798 and ransomed for 2,500 pesos; and in 1823 the Provincial of the Recollects, Pedro de Santa Eulalia, was seized with another friar while making his annual *visita* and the Order had to pay a ransom of 10,000 pesos for the two of them.[12] The ransoming of priests and other Europeans at Jolo was a common practice in the eighteenth century, and the sultan took an active part in such negotiations, especially in cases that involved the governor of Zamboanga.[13]

The 1838 captivity narrative of Cornelius Zacharias Pieters, captain of an ill-fated Dutch merchant vessel, the *Petronella*, plying the waters of northern Sulawesi, reveals the value placed on Europeans in positions of power who were held for ransom. Pieters's cutter was seized after a bitter sea battle in which members of his crew were killed or wounded. Just prior to his capture, he attempted to ensure he was passed off as an ordinary person rather than as the Dutch captain of the vessel. In organizing this desperate ruse, Pieters warned his surviving crew and slaves to call him Jumaat or Domingo and to be careful not to show him any marks of 'respect', because he had heard that people of 'superior origin' demanded a higher price.[14] By choosing the names Jumaat (Malay for Friday) and Domingo (Spanish for Sunday) Pieters seems to have been distancing himself from his Dutch identity, while at the same time aligning himself with the Malayo-Muslim and Spanish worlds of Islam and Hispanic Catholicism.[15] As it transpired, he 'fell to the share of a man called Baludin' who immediately named him Kantores – thereby separating Pieters even further from his own Dutch identity and pseudonyms.

Ransom Negotiations

The Iranun and Balangingi sometimes permitted people they seized to redeem themselves by ransom. Often, redemption occurred soon after seizure, but some *banyaga*, after having spent a considerable amount of time in captivity, were also ransomed to visiting merchants by the Taosug. Indeed, Iranun slave raiders went out of their way to take captives for whom ransoms might be obtained. As Joachim Zuniga observed, wealthy chiefs and religious missionaries were favoured because their families or associates had the ready cash the Moros required.[16] Curiously, the slave raiders always entrusted a *banyaga* to fetch the ransom.

On the Spanish side, negotiations to free a Spanish priest or high-ranking official by payment of a ransom were frequently conducted by a hand-picked emissary. Even so, ransom negotiations were often fraught with difficulties and dangers, as became all too evident in 1757. That year, the Iranun had stormed the town of Ticao, on Ticao Island, burning and looting the church and *convento*, and forcing the terrified populace and local friar to flee. Unfortunately, the barking of Fray Manuel de Sta Catalina's pet dog betrayed their attempted escape. The friar persuaded his captors to ransom him at the fort of Masbate, however, and a ransom of 500 pesos was negotiated. Before reaching the safety of the fort, the hapless man of God fell victim to duplicity: even though he had been assured safe conduct by the Iranun, the ten men who left the fort with the ransom advancing under a flag of truce were seized. The conduct of the ransom negotiations had been too *laissez faire* and the Spaniards, who had been observing events from the fort parapets, watched helplessly as the Iranun raiders herded the fresh captives aboard their vessels and weighed anchor. The flagrant violation of ideas of justice and personal property at stake in this case with respect to the conduct of ransom negotiations led the Spanish to send the merchant captain A. Pedro Gaztambide to Lanao to ransom the deceived friar for 800 pesos. Gaztambide, on his southbound journey, called at the island of Ticao, where he collected the funds to pay the ransom to free the Augustinian friar.[17]

While religious orders were keen to ransom their own, efforts were rarely made by *kerajaan* to liberate captives by force, negotiation or ransom, although aristocratic kin sometimes managed to gain their release by ransom.[18] This was often done on the spot through intermediaries who conveyed messages between the captives and their families, made credit arrangements, ensured the ransom took place as planned and secured the passage home for the ransomed captives. After seizing large sailing vessels, the Iranun, occupying a position of strength, often called for a parlay to ransom the *nakodah* for booty. Frequently, most of the ransom came from the fortunes of the prisoner's family or business interests and could include pieces of gold and silver, gold dust, jewellery, opium, silk and other textiles.

It would be wrong to suggest that the captives themselves had no say in their ransom negotiations. Before 1850, European slaves in Jolo were regularly ransomed by ships' captains who traded there – which brings us back to the plight of Pieters and the difficulties he faced over the price set for his ransom. It transpired that his Balangingi captor eventually sold Pieters to a Taosug named Unkud for a comparatively small price (half of what he would have received on the open market if his true identity had been known); his new master gave him a pair of trousers, a Chinese *baju*, a sarong and head-kerchief.[19] The wife of Unkud, who subsequently uncovered Pieters's real identity, told him to be very careful to conceal his name as she was

> very afraid they will sell you, for every day men from a certain kingdom in Borneo …
> come here to buy men for large prices and these men have the custom whenever one
> of their relatives dies of killing a slave. If they don't do this, they must remain, however
> long, in a state of mourning.[20]

Unkud tried to sell Pieters to various people in the harbour. In the first instance he was offered to a Chinese trader in exchange for tobacco and tea – but Pieters was not amused and refused to be sold. Secondly, Pieters was offered to Captain Escrebano of the Spanish brig *Leonidas*, but 'they could only speak Spanish there', which suggests that Pieters's Spanish was not good. On the third attempt, Pieters was offered to M. A. Somes, the master of the American barque *Minerva*. But the price that Unkud was asking ($1,000) was too high for the American. Pieters does not lose all agency in this proposed transaction. He wrote, 'I agreed with the captain that the amount was too great, and I knew that I would never be able to repay him such a sum'. He continued, 'I said I would return in a couple of days to inform him [Somes] of my wishes regarding the matter',[21] before the 'dis-spirited' Pieters was taken back to the shore and left to further ponder his fate.[22] And ponder he did. As he put it:

> After a time, it occurred to me that the best plan was to feign sickness. I therefore sat the whole day before the door with my eyes fixed upon the sea. When they [his master and his wife] called me to dinner, I said that I could eat nothing as my old sickness had returned upon me.
>
> Afraid that I might grow worse, both Unkud and his wife besought me to take something. I told them, however, that when labouring under this kind of sickness I could eat scarcely anything, as it prevented my breathing.[23]

Pieters refused to eat during the next several days, and his worsening health and depression was the cause of real concern to his master. Three days after he had begun the hunger strike, Unkud ransomed him to Captain Somes for 300 Spanish dollars.[24]

After having been ransomed, the Dutch captain went to Zamboanga in the hope of finding a passage home to Menado on two whaling ships which were said to be anchored there, but they had set sail the day before he arrived. Discouraged, Pieters returned to Jolo before being taken by Captain Somes to Manila, where he resided for several months. The stranded Pieters then finally located a vessel bound for Menado, arriving home safe but impoverished in late June 1839.[25]

Ransom: Port and Passage

As with Pieters, the vast majority of captives were ransomed on the deck of foreign merchant vessels anchored in the Port of Jolo. Most slaves, or recently-arrived captives, especially those from the Philippines, either begged their masters to ransom them to a resident or a visiting merchant trader, or they escaped to a visiting vessel. Fugitive captives hoped to obtain their freedom, and a homeward-bound passage, upon setting foot on the deck of a merchant ship. But their new-found experience of freedom invariably brought some degree of misery. The payment of a ransom in port as the price of escape frequently entailed debt repayment in some form, and a passage that also entailed a long, roundabout route home.

In the early 1830s, the Spanish authorities in Manila encouraged formal trade relations and peace between Manila and Jolo. Hence, from the mid-1830s larger numbers of European trading vessels from Manila, along with those from Macao, Singapore and ports like Menado and Makassar in the Dutch East Indies, regularly arrived at Jolo to collect cargoes bound for Canton, Makassar and Singapore.

The statements of the fugitive captives of the Sulu Sultanate recorded by Spanish naval officers and local municipal authorities provide insight into how captives were ransomed. One of the most active figures in this sector was William Wyndham, an individual who had firmly established Sulu's trade links with Singapore by the early 1840s. By 1842, Wyndham had settled at Jolo and owned his own schooner, the *Velocipede*. Married to a *mestiza* from Iloilo, Wyndham spoke fluent Taosug and Visayan and had acquired considerable status and authority in Jolo. In 1848, Spenser St John described him as being 'dressed in Malay costume and from long residence among them, he assumed much of both the appearance and manner of a native'.[26]

This enigmatic individual, who lived for at least fifteen years in Jolo with his wife and daughter, possessed great influence with the Taosug, who made him a *datu*. He ransomed dozens of captives from his trading base at Jolo and acted as an intermediary on behalf of scores of others in their ransom dealings and negotiations with Spanish captains. But he was not motivated solely by humanitarian concerns. Wyndham, like other captains involved in the Manila-Jolo trade and visiting itinerant Chinese merchants, realized that Filipino captives were a cheap, dependent source of labour. Escaped captive Eulalio Camposano explained that Wyndham not only ransomed captives to turn a profit, but also purchased them for his own retinue and labour force. Captives like Camposano were worked hard by Wyndham in the *tripang* and pearl fisheries of the neighbouring islands or as crew members on his trading schooner before eventually being released from his service.[27]

Captives ransomed by Wyndham, along with the merchant captains of Spanish trading vessels, were a key source of intelligence for the Spanish about traditional Taosug social systems and everyday life in the slaving port. Merchant captain Juan Bautista Barrera, who was in the pay of the Spanish authorities, moored his vessel in the Jolo roadstead from late May to mid-September 1845, maintaining a confidential daily log of occurrences during his stay.[28] In this period, quite a few fugitive captives escaped to his vessel. Barrera's log lists the dates and cases of those 'unfortunates' whom he was able to ransom, and others either ransomed or brought to him by Wyndham and his brother-in-law. His log notes the arrival on 5 July 1845 of seven *vintas* with seventeen captives. It then states, 'on this same day, an unfortunate woman was ransomed'. She had been captured in March of the previous year while leaving Sorsogon with some relatives and friends to attend a *fiesta* in a neighbouring town, and her ransom was set at 22 pesos fuertes. Barrera closed the entry as follows: 'At the same time, I ransomed two men – who arrived with her. These men cost me 12 pesos'. The price set for the ransom of this woman was almost double the amount paid for the two male captives who had been brought with her, reflecting the high status of female slaves in the mid-1840s.[29]

Escape

For many *banyaga* among the Taosug and Samal, escape remained their main goal. From the statements of fugitive captives, it is clear that women were less likely than men to attempt to escape and more apt to be resigned to their captive condition. Nevertheless, escape was more likely among *los nuevos*, the newly enslaved – particularly in the case of Filipino men who had been separated from their families, or who had clung to their faith.[30] Male *banyaga* who retained memories of another home were more prone to escape than slaves who had been seized in their youth and thus were more easily acculturated to the Taosug social system.[31] Francisco Augustino, who had been purchased by 'the moro Ande', explained that 'although I was well treated by him, I felt that I had to escape to return to my family and village'.[32]

For some first-generation *banyaga*, the initial social isolation created by differences in language, customs and status exacerbated the loneliness and yearning for a lost past. Some never did find the 'indispensible margin of social and psychological space' necessary to overcome the trauma of transition and settle down. They constantly reworked their past lives; the memory of their towns or villages, family and companions did not fade away.[33]

It appears that one to two hundred *banyaga* fled from captivity annually.[34] Once the decision had been made to escape, a *banyaga* often sought out another slave from the same ethno-linguistic group or province with whom to make plans. Such a compact was usually made between *banyaga* belonging to the same master or ones living in contiguous settlements. Obviously, common heritage was important in maintaining the secrecy and cooperation necessary for a successful escape.[35]

One of the easiest modes of escape for *banyaga* in Jolo, and one which could be accomplished alone, was to swim or row out to a visiting European vessel. The usual plan was 'to sneak alongside at night, cling hold of the chain plates ... and then make a noise until helped up the side'.[36] The timing of the venture was crucial. *Banyaga* escaped to merchant vessels only at the close of the trading season, as their chances of being granted asylum were greater when their presence on board was less apt to become an issue and disrupt trading.[37] Despite such precautions, *banyaga* were sometimes turned away by European and Chinese traders or given to another *datu* as a 'gift'.[38] In 1834, the American brig *Margaret Oakley* was at anchor off Siassi and was approached by 'a naked Malay, with kreese on his hand ... [who] begged us to protect him and take him to the country whence he had been stolen'. Rather than offering him the protection he sought, the crew of the *Margaret Oakley*

> half suspected that he had swum off to steal our boat; if we had anything to do with him we might find ourselves in trouble ... we gave him something to eat and drink and put him in the boat and rowed near the beach where we told him to jump overboard. He did so and swam to the shore.[39]

In contrast to the uncertainties of escape to trading vessels, fugitives were assured protection on European warships. After the 1830s, when the Spanish warships began to frequent the area, larger numbers of *banyaga* risked escape. More than fifty Filipino slaves from every island group in the archipelago were taken on board the vessels of the Spanish fleet that visited Jolo in 1836.[40] The longer the war vessels remained in the Jolo roadstead, the more prone were *banyaga* to attempt to escape. When *datus* become aware that once *banyaga* had set foot on board a warship they were free, they began to take precautions. Newly acquired *banyaga*, in particular, were herded together and locked up at night, or marched into the interior until the departure of a squadron. In 1836, all small canoes were taken off beaches and sentinels patrolled the shore after dark. *Banyaga* who failed in a bid to escape could be in danger of being beaten or killed, though it was more usual for the owner to sell them.[41]

The Assisted Passage Scheme

While the Taosug were orchestrating a growing trade between China, Manila and Jolo, the incidence and violence of maritime slave raiding continued to grow in the Philippines with potentially horrific demographic consequences. There was an urgent need for the Spanish to come up with innovative means of assisting the repatriation of escaped captives beyond relying on merchant traders to ransom them and exploit their labour, or the cooperation of the commanders of war vessels. By the mid-1840s, the civil government in Manila decided that an assisted passage scheme was a more effective and less expensive means of returning fugitive captives home safely. At the same time, it was apparent that the administrative mechanisms for establishing such a scheme were not well developed, particularly in the southern areas of the Philippines. In order to adequately address the dual threats of the captivity for ransom business and the rapid scouring and depopulation of particular coastal areas of the archipelago, the Manila government attempted to institutionalize inter-archipelago cooperation at state and local levels to deter the corruption and exploitation that had sustained the captivity-for-ransom business.

From the mid-1830s onwards, captives from various provinces in the Philippines who asserted that they had been captured and sold by the Balangingi or enslaved by the Taosug had been presenting themselves in the Plaza of Zamboanga. They asserted that they had managed to escape from Jolo and other places on neighbouring islands, but that they lacked the means to return to their homes. In the past, the political-military governor of Zamboanga had placed them on board merchant ships that left the *presidio* for Manila. However, by the mid-1840s all the ships' captains involved in the coasting trade were reluctant to take fugitive captives on board because they did not pay the passage fare and they had to be fed during the course of the journey.

In June 1841, an attempt was made to place escaped captives detained in Zamboanga on board the *pontin* of the town. Its captain, Don Antonio Rico, asked for a fare of 5 pesos per head, and the destitute ex-captives, not having enough money, were unable to board his ship – much to the chagrin of the authorities. In July, the Governor sent fourteen of these escapees to the *pontin Dolores*, whose captain was Arcadio Sebastian. The Governor provided a certificate of proof or 'transport' on behalf of each passenger, so that a fare could be claimed by the captain at the government offices in the capital. But all did not go according to plan. No payment was made because, according to Manila officials, the Governor of Zamboanga did not have the authority to issue such certificates without his superior's consent. The dumbfounded captain of the *Dolores* angrily complained about having dutifully submitted his claim in the capital and receiving nothing for his efforts. He was informed that these 'transports' were the sole responsibility of the ship owned by the provincial port, in this case, Zamboanga. By the mid-1840s, it was apparent to all concerned that an efficient and effective means of returning escaped captives detained in Zamboanga, Iligan and Misamis to the 'bosom of their families' had to be adopted.[42]

The newly-conceived assisted passage scheme was meant to achieve two goals: namely to provide reasonably-priced transport home, and to partially support the economic and demographic development of Zamboanga and other similar frontier establishments. Escaped captives were to be taken on board the ship contracted by the town without any objections, providing that the vessel did not make more than one such official 'transport' trip to Manila per year. Those unlucky enough to have escaped from the Taosug and Balangingi after the scheduled departure of this ship had to remain in Zamboanga, or other such establishments, until the following year. The captain of the contracted vessel transporting escaped captives received 3 pesos for each person taken to the Visayas or 4 pesos for those taken to Manila after presenting prior certification of each 'transport' and evidence of having fed each one a ration of 2.5 chupas of rices with 6 ounces of dried meat or fish daily. The captain of the vessel also had to present a certificate of accreditation from the parish priest of Zamboanga on behalf of the captives being returned to their towns in order to be paid by the National Treasury – a document also requiring the signature of the Governor of Zamboanga.[43] To encourage further the success of the passage scheme, the Spanish offered the Sultan of Sulu 2 pesos for each captive 'rescued' and returned to Zamboanga.[44]

The journey home from Zamboanga could be quite complicated for escaped slaves depending on their origins. An example of just such an odyssey is that of Mariano Francisco, who had been a servant of Datu Mhd. Moloc until he was able to escape by swimming out to a naval schooner at night. He stayed on board for several weeks until they reached Zamboanga. Later, the political-military Governor ordered his embarkation on the schooner of Don Manuel Garay bound for Iloilo. From there, he went to the Island of Negros, then by land on foot until he reached Bais, and from there took a *banca* to Bolhoon, whence he went overland to the city of Cebu.[45] The statements of rescued and escaped captives reveal the difficulties that confronted local officials in sending them directly to their respective home provinces because of the scarcity of ships that travelled to some of these places.[46] In May 1838, for example, frigate captain Halcon entrusted three captives to the care of the Governor of Camarines Sur so that they could be sent to their home provinces. However, after having under-taken a summary verification of their origins, it was found that all the ex-captives turned over to him were from the Visayas, and not Luzon. From Camarines Sur, there was no opportunity to send them south again, so the Governor of Cama-rines Sur was forced to send them on to Manila so their fate could be determined there.[47] In such cases, former captives, desperate to return home and running out of patience and hope, sometimes took matters into their own hands. Two female captives from Albay, freed from Balanginji, had been taken to Manila by the brigantine *La Guardia* and were handed over to the captaincy of the Port. The arrival of Silveria Constantino and Maria Candelario in Manila caused some consternation, however, as the two women from southern Luzon had masquer-aded as Visayans in order to take advantage of the opportunity to embark with a boatload of Visayan 'transports' bound for Manila. They were apprehended, questioned and 'appropriate arrangements' were eventually made so that both women could be returned to the province of Albay. Constantino and Candelario were 'brought to the *alcalde mayor* of Tondo and placed under his jurisdiction until the appropriate orders were issued for their assisted passages'.[48]

Under the assisted passage scheme, fugitive captives who presented them-selves in smaller towns or remote places frequently found it far more difficult to obtain transport home, official or otherwise. Three individuals, Antonio Qui-lino, Antonio Silvino and Amad, had escaped from the Iranun to the town of Misamis. The *alcalde mayor* of the town sent them, via the schooner *Concepcion*, under the command of Captain Don Andres Ysiderio, to the fortress settlement of Iligan. They remained on board 'the galley of this plaza' while a summary report was prepared about their ethnicity and birth place, before they were eventually released from service on the galley and despatched to their places of origin.[49] Captives transported to Manila had to be detained for questioning about their current status, beliefs and responses to captivity before being returned to their home towns and villages. Most of the former captives were held for questioning in the prison in Tondo, or sometimes turned over to the Hospico Pobres de San Jose or another detention site, until the case had been thoroughly examined and new instructions issued. Ordinarily, if nothing was found against these men and women after inquiries were conducted, the Captain of the Port of Manila and Cavite would remit the sworn statements of the captives to the offices of the Governor General for the final stamp of approval. While the ex-captives were detained, they remained under the jurisdiction and care of the *alcalde mayor* of Tondo. Once the sworn statements had been ratified, a state department official wrote to the *alcalde mayor* of Tondo to release the passports of the ex-captives so that they could be returned officially to their provinces.

This process of verification of identity and citizenship often proved lengthy and time consuming. For example, in early July 1850, three different boat loads of 'transports', or former captives, arrived in Manila on board the Spanish warship *El Cano*, the Spanish frigate *Magnolia* and the brigantine schooner *Ramon Rapido*, and their passports were not remitted to them until the end of November, nearly five months later. Invariably, there was a sense of uncertainty surrounding the time and date of their departure from Manila on the final leg of their homeward-bound journey. In April 1848, twenty-three captives arrived in Manila aboard the brigantine schooner *Guardiana*. Nineteen of these were from the province of Albay and four from Camarines Sur. Manuel Paes, who held the captaincy of the Port of Manila and Cavite, stated that they 'would embark on a ship bound for these provinces at the first opportunity', and that he would coordinate this measure with the Alcalde Mayor of Tondo.[50] However, he could not tell the captives when exactly that might occur.

Zamboanga: The Second Captivity

The Spanish *presidio* of Zamboanga, first established in 1635 to contain Muslim raiding, was located deep within the Sulu Zone, and occupied a position of strategic importance at the southern tip of the Zamboanga Peninsula in the western-most region of Mindanao.[51] Immediately after its re-establishment in 1719, it became one of Spain's most important frontier communities with a large, permanent garrison and developed commercial contacts with Cotabato and China. But by 1800, in the face of the ascent of the Sulu Sultanate, few ports in the region had less trade than Zamboanga. As it failed to attract foreign commerce or control trade into the interior of Mindanao in the latter part of the eighteenth century, Zamboanga itself was placed in a position of economic dependence and became part of Sulu's hinterland.

In the first four decades of the nineteenth century, the Maluso Samal and Iranun of Basilan harried the settlers of Zamboanga who attempted to trade with Jolo or Cotabato. Houses beyond the *presidio* walls were scattered, and the Iranun and Balangingi often attacked them at night. Sometimes after dark fishers and other inhabitants had to leave their huts out of fear and seek refuge behind the walls of the *presidio*. In 1842, the American Naval Captain Charles Wilkes wrote:

> One or two huts which were seen in the neighbourhood of the bay, are built on posts twenty feet from the ground, and into them they ascend by ladders which are hauled up after the occupants have entered. These, it is said, are the sleeping huts, and are so built for the purpose of preventing surprise [attacks] at night.[52]

The slaving raids made it impossible for townspeople to fish, ironically driving the inhabitants of Zamboanga to become dependent on its assailants, the Iranun and Samal of Maluso, for fresh supplies.[53]

Escape from Jolo and neighbouring islands to Zamboanga was rather easy. Zamboanga's proximity to, and commercial dependence on, Jolo offered *banyaga* ample opportunities to reach the *presidio* on trading *prahus* or by small canoes. While the Iranun and Balangingi were conducting their methodical and wholly successful slave raids against the islands to the north of Zamboanga, the fugitive captives of Jolo who had reached Zamboanga in a bid for freedom once again accepted the Spanish yoke and lived there in bondage as overburdened domestic servants, manual labourers and tillers of the soil for indefinite periods of time.

The tale of Feliciana Maria presents a typical case of the systematic exploitation of fugitive captives. The thirty-five-year-old miner from Surigao had been captured at sea by the Balangingi, and after two months she was sold in Jolo to Datu Muhamed, in whose house she remained for six years. She eventually managed to escape in the company of Josef Clemencia, stealing a *baroto* and voyaging to Zamboanga. There, Feliciana Maria was detained for one year, working as a domestic servant in the house of Don Vincente Yndan, who eventually took her to Dumaguete under the assisted passage scheme. In June 1849, she disembarked from her master's vessel at the Visayan Port and made her way overland to the Casa Real of Cebu City where her statement was taken.

Captive detainees quickly realized that their new masters in Zamboanga tended to retain their services for as long as possible and treat them poorly, exacting far more surplus value and labour from their services than they had experienced under the traditional Taosug social system. This form of exploitation was at its worst when there was no opportunity of ships arriving to transport them to their respective provinces and towns.[54] Few fates can have been as cruelly deceptive as the one experienced by the *banyaga* who escaped to Zamboanga. Most *banyaga* who fled one form of servitude were forced to remain in Zamboanga and enter another – a second captivity. It was a standard practice of the Governors of the *presidio* to delay the return of Filipinos to their villages for years at a time in order to exploit their labour.[55] Denied any opportunity to practise a trade in Zamboanga, Filipino fugitives from the Sulu Archipelago were integrated as a residual source of labour power into the lowest stratum of Zamboanga society, alongside criminals, deserters and *deportados*. Men were forced to work on the fortifications, manufacture salt, collect firewood and tend the carabao. The women were forced to work in the fields, a fate also shared by some men, but many were forced to become prostitutes for the garrison and coastguard force.[56]

It is not surprising that Zamboanga developed an infamous reputation among *banyaga* in the Sulu Archipelago. It was a commonly held opinion that the nature of the servitude experienced in Zamboanga was far worse than that among the Taosug.[57] A group of twenty Filipino women in Jolo confronted a Spanish naval officer, intent on transporting them to Zamboanga, with the following ultimatum:

> Senor Commander, if you wish to take us someplace other than Zamboanga we wish to be manumitted; but if we must first go to Zamboanga, where we will be assigned to people's houses as domestics while waiting for a boat to repatriate us and treated worse than slaves, then we prefer to remain as captives among the moros for the rest of our lives.[58]

Similarly, when an English frigate picked up a boatload of fugitive slaves midway between Jolo and Panay, they begged the captain not to take them to Zamboanga, threatening to throw themselves into the sea if he persisted.[59]

The arrival of so many *banyaga* at Zamboanga gave rise to an unusual social situation. The fugitives established themselves with impoverished Chinese and vagrants in a community some distance from the *presidio*. Originating from different parts of the Philippine Archipelago and lacking a common language, the *degradados* developed their own Spanish-Creole dialect – Chavacano – with which to communicate. A large percentage of the surrounding rural population labelled Zamboangueno at the end of the nineteenth century were descendants of fugitive slaves who had lived on the margins of the *presidio* as social outcasts.

Conclusion

Very little is known about the fate of those Filipinos who actually managed to return to their villages after having been captured by the slave raiders. Published records concerning repatriation at the town level are rare. In the 1840s, private traders and the vessels of the *Marina Sutil* were instructed to assist fugitive captives in Zamboanga to reach the Visayas and the port of Manila. At the port of their province, they were handed over to the *alcalde mayor* or *corregidor*, who was responsible for returning them safely to their home towns or villages.[60] But the assisted passage scheme was never regulated properly, particularly in Zamboanga, and fugitive captives were entirely dependent for their future welfare on the goodwill of Spanish administrators, local ship captains and merchant adventurers who often did not hesitate to exploit them for personal gain. Liberated Filipino captives occasionally reached home only to find mounting outstanding debts and unfulfilled reciprocal obligations, some or all of their family dead or their spouse remarried.[61] Many who were ransomed or escaped with the help of assisted passages were left to make new lives, the realities of which were harsher, if not more impoverished, than the ones from which they had fled as *banyaga* in the Sulu Zone.

7 DEBT AND SLAVERY AMONG ARABIAN GULF PEARL DIVERS

Matthew S. Hopper

In July 1928, a pearl diver named Marzuq bin Mubarak fled from Sharjah to Bahrain and presented himself at the British Political Agency. He came seeking a manumission certificate – a document verifying his freedom from slavery and establishing his right to find independent employment with pearling captains. By his own account, Marzuq was a slave. His parents had been brought from Zanzibar to Sharjah where they worked as slaves in the house of one Khalifa bin Rashid. Both of Marzuq's parents had died when he was about five years old, and he grew up working in his master's house, eventually working for him as a pearl diver. The agency staff who recorded his story noted that he looked about twenty-two years old, appeared to be of Zanzibari origin and spoke Arabic. According to Marzuq, his master, Khalifa, was a cruel man who ill-treated him and beat him with sticks. At the end of the most recent pearling season, Marzuq fled Sharjah for Bahrain to seek a new life, and hoped that the certificate he would receive from the British government would allow him to live freely and work for himself instead of a cruel master.[1]

Following standard procedures, the Political Agency in Bahrain forwarded Marzuq's account to Sharjah and requested that the local Residency Agent there, Isa bin Abdul Latīf, enquire into the truthfulness of his testimony. Several weeks later, the Bahrain office received a reply from the agent, which included a letter from the ruler of Sharjah claiming that Marzuq's statement was completely false. Sheikh Sultān bin Saqar Al-Qāsimī explained that Marzuq was in fact not a slave at all, but a free diver who had worked for many years for a diving captain (*nakhuda*) named Jabir bin Abaid and owed him a great deal of money on account of large advances he had received. Furthermore, the sheikh explained, Marzuq had been previously punished for attempting to commit adultery with a married woman and then fighting with her husband when he caught Marzuq in his house. 'He has run away now and claims slavery in order to avoid paying the claim of the Nakhuda Jabir bin Abaid', the sheikh explained. 'If his statement is heeded to, it is certain that after this we cannot punish those who commit irregular actions'.[2] He requested that the British administration return Marzuq to Sharjah so his case could be adjudicated there and his debts settled. He further remarked:

> In coastal Oman there are many slaves who are free born Muwalid and who work with the Nakhudas in diving and are indebted to them. And in these circumstances it is certain if any of them made a mischief and is punished he will run away and take refuge and misrepresent and his request be granted, then my tribe will lose its wealth.[3]

In support of his argument, the sheikh submitted four documents that purported to be annual debt contracts against Marzuq. Each document appeared to include Marzuq's signature and the verification of three witnesses, and three of the documents contained the sign and seal of Sheikh Sultan bin Saqar himself. The documents attested to a substantial debt owed by Marzuq to Jabir bin Abaid Al-Suwaidi, which amounted to 2,000 rupees in 1925 and grew each of the following years until Marzuq absconded in 1928. The accounts showed that Marzuq's debt grew each year despite the money paid back each season from his annual pearl diving earnings.[4]

The evidence against Marzuq looked convincing, but the Political Agent in Bahrain was unmoved. He wrote to the Political Resident in Bushire:

> Blacks escaping from Dubai and elsewhere invariably allege that they are slaves who have been ill-treated. On the other hand, the ruling Sheikhs, anxious to please powerful subjects, always say that the blacks are free men against whom there are heavy debts. A reference to [Residency Agent] Isa bin Abdul Latif, whose job it is to keep in with the Sheikhs and who has no sympathy with the lower classes or diving reforms, will always get the support for the master's point of view. I, personally, am absolutely opposed to returning an unfortunate negro, who has been so lucky to escape from it, to the hell which the life of a slave diver on the Trucial Coast is reported to be. Even if the applicant is really a free man, I am in favour of strengthening his position by the grant of a manumission certificate.[5]

Marzuq's story demonstrates the complex nature of labour relations in the Arabian Gulf during the pearl boom that spanned the half-century before the global Great Depression. Marzuq's story also illustrates the blurry lines between slavery and freedom in an industry driven by relationships of credit and debt. As early as 1863, Sheikh Muhammad bin Thānī, ruler of Qatar, described the complex realities of labour in coastal eastern Arabia to the travelling scholar William Palgrave: 'we are all, from the highest to the lowest, slaves of one master, (the) Pearl'.[6] The sheikh's remark masks the very real disparity between slave and free in the Gulf – there were undoubtedly significant degrees of servility – but it reveals the effects on labour from the growing demands of global markets, which were already being felt in the late nineteenth-century Gulf. Even before the Gulf's lucrative pearl export market reached its ultimate peak five decades later, Sheikh Muhammad could already sense the growing global dimensions of Arabian trade and the intensifying regional dependence on global markets. Sheikh Muhammad's comment also highlights a wider global paradox of the era: the nineteenth century, an era of expanding global markets and expanding abolition of slavery in much the world, also created systems of labour that in many ways mirrored slavery, or were in fact slavery.[7] The structures of debt obligation in the Gulf, around which the massive pearl industry of the late nineteenth century was organized, sparked debate among British colonial officials as to whether all pearl divers were in some way enslaved. At the same time, many divers, particularly enslaved men of African ancestry, faced the double burden of being both enslaved and also indebted. This paper explores the complex labour relationships in the Arabian Gulf surrounding the pearl industry during this period of globalization.

Background

The Arabian Gulf had been a major site for pearl diving since antiquity and had been a leading producer for regional markets centred on India for centuries, but in the late nineteenth century soaring global demand for pearls sparked a worldwide surge in pearl production, and the Gulf became its epicentre. Pearl diving intensified at pearl banks from Mexico to Australia and from Malaysia to Tahiti, but the Gulf remained by far the world's leading producer. Between 1873 and 1906, the value of pearl exports from Bahrain increased more than 800 per cent. By 1905, the value of pearls produced in the Gulf exceeded the production of all other parts of the world combined. At the peak of pearl production, the Gulf pearl banks were worked by more than 3,000 boats employing tens of thousands of men from Muscat to Kuwait. The pearling industry was the largest source of employment in the region, and chronic shortages in labour created a demand for slaves.

Enslaved Africans and free men of African ancestry accounted for a large number of Arabian Gulf pearl divers in the late nineteenth century and early twentieth century. This fact is evident in sources ranging from Western travel accounts to early twentieth century photographs, and British residency records to early twentieth-century manumission records. Captain E. L. Durand, filing a report in 1878, noted that while most haulers in the Gulf were bedouin or Persians, the divers were generally 'sedees', and sometimes 'sedee domestic slaves'.[8] J. G. Lorimer, in his comprehensive gazetteer of the Gulf in 1907, stated that the divers were 'mostly poor Arabs and free Negroes or Negro slaves; but Persians and Baluchis are also to be found among them, and in recent years, owing to the large profits made by divers, many respectable Arabs have joined their ranks.'[9] Paul W. Harrison, who spent twelve years in the Gulf with the American Mission in the early twentieth century, recalled in 1924 that many divers on the Trucial Coast were slaves, but 'they do not number over one-half the divers'. 'Most of these slaves are Negroes from Africa', he explained; 'A few are Baluchees from the Makran coast between India and Persia'.[10] C. Belgrave, who spent the better part of three decades in Bahrain and the Gulf beginning in 1925, recalled that while most divers abstained from eating much during the dive season and were relatively gaunt, 'the pullers were stalwart specimens; many of them were negroes with tremendous chest and arm development'.[11] In 1929, the Senior Naval Officer in the Gulf estimated that there were 20,000 slave divers (roughly a quarter of the total) diving in the Gulf during each season.[12] Bertram Thomas, in his report on slavery in Batinah in 1929, reported that a fifth of the 'army' of thousands of divers that Batinah sent to the diving banks each year were enslaved.[13]

Except for its massive scale, the annual diving season in the nineteenth century looked much like it had in previous centuries. Each diving boat consisted of an all-male crew, including one *nākhuda* (captain, plural *nawākhida*), and an equal number of *ghawāwīs* (divers, singular *ghawwās*) and *siyūb* (haulers, singular *saib*), in addition to an assortment of *radhafa* (assistants or extra hands, singular *radhīf*) and *awlād* (boys or apprentices, singular *walīd*).[14] The captain's responsibilities included gathering the crew and paying them off at the end of each season, selecting the pearl banks to be fished, renting the boat if he did not own it, preparing the necessary provisions for the boat, maintaining order aboard and selling the pearls for the best price possible at the end of the season. Diving began each morning and continued until sunset with only an hour's break in the afternoon. Each diver wore only a loin cloth and was equipped with a pair of horn pincers (a clip similar in shape to a clothespin, made of bone, shell or horn that was worn on the nose to prevent water from entering), leather fingertips and a knife. The pearling enterprise depended in large part on the relationship between divers and pullers, who worked together in pairs. Divers descended to the sea floor with the aid of a heavy stone weight, of which several sizes were kept onboard. The stone weight was attached to a rope and fitted with a loop to the diver's foot. With the aid of the hauler, the diver would slip his foot into the loop, inhale and descend rapidly to the sea floor.[15]

Typical dives would take a diver to depths of between fifty and eighty feet and would last between one and two minutes. When a diver reached the sea floor, he kept his foot in the weight's loop, reached and manoeuvred himself as best he could to collect as many oysters as possible – rarely more than a few from each dive – using his knife to pry the shells from the rocky surface below. For as long as he could hold his breath, the diver put oysters he collected into a net basket tied to his waist with a second rope, which extended up to the boat and was closely monitored by the careful hands of the hauler above him. Before ascending, the diver released the weight, which the hauler pulled back onto the ship, and signalled to the hauler he was ready to resurface by tugging the second rope fastened around his waist. The hauler pulled the diver back to the surface as quickly as possible before his air expired. Divers would rest for only a few minutes before repeating this process.[16]

Diving crews heaped the oyster shells collected into a pile in the centre of the boat and made no attempt to determine which divers collected which oysters. The shells were allowed to sit through the heat of the day and then overnight. Each morning the crews would sit around the pile of shells and, under the supervision of the *nākhudha*, pry open the oysters and search the smelly flesh inside for pearls. Only a small minority of oysters contained any type of pearl (one in five by one estimate), and most of those found were of the smallest variety, but as members of the crew found pearls, they passed them to the *nākhudha*, who placed them in a cloth bag for safe keeping until the catch could be sold. The process continued in this way for 130 days, until the end of the season.[17]

As was the case in the region's other leading export sector, the date industry, free men and slaves worked side by side in the pearl industry. While free divers kept the proceeds from each pearl season, enslaved divers surrendered all of their earnings to their masters. But not even free divers were completely free in the Gulf diving industry. Pearling captains and wealthy merchant boat owners controlled free divers via a credit system designed to ensure their loyal service year after year. Diving crews were consistently lent amounts in excess of their earnings in order to keep them indebted. In addition, they were paid in rice and other staples from a sort of 'company store' which maximized the merchant's profits. Since debts were recorded in debt diaries which the illiterate could not read, captains and boat owners found ample opportunity for abuse and exploitation. Thus, both slave and free divers were exploited, although the degree of exploitation varied.

Cycles of Debt

Even if a diver were free in the sense that he worked for himself and kept his own earnings, his perpetual indebtedness would require him to continue diving year after year, so his situation in many ways mirrored that of a slave. For most of the history of the pearling industry in the Gulf, a diver's debts could also be passed down to his sons after he died, so debt, like servility, could be inherited.

Records of pearl divers' debts that survive demonstrate that debts were nearly impossible to repay. The account of Bashir bin 'Umran bin Abdullah, a diver for one Matar bin Matar of Dubai for 1925, shows that Bashir started the year with a debt of 2,300 rupees. He earned 20 rupees in the winter and 152 rupees in the summer, which reduced his debt to 2,128. He then received an advance after *quffal* consisting of 50 rupees and two bags of rice valued at 25 rupees apiece, followed by a further advance of another bag of rice (25 rupees), a basket of dates (7 rupees), a maund of coffee (7 rupees) and 30 rupees cash. He was also later debited for the cost of one cloak and one table cloth (50 rupees total). The advances amounted to 219 rupees, bringing the total debt to 2,347. Thus, the amount he owed increased by 47 rupees for the year in spite of his earnings of 172 rupees from the pearling season. He was extended credit of about 27 per cent beyond his annual earnings in order to ensure his continued indebtedness, and hence his return the following season. Naturally, Matar bin Matar had access to the rice, dates and cloth at wholesale prices and provided them to Bashir at retail prices, contributing to his profits.[18]

Like their enslaved counterparts, free divers could be purchased, in effect, from their previous employers by paying the employer the debt amount claimed against the diver. For example, a merchant named Rashid bin Abdullah effectively purchased a diver named Ismail bin Sanqah in 1923 when Rashid paid Ismail's former captain, Mohammad bin Ghanem, 1,100 rupees, 'being his claim from Ismail on account of diving'. Ismail's debt record thus begins with the sum of 1,100 rupees, which quickly grew to 1,594 rupees by the beginning of his first diving season with Rashid when Ismail received 340 rupees cash as an advance, plus instalments of two bags of rice (40), a basket of dates (14), and a cloak and shawl (100). In the 1924 season, he earned 233 rupees, which reduced his debt to 1,361 rupees, but he subsequently took 70 rupees in cash at *quffal*, plus a bag of rice (20), a cloak (40) and a basket of dates (16), bringing his debt back up to 1,507.[19]

One reason the starting amount in a diver's debt book appeared so high was because slave owners actually reckoned the purchase price of a slave as the slave's starting debt. A forty-year-old enslaved diver named Jumah Kanaidish who appealed for manumission in Muscat in 1936 provided evidence that his master had been indebted to a merchant for 2,200 rupees and, being unable to pay, sold him to the merchant in lieu of cash. Jumah's new master then wrote his purchase price in his diving book as his debt. Three years later, Jumah still 'owed' his new master 2,216 rupees.[20] Average prices for slave divers varied by location, age and skill level. Spotty evidence from 1910 to 1930 includes prices for divers as low as 600 rupees and as high as 2,000 rupees, with averages somewhere between 900 and 1,500 rupees.[21]

The perpetual cycles of debt for both enslaved and free divers thus created relationships of dependency and entitlement that required divers to work for their captains year after year, limiting their mobility and freedom. Although many divers may not have been literally enslaved, they had to provide for themselves and their families in an economic environment that placed them in perpetual debt servitude. Enslaved divers were forced to hand over their earnings or advances to their masters, but the masters were, in theory, obligated to provide for their sustenance.

British Imperialism, Debt and Slavery

Beginning in 1921, when the Persian Gulf Administration began systematically issuing manumission certificates to runaway slaves in the region, the newly institutionalized forms of freedom presented immediate challenges to Gulf administrators and local elites alike.[22] Fugitive pearl divers sometimes claimed slave status in order to escape their debts, while at the same time enslaved Africans with legitimate histories of enslavement and abuse were often suspected of falsifying their slave status to escape debts, and were therefore returned by British agents to their masters for punishment. The complexities of labour relationships and the systems of debt surrounding the pearling industry led to conflicting and sometimes confused official policies.

The Gulf's dependence on slavery presented a dilemma for British imperialism – a choice between defending either the principles of liberal politics or those of liberal economics. Political liberals at home called for an end to all forms of slavery, while the principles of the free market demanded the uninhibited flow of capital and commodities. As tended to be the case globally, the forces of global markets proved stronger than abolitionism. British policy towards slavery in the Gulf until the 1920s and 1930s, when the Persian Gulf Administration came under fire from the League of Nations and its Advisory Committee of Experts on Slavery, had been to turn a blind eye to it. The issuance of manumission certificates in the Gulf was designed, in part, to preserve the fiction that slavery in the region was an ancient and entrenched institution that was so benign that it could hardly be considered slavery.[23] After 1921, it could genuinely be argued in official circles that anyone who was enslaved in the Gulf must be satisfied to remain in such a condition, since anyone who wanted to be free could apply for manumission at a British agency or consulate. In reality the situation was quite different. Slavery in the region had increased dramatically in the nineteenth century as demand for labour rose with rising global demand for Gulf products like dates and pearls, and treatment of slaves could be very cruel.[24] Many of the slaves imported to the Gulf came from Africa, and most of the enslaved divers of African ancestry in the Gulf had very recent, not ancient, connections to Africa.

Arabia was only one of many regions that experienced a boom in pearl production in the last quarter of the nineteenth century and the first quarter of the twentieth, but the Gulf was the world's largest pearl producing region. The rapid growth of the Gulf's pearl production accompanied the global boom in consumption of gems and precious stones that began in the 1870s with the rise of a class of consumers who were able and willing to pay for them. Particularly in Europe and North America, diamonds, pearls and other precious stones entered mainstream high fashion in the final decades of the nineteenth century and accompanied the rise of the modern fashion industry. The pearl industry expanded in tandem with the diamond industry, but pearls came to surpass diamonds as the gem of choice for fashionable women.[25] As global demand for pearls increased in the late nineteenth century, prices rose and production expanded from Venezuela and Mexico to Australia, Ceylon and the Philippines. In the Gulf, the value of pearl exports rose steadily throughout the last quarter of the nineteenth century. Between 1873 and 1906, the value of pearl exports from Bahrain increased more than eightfold. The rise in production required additional labour, and made the importation of slave labour, originally from East Africa and later from Baluchistan and Persian Mekran, profitable.

In the late nineteenth century, slave traders increasingly imported young boys from East Africa for work in the pearl industry. By the 1870s, the ratio of male to female slaves among captured slave dhows on the Arabian coast reversed previous trends, shifting overwhelmingly in favour of young males. In 1872, the HMS *Vulture* captured a large slave dhow off the coast of Ras Al-Hadd at the entrance to the Gulf of Oman. The dhow was carrying 169 slaves from the island of Pemba in East Africa to Sur and Batinah in Oman. Of the slaves found aboard, 124 were male and forty-five were female; the majority were children.[26] The HMS *Philomel* captured a sixty-three-ton dhow near Ras al-Hadd on 13 October 1884 which was found to have 128 male and twenty-six female slaves aboard (seventy-seven men, fourteen women, fifty-one boys and twelve girls). The dhow was bound for Batinah from Dar es Salaam, having collected the slaves by canoe between Ras Ndege and Kunduchi.[27] In November 1885, the HMS *Osprey* captured a forty-two-ton dhow around Ras Madraka in Oman bound from Ngao in East Africa to Sur with forty-nine male and twenty-four female slaves (eight men, twelve women, forty-one boys and twelve girls).[28] In fact, in the last quarter of the nineteenth century it is difficult to find evidence of any dhow captured off the Arab coast which was carrying more female slaves from East Africa than male slaves.

As a consequence of their substantial presence in the Gulf, African divers made up a large proportion of the petitioners for manumission certificates at the British Persian Gulf administration offices at Bahrain, Muscat and Sharjah. Enslaved Africans on the Trucial Coast (today's United Arab Emirates) are far less visible in the records from Sharjah than Baluchis and others, since the Residency Agent there from 1919 to 1935, Khan Bahadur 'Isa bin 'Abd al-Latīf, a Persian merchant who worked as the British administration's primary 'native' agent in the region, was notoriously unfavourable to enslaved Africans who sought his assistance.[29] Enslaved Africans from Sharjah, Dubai, Ras Al-Khaimah or Abu Dhabi were more likely to appear in the records of Bahrain or Muscat (after finding passage by sea or walking the 230 miles to Muscat) than in 'Isa's records from Sharjah.[30]

As a growing number of enslaved divers began to abandon their masters and seek British manumission certificates after 1921, local merchants and rulers began to fear a massive exodus of pearl divers and a corresponding wave of defaults on the debts of free divers. In the summer of 1925, the ruling sheikhs of Sharjah, Abu Dhabi, Dubai, Ras Al-Khaimah, Ajman and Umm Al-Qaiwain each sent a petition to the Political Resident complaining about runaway divers. The sheikhs explained that a large number of heavily indebted divers were leaving the Trucial Coast for Bahrain, Muscat, Bandar Abbas, Linga and Bushire where they were claiming to be slaves in order to avoid paying their debts. Since the British administration held that slaves could not be liable for debts, they argued, free men who owed local merchants or diving captains large sums of money were taking flight and seeking manumission certificates from the British government by pretending to be slaves in order to avoid paying their debts. Taking their certificates and claiming British protection, these indebted divers sought employment with diving captains at other ports as if their existing debts had never existed. The fact that the returns from the previous pearling season had been poor was driving many divers to this fraud. The situation was exacerbated by the tendency of the divers in better times to take out excessive loans in anticipation of easy repayment only to find that, in poor seasons, the larger loans only increased their indebtedness. Sheikh Sultan bin Salem of Ras Al-Khaimah wrote to the Political Resident:

> As it is not hidden to Your Honor that for the past five or six years divers have gone to extremes in taking advances from their Nakhudas and as a result every diver is now owing sums varying from Rs. 4,000 to Rs. 3,000 and the lowest of them in rank owes Rs. 2,000. For this reason I am faced with the difficulty namely that the capitals of my merchants have thus been advanced to divers and the merchants owe money to His Britannic Majesty's subjects.[31]

The sheikh explained that if the British administration did not stop this trend, the problems would be compounded and would spur a massive exodus of divers, and with them the captains' and merchants' ability to repay their loans. 'As you are aware', he continued, 'the welfare of the Trucial Coast depends first on God's bounty and then on the earnings from diving, I therefore trust that you will bestow your attention on this matter'. He appealed for a return to system in effect during Percy Cox's administration (1904–20), in which divers who received certificates were sent to the Residency Agent in Sharjah, who would ensure the divers had their cases heard in Salifah court. He concluded by appealing to the British policy of justice and the government's interest in ensuring that merchants who were British subjects did not become bankrupt.[32]

A separate letter from Sheikh Sultān bin Saqar, ruler of Sharjah, about two more runaway divers stated that he 'and other sheikhs are extremely inconvenienced from the complaints of our subjects against their divers who run away while they owe them money on account of advances made to them for diving'. Sheikh Sultān named two such divers who had run off to Bahrain, and he provided documents attesting to their debts. Then he contextualized the situation:

> You are aware that our subjects always owe money to His Majesty's [Indian] subjects and this year, as you know, diving business is not paying and prices of pearls are low, consequently divers have not got a quarter of what they have borrowed from merchants. In view of this, I trust the Honorable the Political Resident will give this case his favourable consideration so that God willing our subjects shall not suffer losses.[33]

In response, the Political Agent in Bahrain wrote to the Political Resident in Bushire that he had seen many cases in Bahrain in which masters, desperate to recover their lost slaves, resorted to fraud:

> In the event of a slave escaping with a view to obtaining manumission, the owners frequently allege debts in the hope that this will enable them to recover the slaves. It has been the custom, if it was obvious that they were slaves, to decline to accept claims for money. This being known, there have been cases in which the owners have declared that run away slaves were not slaves at all, but free men, indebted to them and in some cases it has been found that they were in fact slaves, but the owner, knowing that as slaves they could not be indebted, endeavoured to prove a money claim and to support it had to allege they were free.[34]

His suggestion was to grant manumission certificates liberally, and encourage captains who had legitimate claims of debt against divers who absconded to take up the issue with whichever diving captain hired the runaway diver, just as they would for divers who had fled Bahrain for Qatar or Najd.

'The Usual Claim and Counter Claim'

In the margins of a set of typical manumission cases from Muscat, the Political Resident in Bushire wrote:

> Here the slave claims manumission and his owner sets up that he is not a slave but a free man and in debt to him. This is the usual claim and counter claim, as we never admit that a slave can owe anything, so the owner always tries to set up that the man is free and not a slave. It is hard to say which side is lying, but it is safer to err on the side of believing the slave.[35]

In truth, it was nearly impossible to determine whether a diver's status was slave or free, so officials increasing began to 'err on the side of believing the slave'. One reason for this shift was a recognition of the difficulties faced by all divers, enslaved or free, but also a growing recognition by colonial administrators that the circumstances of anyone of African ancestry was particularly difficult even if they were legally free. The secretary to the Political Resident in the Persian Gulf noted in 1925 that:

> Besides the partiality shown by the Salifah Court in the settlement of claims against diving slaves there is another disadvantage under which the diving slaves and the divers in general labour, and that is the fact that their earnings in the majority of cases are not paid to them entirely and whatever out of same is given them is valued at very low prices. These two are the reasons for which diving slaves run away from their Nakhudas.[36]

The Political Agent in Bahrain in 1928 recognized that Africans were the worst off because of their risk of being kidnapped and enslaved. The agent wrote, 'We know how easy it is for any black to be kidnapped and sold by Bedouins'. He continued, 'Less than three years ago, dark-skinned cousins of the sultan of Muscat were seized by Bedouins in close proximity to the Sultan's own territory. If this fate can befall near relatives of the Muscat house, what can the black diver expect?'

By 1931, the secretary to the Political Resident in the Persian Gulf recommended that administration officials not enquire of masters whether a suspected slave was indeed enslaved since 'the master may enumerate a dozen excuses and palliatives that the man is actually a bonded slave and over and above that he owes a heavy sun of money to himself the master or to a Nakhuda'. Adding that 'Slave-owners are in the habit of obtaining bonds from their slaves for heavy sums of money in order to pass them for divers and to retain them in slavery indefinitely'.[37]

The Debt Records of Marzuq bin Mubarak

It is within this context that Marzuq bin Mubarak presented himself to the Political Agency at Bahrain. The documents submitted as evidence against him reveal that his hard work at the pearl banks did little to relieve his burden of debt. Like the 'payday advance' industry in twenty-first-century United States, Marzuq's financier (or master) provided credit at a price that allowed him to make little hope of getting out from under his debt burden. Furthermore, his starting debt is suspiciously similar to the sale price of slave divers in this period. The first document preserved in the archives dates from June 1925.

> I, Marzuq bin Mubarak, admit that I owe Jabir bin Abaid Al Suwaidi a sum of Rs. 2,000/- which is a proved debt against me and that I have to work in diving and make payment whenever God may grant me.
>
> Dated 22nd Zil-Qadeh 1343 (14–6–25)
> Sd. Marzuq bin Mubarak [3 witnesses]

In the month of Rabi II, 1344 (October 1925) account was adjusted and Marzuq's

earning was	Rs. 200
Balance due from him:	Rs. 1,800
Advance taken after Quffal	Rs. 40
1 bag of rice	Rs. 25
1 basket dates	Rs. 10
1 shawl	Rs. 20
Total	Rs. 1,895
Advance taken in	
Zil-Hejjeh 1344 (June 1926)	Rs. 200
Total	Rs. 2,095[38]

There is no indication of how Maruq managed to acquire the initial debt of 2,000 rupees. It may very well have been his purchase price if he was in fact enslaved. Marzuq's advances in cash and kind nevertheless exceeded his share of the revenue from the 1925 dive season, but he (or his master) was evidently extended an even greater line of credit in the following season, as a subsequent document demonstrates:

I, Marzuq bin Mubarak, admit that I owe Jabir bin Abaid Al Suwaidi a sum of Rs. 2,095. I have to work in diving and make payment out of what I earn from diving.

Dated 3rd Zil Hejjah 1344 (14–5–26).
Sd. Marzuq bin Mubarak [3 witnesses]
Sd. & Sld. Sultan bin Saqar Al Qasimi, Chief of Shargah.

Due from Marzuq	Rs. 2,095
Advanced to him while leaving	
Shargah for diving	Rs. 10
Paid to him in Quffal	Rs. 30
Total	Rs. 2,135
His earnings from diving	Rs. 340
Due from Marzuq	Rs. 1,795
Advance taken from him in winter	Rs. 50
2 bags rice	Rs. 50
1 cloak	Rs. 30
2 baskets dates	Rs. 20
2 baskets dates	Rs. 16
Total	Rs. 1,961
Advance taken	Rs. 200
2 bags rice	Rs. 50
Due from Marzuq Total	Rs. 2,211[39]

If the document is in fact authentic, and if Marzuq was in fact lent the money (as opposed to this being a loan to his master or a fraudulent claim by a master on a slave), Marzuq appears to have been lent Rs. 416 on the basis of his earnings of Rs. 340 from the pearling season, more than 20 per cent above his projected income. This kind of predatory lending was designed to keep a diver in perpetual debt. In spite of an increase in his earning the following season, Marzuq's debt increased as the next document attests:

> I, Marzuq bin Mubarak, admit that I owe Jabir bin Abaid Al Suwaidi a sum of Rs. 2,211/-. This is a proved debt and I shall pay it out of my diving earning.
>
> Dated 25 Zil-Qadeh 1345 (27–5–27).
> Sd. Marzuq bin Mubarak [3 wintesses]
> Sd. & Sld. Sultan bin Saqar Al Qasimi, Chief of Shargah

Due from Marzuq	Rs. 2,211
Paid to him in Quffal	Rs. 25
Total	Rs. 2236
Deducted on account of his earning	Rs. 460
Balance	Rs. 1,976
1 ½ bag rice	Rs. 37
Advance	Rs. 60
Coffee	Rs. 12
2 shawls	Rs. 22
Paid to him in cash	Rs. 20
Total	Rs. 2,131
Paid to him in advance	Rs. 150
Due from Marzuq	Total Rs. 2,281[40]

Marzuq thus owed even more following his most productive season. The archives preserve only one more document attesting to Marzuq's indebtedness. Although he appears to have made some headway on repaying his debt, his progress was minimal:

> I, Marzuq bin Mubarak, admit that I owe Jabir bin Abaid Al Suwaidi a sum of Rs. 2,281/-. This is a proved debt against me and I have to work in diving and settle it out of my earning from diving. Dated 2nd Zil-Hejjah 1346 (22–5–28).
>
> Sd. Marzuq bin Mubarak [3 witnesses]
> Sd. & Sld. Shaikh Sultan bin Saqar Al Qasimi, Chief of Shargah

Due from Marzuq	Rs. 2,281
Paid to him as advance when going to diving	Rs. 15
Paid to him in Quffal	Rs. 30
Total	Rs. 2,326
Deducted on account of his earning	Rs. 380
Balance	Rs. 1,946
Paid to in in Quffal	Rs. 25
2 bags rice	Rs. 50
2 baskets dates	Rs. 10

1 Marino cloak	Rs. 30
Total	Rs. 2,061
Paid to him as advance	Rs. 220
Total	Rs. 2,281
Deducted on account of his earning	Rs. 330
Balance	Rs. 1,951
Paid to in as advance	Rs. 40
1 bag rice	Rs. 25
1 basket dates	Rs. 10
Due from Marzuq	Rs. 2,027[41]

After four seasons of pearling, Marzuq was thus back where he started at his original debt amount of around Rs. 2,000. His successful seasons of earning Rs. 300 to Rs. 500 allowed him to make little progress in repaying his original debt, which may in fact have been his original purchase price if he had been a slave as he claimed.

Conclusions

Although it cannot be concluded with certainty whether Marzuq was an enslaved diver who had fled a cruel master who kept all his earnings or a free diver who had simply abandoned his legitimate debts, it is clear that the complex labour system in the Gulf that developed in tandem with the expanding global market for pearls created debt relationships that in many ways mirrored slave relationships. In some ways, free pearl divers worked under coercive conditions as well because their permanent debts forced them to continue diving for their captains year after year without hope of making any progress in repaying their loans. In other cases, merchants, rulers and elites used the existing systems of debt to mask slavery and reclaim slaves as their property just as they would seek to reclaim a debt. In other cases, slaves themselves served as collateral for loans, and were in fact forced to work to repay substantial debts that they had not themselves incurred. Attempting to pay back debts in a system perpetually rigged in favour of lenders made the conditions of free labourers similar in many ways to those of slave labourers. The case of debt and slavery among pearl divers in the Gulf is further evidence of a global nineteenth-century trend of moving away from slave labour and towards forms of labour that were ostensibly 'free', but in reality were little more than slavery by a different name.[42] Examination of the global trends of debt and labour in the nineteenth century in the context of contemporary trends begs the question of how much has changed. Daniel Brook's recent examination of the payday lending industry in the United States indicates that systems of usury and perpetual debt are still as alive as ever. The means of absconding from that debt, however, are perhaps disappearing more rapidly.[43] Both Marzuq and his creditor (or master) suffered from a growing dependence on global markets. Both were, in Sheikh Muhammad's words, 'slaves to one master'. In this way, it could be argued that the difference between them was one of degree, not kind.

8 THE POLITICAL ECONOMY OF DEBT BONDAGE IN CONTEMPORARY SOUTH INDIA

Isabelle Guérin

Every year in the Villipuram District in the southern Indian state of Tamil Nadu, which is ranked one of the wealthiest of India, just after the mid-November Dipawali festival, entire families leave for the outskirts of Chennai to work as brick moulders. They return six months later at the start of the rainy season, with the sole goal of resting and forgetting the suffocating heat of the kilns. A few weeks later, it is the turn of cane cutters to head south. Once again, men, women and children depart for several months, returning equally exhausted by terrible working conditions. In both cases, wage advances push families to migrate and to tolerate deplorable working conditions. The luckiest are able to return with a small amount of savings. Most, however, will not have been sufficiently 'productive'. Some return empty-handed, while others are even forced to return the following year to pay off their accrued debt. This kind of circular migrant is beyond the reach of any census, but there are hundreds of thousands of them, perhaps even millions, in the state of Tamil Nadu alone. Elsewhere in the northwest of the state, far from prying eyes, other families are confined to sheds, their entire lives revolving around drying rice, for which they work around the clock. These individuals are also initially migrants, though they are never able to return home, trapped through indebtedness to their employers.

These workers share a common experience beyond unacceptable working conditions and extremely low wages: their indebtedness to their employers or recruiters amounts to a form of bondage, condemning them to work for their creditors until the debt is repaid. Until recently, labour bondage in India was mainly discussed in relation to the agrarian economy. Indeed, the 1976 Abolition of Bonded Labour Act was intended to end lingering unfree labour practices in landowner–agricultural worker relationships. But bonded labour has turned out to be far from the residue of 'tradition' that disappears with the modernization of production processes and the industrialization of the economy, remaining a surprisingly current practice in India. It may have shifted away from certain sectors, but it has returned to others, sometimes giving rise to new forms of sub-ordination and exploitation.

To date, Indian state initiatives to end labour bondage where it exists have been ineffective.[1] The 1976 Abolition of Bonded Labour Act had virtually no impact, a failure not only due to administrative indifference and an absence of political willpower, but also to the lack of a proper definition of the term 'bonded labour'. The voluntary elements of labour relationships have proven the most prone to controversy. In the case of physical confinement and a total absence of freedom, as with the situation of the rice dryers discussed above, no one disputes bondage as a fact. But if workers are in a position to come and go according to production peaks and have relative 'freedom' of movement, as with the seasonal workers described above, then the existence of bondage is more controversial.

Debt may also be a 'bond of life' or a 'fatal knot', in the words of C. Malam-oud.[2] According to the situations and the type of relationships binding creditors and debtors, debt may equally well express a relationship of solidarity and coop-eration or represent a source of exploitation, oppression and bondage. In the three sectors studied here – sugar cane harvesting, brick moulding and rice dry-ing – debt indeed is a source of bondage, to the extent that it enables employers to maintain extremely low wages and miserable working conditions. As we shall see, a comparison with other methods of recruitment in the sectors studied here leaves no room for ambiguity. The main purpose of this chapter is to analyse the political economy of bondage and the ways in which debt shapes power relationships between creditors and debtors. It draws on intensive fieldwork car-ried out between 2003 and 2009 in Tamil Nadu in several areas of production.[3] Various data collection methods were used: statistical household surveys (for brick moulders and cane cutters), ongoing qualitative interviews with various stakeholders (labourers, recruiters, managers, employers) and monographs on production units and the source villages of workers. As with all sensitive topics, our choice of data collection tools was a balance between the scientifically desir-able and the feasible. Thus, it was, for example, impossible to investigate the rice dryers statistically due to very limited access to the production units, which were almost continuously locked.

How Shall We Define Bondage?

Over the past few decades bonded labour in India has become the subject of lively academic as well as ideological debates which have mostly focused on two major issues that are closely related. The first deals with definitions: what is unfree labour, and what is the distinction between free and unfree labour? Is debt sufficient to prove lack of freedom, or should it be defined by non-economic coercion? Is the line between freedom and unfreedom impossible to draw, as any labour contract necessarily involves coercion?[4] A second, closely related question is that of the links between capitalism and unfree labour. Are arrangements mutually beneficial in an imperfect market context (the neoclassical thesis)?[5] Is unfree labour inherent to capitalism, serving both to control and cheapen labour costs while preventing the formation of class consciousness (the de-proletarianization thesis)?[6] Or is unfree labour a relic of tradition and a symptom of feudal or semi-feudal modes of production which are supposed to disappear with the transition to full capitalism (the semi-feudal thesis)?[7]

Besides these theoretical – and often very abstract – debates, there is a large body of literature inspired by political economics or economic anthropology and rooted in fine-grained empirical studies. Here, the objective is not necessarily to defend specific postures and to establish a universal link between broad categories such as 'feudalism', 'capitalism' and 'unfree labour', but instead to examine the physical manifestations of unfree labour in its diverse forms. It seeks to analyse how it interrelates with other labour regimes, how it emerges, evolves, disappears, or conversely strengthens. This is examined in connection with specific historical contexts, the changing nature of the economy (and in particular the rise of the non-agricultural economy), production techniques and productive forces, both national and international market configurations, state interventions, peasant mobilizations and power relationships.[8] Our own work is very much inspired by the latter school of thought. As far as definitions are concerned, though coercion certainly exists in any wage relationship, we consider that the category 'unfree' is still valid as a category. However, what counts is not necessarily debt as an indicator, as argued by Tom Brass, but rather the consequences of debt.[9] Our view is that bonded labourers are those whose freedom, wages and bargaining power are significantly restricted by debt. 'Significantly' is still, of course, a rather vague term, but it is difficult to be more precise given the diversity of the degrees of restriction. In line with previous work, we recommend approaching bondage in terms of a continuum, from mild to harsh forms.[10]

Both employers (and recruiters) and employees certainly have a specific interest in entering into debt contracts, and I will examine the diversity of their respective motivations. Going against the tenets of neoclassical economics, however, I will also examine the framework of such arrangements, the inequality of power relationships and how these result in extremely high levels of exploitation. Refuting the tenets of the semi-feudal thesis, we argue that unfree labour can go hand in hand with capitalism, and that it can be initiated and sustained by capital itself in order to accumulate surplus value. Going against the tenets of the de-proletarianization thesis, we suggest that bonded labour is not *always* the preferred working arrangement for capitalism. Not all capitalists use bonded labour, and those who do have a variety of motives. Maximizing or sustaining profit is of course the ultimate objective, and the main purpose of bonding labour through debt is to control, cheapen and discipline labour-power. But capitalists also resort to bonded labour in response to various constraints related to production, market and balance of power, as illustrated in the three industries studied here.

Setting: Three Case Studies

The three sectors examined here were primarily chosen because they are all strategic sectors, either in terms of labour (brick) or staple food items (sugar and rice). They also span diverse bondage scenarios: brick moulding and cane cutting are typical forms of 'neo-bondage', characterized by relative freedom and mostly motivated by economic factors, while rice drying typifies 'traditional' forms of servitude, involving coercion, confinement and paternalism.

Brick Moulders and Cane Cutters: 'Mild' Forms of Debt Bondage

The construction sector, including the brick kiln sector, is one of the most dynamic in India in terms of job creation. It is a challenge to obtain reliable data on brick kiln and worker numbers, since many are not legally registered, and those that are only comprise a fraction of their workforce. Data from the National Sample Survey Organisation, renowned as the most reliable on the unorganized sector, can nevertheless convey broad trends.[11] The latest estimate indicates that the state of Tamil Nadu is home to approximately 500,000 brick kiln workers, which is over 12 per cent of the total Indian brick kiln sector workforce. This workforce is in one of the strongest growth phases in the country in absolute terms (7.51 per cent in 1993–4 and 1999–2000), as well as in relative terms (the proportion of brick workers in relation to the global active population increased from 1.15 per cent in 1993–4 to 1.77 per cent in 1999–2000).[12] In Tamil Nadu, production is centred on two regions: the outskirts of Chennai (studied here) and the south of the state (around Madurai).

Sugar cane production in India comprises the second largest sugar industry in the world after Brazil, and India's second largest agro-industry. 2.2 per cent of cultivable land in India is utilized for sugar cane production, totalling around 4 million hectares and 35 million producers. Tamil Nadu is the third largest sugar cane-producing state after Uttar Pradesh and Maharashtra. The two main production areas are in the centre of the state (Villupuram and Cuddalore districts) and the south (Madurai district), with 30 per cent and 10 per cent of cultivable land devoted to sugar cane respectively. In Tamil Nadu, sugar cane harvesting involves around 130,000 workers annually and takes place during an approximately six-month period. Sugar production is a designated priority sector, and has always been carefully organized and controlled by the state. Minimum prices, which are fixed at both centralized and state levels, are a constant source of controversy and tension between producers, mills and the government.

The price concern is raised every year, leading to well-publicized debate over the key issues of maintaining minimum retail prices for a consumer good considered essential and ensuring decent incomes for producers.[13] Strikingly, little interest is ever shown in the often miserable working conditions of harvesters. Public authorities and NGOs both argue that bondage only pertains to the 'informal' sector, and that it is unthinkable that sugar mills, which are not only part of the formal sector but also partly nationalized, could resort to such practices.

Both sectors regularly implement a form of labour management that has been referred to as 'neo-bondage' since the work of Jan Breman. In contrast to earlier forms of bondage, which were embedded within a broad set of rights and obligations among which debt was just one component, neo-bondage relationships are far less personalized, often temporary and non-hereditary and motivated more by economic than social or political factors. Several factors make neo-bonded labour extraordinarily flexible and docile. Such labour is carried out by a migrant, seasonal workforce often comprised of whole households. Payment is by piece rate and issued at the end of the season. Production and processing units do not directly recruit workers and their families, but rather local, native intermediaries who are often from the same community do so. Wage advances attract workers, and are mainly distributed during the slack season. Brick kiln recruiters follow the instructions of the kiln owners, fixing the amount of labour required and paying a portion of the advances. For cane cutters, it is sugar mills, and not farmers, who control the process. During the work season, workers are only given a weekly allowance intended to cover their basic needs. Accounts are settled at the end of the season, with the season's production deciding the total remuneration minus the sum of the advances and weekly allowances. Data collected from 2000 to 2004 not only show that these advances amount to most of the final wage, but that their share has increased over time, a point to which we will later return.

In the case of both industries, most of the workers are Paraiyar, members of an ex-untouchable community viewed as one of the most marginal groups in Tamil Nadu. A household survey of 300 workers from both sectors sheds light on their vulnerability. Whatever the chosen criteria (income, assets, vulnerability), even if there are some disparities, all of the families can be considered 'poor'. In 2004, the annual income of the majority of those surveyed (between 80 and 90 per cent) ranged from 10,000 to 30,000 INR.[14] Seasonal migration income on average represents 60 to 90 per cent of a household's total annual income. This meagre income comes at the cost of very long working days (twelve to sixteen hours for the brick moulders, with half of these shifts spent working at night; fifteen to eighteen hours per day for the cane cutters) and six-day working weeks. For the brick moulders, the demanding nature of the work, ongoing exposure to dust and heat, absence of drinking water and poor quality food leaves them vulnerable to various diseases, in particular dysentery, allergies and skin diseases, fevers, and muscle pains. For the cane cutters, not only is the work extremely demanding, but living conditions are deplorable: workers are grouped together in makeshift tents in which there is considerable overcrowding and a total lack of hygiene.

Among individuals working in the brick kilns, around 50 per cent bring their children and put them to work when they are five or six years old. Child labour helps to increase or speed up production, to pay back the advance more quickly and also to get a larger advance (approximately 1,000 INR per child in 2004), and the parents are very clear as to the added value of child labour. As for the cane cutters, most children accompany their parents but do not work, or only work very little, as the work is too demanding. In the later stages, they help by collecting dry leaves and tying up bundles of cane stalks. None of these children receives an education.

In both the sugar cane and brick production industries, according to a survey of 300 workers, most suffer from harassment, which is mainly verbal (two thirds), but also physical (one third) and sometimes sexual (in a few cases). The main sources of conflict are the fact that they are not 'productive' enough, and that they wish to leave the production site for a few days, for instance due to illness, festivals or village ceremonies. One third state that they have no freedom of movement, while the others report that they are unable to negotiate more than an exceptionally few days off.

Rice Drying: A Severe Form of Bondage

Rice, like sugar cane, is one of India's priority commodities, being grown on more than 20 per cent of cultivable land. In contrast to the previous cases, workers are hired permanently and live permanently at the production site. There is no intermediary or sub-contractor, and the relationship between employees and their employer is typical of certain forms of paternalism, in which over-exploited workers continue to express their gratitude to an employer who is considered a 'protector'. Rice mill owners represent a protective figure in a hostile and insecure environment, though the employers are, in fact, the ones who create the labourers' vulnerability. Whole families are confined in locked production units made up of storage sheds and courtyards for rice processing. Men, women and children work day and night in shifts to boil rice, spread it out in the sun and monitor the drying. Preventing damage and mould demands ongoing, constant vigilance, and workers have no choice but keep up with the relentless pace of rice drying work in shocking conditions. The social exclusion of these workers, whose families in some cases have worked in this profession already for over two or three generations, is almost total. Not only does their confinement cut off all ties to the outside world, their family and native village, but the exhausting pace of work and living conditions prevent any form of family life.

Opportunities to leave the enclosures are extremely rare and strictly controlled. However, many workers do not even feel the need to do so, owing to a lack of contacts and fear of an external world which many of them have never known. Working days are from thirteen- to sixteen-hours long, partly stretching into the night, and sometimes longer for very big orders. Payment is piece rate, partly in cash, partly in kind. In 2006, workers were paid 36.8 INR per day on average (2.54 INR per hour).[15] Under NGO pressure, some makeshift schools have been organized around production sites, but it seems that most of the children of rice drying workers themselves work regularly. They have no specific tasks, but help their parents to clean the drying area and then to spread the paddy. Housing and sanitary conditions are often extremely poor, and there are very frequent cases of tuberculosis due to overcrowding and a lack of proper hygiene conditions, especially among young children and the elderly.

Here, too, debt is a central element of the labour relationship. Recruitment is not only often based on an initial advance, but extremely low wages also force the workers to request regularly new advances. Total debts often amount to several years' wages, and are thus impossible to pay back. Here, our focus is on rice mills located in the suburbs of Chennai (Tiruvallur district, which has 200 to 300 units of manual drying areas, and employs approximately 10,000 workers); across the whole of Tamil Nadu, it seems that this is the only area in which bonded labour is employed.

Where Does Bondage Come In?

We have already shown elsewhere with respect to the brick industry that advances are the major focus of negotiations between employers and recruiters.[16] At the time of our field work, the construction sector was booming. Wages were rising, but more slowly than advances. As a consequence, migrants' dependence on the sector – both in terms of the number who are actively involved and their debt levels – is growing. Families are increasingly likely to accumulate debt by the end of the working season: those who did so were a minority in 2000 (nearly 4 per cent), while in 2004 they represented almost a third of our sample (29 per cent), and it is likely that this proportion has continued to increase in recent years. We have equally observed that the number of migrants in a family unit increased among one third of families, while the opposite trend was exceptional (3 per cent). Another survey was carried out in 2009 which found that real wages had increased by 15 per cent, slightly more than the advances, and the number of migrants per family unit was largely unchanged from 2004. Though the proportion of families coming back with debt had reduced, it was still high (20 per cent).

Cane cutters face a similar scenario. Cane production has risen sharply over the past ten years, but this has primarily led to increases in the amounts of advances paid, and thus to an increase in workers' dependence on recruiters. In 2004, this advance amounted to almost 77 per cent of wages (as opposed to 64 per cent in 2000) and the weekly allowance was 27 per cent of wages (as opposed to 35 per cent in 2000). End-of-season balances were slightly positive in 2000, but then declined to the extent that in 2004, workers were returning home with an average debt of around 420 rupees.

The use of migrant labour is not universal, however, and local workforces are better paid than migrants. Our observations show that the difference in remuneration between migrant and local labour varies from 40 to 85 per cent. Two main factors account for this: debt levels and whether or not intermediaries are involved. Locally hired workers do not receive advances. They negotiate directly with the landowner over their employment conditions and wages and are paid straightaway. By contrast, migrants have little direct contact with landowners, dealing instead with recruiters who negotiate on their behalf. Recruiters are the leading figures of seasonal migration, but the cost of their intermediary role is fully borne by workers.

Migrant and local workers' wages differ in two ways, due to the differences in their specific geographical areas. Piece rates are significantly higher for the local workforce (30 per cent), due both to different technical constraints and variable degrees of bargaining power. Bonded labourers' production areas are more spread out and smaller in size, which implies higher production costs. The recruiter is supposed to negotiate for the workers, but in practice bargains mainly for his own salary, which is a bonus calculated on the total production of the workers under his charge. Recruiters also deduct a commission from the piece rate paid to the workers amounting on average to 10 to 30 per cent of workers' wages. Recruiter deductions and commissions ultimately amount to a 40 to 85 per cent shortfall in income for migrant workers.

The relationship between recruiters and workers is highly ambiguous, as the workers' attitudes convey. Some complain of exploitation, for instance stating that the recruiters live off their backs, that the system is unfair and that they are treated like 'dogs'. They also express, however, gratitude and appreciation in the hopes of obtaining favour and privileges in return. Workers' responses equally vary according to their frame of reference, group/caste membership and previous life experiences. Some workers, for instance, 'chose' sugar cane work to escape from working as bonded labourers for landowners who restricted their freedom of movement to an even greater extent. Different employers meanwhile elicit varying responses. While working conditions are mostly extremely poor, some employers are worse than others: some, for example, do not hesitate to use physical violence against 'rebellious' or 'lazy' workers, to quote such employers. In other cases, workers feel well treated and deny suffering violence. Beyond this heterogeneity of experience, workers always express at least some sentiments of gratitude and bitterness; such sentiments are evoked by a system in which relationships of protection, assistance and support can suddenly switch to those of domination, and vice versa. As regards the systematic harassment discussed above, in over two thirds of these cases it is the recruiters who harass workers. Workers are aware of being cheated and, here too, over two-thirds complain of such mistreatment, usually attributing the problem to a lack of transparency in accounting systems. Ninety per cent, however, also state that they trust their recruiters. These limited data, subject to all of the limitations of a quantitative questionnaire on highly complicated and subjective issues, nonetheless high-light the ambiguity of workers' feelings towards their recruiters.[17] Rice-drying workers are completely dependent on their employers, which precludes any form of discussion and makes the very idea of negotiating unthinkable for them. If they dare to try to negotiate, employers normally respond by appealing to the shelter and regular advances they provide.

In all three sectors, a lack of transparency further lowers wages. Brick kiln employers routinely deduct a certain percentage of production, usually 5 per cent, to cover for 'damaged' bricks. Wage negotiations are unheard of for cane-cutting workers: our surveys indicate that 85 per cent of cane workers are unaware of the going piece rate, which is calculated by weight; cane stalks are not weighed in the fields, but rather at sugar mills, and so cutters have no way of verifying measurements. Tacit arrangements between recruiters and sugar mills, in which recruiters underestimate the tonnage and in return receive a better commission, are extremely common. Last but not least, wages are part of a global 'package' that includes transport, lodging and medical expenses, the responsibility for pro-viding which is divided between recruiters, landowners and/or sugar mills; as a result, workers are usually unsure who is actually obligated to pay them. In the rice mills, bags of dried rice are infrequently counted every two or three weeks rather than following each three-day production cycle, while storage spaces are limited in size, and new bags are mixed with old. Thus, here too the counting process lacks all transparency.

Debt Bondage as a Labour Management Strategy

Some production systems are more suited than others to bonded labour owing to technical constraints. In agriculture, for example, manual labour constraints have long been used to justify the use of permanent labour, and bondage is an excellent way of ensuring a low-cost, round-the-clock workforce.[18] Manual rice drying is similarly restrictive, demanding intensive, continual labour that determines the final quality of the rice, the amount of broken rice, conservation longevity, texture and taste. The rice is dried in the sun immediately after soaking and boiling to pre-vent mould. The grains are spread under the sun for several days, but turned over very carefully to prevent chipping and guarantee grain homogeneity. In Tiruval-lur, labour is organized such that the same workers carry out this channel activity (soaking, boiling, drying), which demands their continuous presence. Soaking and boiling take place at night so that drying can begin at sunrise. Each cycle lasts for about three days and is repeated without a break to optimize operations. Seasonal agricultural and open-air tropical climate industrial activities also use debt bondage to ensure workforce loyalty over limited periods. This technique is all the more effective when production processes are ongoing with little scope for interruption, as with brick moulding and cane cutting.[19] Moulded bricks are destined for firing in kilns within the same sites, and supply disruption would raise production costs considerably. Likewise, cane has to be pressed and pro-cessed into sugar in the rice mills as soon as it is cut, so that supply disruptions are also costly. The advances and end-of-season payments guarantee the presence of workers throughout the season, and the piece rate ensures a certain degree of productivity while transferring most of the risks onto the workers.

Debt bondage as a labour management strategy is well suited to labour-inten-sive industries,[20] but the adoption of new technologies has caused it to disappear from many sectors. This trend, however, is still far from universal. In some cases, intensified capitalist modes of accumulation, far from leading to secure and improved working conditions, have proved entirely compatible with labour over-exploitation and continued bondage.[21] This is precisely the case with the sugar and rice sectors discussed here, which are among India's biggest agro-industrial sectors. Differences between migrant and local labour systems in the sugar sector are due to distinct modes of accumulation, and more precisely to a varying degree of vertical integration of the value chain. The sugar cane industry is based on a triadic system comprised of landowners, sugar mills and public authorities (and of course workers, who, however, have little say in the sector's organization).[22] In the first part of the system, public authorities supervise production very closely and play an essential, incentivizing role with respect to producers, in particular via guaranteed minimum prices and subsidized credits. This is also the case for the sugar mills, which are provided with tax exemptions and various subsidies. In turn, producers depend on the sugar mills to accept their production and to begin the cutting only when a contract between the two parties has been established. In the 'local labour' system, farmers are relatively independent of the sugar mills, and most use a local work force. This is, for instance, the case in the districts of Villupuram and Cuddalore, which converted to sugar cane production half a cen-tury ago and are today situated in the sugar belt. In the 'migrant labour' system, by contrast, farmers are much more dependent on the sugar mills, in particular for labour force management. The mills take care of the workforce as far as most of the farmers are concerned, whether in terms of recruitment or payment, but their only points of contact are with the recruiters, who are officially registered by the sugar mills. This labour system is found in the south of Tamil Nadu (Madurai district), in which, according to our estimates, 80 per cent of sugar cane cutters are migrants, mainly from the Arcot region.

Only a historical analysis of the social construction of the two systems can account for the discrepancies between these two modes of labour management. In zones where local labour is used (Villupuram and Cuddalore), cane production is a relatively long-standing enterprise which today takes up 30 per cent of cultivated land, and which has involved farmers and harvesters for almost half a century. Production remains cyclical and alternates with rice farming according to climate and public incentives, which fluctuate annually but nonetheless regularly bring farmers back to this activity. The regions' refineries, including public ones, are reputed for their reliability, a determining factor for farmers given that they are thus guaranteed the sale of their production. In zones in which migrants are employed, such as the district of Madurai, the choice of labour management mode evolved gradually. Large-scale industrial cane production began in the 1970s, initially at the behest of government refineries, but the industry remained underdeveloped for a long time. Numerous technical difficulties at the government factory level caused regular activity stoppages, which discouraged producers from permanently converting to cane farming owing to a lack of reliable opportunities. At the time the workforce was essentially local, but demand was in any case limited. Cane production is still a secondary activity today, taking up only approximately 10 per cent of land usage, but from the 1980s, private sector involvement increasingly changed the state of play. Local workers employed up until then were known for being 'undisciplined', unmotivated and lazy. It could have scarcely been otherwise given that the work supply was erratic and limited to very short timeframes owing to the tiny amounts of land cultivated. The private sector thus opted for a migrant workforce, the simplest option being to turn to labour intermediaries from traditionally productive zones. Migration channels to the south gradually developed and were managed from the outset by intermediaries, who attracted migrants with advances. These migrant workers were already experienced in cane cutting and recruited for this reason. They moved either because of scarce local work opportunities due to landowners abandoning developments, or because they were attracted by advances.

Diversified labour management systems were also found in the rice sector. While the previously discussed rice mills in north-west Tamil Nadu (Tiruvallur District) widely resort to bonded labour, those in Villupuram district (about 200 km further south) and the state of Puducherry (also located about 200 km further south) hire day labourers. Hence, while Tiruvallur rice mills have opted for a continuous production process carried out by the same workers, who are therefore obliged to be present at all times, the rice mills of Villupuram and Puducherry have opted for either labour rotation for each production cycle

(Villupuram), or the division of labour between men and women (Puducherry). In both cases, workers are neither bonded nor indebted and are paid regularly. Most also engage in other income-generating activities, with rice drying a secondary occupation. Wages are just as poor (between 2 and 3 rupees per hour), but the working conditions are much better, and workers are willing to be poorly paid for this secondary employment. Technical constraints firstly account for this, as the two production systems differ in various aspects, the first of which is quality. Bonded labourers are used for higher production quality, which requires meticulous drying and permanent monitoring. Space constraints also come into play. Rice mills in Tiruvallur district are further away from rice plantations, resulting in added expense and all kinds of cost-cutting strategies. Meanwhile due to their proximity to large urban centres and a more active job market than elsewhere, mills struggle to retain their workforce. Employers have got around this difficulty by recruiting from the Irular community, which is renowned for its rice-drying expertise, but also its social exclusion, as discussed below.

Over the past few years, the rice sector has changed in two ways. Firstly, the number of drying units with bonded labourers has decreased, but working conditions are worse than ever in the places in which bonded labour is still in use. This is in part due to advances in mechanization (mechanized drying units are rare but do exist); this is mostly, however, a survival response to a rapidly changing sector, characterized both by liberalization and increased vertical integration. Rice processing units are highly diversified according to their position in the treatment process: some specialize only in one stage (drying or hulling), while others deal with all stages, which also depends on the degree of mechanization; furthermore, some plants use a completely manual process, while others are partially or entirely mechanized. Diversification depends on their position in the supply chain, which in turn depends on their storage capacity and their degree of reliance on intermediaries. A diversity continuum spans the most modern to the most traditional plants; at its extremes are the following scenarios:

i.   Rice mills with sufficient capital to buy, process and sell paddy independently in the market. They are also able to modernize and are assisted by various governmental industrialization measures (especially soft loans from the Tamil Nadu Industrial Investment Corporation). They, moreover, benefit from a very strong position in the value chain, are able to play with prices and speculate, and are capable of developing their own brand. They can also supply the public market by meeting its high production capacity requirements.

ii. Rice mills depending on paddy merchants that only undertake sub-contracting: these sub-contract for the dry stage if they have a nerkalam (manual drying), and/or for hulling, polishing, etc. They have little room to manoeuvre since prices are imposed by paddy merchants.

Paddy merchants also have little room to manoeuvre since they in turn depend on the rice and paddy markets.

The most marginalized units specialize only in nerkalam, and are mostly small, traditional processing units. Debt bondage prevails here, and recent changes in the market have further increased pressure on workers for two main reasons. Firstly, consumers have increased quality expectations. However, far more than for the other processing stages, the quality and uniformity of the drying process are critical for the taste, appearance and conservation quality of the rice. Mechanization is completely out of reach for small units owing to excessive investment costs. The only alternative is to demand even greater worker presence and vigilance than before. The second reason for increased pressure on workers is the growing role of intermediaries. These are either merchants or some of the modern processing units described above. Intermediaries seek all possible means to cut costs when faced with intense competition from the liberalization of the sector and do not hesitate to crack down on production units and harass workers to accelerate the pace of work. It can of course be argued that small-scale units are doomed to disappear and that their disappearance will de facto solve the bondage problem. This may be true, but how many generations will be sacrificed before reaching this point?

Bondage and Social Hierarchy

Bonded labourers are members of marginalized communities, while employers operate within the higher echelons of society, as numerous studies have documented.[23] This skewed arrangement is partly due to the fact that scheduled castes and tribes are over-represented among the poor, underemployed and landless.[24] The social gap between employers and workers is also a factor, however. While their working relationship is mainly economic, bondage occurs only in communities in which historically and socially embedded verticalized ties of subordination are still sufficiently strong in employers' and workers' memories to make subordination acceptable.[25]

In the brick kiln sectors, most employers are Reddiars, who are former big landowners and members of the most dominant caste in Tiruvallur District. They depend on various alliances that preclude any form of dissidence: alliances with the migrants' village leaders, who intervene in the owner's favour if a worker escapes; and alliances with the leaders of the villages in which the brick kilns are located, achieved principally through temple donations and investments in local infrastructures (especially roads), which prevent or limit any potential reticence towards the employment of a migrant work force. Alliances are also forged with political parties, which protect the employers against potential sanctions from the public authorities.[26] Some owners also forge alliances with political parties defending the lower castes, in order to protect themselves from potential group actions in the fight against lower caste discrimination. The political protection of rice mills is similar. All such facilities are owned by the dominant castes, mostly Chettiars (mainly Beri Chettiars), Naidus, Mudaliars and Nadars.[27]

The owners of both brick kilns and rice mills often rely on charity, which increasingly takes the form of donations to local NGOs for projects such as nursery construction and event sponsorship, to maintain their positions in society. Brick kiln owners are important local figures owing to their involvement in public projects, which is often presented as a contribution to local social harmony.[28] Owners' generosity in no way benefits the migrants, however: the purpose of such actions is to buy social peace with neighbouring villages in order to prevent opposition to the employment of a migrant work force – and to fend off organizations likely to intervene against bonded labour and political parties defending the dalits. Beyond numerous political alliances and the degree of protection they provide, positive public opinion and their image as benefactors protect them from local authorities, in particular labour inspectors.[29]

The workers in the three sectors discussed in this chapter are members of the most marginalized communities in Tamil Nadu: Paraiyars for brick kilns and sugar cane, and Irulars for rice drying. Paraiyars belong to the largest and lowest-caste community in Tamil Nadu. Although their economic and political position varies greatly within the state's sub-regions, they still generally suffer from considerable levels of discrimination.[30] Irulars, on the other hand, are a tribal group. Employers seek them out in the small outlying villages in their region of origin (Salem District, Tamil Nadu). Employers firstly cite 'technical skills' to justify their prioritization of Irulars for recruitment, and the group is indeed known for its expertise in paddy hulling.[31] However, besides these so-called technical skills, which are often given as a poor justification for exploiting vulnerable communities, the social hierarchical difference between the Irulars and their employers is clearly crucial. Traditionally, Irulars were forest dwellers who specialized in hunting rats and snakes; gathering honey, beeswax and medicinal plants; and tree root digging. Some were also agricultural coolies. Since the 1950s, as with many other communities specialized in forest activities, they have been forced gradually to move to the plains and to take up other occupations. Most have faced a number of difficulties in terms of labour and social integration. Irulars are generally regarded as poorly educated, 'rustic' people. They are very dark-skinned (*irul* means darkness or blackness), and generally only speak Telugu (which is also spoken by many rice mill owners native to Andhra Pradesh), rather than the local language of Tamil. Last but not least, most of the Irulars live in thatched huts in very small communities on the outskirts of villages. Their settlements are rarely permanent, and they tend to migrate from one village to the next after a few years according to the work they find. As such, they have no true native place of origin, and very few have property titles. In this context, they have extremely limited employment alternatives. Employers point out the vulnerability and 'roughness' of the Irulars to enhance their image as 'protectors', commonly describing their staff with terms such as 'alcoholic', 'ignorant', 'naïve' or even 'simple-minded', displaying an astonishing degree of paternalistic contempt.

Conclusion

These three case studies show that labour markets emerge within a historically and socially produced and instituted process, on which technical, social and spatial factors have an important impact. Though debt bondage is far from unique to India, it is clear that the prevalence of hierarchy and caste facilitates the maintenance of these forms of exploitation. Echoing a large body of evidence,[32] this study finds that the owners of capital are exploiting intensively caste institutions to control labour in India. Technical aspects also clearly have an impact on labour relationships, however. For employers, debt bondage is without question a way to cut costs. This method of labour management is particularly suited to low capital-intensive and cyclic production. It plays an adjustment role by securing workers' loyalty in the event of increased production and labour force shortage, as is illustrated by the brick kiln and sugar cane sectors over the last few years. Debt bondage equally facilitates cost cutting and resistance to competition, as the example of the rice mills demonstrates. Space is also a factor. Several studies have highlighted the frequently central role of space in the social fabric of the Indian economy's diverse forms of accumulation, and the presence of clusters of competing or complementary production or processing units. While the positive dynamics of these clusters of productive units are often highlighted, here the negative effects are highly apparent. As Barbara Harriss-White has argued, one feature of Indian clusters is the 'social acceptance of vast negative externalities'.[33] This is particularly the case in the Red Hills areas where the brick kilns and rice mills are located.

Debt bondage is, however, far from the inevitable result of such conditions. The coexistence of distinct modes of production and labour management within the same sector in different geographical areas reveals the extent to which debt bondage is a social construction. The diversity of modes of accumulation, defined here as the method of organizing production and distributing surpluses among the various stakeholders, is critical. It is also interesting to observe that the development of capitalistic and 'modern' regimes of accumulation, far from offering security and improved working conditions, has come hand in hand with overexploitation of the work force and a perpetuation of bonded labour relations. The transformation of the accumulation regimes has in fact relied on a migrant work force reputed for its discipline and docility, and well suited to the needs of ongoing and faintly capitalistic cyclic production systems.[34] For labourers, continued bondage is closely linked to the increased informality and casualization of labour, which concerns about 90 per cent of the Indian workforce, and growth in labour migration.[35] Underemployment in India is not only chronic but increasing, affecting about a third of the workforce today. Employment is erratic due to the effects of weather conditions on agriculture, but also due to the fact that many activities are open-air and therefore seasonal. As a consequence, workers have no bargaining power and have no other choice than to accept these forms of exploitation.[36]

Labourers are both materially and non-materially vulnerable. They lack secure jobs and social protection. Social identities erode, both because of agricultural crises and the emergence of a consumer society which is now almost within grasp but still inaccessible.[37] A culture of daily violence also feeds into vulnerability, as formal institutions fail to guarantee basic rights. In such a context, clientelism and paternalism – of which bondage is constitutive – often appear to be the only possible protection and assistance for the poor. Debt bondage, as much a form of slavery as it is, is both a guarantee of employment and protection against the vagaries of daily life: advances granted by recruiters or employers are by far the best source of access to cash for poor labourers. This is why workers are confused by initiatives proposed by NGOs,[38] believing that such movements will force them out of work in order to free them. Should we therefore consider the system to be 'mutually beneficial', as some economists argue? Clearly this is not the case, for both ethical and economic reasons. At a sectoral level, we have observed that that bondage is far from unavoidable. In all three sectors, bondage is one form of labour management among others which is used for specific modes of accumulation. At a macro level, it seems clear that bondage globally lowers wages and creates casual labour trap production systems in a vicious circle of low demand, low productivity and low capital intensity.[39]

9 THE NAME OF THE SLAVE AND THE QUALITY OF THE DEBT: WHEN SLAVES ARE NOT DEBTORS AND DEBTORS ARE NOT SLAVES IN THE FAMILY NARRATIVE OF A FILIPINA COMFORT WOMAN

Michael Salman

Indebtedness and slaving are protean practices that straddle boundaries, respectively, within and between communities. Fathoming the relationship between debt and slavery in a wide comparative perspective requires a consideration of both historical specificity and the extent to which cultures are porous, malleable and may reciprocally inform each other as well as misinterpret each other, both historically and coevally.

As M. I. Finley and Gyan Prakash have expounded, debt has entailed servitude or bondage only under particular historical and cultural conditions. In writing about ancient Greece, Finley noted that 'it was only between classes, between rich and poor, to put it in loose and simple terms, that debt led to bondage', and that bondage was a condition of the loan rather than a punishment for default.[1] Revisiting Finley's thesis, Prakash underscored that '[i]t was not the power of money that bonded people but the fact that persons advancing and receiving money were of unequal ranks', and then elaborated that 'debt bondage's claim to universality is untenable'. Rather than being 'ontological facts', Prakash explained that the theory of a natural state of freedom cancelled by monetary debt contains key constituents of the hegemony of Enlightenment political philosophy and bourgeois capitalism, both of which are historically specific and culturally rooted in Europe (or, as some put it, the West). Writing about Bihar in colonial and post-colonial India, Prakash traced the genealogy of how British colonialism first inscribed and even required the performance of monetary debt relations as an explanation for what officials considered the unfreedom of *kamia* labourers' enduring subordination to *maliks*; the latter were first understood as landlords, and then later the British tried to forbid these very same debt relations because they were assumed to be the cause of *kamias*' unfreedom. Prakash rejected the notion that the British colonial history of inscribing, regulating and then attempting to abolish debt bondage should be dismissed as nothing more than an ephemeral misunderstanding of India from the outside, a mistaken gloss that slipped off an indelibly indigenous tradition of social praxis. Instead, he focused on 'how historical practices gave a real existence to this misrecognition', and thus 'how freedom and commodity fetishism came to don the garb of naturalness in Indian history', all while the *kamias* and the *maliks* persisted in maintaining hierarchical relations that resisted successive denunciatory definitions of their relationship as slavery, debt bondage and a psychological problem hindering the development of Indian modernity.[2]

The Comparative Frame of Classic Scholarship on Debt and Slavery in Southeast Asia

The histories and ethnographies of Southeast Asia furnish opportunities to engage comparative studies of the relationship between debt and slavery in several interesting ways. First of all, the classic scholarship on slavery in Southeast Asia casts it in a subordinate role to debt and debt bondage. Although Anthony Reid found servitude to be widespread in Southeast Asia, he characterized Southeast Asia as what might be called debt societies, even where slavery existed. In Reid's words, the distinction between debt-bondage and slavery 'is not of primary importance in the indigenous Southeast Asian context'. Instead, and with an erroneous if understandably dated gender referent, Reid declared that '[f]rom very ancient times to surprisingly recent ones, men have worked for someone else because of an accepted obligation, and not in payment of a wage ... If we seek a single origin for this system of obligation, it appears to be debt'. Rather than slavery versus freedom or belonging versus alienation as primary oppositions in the logic of social relations in Southeast Asia, Reid stressed that '[w]hat was universal was the association between debt and bondage'.[3] This continued the long tradition of beginning analyses of Southeast Asian slavery with a comparative framework that emphasizes difference from modern, 'Western' slavery– but what of debt?

When the classic academic literature on slavery in Southeast Asia discussed debt and slavery, it almost always construed debt in a material sense that was monetary. Even when and where money did not exist, servitude was construed as a payment for debt that it treated as calculable in measurable equivalences of the sort that money represents in a master form. Bondage in this sense is seen as a substitution for the debt. As Reid put it, '[i]f a debt or a fine could not be paid, the debtor or one of his dependents had to be transferred into bondage to the creditor'.[4] In this respect, the explicit comparative logic of differentiation that dominated many analyses of slavery coexisted with an implicit comparison that assumed sameness by treating debt as a fundamentally economic logic that appears universal.

Oddly, and this is the third and final theme of the classic scholarship that I wish to introduce here, the economic reading of unpaid debt as the route into bondage exists side by side an emphasis on the centrality and near timelessness of hierarchy in Southeast Asia. Returning to Reid both as a leading author on slavery and a representative synthesizer of scholarship on Southeast Asian history and society, we find his explanation 'that vertical bonding is at the heart of many Southeast Asian social systems'. Once again the discussion picks up the explicit logic of differentiation. We are advised that '[i]t requires effort for modern Westerners to understand a situation where unequal relationships can be both cooperative and intimate', and that this difference – the centrality and omnipresence of vertical bonding, the absence of ideas of equality in 'Southeast Asian high cultures', and the celebration of 'a mystical unity between master and servant' – indicates 'that the various systems of bondage encountered during the last eight centuries of recorded history [in Southeast Asia], including those we recognize as slavery, are indigenous developments having their origin in a characteristically Southeast Asian acceptance of mutual obligation between high and low, or creditor and debtor'.[5]

This representation of the difference of Southeast Asian bondage structured by debt is interesting to me precisely for its need to be substantially revised. Newer historical and ethnographic studies have reconsidered the operations and meanings of indebtedness, reciprocity and the unstable dynamics of hierarchy rather than assuming a consistent and smoothly functioning conception of selfhood, culture and hierarchical structure. Instead of comparisons that polarize differences and similarities between histories and cultures, the discussion of debt and slavery in Southeast Asia needs to keep in mind the reversibility of comparisons, enabled by the dialogical and dialectical relations among peoples whose cultures are and have been porous, internally variegated and invariably hybrid. Not only do the workings and range of relationships of bondage and indebtedness in Southeast Asia need to be recognized as more diverse, more fluid and more contested than generally posited in comparative discussions, but some scepticism is warranted about many reciprocal claims of categorical differences between Southeast Asian and other regional formations of bondage, especially those glossed as European, Western or of the modern Americas.

Slave of Destiny, the Narrative of a Filipina Comfort Woman

To make this critique more concrete and to enable it to stand as its own historical narrative and interpretation, I will relate and analyse an especially important first person narrative about varieties of servitude in the Philippines. Maria Rosa Henson's *Comfort Woman* was initially published in the Philippines in 1996 with a subtitle of her own creation, *Slave of Destiny*, but then reissued in an international edition in 1999 with a less poetic and prophetic subtitle chosen for the international market, *A Filipina's Story of Prostitution and Slavery under the Japanese Military.*[6]

Comfort Woman is a distinctive text in some respects. It is the only published autobiographical account of a Filipina comfort woman. During the Pacific War, comfort women were held in sexual slavery to serve Japanese soldiers throughout the empire and occupied territories. Rosa Henson used the word 'slavery' to describe her experience as a comfort woman. She also recounted her mother's and grandparents' history of living in a relationship of indebtedness to their landlord who, by raping Rosa's mother Julia, fathered Rosa. The value of this extraordinary text for reconsidering interpretations of the workings of debt and slavery derives from the continuities and disjunctures of these intergenerational stories of servitude.

Rosa described her grandparents' and mother's relationships with their landlord in fraught terms, especially the repeated rape of her mother Julia, which started when Julia was fifteen and went on for years. But Rosa never described those relationships with words like slavery, debt bondage, servitude or any other terms along that spectrum. In fact, she did not give the relationships a name at all. Instead, she described a family drama that included an analysis of her mother's and grandparents' reasoning, without representing the relationships as a social form or structure repeated in other families. In other words, unlike her condemnation of her own torment as a comfort woman in terms of slavery, a category that serially extended to and recognized other women tormented and exploited alongside her, Rosa related her grandparents' and mother's story only as an empirical narration of their personal relationships, as if it were a drama unique to her family.

Rosa did not describe debt as a widespread social phenomenon, although it certainly was just that during her grandparents' and mother's lifetimes in Pampanga Province in Central Luzon, from approximately 1900 through the 1930s. Rosa referred only once to debt in an economic sense – that is, to debt of a monetary kind that could be paid off, the kind of debt that could be experienced serially by all people of a similar social and occupational station, namely landless farmers working as share-tenants. She made many other references to debt, but these were specifically to indebtedness, which is to say gratitude and obligation that were not the kind of thing that could be paid off, even when the specific indebtedness was for monetary disbursements. This kind of indebtedness was subject to the micro-politics of strategic manipulation in both directions by utilizing the leverage of intimacy, shame and reciprocal need. This kind of indebtedness could not be quantified, translated through money and exchanged through equivalencies, although its terms could be contested and even broken.

The painful stories of rape at the centre of the lives of Rosa and her mother did not cause Rosa to label her ordeal and her mother's with the same designation. Rosa's experience was slavery; her mother's she narrated without a name. Nevertheless, both of these parts of Rosa's narrative feature the strategic uses of indebtedness. Across their different circumstances, Rosa, her mother and her grandparents all attempted to manoeuvre through relations of indebtedness and even to create them when they were in their most abject conditions, precisely because these relationships offered the possibility of manipulating intimacy, shame and reciprocal need for the purposes of survival, protection and even resistance.

As a historical source, Rosa Henson's *Comfort Woman* presents interpretive problems that are well known in slavery studies. The book partakes of the literary genre we know as the slave narrative. Rosa describes passages through changing social relationships, some fond memories of childhood, a descent into abject conditions of servitude, attempts to negotiate through and/or resist the worst features of bondage, a dangerous escape and then a new life as an advocate for the enslaved. In Rosa's case, this last phase did not begin until almost fifty years after her enslavement, and it was advocacy for redress rather than abolition. The plot form of the genre is not accidental, and any such assemblage of first person and parental stories written down fifty to seventy years after the events must also be affected by problems of memory and the influence of the political purpose for which it is written. There are other problems more specific to the Philippine context, including emplotment within local literary forms and language issues, since the book is written in English with a smattering of Kapampangan phrases and songs. These are interpretive problems, however, and not necessarily insuperable barriers against validity.

Two features of the intergenerational nature of Rosa's autobiography lend special credence to her narrative. First, Rosa's retelling of her mother's experience of repeated rape by the family's Filipino landlord resists any reduction of the text into a simple polemic dominated by the drive for redress from Japan. Secondly, the identification by name of the landlord is indicative of a political bravery that extends beyond the extraordinary emotional bravery Rosa needed to tell her own story of the war years. Rosa's grandparents lived in the barrio of Pampang in the town (later city) of Angeles, in Pampanga Province, about eighty kilometres north-west of Manila. Their landlord, and Rosa's father, was Don Jose 'Pepe' Henson (1869–1947), a member of a prominent Chinese–Kapampangan mestizo clan descended from an eighteenth-century Chinese migrant named Eng Son, Hispanicized to Henson. The Henson clan was related by marriage to the late nineteenth-century paternal great grandmother of Benigno Aquino, Jr, the late twentieth-century politico and martyr, whose widow, Corazon Aquino, became President of the Philippines in 1986. Don 'Pepe' was a large landowner, a sugar planter, the owner of a pharmacy in Binondo (the Chinatown/business district of downtown Manila) and then the founder of Don Pepe Henson Enterprises, a major real estate and development company that increased the family fortune in the post-war years through, among other things, profitable dealings with the American military and its personnel at the Clark Air base located in Angeles until its closing in 1991. Don Pepe Henson Enterprises still exists; Angeles has a Henson Street and a district named Hensonville. The old barrio of Pampang, home to Rosa's grandparents, has a Don Pepe Henson Memorial School. By naming Don Pepe as her father and the man who raped her mother, Rosa had nothing to gain except powerful enemies.

Rosa's Enslavement, the Politics of Intimacy and the Recovery of Self

Rosa had recently turned fourteen in December 1941, when Japan began its invasion and occupation of the Philippines. She, her mother and her two uncles were living in a rented house in the Manila suburb of Pasay, but promptly fled to the neighbouring provinces to the North, obtaining money along the way from her father, the family's long-time landlord in Pampanga and their patron in Manila. Another uncle, now eighteen, was living at the landlord's house in Pampanga as a house servant.

After the American General Douglas MacArthur and Philippine President Manuel Quezon declared Manila an 'open city' on 26 December, relinquishing it to impending Japanese control without a fight, Rosa's mother brought her back to Pasay, thinking it would be safe. One day in February 1942, Rosa was gathering firewood near Fort McKinley, which had been an American military base before the Japanese occupation, when two Japanese soldiers grabbed her. These men held her while she screamed, which caught the attention of a Japanese officer. He upbraided the soldiers, calling them *baka* (stupid), then took Rosa and raped her before turning her back to the two soldiers, who also raped her. Traumatized, bloodied and unable to stand, Rosa was taken in by a farmer and nursed by his wife for two days before she could return to her mother. Her mother recommended remaining silent about the incident and being thankful that she was not killed. In her autobiography, Rosa wrote, 'I kept thinking, why did this happen to me? I remembered the landlord who had raped my mother. Did I inherit my mother's fate?'[7]

Two weeks later, Rosa went gathering wood with her uncles and some neighbours, and the group encountered several Japanese soldiers, including the same officer who had raped her. The officer proceeded to grab Rosa, in front of her uncles and neighbours, and raped her again. Her mother then took her back to the family's barrio, Pampang, in Pampanga Province. The province was a centre of activity for the Hukbalahap, the People's Anti-Japanese Army which had developed out of pre-war peasant unions and would re-emerge after the war as a revolutionary army with some ties, often strained, to the Communist Party based in Manila. Rosa and much of her extended family joined the Hukbalahap, participating in meetings, support and guerrilla attacks during the resistance against the Japanese, and later in the Huk's revolutionary movement.[8]

Fifty years later, Rosa could still sing a Kapampangan song from the Huk's resistance against the Japanese occupation that included these stanzas referencing national enslavement and rape:

> Pamisan metung a panig mitatag ya
> Lalam nang bandila ning balen tang sinta
> Bang mayatbus lubus ing katimawan na
> Ning panga bansang Pilipinas

> Once a group was formed
> Beneath the banner of our beloved land
> To free from slavery
> The Philippines, our country

> Dapat lang itabi ding pasistang Hapones
> A berdugo ning lahi
> Kinamkam king pibandian
> Lepastangan da ing puri deting babai

> Viva Hukbalahap! Makanian tang igulisak

> King purinang mesintang ning balen tang meduhag.
> Dakal lang Taong mengayalang kalma
> Karing penabtab da batal
> Kaybat depatan ngara e tala kalaban
> Hiling kabalat tula naman.

> We must vanquish the fascist Japanese
> The scourge of our race
> They seized all our wealth
> And raped our women.

> Viva Hukbalahap! Let us shout.

> They shattered the dignity of our oppressed land
> They blighted our people with misfortune
> They killed those who opposed them
> Yet they say they are not our enemy
> Because we belong to the same race.[9]

For Rosa, the song caused a peculiar and painful sensation, like an out-of-body experience as she sang words written by others that described herself in the most intimately excruciating way.

> Whenever I sang the Hukbalahap song with my comrades, I felt deep hurt. There is a line in that song ... 'they seized our possessions and raped our women' ... When I

sang that line, I whispered to myself, 'I am one of those women'. But nobody in the organization knew my secret.[10]

The taking of women by American and Spanish colonizers (including priests) was a staple of nationalist literature and dramas of the late nineteenth and early twentieth centuries, sometimes figured as acts of rape, and other times as nuanced allegories of courtship by characters representing the colonizers in competition with Filipino nationalists.[11] Although discourses connecting rape, slavery and colonialism were not new during the years of the Japanese occupation, nothing could have prepared Rosa for what happened to her in 1943.

In April 1943, Rosa and two Huk companions were transporting weapons on a cart loaded with dried corn when they were stopped at a checkpoint. The weapons were not discovered and her fellow guerrillas were allowed to pass, but Rosa was taken by the soldiers to the town's hospital, which had been converted into a garrison and comfort station. There she encountered six other women, who were kept in bamboo stalls partitioned with curtains. The next day, she was raped by two dozen soldiers, and this continued day after day. The women were held under armed guard, given minimal rations and allowed out to bathe once each day under the gaze of laughing soldiers. A doctor inspected them every week. The women were not raped for four or five days each month when they had their period, but Rosa was not menstruating, so she was not accorded even that relief.[12]

Rosa's account of her trauma is graphic and harrowing. Soldiers beat her, tied her up and assaulted her even more viciously when they ejaculated too quickly or were impotent. Rosa wrote that '[e]very day there were incidents of violence and humiliation', noting that this was not just her experience but also that of the 'other women there'. She described this as a serial experience, repeated in the case of all the women, continuing for the three months that she was captive at the hospital building. It was a dehumanizing experience. Rosa recalled that she 'felt like a pig' when the soldiers raped her, sometimes tying her 'right leg with a waist band or belt and hung ... on the wall as they violated me'. She wrote, 'I was angry all the time. But there was nothing I could do. How many more days, I thought. How many more months? Someday we will be free, I thought, but how?' But she also said she considered suicide and that the only thing that prevented her was the thought of her mother.[13]

From the hospital, Rosa and the other women were transferred to a nearby mill on Henson Road, on land owned by her father. Her torment continued unabated for four more months, a time period about which she added no further details. Then, in December 1943, a new set of officers took over command of the garrison at the mill. One officer looked familiar to her and called her over, asking, 'Are you the girl I met in Fort McKinley?' It was the officer who had raped her first; he introduced himself as Captain Tanaka.[14]

Rosa and the other women were now occasionally transported to the estate houses the officers commandeered for their quarters, where they were raped by the officers. These houses included her father's house, where he had raped her mother and impregnated her sixteen years earlier. Rosa emphasized that on these occasions she was always raped twice by the commanding colonel, while Captain Tanaka was there, presumably raping another woman.[15] And it is just after relating this that Rosa begins the passage in her account of her experience as a comfort woman that is central to my analysis:

> Tanaka seemed to be fond of me, but I did not like him. He took pity on me. It seemed that if he could only stop the soldiers from raping me, he would. Sometimes, if the colonel was not there, he asked me to make some tea for him. He told me that he was from Osaka. He was about thirty-two years old, with eyes so small that they disappeared when he smiled.
>
> From the time he recognized me as the girl he had raped in Fort McKinely, Tanaka became very kind to me. He could speak a little English, and he talked to me often. He asked me my name. 'My name is Rosa', I answered. 'Rosa means a flower, a rose'.
>
> From that time on, he called me Bara which means rose in Japanese, he said. He also asked how old I was. I told him fifteen by making a sign with my fingers.[16]

Rosa had 'served thousands of soldiers', by her estimation, but now she had also begun to develop a relationship with Captain Tanaka. It was a relationship based on his feeling of 'pity' for her, according to Rosa, and thus, she expected, a relationship that would develop mutual indebtedness and potential protection for her. She made tea for Tanaka, talked with him and, although she did not like him, she welcomed his pity and kindness. Then one day Captain Tanaka called Rosa into his room in the morning, when he was writing with a fountain pen. She sat at his table while he dipped the pen in ink and used it to pierce the skin on her chin. 'It was painful', Rosa recollected, also noting that '[t]o this day, that ink mark is on my chin'. Was it a brand by tattooing to signify ownership? Rosa only wrote, 'I do not know why he did that', and then she described how he ran his fingers through her hair. The colonel arrived and took Rosa to rape her. She continued to be raped by ten to thirty soldiers on a daily basis.[17]

Sometime after that, Rosa developed malaria, with a high fever. Captain Tanaka took Rosa to his room and gave her medication. The colonel learned of her illness and visited the captain's room, instructing him that Rosa should have the day off. She spent the day in Tanaka's room and was brought dinner there but could not eat. The captain, she wrote, 'looked at me sadly'. That night she went back to her room and could not sleep. She cried, remembering 'my mother again and the thousands of soldier who raped me. I felt very weak'.[18] And then, again, at exactly this point in the narrative, Rosa returns to the subject of Captain Tanaka and feelings of pity:

> I felt then that only Captain Tanaka understood my feelings. He was the only one who did not hurt me or treat me cruelly. But inside my heart I was still very angry with him.
>
> Sometimes, when the colonel was not in the garrison, Tanaka went to my room to talk to me, asking me if I felt better after my malaria attack. He would hold my face and look straight into my eyes. But I did not look at him. *Sometimes I pitied him.*[19]

Having felt pity and kindness from Tanaka, Rosa felt indebted to him and so – despite the fact that he was the first to rape her, and had done so twice, and had tattooed her painfully with his pen – she now sometimes pitied him. In the very different circumstances of Bikol Province in the 1990s, the anthropologist Fenella Cannell found that poor rural women often told stories about how they were frightened at the outset of their marriages, but this changed as they began to feel pity for their husbands. Familiarity can open the door to seeing weakness, burdens and even fear in the other, who may have initially seemed threatening and dangerous in unknown ways as a man. Pity in this sense does not imply disdain, but rather recognition of suffering, and in this way it catalyses emotional intimacy in marriages.[20] In an earlier context, brilliantly and generatively interpreted by the historian Reynaldo C. Ileto, feelings of pity for martyrs executed in 1872 and later for Jose Rizal, executed in 1896, played a crucial role in precipitating a new sense of national belonging and the potential for revolution against Spain. All of this, Ileto demonstrated, was woven from Tagalog translations, localizations and appropriations of the story of Christ's Passion. Jesus's suffering evoked pity and thus identification, as well as indebtedness for his sacrifice. In return, there was the potential for transformation.[21]

Returning to Rosa Henson, it is at this moment of the narrative when she muses on reciprocal feelings of pity that she tells us that she 'pleaded with [Tanaka] to allow me to escape'. Only when she felt pity for Tanaka could she feel that she was a person whom he could recognize as such, and perhaps help to liberate. Her feeling of pity for Tanaka was a response to his pity for her, confirming her personhood. This enabled Rosa to ask the Captain to help free her. Tanaka explained that he could not because it would violate his vow to the Emperor. 'Then he embraced me and kissed my cheeks and neck tenderly', Rosa recalled. 'Maybe he pitied me but could do nothing', she wrote. Rosa understood the politics of indebtedness and obligation.

Soon afterwards, while she was still weak from malaria, Tanaka came to her room, began to caress her and kiss her hair, then brought her to the bed and raped her. She recalled that she 'was very angry', and that 'although he was not as rough as the others, he still took advantage of me'. After the rape, Tanaka said, '"*Arigato*" and then left'. Rosa recalled, 'I understood what he meant. "Thank you", he said for the first time'.[22] That their expectations and uses of reciprocity did not match did not negate the existence of intimacy within their relationship, but it did mean that Rosa's strategy was only partially successful. Their relationship continued.

Captain Tanaka nursed Rosa a second time, after what may have been another malaria attack and a bout of severe vaginal bleeding, protecting her and preventing her from being raped during this time. As she recovered, Rosa began to provide domestic services. One day, when she brought tea for the captain and the visiting colonel, she was able to make out that they were talking about a raid on Pampang, her family's home barrio, and the plans included the word *zona* (meaning free-fire zone) and the Japanese word *moyasu* (burn, as in burning the barrio). The next day she was allowed outside and managed to convey the information to a passer-by. The barrio was empty when the Japanese soldiers arrived, leading the colonel to conclude that Rosa had communicated the information. She was tortured, left to hang with her arms suspended from the wall. After Captain Tanaka brought her tea, she passed out, regaining consciousness only when she was rescued by a Hukbalahap raid. 'It was January 1944', Rosa wrote. 'I had been held captive as a sex slave for nine months'.[23]

Rosa's Mother and Grandparents

Rosa Henson never used the words 'slavery', 'bondage' or 'servitude' to describe her family's cross-generational relationship with their landlord, Don Pepe Henson. But Rosa's family attempted to cope with, cushion and even gain some advantages from their subordination to Don Pepe by using the same grammar of relationships that Rosa attempted to use with Captain Tanaka. Rosa's grandparents worked to turn rape and the family's debts and services to Don Pepe into a relationship of greater intimacy and reciprocal commitment. Rather than flee, they moved deeper into the relationship in order to draw on Don Pepe for support, which only increased their indebtedness and, they hoped, their ability to draw on his sensibilities of pity, shame and obligation.

After Rosa's grandfather Alberto Luna had courted his beloved Carmen Salas and served her parents for one year to prove 'the sincerity of his intentions through hard work', they were allowed to marry in 1906. Their daughter Julia, who would become Rosa's mother, was born in April 1907. This all transpired in the barrio of Pampang, where Don Pepe was the great owner of the farmlands that peasants worked as share tenants. In 1920, when Julia was thirteen years old, Don Pepe visited the barrio one day and sought shelter from a sudden storm in the thatched house of Albert and Carmen. They were huddled in a corner with five of their six young children because the roof leaked everywhere else. Alberto kissed Don Pepe's hand and offered him his own *salakot* (a conical rattan hat) to keep him dry. Don Pepe said it would be better to save money, even by skimping meals, in order to fix the leaking roof, which was bad for such young children. Alberto, Rosa tells us, 'was so shamed he could not say anything'. Just then Julia, cold and wet, came in from an errand to borrow rice for dinner, since the family had none. Don Pepe inquired about her age and then quickly proposed that Julia should be sent to work as a maid in his house, 'Just for me and my wife', he added, 'because my children have their own maids'.[24]

Alberto agreed to discuss the proposal with Carmen. Don Pepe inspected all the barrio houses for leaking roofs and gave the residents money in advance for repairs, which the tenants, Rosa says, 'paid him during the harvest season when they got their share of the crop'. The next day Alberto and Carmen told their daughter about the proposal, which made Julia sad because she 'would no longer see her playmates and cousins'. Days later, Don Pepe returned to receive an answer. As Rosa relates the story of the exchange in an interesting construction she refers to Julia's willingness to leave before suggesting that there was no other option: 'Alberto and Carmen said yes, Julia was willing to be the landlord's maid. They had no choice. They thought that if they disagreed, Don Pepe might not allow Alberto to work the farm. And where would they go if that happened?'[25]

Julia was brought to the estate house the next day and her parents were received in the impressively furnished grand hall. Julia would be paid five pesos each month, and her father was given 120 pesos in advance, two years' pay for Julia. Two years later, when Julia was fifteen, Don Pepe raped her for the first time, ordering her not to tell her parents or he would kick them off his land. Don Pepe was fifty-three. Several days after, Julia told her parents what had happened, to their disbelief. Her father Alberto declared, 'Don Pepe is a religious man, he would not do that'. However, the story was conveyed to Rosa with the understanding that Alberto 'knew in his heart that [Julia] was telling the truth'. Julia only learned later that 'her father was bitter and angry, too', because he felt that this was 'happening to us because we are poor'. Like Rosa's reaction to Captain Tanaka raping her during her recovery from illness, Alberto was angered by the feeling that Don Pepe was taking advantage of his family's debility and poverty.[26] Julia was distraught. She feared that her parents had ceased to love her and '[s] he wanted to run away somewhere, anywhere … But she was afraid'. And so she returned to Don Pepe's house, 'her heart full of anger and resentment'.[27]

Rosa interjects her own first person voice into the narrative at this moment to authenticate the tale. 'This story came from my mother's own lips', she wrote. 'She told me all that happened to her before I was born. She told me not only once but many times. That is why this is written in the diary of my mind'. It was a traumatic experience for Julia and also her parents. Alberto was broken by it, in spirit and physical health, and Carmen was deeply pained, too. Alberto grew depressed, stopped eating and then contracted a severe fever, for which he could not afford medical care. Then Don Pepe passed through the barrio and saw Alberto sick in bed. He gave Carmen money and instructions to take Alberto to the hospital in town, where it was discovered that he had pneumonia. After two weeks in the hospital, he was released with orders not to work the fields anymore.[28]

Julia's parents were now completely destitute and dependent upon Don Pepe. Julia learnt about her parents' situation from a friend who visited her. She broke down in tears when she saw her parents and 'learned it was Don Pepe who was providing for her family's daily needs'. She understood now that she could not run away, and '[s]he cried secretly when she remembered Don Pepe's cruelty. She could not protest against his advances anymore'. Without Don Pepe her father might have died, and now the money he 'gave her family kept them alive'. Julia still did not want to go back to the estate house, but her mother told her that she must or 'the landlord might be angry and call them ungrateful'. This was not a monetary debt to be paid off, but indebtedness that demanded reciprocation through actions signifying gratitude in a continuing circuit of exchange.[29]

For the next three years, Julia worked as a maid at the estate house. During this time Don Pepe did not molest her, but he began to rape her repeatedly when she turned eighteen. This time, however, Don Pepe visited Alberto and Carmen to tell them about it, because, according to him he had fallen in love with their daughter. He intended to continue a relationship with Julia, and tried to ease this with her parents by telling them, '[d]o not worry too much, I promise I will support you and your family'. Two months later, he sent Julia home to her parents for fear that his wife would discover his sexual relationship with the house maid. At home, Julia's parents quickly barred the door to suitors, and her mother told Julia about Don Pepe's proposal to 'provide for our financial needs if we will agree to let you live with him'.[30]

Julia protested that she did not 'love that old man. He is older than my grandfather'. But her mother slapped her and retorted that she should obey her parents. 'We are grateful because he helped us when your father was sick', she said, and 'without him, we will have nothing to eat'. Later, Carmen tried to comfort her daughter and apologized for striking her, but she stood her ground, emphasizing that Julia's father agreed and that the landlord 'promised to give us all the things we need'. Julia remained silent and stayed in her room without food for three days, prompting another angry confrontation from her mother: 'If you refuse what the landlord wants, then go and pay all our debts and give us the benefits that the landlord is giving us now. Otherwise, your father and I will despise you. You are not a good daughter. You are selfish'.[31]

Carmen's verbal assault and, indeed, all of the talk about gratitude and shame played on the Filipino conception that is best known by the Tagalog phrase *utang na loob*, literally 'debt of the inside', usually glossed in modern translations as 'debt of gratitude'. The ur-model of an *utang na loob* is the debt one owes to one's mother which can never be repaid. But the phrase applies to all manner of obligations that are sustained over time, often beginning with a great favour (in fact or at least narrative), then perpetuated by succeeding rounds of acts of gratitude from the recipient and further benefactions, or advances, from the benefactor. The failure to honour *utang na loob* relationships would indicate that one was *walang hiya*, literally 'without shame'.[32] This is precisely the key that Carmen struck to play off of Julia's sense of indebtedness and bring her in line with her parents' direction. And it worked. Julia told her mother she would protest no more. Carmen told her, 'It is for your own good, Julia'.[33]

The modern gloss of *utang na loob* as 'debt of gratitude' is both illuminating and sometimes misleading, tied to the strange historical career of the word *loob*. Before Spanish colonization, *loob* simply meant 'inside', which was the opposite of *labas*, 'outside'. Debts of or from the inside came from the outside, from relationships with other people; thus, one's *loob* in the sense of one's inner self was constituted by transactions with the outside, first with one's mother and then other kin and other people encountered in life. Rather than being fixed, identity was fluid. As relationships changed, expanded and contracted, so did one's name, social standing and being. The early Spanish Friars, committed to converting the natives to Christianity through the native languages in the sixteenth and seventeenth centuries, recognized the importance the Tagalogs placed on *utang na loob*, but burdened the word *loob* with their own theological and cultural assumptions by rendering it to mean one's soul. From the Friars' point of view, where else but from the soul could one owe their greatest debts? Debts of the *loob* bound a person to their parents, their benefactors and, indeed, their saviour, who would cleanse their immortal souls in exchange for faithfulness, confession and penance. The problem was that there was no concept of soul in indigenous cosmologies and no related singular sense of a consistent self created at birth. Rather than discrete souls created by the one god of monotheisitic Christianity, the polycentric animists of the islands understood their selves to be transactional and shifting fluidly as they entered new relationships or changed the terms of old relationships over the course of their lives. Benefactions from the outside, when taken in, would become *utang na loob* (debts of the inside) requiring reciprocity that confirmed and continued the relationship. Belonging and human being derived from these relationships, as did power for the strong and protection for the weak. But as a transaction with no third-party god, king or state apparatus to enforce it, *utang na loob* relationships could always be broken. Promises could fail, demands could become excessive and the strong could become weak or displaced.[34]

In recent Bikolano usage (the language of the Bikol Peninsula on the southern end of Luzon), people speak of monetary loans as being *sa laog* ('on the inside') or *sa luwas* ('on the outside'). In the former, the lender–borrower relationship is more fully social and there is a potential for 'talking things over' for extensions and changes of terms, since the indebtedness of the relationship stands before any specific monetary debts that could be paid off. The latter class of debts are typified by bank and government loans that bring with them 'the terror ... of foreclosure without negotiation', and thus an absence of a relationship that exceeds the monetary debt.[35] An inflexible relationship that could be terminated is fear inducing, while a dynamic and ongoing relationship with a creditor is reassuring.

Not long after Julia acquiesced to her parents' wishes, which were also Don Pepe's wishes, she discovered she was pregnant. 'When she told her mother', Rosa reports, 'Carmen was happy, because a baby meant that the landlord would remain their benefactor for a long time. Alberto was glad, too'. Julia's helpless subordination to rape by Don Pepe was being turned from an abuse of the family's poverty and indebtedness to a source of Don Pepe's obligation to them. During the first months of her pregnancy, Don Pepe would bring her to a hotel for sex twice a month. Julia cooperated, but, Rosa writes, she 'did not love him and hated having sex with him'.[36] This was not a complacent relationship founded on a 'mystical unity of master and servant'.[37]

Don Pepe moved Julia, her parents and their other nine children to Pasay in the Manila suburbs in 1927, and Rosa was born in December of that year. Five more relatives from Pampanga came to stay with them in Pasay, and Don Pepe paid for it all, including schooling for Julia's four brothers, and then for Rosa's education at a church-run school. Don Pepe visited regularly, and young Rosa told him that money was short for her school supplies and asked why he did not live with them. Rosa recollected that she later learned that her father 'had his own family. My mother told me the things that had happened in her life. I pitied her very much, especially because she could neither write nor read. She did not even know how to count. I worried about her. I studied very hard because she was illiterate. My dream was to redeem her sad life'.[38]

Soon the teachers learned of her illegitimacy and the students began to tease her. Rosa wrote that 'I sobbed, because I pitied myself'. She studied harder, and 'wanted to be humble and did not want to argue with those who wanted to hurt [her]', but she 'could not endure the taunts'. Rosa wrote that the 'truth was that I loved my father, and I was eager to embrace him and to talk with him even though I knew all about his own family'. She also knew about her mother's rape. Although her family family was provided with resources for housing, food and schooling far beyond what they had back in the Pampanga barrio, Rosa also wrote that her 'childhood memories are very painful. We lived in poverty even if I was a landlord's daughter. I was bitter about my mother's situation. I resented my grandmother's greed. She did not even give my mother a chance to be happy'.[39]

It was probably in the years just before the beginning of the war, when Rosa was in her early teens, that her mother told Rosa the family story. Rosa wrote, 'From my childhood, my mother told me the story of her life'. Julia told her that she had 'no regrets because of you, Rosa, and also my brothers and sisters who benefited from the landlord'.[40] Julia's mother had died. One of Julia's brothers, Pedro, had been 'instructed to work in the big house so that my father and I could remain in touch after my grandmother's death', but surely this act of servitude for the landlord who paid for Pedro's schooling was also about the larger continuing relationship of indebtedness.[41] This was a relationship fraught with severe costs and previously unimaginable rewards for Rosa's family. It was a relationship that could not be rejected or escaped, and it was unstable with conflict and shifting demands that were sometimes excessive. However, at its most abject moments for Julia and her parents, it was a relationship that they tried to make more intimate precisely to gain some control over it.

The war would bring a new experience to Rosa. Despite its echoes of her mother's travail of repeated rape and her use of a similar grammar of intimacy and reciprocity to cope with abjection, Rosa characterized her experience in a way that she did not do for her mother's story. One was slavery. The other Rosa did not label, but simply told as her mother's story. Shall we call it a family story, one that is about kinship, servitude, indebtedness, rape and the construction of new intimacies to manage a condition of abjection?

Comparative Reflections

The one-sided emphasis on monetary debt in the classic scholarship on Southeast Asian debt bondage needs to be replaced by consideration of the wider range of meanings ascribed to debt, many of which may be better understood when glossed as indebtedness. Unlike the economic logic of debt bondage, which imagines calculations of equivalent exchange for labour power, thinking about indebtedness allows us to speak of a micro-politics based on intimacy and obligation that can be pulled, unequally, in multiple directions. As Indrani Chatterjee advised, 'It is imperative for historians not to talk of terms of service alone but of terms of endearment'.[42]

The question of why Rosa Henson regarded her experience as a comfort woman as slavery while her mother's rape and her family's servitude received no comparable label is a matter that merits further reflection. Rosa Henson's grandparents were indebted and in debt to Don Pepe Henson, who was rich and from a distinguished family. He wielded tremendous power over their lives, to the extent that he could requisition and retain their daughter's body for rape with their full knowledge. Yet Rosa did not see her grandparents or her mother as slaves or bondspeople. Later, in Rosa's own horrific experience during the war, she was subjected to a new and alien master that held her in inhuman subjection. In Rosa's words, she became a slave. In contrast to the most common historical experience of slavery through natal alienation, Rosa was not carried away from her native land and kinship ties; she was effectively stripped of all such ties while still geographically on her own fathers' land. But then she was always partially alienated on his land. She was his daughter and used his surname. He was fond of her and paid for her schooling, an unimaginable social leap for Rosa's grandparents. Yet she was a semi-secret illegitimate daughter, denied recognition and reception by Don Pepe's powerful family.

The stories Rosa Henson told about negotiating and attempting to tame and cope with servitude through strategies of intimacy and obligation are not unique – certainly not unique in the Philippines and Southeast Asia, or in India as we know from Indrani Chatterjee, but also not wholly distinctive from many experiences and accounts of slavery, servitude and imprisonment in Europe and the Americas. Not unique, and not wholly distinctive, but not exactly the same, either.

10 TWO BONDED LABOUR EMIGRATION PATTERNS IN MID-NINETEENTH-CENTURY SOUTHERN CHINA: THE COOLIE TRADE AND EMIGRATION TO SOUTHEAST ASIA

Ei Murakami

This chapter compares two types of bonded labour emigration, the coolie trade and emigration to Southeast Asia, and reconsiders the reasons for the decline of the former. Given the global expansion of migration, interest in emigration throughout history has increased, and the Chinese diaspora has recently also begun to attract more scholarly attention. However, work on the coolie trade, which became a research focus in the field of Chinese modern history by the 1980s, has declined because of the shift in interest from the coolie trade to Chinese emigration to Southeast Asia and North America. Nonetheless, many aspects of this trade have received attention. For example, P.C. Campbell's *Chinese Coolie Emigration to Countries within the British Empire* (1923) considered the coolie trade in the British Empire, while E. C. Arensmeyer in 'British Merchant Enterprise and the Chinese Coolie Labour Trade 1850–1874' (1979) studied the role of the British government in the coolie trade and its relationship with British merchants. Qing government policy against the coolie trade has also attracted the attention of scholars.[1] Furthermore, the emigration system,[2] resistance against the coolie trade[3] and the rescue of kidnapped persons[4] have already been analysed, along with the situation in the area of immigration.[5]

However, although many scholars have studied this topic, some issues remain unexamined. For instance, most studies focus on the coolie trade but overlook the relationship between its emergence and economic and social changes in China's coastal areas during the mid-nineteenth century. While they highlight the problems associated with the coolie trade, such as fraud and kidnapping, these studies have failed to analyse fully the reasons for these problems. Moreover, most have not addressed why only the coolie trade became a social problem, despite the fact that other forms of human trafficking were also common within China or from China to Southeast Asia. As for the studies on the regions central to emigration to Southeast Asia, such as Guangdong and Fujian, many focus on the period after the late nineteenth century, paying little attention to the mid-nineteenth century. Finally, there has been insufficient comparison between the coolie trade and emigration to Southeast Asia.

In this chapter, I will firstly analyse the reasons behind the emergence of the coolie trade, placing special emphasis on economic and social changes that took place in China during the mid-nineteenth century. Secondly, I will analyse the problematic nature of the coolie trade by focusing on the brokers (*ketou*) who recruited coolies. Finally, I will compare the coolie trade with the emigration system to Southeast Asia. This analysis particularly focuses on the treaty port of Amoy, in which this trade both began and declined earlier than elsewhere, and which was also the main port for emigration to Southeast Asia. Because trade, and the coolie trade in particular, in nineteenth-century Amoy was mostly funded by British capital and undertaken by British merchants,[6] this study relies mostly on the British Foreign Office archives as its primary sources.

The Rise of the Coolie Trade

The Rise of the Amoy Coolie Trade

As is well known, Britain, yielding to the actions of the antislavery movement, abolished the slave trade in 1807 and passed the Slavery Abolition Act in 1833. Other European countries soon followed suit. There was no change in the demand for labour in the plantations of Latin America, however, and the demand for labour in North America and Australia actually increased at this time because of the discovery of gold. As European workers alone could not satisfy this demand, Asian labour was imported, sparking the coolie trade.

In essence, the coolie trade was a form of contract emigration in which the contractors (coolies) worked for a fixed period under fixed conditions. At first, the counterparty bore the fee of transportation, causing the contractors to incur debt; consequently, the rights of many such contractors were limited. For example, emigrants to California were bound to repay their debt at an interest rate of 4–8 per cent compounded monthly, causing many to take years to repay their debt.[7] In general, migrants were recruited from November to March, which was monsoon season and the farming off-season.[8] The ports of departure, although they changed over time, were typically Amoy, Swatow, Hong Kong, Macao and their surrounding districts. The principal destinations for emigrants were the West Indies and Peru, where labour was required to replace slaves, and America, Canada and Australia, where labour demand had started to increase.

The coolie trade began in Amoy with a shipment of coolies to Bourbon (Réunion) Island on a French ship in 1845. The transportation of Chinese workers from the Straits Settlements to Bourbon Island by the French is said to have contributed to coolie emigration,[9] but in fact, attempts to introduce Chinese emigrants from the Indian Ocean into Latin America influenced the beginnings of the coolie trade more significantly. By August 1852, some 6,255 coolies had departed from Amoy: four British ships carried 3,946 coolies, two Spanish ships carried 850, and a French, American and Peruvian ship each carried the remainder. Their destinations were principally Australia (2,666 coolies) and Cuba (990).

Reasons Underlying the Rise of the Coolie Trade

Why did the coolie trade develop so early in Amoy? One possible factor is that because imports to Amoy vastly exceeded exports, merchants transported coolies as ballast for their return journeys.[10] Another is that local officials were less powerful in controlling commerce in Amoy, which was not a provincial capital.[11] However, the latter is somewhat implausible, given that the coolie trade also developed at this time around Guangzhou, the provincial capital of Guangdong. Considering the fact that the coolie trade did not develop in other treaty ports, such as Shanghai, Ningpo and Fuzhou, it is conceivable that factors in existence already before the opening of the treaty ports can explain its development. For example, there was a tradition in Amoy of emigration to Taiwan and Southeast Asia, and the credit ticket system that came to be widely used in the coolie trade and emigration to Southeast Asia, in which emigrants borrowed passage from owners or captains of junks and repaid the money with monthly deduction from their wages, emerged first in Taiwan.[12]

In Amoy, human trafficking to Southeast Asia already took place before the Opium War. For instance, on the eve of the war, while xenophobic sentiments were rising, some officials complained that foreigners and foreign ships bought girls in coastal areas. In response, Wu Wenrong, the governor of Fujian, carried out an investigation, stating in a memorandum on 27 October 1839 that there was no evidence of this practice. However, Wu did admit that human trafficking to foreign countries took place, stating that poor people living in coastal areas sold their children to interested buyers in the Philippines and Singapore when they suffered from famine.[13] This suggests that there was no effective control at this time of human trafficking, regardless of the ban on emigration abroad. Indeed, following the opening of the port, C. A. Winchester, the assistant British consul in Amoy, observed that approximately 100 to 200 women with 'large feet (i.e. who had not had their feet bound)' were sold and shipped from Amoy annually.[14]

Systems of emigration to Southeast Asia, such as the credit-ticket system and human trafficking, were therefore in place before the opening of the treaty ports and were perpetuated afterwards. Foreign firms that were later involved in the coolie trade, such as Tait & Co. and Syme, Muir & Co., were already in Manila and Singapore, ports that had close relationships with Amoy in both immigration and trade, before the opening of the treaty ports.[15] Thus, what allowed the coolie trade to form was weak governance over these activities.

The similarities between the coolie trade and the opium trade, both of which expanded from the beginning of the nineteenth century onwards, are also important. The coolie trade system in Amoy involved foreign merchants, Cantonese great brokers (multilingual individuals who were agents of foreign merchants[16]), Fujianese brokers and Fujianese coolies. This is remarkably similar to the structure of the opium trade that took place in Fujian, which involved foreign merchants, multilingual Cantonese and Fujianese brokers and Fujianese opium retailers.[17] Clearly, the development of trade in Guangzhou since the second half of the eighteenth century had broadened the role of Cantonese brokers in connecting with foreigners.

After the opening of the treaty ports, it became easier to deal in coolies than opium, since the latter had to be traded outside the major ports in order to evade the control of the Qing government, which led to Cantonese migrating to Amoy to act as compradors for foreign firms. In the period leading up to the Opium War, the Qing government's governance in coastal areas collapsed;[18] after the opening of the treaty ports, confusion and disorder in coastal areas caused by smuggling and piracy only increased, and the government soon found itself unable to re-establish its rule.[19] Moreover, at this time trade stagnated and economic conditions deteriorated due to the shortage of silver.[20] Thus, the main causes of the rise of the coolie trade were a strong tradition of emigration, loose governance, the utilization of a trading style similar to the opium trade, the presence of mediators between foreigners and emigrants, the collapse of order and the ensuing depression in coastal areas following the opening of the treaty ports. But why did this trade become such a massive problem?

Problems with the Coolie Trade

One of the most significant side effects of the growth in the coolie trade was the widespread mistreatment of emigrants. This included instances of cruelty in barracoons (barracks for temporary confinement) where coolies were held or confined, poor conditions and high mortality rates during sea voyages, long working hours, low pay and mistreatment upon arrival (especially in Cuba and Peru), which have already been discussed in many earlier studies. This chapter focuses on the problems caused by the brokers who recruited emigrants, as their behaviour provides insight into the nature of society in the coastal areas of China.

Brokers

While some have argued that the brokers who played a crucial role in the system of recruiting coolies originated among the headmen who recruited emigrants to Taiwan,[21] such intermediaries certainly existed in the areas around Amoy before the expansion of the coolie trade. Interestingly, the majority of brokers did not come from a mercantile background; rather, they were mainly poor young men without families,[22] regarded by most as a lower class in the coastal area. The poor reputation of such men worsened when official efforts to curtail brokering became stricter, forcing many reliable agents who feared execution to leave the trade, opening it to people of 'the worst character'.[23]

Rewards for brokers varied. Reportedly, they received 50 wen for each man caught, while the *guerdon* (reward) on each coolie actually shipped was one dollar.[24] The money was advanced first by foreign merchants to great brokers (the leaders of groups of brokers), and then paid out by great brokers to subordinate brokers. In Macao, if great brokers could not obtain the contracted number of coolies for their foreign clients by the due date, they were obliged to repay ship charter and food expenses plus whatever money they had already advanced, as well as interest on each expense item. In the case of such a shortfall, great brokers would demand compensation from their subordinates.[25] In a sense, both great brokers and the brokers beneath them were bound by debt. While brokers could run off with the money advanced to them, pressing for repayment could be effective in Macao because all the great brokers, brokers and coolies were Cantonese, and thus it was easy to govern their interactions. By contrast, the coolie trade in Amoy principally involved foreign merchants, Cantonese great brokers and Fujianese brokers and coolies. The different backgrounds of the agents involved thus weakened the bonds of trust and authority within the Amoy coolie trade system. Why, then, did the brokers in Amoy still conduct illegal recruiting?

Secure Labour

The main demographic targeted for recruitment in the coolie trade were men with experience in cultivation, obviously because of the demand for manual labour; thus, for instance, Tait & Co. in 1847 specifically sought farmers who wanted to emigrate.[26] In terms of local wages, Amoy workers earned some 80 to 100 wen per day: 160 wen per day for first-class agricultural labourers and skilled craftsmen, 25 to 40 wen (with food) each day for agricultural labourers on long-term contracts (i.e. one year), and 75 to 100 wen (without food) for day labourers.[27] By contrast, there were instances of coolies being paid 3 to 4 dollars per month in the country to which they emigrated,[28] though in other cases, the wage of a person who was tricked into becoming a coolie was 80 or 120 wen per day.[29] At the time, a tael was worth more than 2,000 wen due to the shortage of silver,[30] and a dollar was worth more than half a tael, or over a 1,000 wen. Thus, the wage of a coolie was clearly not too low at 3 to 4 dollars per month, because this was the equivalent of more than 3,000 wen, or more than 100 wen per day. Nevertheless, the wages offered to coolies were not very attractive for skilled workers, and if we consider the deduction of fees for passage, clothing and food, the real wages of coolies overseas were probably lower than those of labourers who remained in Amoy.

Coolie emigration was made less attractive by the fact that information about the conditions of coolies who had already emigrated did not often flow back to those planning to emigrate because the trade was mainly conducted by foreign merchants. For instance, at the time of the Amoy riot, a placard declared that coolies would not be able to communicate with or return to their families, and that they would be cut off from their family's line of succession if they did so.[31] Relationships between coolie emigrants and their relatives still at home often deteriorated because of this poor communication, and this situation became even more serious with the kidnapping of coolies. In 1866, the British Emigration Board put a halt to the remittances sent by emigrants in the West Indies to their families and relatives. In response, the relatives protested this order,[32] but many coolies denied sending remittances.[33] One possible explanation for this is that the coolies had never intended to send remittances in the first place;[34] another is that some coolies were sold by their own relatives into the trade. In either case, the distrust engendered in many cases between emigrants and their families back at home by an inability to communicate was undeniable. Nevertheless, information about the cruel treatment of migrants still leaked out. For instance, José Villate, a Spanish doctor in Havana, posted and circulated Chinese-language handbills and placards describing the poor treatment of coolies carried to Cuba by the ship the *Duke of Argyle* and contracted by Tait & Co.[35] When these circumstances were made public, coolie emigration became much less attractive to the average labourer.

In the eyes of those who recruited coolies, the quality of emigrants was also often disappointing. On 25 February 1847, the British consul in Amoy stated that most of the young Chinese who emigrated were outcasts, gamblers or thieves who cared little about what they had signed up for, whether they would return in three years or eight, or if they would even return at all.[36] Reports like this were not unique to Amoy. The report of 4 August 1847 from J. T. Crawford, the British consul-general in Havana, also provides an account of the emigrants transported from Amoy to Havana:

> It seems, however, that little or no care has been taken in the procuring of these people in China. They are almost all fishermen from the coast near Amoy, unaccustomed to hard work, and already they have shown a determination not to work with Negros

in the field. Four hundred of them were brought from China in a British ship, 'The Duke of Argyle.' The Master informs me that they are almost all bad and worthless, and from what I learn of those which first arrived and have been tried, their acquisition will not be at all valuable to the island.[37]

In addition to those enticed by profits, many coolie emigrants were debtors, prisoners of clan fights, or indebted gamblers.[38] A Chinese man living in Hong Kong described the coolie trade in Macao as follows:

A great many of those who are willing to proceed to foreign countries to engage in labor are poor men, and a great many are bad men, who, when in their native place, have consented to go, and have received from the Coolie catcher clothes and money for their expenses, but who, when they have got to some place half way, run away or get their companions to rescue them forcibly. The Coolie catcher has no means whereby he can refund the money. This is another cause which makes him resort to kidnapping.[39]

In short, the unpopularity of the coolie trade caused a shortage in the supply of 'good quality' labour, driving indebted brokers to secure 'good quality' labour through 'seduction, fraud, gambling, human trafficking and kidnapping'.[40]

Antipathy towards Brokers

As previously noted, although there was human trafficking around Amoy, it never became a major problem. Emigration to Southeast Asia based on the credit-ticket system was much more predominant and did not lead to friction. Why then did the illegal acts of brokers become problematic? Those who became victims of brokers were often trade tailors, barbers, artisans, woodcutters, chair bearers, porters, husbandmen and drug collectors. These were individuals travelling by land or water,[41] often of low social status, many of whom left their homes to seek jobs in the city.[42] Thus, most of those kidnapped by brokers were already regularly away from home for long periods of time, causing little attention to be brought to this practice.

There were, however, those whose kidnapping caused alarm, even though they also were living away from home. In 1858, the magistrate of Tongan county wrote to the British consul as follows:

In the miserable situation, wives mourn for their [kidnapped] husband and parents mourn for their [kidnapped] children. And in bad cases, if the family's living entirely depended on him and he was kidnapped, the family would lose their livelihood. If he is the only successor in some generations, the family line would fail if he is kidnapped. It is a pity to talk about these kinds of things, the story of which should engender compassion.[43]

This indicates that problems arose with the kidnapping of men responsible for their family's livelihood or the continuation of their family line. These problems were especially serious if the only son of a widow was kidnapped, as demonstrated by the case of one such widow named Ye who appealed to the Sub-Prefect of Amoy on 4 July 1859 that her only son, twenty years of age, had been kidnapped by brokers in Liuwudian on 18 May.[44] The coolie trade only began to garner more attention, however, when a local leader's relatives were kidnapped, as indicated by the case in which a coolie broker kidnapped the nephew and son of a local leader named Yan Qing in 1857.[45] Trafficking in lower-class men and women was thus not considered a serious problem until it involved those who provided for their families, successors to family lines or relatives of local leaders.

Not surprisingly, these practices caused hostility towards brokers to intensify. Those who initiated the Amoy riot expressed the belief that foreign merchants instigated human trafficking, thus attracting bandits (*jianfei*), who in turn kidnapped good men to sate demand.[46] The British officials who were dispatched in this particular incident also regarded brokers as 'men of the lowest possible character',[47] viewing them with the same contempt as the coolies themselves. Antipathy towards the Cantonese in their role as great brokers was especially strong. For instance, the petition of the local men involved in the Amoy riot requested compensation for an incident in which the British shot and killed innocent people while protecting 'Cantonese vagabonds'.[48]

In sum, the coolie trade, the ruthless acts of coolie brokers that it caused and smuggling and piracy undermined the stability of the treaty ports and their surrounding districts after these commercial centres were first opened.

Decline of the Coolie Trade

On 22 November 1852, a riot broke out in Amoy, mainly caused by outrage over the actions of those involved with the coolie trade who worked for Syme, Muir & Co. The trigger was a request by F. D. Syme for the release of Lin Huang, a broker who had been arrested and taken to the police station (*canjiang yamen*) that day. On the same day, all shops in Amoy closed, many gathered in the city from neighbouring villages and both the gentry and officials petitioned the Circuit Intendant (*daotai*) to take control of the outlaws. On 23 November, British marines fired into the assembled crowd, resulting in twelve dead and twelve to sixteen wounded. In the wake of this incident, negotiation between the British consul and the Circuit Intendant and Sub-Prefect led to the opening of the British Consular court and the conviction of Syme, while fines provided compensatory payments for those killed or wounded.[49] While the Amoy riot was a relatively small-scale incident, the details relating to it help illustrate the attitudes of people in the treaty ports towards the coolie trade.

Arguably, the main conflict in the coolie trade was between a small group of foreign merchants, Cantonese great brokers and Fujianese brokers on the one hand, and local people, gentry, foreign and Chinese merchants, Qing local officials, British diplomats and foreigners in Amoy on the other. As a whole, the former group was weaker. In addition, those comprising the former group did not trust one another. By contrast, the latter group included officials and local leaders who shared a mutual interest in stabilizing society and bringing an end to the criminal acts of those involved in the coolie trade. Furthermore, xenophobic sentiment was uncommon around Amoy, so that, for instance, frequent negotiation took place between Qing local officials and British consuls. The riot made the importance of resolving the problems of the coolie trade through diplomatic channels evident to all.

After the Amoy riot, the coolie trade in Amoy declined due to various factors: cooperation between the British consul and local officials, who targeted foreign, mainly British, merchants involved in the coolie trade; the Act for the Regulation of Chinese Passenger Ships, which controlled emigration through British ships; and the suppression of Cantonese pirates who were connected with the coolie trade.[50] This contrasts starkly with conditions in Guangzhou, where the coolie trade rapidly increased up until 1859.[51] Cooperation between Qing local officials and foreign diplomats spread to Guangdong province by way of controlled emigration under military pressure from the allied British and French armies occupying Guangzhou. Emigration then expanded to Swatow.[52] However, the coolie trade took longer to eliminate in the coastal areas of Guangdong because the network of Cantonese brokers there, working through major trading centres such as Hong Kong and Macao, was more developed than in Fujian. The coolie trade in Guangdong finally ended in March 1874, when human trafficking was stopped in Macao.

The Concentration of Emigrants in Southeast Asia

According to Qing officials, 50,000 people emigrated from Fujian annually, with at least 5,000 of those moving to the Straits Settlements.[53] Emigration to Southeast Asia was thus much more significant than the coolie trade, which involved the transportation of about 6,000 people annually until 1852. Emigrants to Southeast Asia faced conditions similar to coolies, including debt slavery when they were unable to pay the money owed for their passage,[54] but Southeast Asian emigration never became as much of an issue as did the coolie trade. What, then, was the difference between this form of emigration and the coolie trade?

The Attitude of Qing Local Officials

Chinese emigration to Southeast Easia was favoured by many foreigners, but the Qing government banned emigration, and Qing local officials were thus tasked with obstructing the traffic of Chinese to Southeast Asia. In fact, however, Qing officials turned a blind eye to human trafficking abroad upon the opening of the treaty ports, as stated above.

On 5 July 1858, in a meeting with the American consul, the Circuit Intendant stated that emigration should be allowed, provided the emigrant and his kin consented.[55] His successor also stated that there was no desire to obstruct voluntary emigration.[56] Local officials therefore largely ignored emigration to Southeast Asia, as it was more self-motivated than the coolie trade. Nevertheless, it was important for local officials that this population movement not disrupt the stability of local society or weaken their governance of the area. There were several reasons for this.

The Coolie Brokers and Information on the Migration to Southeast Asia

To begin with, the brokers involved in emigration to Southeast Asia were unlike those involved in the coolie trade. By 1860, many brokers who handled emigration to the Straits Settlements had visited foreign countries,[57] and many were Chinese who had returned from Southeast Asia.[58] Thus, many of the brokers involved in emigration to Southeast Asia had at least visited the destinations to which they sent emigrants. In this way they differed from the coolie brokers, who often had not emigrated themselves, let alone visited the destinations to which they sent many. In general, reports from the Chinese who returned from Singapore and Sydney, unlike those who emigrated to work as coolies, encouraged emigration.[59] Many of those who emigrated also had relatives in the countries to which they moved,[60] which meant that they had extra first-hand information.

Many emigrants to Southeast Asia, however, did not take their families with them. This was because they could return to their homes frequently and continue their ancestor worship.[61] The ability to communicate with their families at home also distinguished the experience of many emigrants from those of coolies. This contact between home country and destination reduced information asymmetry between emigration agents and emigrants; indeed, in Fujian, many emigrants were recruited by trusted individuals, unlike the system of coolie emigration, which was based on a chain of distrust. Emigration to Southeast Asia therefore did not cause the serious conflicts in southern China that the coolie trade did, and few factors disturbed the process of emigration, thus causing this movement of people to grow.[62]

Utilization of Foreign Ships

The most significant change in emigration during this period came with an increase in the utilization of foreign ships in transporting emigrants to Southeast Asia, many of which were owned or chartered by the Chinese in Singapore; this practice also differentiated the trafficking of emigrants from the coolie trade. The origin of this development lay in the desire to tighten security against increasing piracy along the coast of China. Examples of such voyages include the 1846 voyage of the *Sophie Frazer* from China to Singapore that resulted in its wreck, organized by a Chinese broker from Singapore, Hong Sing,[63] and the five voyages that sailed to the Straits Settlements in November 1860.[64] By 1867, the British consul reported that Chinese British subjects owned nearly all of the carrying ships.[65] With regard to emigration to the Philippines, although the steamships used to transport emigrants were owned by foreigners, their voyages were still under the control of Chinese individuals.[66]

Although Chinese brokers controlled foreign ships during this period, the number of ships transporting emigrants that belonged to non-treaty countries or countries that did not strictly control their ships also increased steadily at this time. In response to this, W. H. Pedder, the British consul in Amoy, opposed the application of the Act for the Regulation of Chinese Passenger Ships to Southeast Asia because it would have benefited the ships of other countries over British ships.[67] During the 1870s, however, British ships became the exclusive mode of transport for emigrants due to the development of British steamship companies,[68] thus making the owners of these vessels also their managers.

Despite this, however, the problem of overloading continued, as increasing demand led many to attempt to increase profits illegally. An illustrative example of such an incident occurred in 1881, when the Spanish consulate, trying to load as many emigrants as possible onto a Spanish ship bound for Manila in order to maximize the division of emigrant taxes among consular officers, resulted in severe overcrowding.[69] By the early twentieth century, many of the same issues that plagued the coolie trade became prevalent during emigration to Southeast Asia, and it took a long time for them to be addressed.[70]

Although many of these problems remained unresolved, emigration to Southeast Asia, mainly organized by Chinese brokers and based on relationships of trust, did not cause major problems in destination countries, induce large-scale conflict or undermine governance in the points of departure in China, causing local officials largely to ignore this kind of emigration. The popularity of this attractive and somewhat less problematic form of emigration thus likely spurred the decline of the coolie trade in Amoy, resulting in a growing concentration of emigrants in Southeast Asia from as early as the late 1850s. Ultimately, this led to the establishment of a significant Fujianese presence in Southeast Asia.

Conclusion

The coolie trade in Amoy arose due to the development of the credit-ticket system in the eighteenth century, the emergence of cooperation between foreigners and Chinese brokers in the early nineteenth century, and the chaos prevailing in coastal areas during the mid-nineteenth century. The increase in the demand for labourers and the unpopularity of serving as a coolie created a gap between the supply of and demand for labour. Thus, coolie brokers, often indebted, turned to criminal acts including kidnapping to secure desired labourers. Brokers often kidnapped men at random, causing major disruption in the communities from which these individuals hailed. This led to waves of outspoken opposition, which eventually helped put an end to the coolie trade. The Amoy riot gave China a reason to cooperate with Britain in the region, and this cooperation struck hard at the coolie trade by expelling Cantonese individuals involved (such as great brokers and pirates) and putting pressure on non-British ships to cease transporting coolies. By contrast, emigration to Southeast Asia, which was also bonded labour emigration employing the credit-ticket system, did not provoke the same level of conflict as it was based on relatively reliable relationships. As a result, local officials generally overlooked this practice despite its legal prohibition. This led to a concentration of emigrants departing from Amoy in Southeast Asia.

We can understand well the problems relating to the coolie trade from the recorded conflicts and negotiations between foreigners and Chinese brokers. Conversely, we know little about the problems relating to emigration to Southeast Asia because this kind of emigration was organized by Chinese networks, and thus did not cause problems for the authorities. Similarly, many emigrants became indebted in other ways, but Chinese officials and elites did not consider these as problematic, and so we know little about the issues surrounding them. It thus should not be forgotten that the experiences of the majority of bonded Chinese labourers who went abroad have been left out of official and private records.

11 DEBT SLAVES IN OLD KOREA

Bok-rae Kim

Introduction

The word 'family' (from the Latin *famulus*, 'domestic slave') originally referred to a group of slaves belonging to one man, then, by extension, to all persons ruled by one man or his descendants and, finally, to all persons living together in a man's household, including servants, wives, children, parents, grandparents, other close and distant relatives, friends and permanent guests.[1] In patriarchal societies, a man's wife and children are often treated like the slaves of their husband and/or father, thus making the father not a family member, but a master of the household.

In China, traditional customs of wife-lending, wife-mortgaging and wife-selling existed until the Chinese Communist Party came to power in the twentieth century and banned them. However, wife-selling was still occasionally reported in rural areas of the country, and a well-known example comes from Pearl Buck's novel *The Good Earth* (1931), which depicts the practice of selling children into slavery due to extreme poverty. In Japan, posters advertising the sale of a daughter were occasionally posted on telephone poles during hard times, even up to the modern period.[2]

Such practices were also common in Korea under the Chosun dynasty (1392–1910). Documents pertaining to *nobis* (slaves) record the case of a man named Jong Il-jae, who found that due to a poor harvest he had no means of fulfilling his filial duty to support his eighty-year-old father.[3] Consequently, Jong sold his six family members, namely his forty-seven-year-old wife, four sons ranging from three to twenty years old, and sixteen-year-old daughter to the noble Choi family for fifty nyangs (a unit of old Korean coinage), which translates to about one million won (a Korean monetary unit) calculated in rice prices, though he did not sell his eldest son so that he could continue the Jong family line and perform his ancestral rites.[4] Families in dire poverty abandoned children who might become, or be forced into becoming, *nobis*, and *in extremis* the father of a household would also sell himself into slavery. Indebted *yangmin* (commoner) farmers often arrived at such poverty because annual interest on loans during the Chosun dynasty could reach up to 50 per cent.

Debt slavery already had a long history in Korea by the Chosun period, however. For example, a person convicted of theft under the Koguryo kingdom (37 BC–AD 668)[5] was obligated to repay the amount stolen tenfold, and if anyone could not pay off their debts, they could be forced to sell their children into slavery.[6] Likewise, under the Silla kingdom (57 BC–AD 935), men of influence who lent grain at high interest rates would often enslave their defaulting borrowers.[7] Thus, debt slavery was a well-established element of Korean society by the beginning of the Chosun period. This essay therefore does not examine the origins of debt slavery in Korea, but rather how this practice changed during the latter half of the second millennium AD and ultimately came to an end.

Debt *Nobis* under the Chosun Dynasty (1392–1910)

The *nobi* system needs to be examined within the context of Chosun society, and in particular its status system. The historian James Palais characterized Chosun society as a slave society on the grounds that one third of the population belonged to the *nobi* class.[8] Scholars Yi Young-hoon and Yang Dong-hyu have highlighted, however, that although they were possessions that could be sold and inherited, a considerable number of *nobis* were 'small, independent farmers who retained property rights, civil rights, and, as time passed, acquired a legal capacity like *yangmins*'.[9]

During the Chosun dynasty, four distinct social strata developed: (1) scholar-officials, collectively referred to as the *yangban*; (2) the *chungin* (literally 'middle people'), comprising technicians and administrators subordinate to the *yangban*; (3) the commoners or *yangmin*, a large group composed of farmers, craftsmen and merchants; and (4) the *chonmin* (literally 'despised people'), those at the bottom of society. The *nobi* class belonged to the last social category. To ensure stability, the government devised a system of personal tallies that helped to identify people according to their social status. The *nobi* was recognized as a human being, but commonly regarded as a 'living instrument'. The *nobi* system was generally divided into two categories: public *nobis*, who belonged to the government, and private *nobis*, owned by individuals. Private *nobis* were also divided into resident *nobis*, who lived with their masters, and more independent externally resident *nobis*, who lived away from their masters' homes.

The *nobi* system was perpetuated in two ways: by the enslavement of non-*nobis* and the reproduction of the *nobi* population through hereditary bondage.[10] From the Koguryo to the Chosun period, the traditional method of increasing the *nobi* population was through enslavement as a form of punishment. As time went on, however, this method of enslavement declined markedly, though it still remained a main source especially of public slaves during the Chosun period. War captives were the main source of *nobis* from the early period of conquering wars to the Three Kingdoms period (57 BC–AD 668), when the enslavement of war captives reached its peak due to frequent warfare between the three rival kingdoms; enslaved war captives almost disappeared completely during the Chosun dynasty, however, because Korea was relatively peaceful during this period. As the demand for *nobis* grew, different forms of enslavement were progressively developed. Overall, there emerged seven ways by which people could be enslaved: (1) punishment for a crime; (2) capture in warfare; (3) indebtedness; (4) human trafficking; (5) naturalization; (6) enslavement of commoners (*yangmins*); and (7) birth. As stated above, during the Chosun dynasty, the majority of *nobi* repopulation occurred through birth and/or the enslavement of *yangmins*. People mainly became private *nobis* due to impoverishment: a bad harvest could push many *yangmins* to sell their children or offer themselves as *nobis*. When *yangmins* changed status and became *nobis*, their new status was inherited by their descendants, and thus passed from generation to generation. On the other hand, some *yangbans* abused their power arbitrarily to make poor *yangmins* into *nobis*. Enslaving *yangmins* was the cause of serious financial loss for the government, however, as it reduced the number of *yangmins*, who were the main source of tax revenues. It is estimated that a very small proportion of the *nobi* population was enslaved due to human trafficking, naturalization or debt. However, it is the last category which will be analysed here.

Under the Koryo dynasty (918–1392), if a *yangmin* became indebted and could not pay off that debt, he could legally be sold into slavery by his creditor. However, in 1392, King Tae-jo (the founder of the Chosun dynasty) abolished the enslavement of indebted *yangmins*. As he stated, 'the (discriminative) law of *yangmin* versus *chonmin* in Korea is very rigorous. Enslaving a *yangmin* who cannot pay off his debt is against the natural law'.[11] According to this measure, if a commoner failed to repay a debt, he was forced to work for the equivalent of the total amount of debt owed, and was subsequently acquitted of that debt. Nevertheless, it is apparent that the ban had limited impact, for a document in the *Annals of King Jong-jo*[12] refers to the difficulties encountered by the judicial government office of *nobis*, which officiated in all legal disputes involving *nobis*, in punishing rich or influential people who grew wealthy by enslaving indebted *yangmins*; the inability of the office to enforce the law stemmed from the fact that the official who headed the office was of lower rank than those he was attempting to prosecute. Another document confirms both that indebtedness was widespread among poor *yangmin* farmers at this time, and that it was common to enslave those who failed to repay their debts. The document states that in the year 1475, a subject informed king Song-jong that the price poor *yangmins* had to pay for renting one kyol (an ancient unit of the rice or dry field) of a rice field from a *yangban* family was working seven kyols of their landlord's fields:[13]

> During the busy farming season, they cannot farm rice. In autumn, they have nothing to harvest; therefore, they have to live off debt. Next spring, they pay all their debts by selling their whole fortune (house and fields). It is a great pity that they have no choice but to live off of a powerful family, and they are in the end reduced to becoming *nobis*.

This text shows how the practice of demanding seven kyols of corvée in exchange for the right to cultivate one kyol of rice or dry field could have severely undermined the livelihood of poor *yangmins*, driving them to the point of bankruptcy, and consequently enslavement.

The distinction between *nobis* and those of higher status was great; indeed, the *nobi* was called 'another sort'. Scholars differ in their estimates as to the size of the *nobi* population in any one period, but in the fifteenth and sixteenth centuries they are estimated to have comprised 30 to 40 per cent of the total population. Some *yangban* families possessed hundreds of *nobis*: in one extant document enumerating the inheritance and distribution of the Shin clan, a *yangban* family, 162 *nobis* are listed who were widely dispersed throughout Korea. Under the reign of King Myong-jong (1534–67), the *yangban* family of Yi Hwang (1501–70)[14] owned 367 *nobis*.[15] Yi Yong-hoon asserts that among the *yangban* class, the most popular method of obtaining more *nobis* was to enslave *yangmins* illegally, or to marry their male *nobi* (*no*) to a female *yangmin*. Under the Chosun dynasty, if a female *nobi* (*bi*) gave birth to a baby, this child became the possession of the *bi*'s master. Therefore, it was unpopular for a *yangban* to marry his *no* to a *bi* belonging to another *yangban* family. *Yangbans* rather preferred to marry their *nos* to female *yangmins* in order that they would own any offspring. In the mid-seventeenth century, a *no* called Ke-ryong[16] of the *yangban* Yun family was married to a *bi* of another *yangban* family. The couple had a large number of children, but they all belonged to the *bi*'s master. In Chosun society, the status of a child followed that of his or her mother (*partus sequitur ventrem*). Thus, Ke-ryong apologized to his master Yun by bowing many times and saying 'I have committed a grave sin against you. To die a thousand deaths would be too good for the likes of me', in addition to offering some of his wealth to his master.[17] Thus, many masters attempted, if possible, to marry their *no* not to a *bi* of another *yangban* family, but to a *yangmin*'s daughter. For this reason, very many *nos* remained unmarried for long periods while their masters searched for a female *yangmin*. Nevertheless, the status of Chosun *nobis* was better than that of Roman slaves. They could establish their own families, for instance, even though they were not truly independent, especially *nobis* living with their masters. By contrast, it was very difficult for Roman slaves to get married, except slaves of special status. *Connubium*, or the Roman right of marriage, was reserved for Roman citizens; *matrimonium* for other non-citizen free persons; and *contubernium* for slaves. The former two were legal statuses, however, while the latter was a *de facto*, and not a *de jure* status.[18]

Most *nobis* were farmers and weavers. *Bis* engaged in silk farming during the middle of the summer, and weaving hemp cloth when it was not farming season. Indeed, masters profited greatly from the work of their *nobis*, but a significant portion of *nobis* were also engaged in directly supporting the luxurious lifestyle of both men and women of the *yangban* class. For instance, *yangban* ladies, governed by social conventions of strict gender segregation, were not allowed access to the reception room for male guests in their own houses, and so female *bis* were responsible for serving male guests. According to a historical tale, during cold winters a *yangban*'s *bi* warmed a blanket with her own body heat for her master's comfort. It was common for a *bi* to bear her master's children as an unofficial concubine. Nevertheless, it was very rare for a *yangban* to declare himself the father of an illegitimate child in his family register or diaries.[19]

During much of the Koryo dynasty (918–1392), *nobis* were relatively few in number. In the second half of Koryo dynasty, however, the *nobi* population began to increase due to the introduction of the law of mixed marriage between commoners and *nobis*. During the first three centuries of the Chosun dynasty that followed, when the *yangban* class became well established, the number of *nobis*, who served as markers of social privilege, increased greatly. During this period, the *yangmins* were legally free, but they had to pay taxes to the state and were liable for military service, while, at the same time, they were exposed to the arbitrary and illegal exploitation of the *yangban* class. By contrast, the *nobis* were not free, but they only had economic obligations to their *yangban* masters. Some *yangmins* were so exploited that they considered it more economically beneficial to live as a *nobi*, renouncing their free status and attaching themselves to powerful *yangban* families. As a result, the *nobi* population increased, notably in the sixteenth century.[20]

Again in the late eighteenth century, due to a deterioration of living standards, *yangmin* farmers increasingly sold themselves and their families into slavery. Only a small proportion (0.6 per cent) of the *nobi* population entered bondage in this manner, but their number grew rapidly, so that by the late nineteenth century nearly half of all *nobis* were self-sold.[21] Traditionally, the market for *nobis* was small, but as voluntary enslavement increased, so did *nobi* sales. Because slave dealing was considered a disreputable activity, however, and also because the *yangban* class maintained that the relationship between master and *nobi* was akin to the relation between father and son according to Confucian ethics, masters usually arranged for other *nobis* to sell their *nobis* on their behalf.

Nevertheless, the total number of *nobis* began to decline during the eighteenth century. This was due less to a growing abolitionist sentiment among enlightened scholars than to an increase in the flight and violent resistance of private *nobis* during the latter part of the Chosun dynasty. Runaway *nobis* would sometimes kill their masters or policemen during attempts to re-capture them, and such efforts ultimately wearied *yangbans*, who were forced to devote increasing efforts to keeping their *nobis*. At this time, secret tricks believed to be able to stop *nobis* from flight proliferated, often being quoted at the end of old family encyclopaedias or picked up here and there from Chinese texts. For example, it was believed that if hairs collected from a runaway *nobi* were placed around a cartwheel which was then turned, the fugitive would become dizzy and disorientated. Another trick advised the master to pin the name tag of a runaway *nobi* on a crossbeam of his or her house or to place a magnet in the pocket of the fugitive's clothes and hang them in a well, thus causing him or her to return.[22]

Nobi flight reached its zenith in the eighteenth century. Even though there was no systematic resistance in the form of group rebellions or armed uprisings, the number of *nobis* who fled state control alone left the Chosun royal family no choice but to emancipate 66,000 public *nobis* in 1801, though some *nobis* were still bound to government offices thereafter. Nevertheless, private *nobis*, whose numbers were far greater, remained unaffected by this emancipation. It took until 1886 for the transmission of *nobi* status from parent to child to be abolished, and the complete emancipation of all public and private *nobis* was only accomplished through the Gabo reformation of 1894. But while slavery became illegal, it remained entrenched in Korean society. During the Japanese colonial era (1910–45), there are still reports of *nobis* fleeing their masters, sometimes with their entire families, because they were unable to repay their debts. During this same period there are also reports of *nobis* returning to their masters because they were unable to make a living on their own. Some residual *nobis* remained even after the 1944 liberation of Korea, but by the end of the Korean War (1950–3), the institution had disappeared completely.

Thus, the hereditary *nobi* system was reinforced throughout the Koryo and Chosun dynasties, and only gradually disappeared in the latter part of the eighteenth century. This distinguished Korea from neighbouring Japan and China. In Japan, the *nobi* (*nuhi* in Japanese) system[23] was abolished in the 900s, though this merely caused slaves to be replaced by bonded *chonmins* (low people) until their emancipation in 1871. In China, the *nobi* system (*nubi* in Chinese) persisted until 1909, but it was at its zenith during the Tang dynasty (618–907), and began to decline significantly after the Song dynasty (960–1279).[24] It was only because of the implementation of a series of anti-slavery policies established by the Chosun government (such as the emancipation act of public nobis in 1801), which hindered the enslavement of yangmins to increase tax revenues, that it became relatively easy for nobis to free themselves by running away, marrying a commoner or buying *yangban* status. The *nobi* population thus began to decrease, but from the late eighteenth century onwards the number of self-sale *nobis* rapidly grew as a proportion of it. Thus, the *nobi* system was dissolving, but self-sale continued to function on a small scale in spite of the fact that it became prohibited by the Chosun government.

Nine years after the complete abolishment of slavery in Korea, a man named An Chang-ho posted this announcement in a newspaper:

> On the night of April 13th, my *bi* ran away and has not yet returned. I have not been able to find her, so I am advertising for help. She was wearing blue hemp clothes and shoes riddled with holes. This *bi* is a good speaker and now fourteen years old; she has a white face without scars and a black wart around her left eye, and she wears Chinese powder on her face. If anyone finds this girl, please let me know. I will gladly pay you twenty wons in compensation without haggling. From An Chang-ho.[25]

This advertisement demonstrates that many *yangban* families still owned domestic *nobis* despite the emancipation act, and that such advertisements looking for a runaway *nobi* were still openly posted in help-wanted columns. According to the *Record of Silla* related in the *New History of Tang Dynasty* (*Xin Tangshu*), 'someone lends grain to another, and if the latter cannot pay off his debt, the former enslaves him'. The following is another example of a mortgaged girl from the late Chosun dynasty:[26]

> Scores of years ago, a *yangban* called Suh Do-sa who lived in Namchon lent seventy nyangs to a *yangmin* living in the same village. When the commoner was unable to pay, Suh seized as repayment this commoner's nine-year-old daughter to work as a *nobi*. Her parents, in surprise, managed to scrape together the sum owed; but when they offered to pay their debt in exchange for their daughter, the latter refused. For fear of the *yangban*'s power, their daughter remained silent about her situation. She then lived as a *bi* in Suh's house for thirty years, eventually giving birth to a daughter. After offering her daughter to Suh as a substitute, she was able to escape his house. Her daughter, however, suffered from cold and hunger and eventually escaped to her mother's house. At this time, Suh demanded 5,000 nyangs as ransom for her daughter. The mother sold the entire family fortune, barely amassing 400 nyangs, and gave him this money. Suh, however, said that this sum was only sufficient for the mother's ransom, and demanded again a new ransom for her daughter.
>
> The criminal act of enslaving *yangmin* can be punished by law, but Suh seems to ignore the new *nobi* emancipation act. People have spoken with one voice that using a human body as collateral instead of money is wrong, and that demanding a daughter's ransom is an unseemly thing to do.[27]

Numerous articles can be found from the end of the Chosun period relating stories of poor parents who sold their children as *nobis*.

If we compare the two above-mentioned documents, written a thousand years apart in the Silla and Chosun periods, we find little difference in practice. Slavery was only able to persist due to poverty, which caused many to become enslaved, and prevented many others from obtaining their freedom. Indeed, the French missionary Félix-Claire Ridel, consigned to prison in Korea during the nineteenth century, noted that a third of his fellow prisoners were debtors.[28] Debt was thus ultimately the last fetter to entrap poor Koreans as *nobis*.

12 THE DEBT-SERVITUDE OF PROSTITUTES IN JAPAN DURING THE EDO PERIOD, 1600–1868

Yoko Matsui

Introduction

During the Edo period (1600–1868), the trade in human beings was totally banned in Japan and gradually disappeared. Thus, those who had to work to repay their debts became indentured servants for only a specific period of time. However, the contracts of prostitutes persisted in keeping them in slave-like conditions. Most of the girls who belonged to licensed or unlicensed brothels in this period had been sold as apprentices by their parents or relatives and were subsequently forced to work as prostitutes in order to repay the advances their parents received as payment for their 'apprenticeship'.

In this chapter I will first provide a general overview of human trafficking and the custom of debt servitude throughout Japanese history, as well as the history of prostitution in the Edo period. Then I will shift my focus to the prostitutes of the licensed brothels in the port city Nagasaki, which was the only city in which foreign trade with the Chinese and the Dutch was conducted. I will examine their contracts, working conditions and lives, as well as the social structure in which this system was approved.

'The Trade in Human Beings' throughout Japanese History

In Japan, human trafficking has generally been prohibited since antiquity.[1] However, this does not mean that such trade did not exist. Under the ancient *ritsuryō* legal system, persons of the lowest social strata, who could be considered slaves, could in fact be bought and sold. There are many stories about frequent abductions and ubiquitous 'people merchants' in medieval literature. The Kamakura Bakufu (shogunate) enforced strict regulations on those who trafficked in human beings. On the other hand, the government seems to have had no choice but to consent to the enslavement of people who had sold themselves to escape from starvation during the great famine of 1231.[2] Selling as well as pawning oneself or a family member for a legitimate reason, such as paying the land tax, was an accepted and prevalent form of solving monetary problems;[3] those who were pawned became slaves after defaulting. Some researchers insist that this kind of enslavement of ordinary peasants increased during the medieval period.[4] During the age of civil wars, that is from the latter half of the fifteenth century onwards, prisoners of war were also traded.

When the Jesuits came to Japan in the sixteenth century, they found that Portuguese merchants exported great numbers of Japanese slaves, a practice which they feared would interfere with the propagation of their faith. The Jesuit Gaspar Coelho wrote in 1587 that the Portuguese bought Japanese people because other Japanese individuals sold them, so that the Portuguese only followed the Japanese practice of buying and selling slaves.[5] We can identify three major sources for this supply of slaves: firstly, the capture of prisoners of war both within and without Japan; secondly, the enslavement as criminals and their kin as punishment; lastly, enslavement for economic reasons, i.e. defaulting on a debt.[6] As most wars were fought in Japan during this period, most of the slaves for sale in Japan were also Japanese, and their masters' attitudes towards them tended to be rather lenient.[7]

In the course of his war to reunify Japan, Toyotomi Hideyoshi reissued a ban on human trafficking in order to prevent the Portuguese from exporting Japanese slaves and to return all those fleeing the war to their homes.[8] The Tokugawa Bakufu also banned human trafficking. The sale of those put in bondage permanently was generally prohibited for all social strata. This prohibition was put in place in order to save the peasant class from impoverishment, perpetuate a fixed class structure and maintain a functional tax collecting system, all indispensable instruments for maintaining power. Although no clear ban on fixed-term sales was issued,[9] the main force in agriculture shifted from the labour of bonded servants attached to patriarchal families to that of the members of smaller families complemented by indentured servants. Thus, human trafficking was no longer the main source for agricultural labour. At this time, apprenticeships also gradually came to be recognized as contracts stipulating the sale of labour for a fixed period of time, rather than contracts that bound the apprentice to repay his debts with his labour.[10] Prostitution apprenticeship, however, maintained such slave-like conditions.

Prostitutes in Edo Society

The Licensed Quarters of the Edo Period

The social structure of early modern Japan was based on a status system that ranked warriors as the ruling class, followed by a separate class of commoners, that is peasants and townsmen, the latter composed of the two categories of artisans and merchants. The Bakufu also defined discriminated classes; these individuals formed autonomous communities of outcasts, though they were not the objects of human trafficking. The power of the Bakufu was based on a rice-dominated economy; however, the mid- and late Edo period (around 1700–1868) witnessed the rapid growth of three central and numerous other provincial cities as well as the development of a monetized economy. During this period, the gap between the rich and the poor grew wider, producing a large stratum of impoverished people both in the cities and the countryside who depended on cash incomes.

Under the patriarchal family system prevalent at this time, when and whom a young person was to marry was decided by his or her patriarch. It was considered ideal at this time for a full-blood son to become the family head after the death of his father, inheriting the family business in the process. As such, only wives were expected to be chaste, and adulterous relations were consequently severely punished. On the other hand, there were many poor lower-class men and women who could not get married or live together because of their long-term live-in apprenticeships or the instability of their short-term employment.

Because of these conditions, it was considered socially acceptable for men to pay to satisfy their sexual desires, as there were no strong religious or ethical norms condemning the institution of prostitution itself.[11] The resulting commodification of women's bodies and the pervasiveness of this business among ordinary people indicates that prostitution became widespread in the Edo period.[12]

Some major cities under the direct control of the Bakufu, such as Edo, Kyoto, Osaka and Nagasaki, had *yūkaku*, or 'licensed quarters', districts containing brothels, teahouses and other facilities related to the services of prostitutes. Some of the *daimyo* (territorial lords), like those of Kanazawa and Mito, also established such districts in the castle town of their domains. The prostitutes who belonged to these licensed quarters were called *yūjo*.[13] In the post-station towns and port cities along major routes, some inns and teahouses hired prostitutes officially called *meshimori-onna* (rice-serving girls) or *chatate-onna* (tea-making girls), although their numbers were restricted.[14] These girls worked as the innkeeper's apprentices, and as such they were legally employed, though this was merely a cover for their work as prostitutes.

In spite of the severe prohibitions against prostitution in place, this practice was tolerated within the licensed quarters. The most famous licensed quarters in the Edo period were the Yoshiwara in Edo, the Shimabara in Kyoto and Shinmachi in Osaka.[15] The brothels were concentrated in a fenced quarter, or *kuruwa*, on the outskirts of the city. They formed exclusive guilds of prostitution businesses licensed by the Bakufu, who recognized them because such institutions paid high licensing fees and were useful for the authorities in maintaining security and controlling public morals in the early Edo period. In these licensed quarters, prostitutes did not engage in their business individually, but served as the servants or apprentices of a brothel. As a result of the approval of licensed quarters by the authorities, prostitution was socially recognized both as a business and as entertainment.

Prostitution and Human Trafficking

While some girls or women came into brothels after having been kidnapped or punished, in most cases girls were sold into prostitution under the guise of assuming an apprenticeship. Under the strong patriarchal family system of the Edo period, the patriarch of a family had the right to submit his daughter to any kind of apprenticeship he wished.[16] This practice was encouraged by the fact that it was considered a virtue for a girl to help her family to escape poverty by becoming a prostitute.[17]

Apprenticeship contracts in the Edo period took the form of a *ukejō* (surety bond), in which the guarantor assured the master that the apprentice would work as specified in the conditions of the contract. Prostitution contracts were similar, though a few important differences reflect the nature of these transactions:[18]

(1) All remuneration was paid in advance and in some cases it was called 'the girl's price' rather than her 'salary'; such payments were often higher than for other apprentices.

(2) In addition to the regular guarantee of compensation for any loss caused by the apprentice, the guarantor assured that there were no persons concerned, such as relatives, a fiancé or a former master, who might protest against this apprenticeship.

(3) If the girl died during the term of service, the master was allowed to bury her without prior notification.

(4) If a man wanted to take the girl for a wife or concubine and agreed to pay her advance and additional expenses, the master could take the money and hand her over to that man. This condition seems to cede the right to decide the girl's marriage, considered otherwise to be the exclusive right of her guardian.

(5) The master was allowed to transfer his apprentice to another master, i.e. to resell her. On the other hand, the apprentice was not allowed to arrange for a surrogate to take her place if she could not perform her duties.

(6) These contracts often stated that the apprentice herself had agreed to work as a prostitute.

The wording and conditions of the actual contracts differed depending on when and where they were written, but in all cases the contracts of the prostitutes were signed first by a guardian, such as her father or elder brother, then by her guarantor and finally by the apprentice herself; this is unlike the contract for an ordinary apprenticeship, in which the guarantor would sign first.

The Prostitutes of Nagasaki

Nagasaki: A City of Foreign Trade Directly Controlled by the Bakufu

The port city of Nagasaki, located on the west coast of Kyushu, Japan's south-western island, was opened in 1571 as the port of call for Portuguese trading vessels. This city developed rapidly when large numbers of Christians and merchants who wanted to participate in the foreign trade began to settle in it. In 1580, the lord of Nagasaki Ōmura Sumitada ceded the settlement to the Society of Jesus, but Toyotomi Hideyoshi later took control of it when he advanced into Kyushu in 1587. After his death, the Tokugawa Bakufu in its turn controlled Nagasaki as part of the Tokugawa domain.

At this time, the Bakufu gradually stepped up its prohibition of Christianity. To prevent Nagasaki's citizens from interacting with Christian Europeans, the Bakufu constructed a fenced artificial island, called Deshima, in the bay of Nagasaki and quarantined all Portuguese traders there in 1636. In 1639, in the aftermath of a Christian peasant rebellion in Amakusa and Shimabara not far from Nagasaki, the Portuguese were banned from Japan. Two years later, the Dutch were transferred from Hirado to Deshima, while private merchants from China were also restricted to trading in Nagasaki.[19] The trade of Nagasaki was at its most prosperous in the seventeenth century, and at its peak the city was home to more than 64,000 people.[20] Although from around the middle of the eighteenth century the total amount of trade conducted in Nagasaki was restricted and its population decreased about 50 per cent, the city maintained its unique position as the only port permitted to trade with the Dutch and Chinese during the Edo period.

Yūjo in Maruyama-machi and Yoriai-machi

The licensed quarters called Maruyama-machi and Yoriai-machi were situated on the outskirts of the city of Nagasaki.[21] The *yūkaku* was enclosed by walls and escarpments and segregated from the rest of the city by double gates. Another gate at the rear of the quarter was called the 'never-opened gate', *akazu-no-mon*.

Maruyama-machi and Yoriai-machi were two of the eighty *machi*, or wards, which comprised the city of Nagasaki, functioning as neighbourhood organizations as well as administrative units. The local officials of the two wards maintained and supervised the streets and their residents and also represented the licensed quarter in dealings with the city authorities. According to statistics of the late eighteenth century, Maruyama-machi comprised 2,993 tsubo, or 0.9877 hectares, and contained 130 houses with a population of 522 people (of which 159 were male and 363 were female). Yoriai-machi was 4,664 tsubo in size, or 1.5391 hectares, and had eighty-eight houses with a population of 842 people (of which 146 were male and 696 were female).[22]

The average number of brothels in the district was between twenty and thirty during the eighteenth and nineteenth centuries, and the *yūjo* who belonged to them numbered over 400, though this number does not include the one or two hundred *kamuro*, or girls under fifteen, associated with these businesses. The number is likely to have been larger in the seventeenth century, when this industry reached the peak of its prosperity.[23] According to a document of 1732, there were twenty-seven brothels in Yoriai-machi, whose population was 1,058, of which 246 were male and 812 were female. The number of *yūjo* in this district was 330, of whom 294 had grown up in Nagasaki or its suburban villages.[24] In many cases, these girls and women were not completely cut off from their families, which is in striking contrast with the situation in other cities, in which girls were often sold by their parents with documentary proof of a transfer of ownership. In Nagasaki, many families chose to keep supporting their daughters and to rely on their earnings in perpetuity instead of transferring ownership of their daughter for a one-time advance payment.

Yūjo were divided into different ranks.[25] The highest among them, the *tayū*, were advertised as the most beautiful in appearance, the most excellent in accomplishments and the highest in price. In the late seventeenth century in Nagasaki, there were three ranks: *tayū*, *mise* and *nami*. From the late eighteenth century onwards, only the first two ranks appear in documents. The prices charged varied according to rank – 15 momme for *tayū*, which was one sixth of what was paid in the Yoshiwara, and 7.5 momme for *mise*.

In Edo, Kyoto and Osaka, *yūjo* were prohibited from leaving the *yūkaku* to see clients from the 1630s onwards, while other outings were also heavily restricted. This was seen as a means of keeping the peace and protecting public morality, the principal aims of the recognition of these quarters, and such measures suited the brothels' interest in preventing the *yūjo* from escaping. In Nagasaki, however, *yūjo* were called to Deshima and the Chinese compound on a daily basis. Prostitutes could also pass through the gate of the *yūkaku* to return home to see their parents or to visit temples, graves and shrines during memorial services or festivals. Some *yūjo* were also able to return home on account of illness or pregnancy, and it was difficult for the brothels to make them return quickly. This freedom to leave the district, a distinctive feature of the *yūjo* of Nagasaki, continued until 1843, when the Governor of Nagasaki prohibited prostitutes from leaving their *yūkaku* altogether.[26]

Relations between Yūjo and Foreigners

From the 1630s onwards, the Bakufu established a strict policy of prohibiting Christianity and maintaining close control over foreigners' access to Japan, later called 'Sakoku', or 'National Seclusion'.[27] Under these circumstances, foreigners could only stay in Japan for the duration of their business. Furthermore, they could not establish families and were forbidden from having intercourse with Japanese women, except for prostitutes.[28] For this reason, Nagasaki *yūjo* became famous for their foreign clientele.

The Dutch established such relationships with *yūjo* soon after they were moved to Deshima. The Dutch began to call *yūjo* to their quarters soon after they were moved to Deshima. Already by 1649, such relations had become so common that the chief factor, who worried about the trouble caused by such affairs, asked the governor of Nagasaki to prohibit prostitutes from visiting Deshima at least during the trading season.[29] Chinese merchants could stay in their business partners' houses in Nagasaki until 1685, when the Bakufu ordered that they, too, were to be confined to one compound, known as the *Tōjin yashiki*, or the 'Chinamen's Mansion'. Without this quarantine, it was believed to be impossible to sever completely their contact with ordinary Japanese women. The authorities of Nagasaki repeatedly issued orders restricting the Chinese from forming romantic relationships with ordinary Japanese women in the city in defiance of the standard procedure of calling *yūjo* to their lodging.

The relationships between port town prostitutes and foreigners who stayed for only a short period of time were originally intended to be transitory in nature, and it was assumed that children would not be born of such unions. However, in some cases children were born. The ordinance issued by the governors of Nagasaki in 1715 that the pregnancies, births and deaths of children sired by foreigners were to be reported to the government clearly recognizes this reality. These children could be brought up by their fathers in Japan, but never taken out of the country, and were expected to be brought by the mother's parents or by the mother herself in the brothel.[30] In other parts of Japan, the *yūjo* of Nagasaki were famous for their exotic aura, luxurious costumes and food, and their relations with foreigners were the object of a great deal of curiosity.[31]

From 1715 onwards, only two Dutch ships per year were allowed to come to Nagasaki. Each ship was manned by about one hundred crewmembers and anchored in the bay of Nagasaki for four to five months, though few members of the crew could come ashore. After the ships departed, less than twenty people were left on Deshima. As such, the main clients of the *yūjo* were the higher-ranked residents of the island, such as the chief factor, the doctor and the upper echelons of the trading staff. It was common practice for such men to keep their favourite *yūjo* at their side and give them gifts in addition to their regular payment. In many cases, the family of the *yūjo* also depended on this additional income.

Highly-ranked Chinese residents, like the owners or masters of the ships and rich merchants, also maintained *yūjo* in their compound. In the case of the Chinese, all the passengers and crew of each junk would come ashore and stay in the compound. From the late seventeenth century onwards, many Chinese passengers travelled to Japan not for trade but for pleasure, with the *yūjo* being their main attraction.[32] Ordinary sailors and servants could also call *yūjo* to their compound for short periods of time. It is said that in the nineteenth century many sailors spent their fortunes made in private trade on *yūjo*.

In 1685, the Bakufu set upper limits for the amount of foreign trade that could be conducted in Japan each year, making smuggling commonplace in Nagasaki. *Yūjo*, because of their contacts with foreigners, were often used by smugglers as a means of communication and transportation. In an effort to prevent such involvement, officials examined *yūjo* at the gate of Deshima and the Chinese compound every time they entered and left and required them to declare officially any gifts received from foreigners. *Yūjo* also swore an oath sealed with their blood to the authorities of Nagasaki every year, just like local officials who had working relationships with foreigners. They pledged that whenever they entered the foreigners' compounds, they would never facilitate or participate in smuggling or any other secret contact between Japanese and foreigners, and also that they would report everything to the officials.

Whenever foreigners wanted to see *yūjo*, they submitted a request to the *otona*, or supervisor of the compound, who then transmitted the request to a brothel. The officials of both wards of the licensed quarters in turn confirmed the order and prepared the necessary documents. The payment for the *yūjo* was also managed through official channels, with the brothels receiving money from the *kaisho*, or accounting office, of Nagasaki. It was peculiar to Nagasaki's administration that these procedures did not directly involve the clients of the *yūjo* and the brothel owners, but rather the local officials who supervised the foreigners' compounds and the licensed quarters.[33]

The Indenture Contracts of Nagasaki Yūjo

The terms of the contracts for *yūjo* in Nagasaki were 'to raise the girl for several years without payment, then have her serve as *yūjo* for ten years in exchange for advanced payment'. In other words, these girls first began working in brothels as *kamuro*, or the maids of *yūjo*, before, at the age of fifteen, beginning their ten-year term as *yūjo*. The price paid for such girls varied greatly according to conditions.

Included below is an example of a typical contract of a *yūjo* in Nagasaki around the end of the eighteenth century:[34]

(1) This is my real daughter named [name], [age] years old. Recently, I asked you [brothel owner] to take her on as an apprentice *yūjo*, but you refused because she is too young, and thus unable to serve as *yūjo*. I and the guarantor asked too much and you agreed to feed her from [date] to [date] without pay.

(2) When she becomes fifteen on [date], you can make her serve as *yūjo* for ten full years until [date]. In exchange for that price, I acknowledge having received [amount of advance] now. Thus, parents, brothers and any one else from the outside will not make any objections to this girl's apprenticeship. If such trouble occurs, we [the undersigned] will be responsible for resolving it. If she is not obedient and neglects her work, you may admonish and punish her as you see fit. If

she is useless as a prostitute, you may use her for any other dirty work until the end of her term. If she runs away, we will not hide her but bring her back to you. In any case, we cannot unilaterally cancel this apprenticeship before the end of the term. If she escapes with stolen property, we will be responsible for finding her and returning the goods with her. We do not care if you pawn her or send her to some other place for money as long as she will be released once her term of duty is over. If some man wants to take the girl as a wife or concubine and agrees to pay her advance and additional expenses, you do not have to notify us beforehand, and it is of no concern to us how much money you receive.If she dies during her term, both sides will bear the losses, and each will not claim compensation from the other.

(3) We affirm this girl's religious sect is [name of sect] and she is a parishioner of [name of Buddhist temple].[35] We pledge to take responsibility for any other public or private troubles and never cause you any inconvenience.

[year and date] [address]

	parent and contractor	[name and seal]
	guarantor	[name and seal]
	apprentice	[name and seal]

Maki Hidemasa, a scholar of legal history, has pointed out that the Nagasaki indenture contracts reflect the traits of human trafficking much more strongly than those of other regions. For instance, the conditions were more advantageous to the brothel owners than to their employees, while the payment was called 'her price'.[36] Some of the indenture contracts of the nineteenth century added more detailed conditions. For example, some stipulated that the apprentice and her guardian would not protest if she was injured by her master through physical or sexual abuse; that if she had a child, her guardian had to take care of the baby in order not to disturb her work; and that if she were to neglect her work or borrow money from her master, the term of the contract would be extended.[37] Judging by the terms of these indenture contracts, conditions became worse for *yūjo* apprentices over time. On the other hand, local historians who have investigated documents from other sources, such as lawsuits and the city's administration, assert that these terms were countermeasures taken by brothel owners against the 'rudeness' and 'selfish actions' of these *yūjo* and their parents.[38]

Prostitutes in the Social and Economic Structure of Nagasaki

The official recognition of licensed quarters led to the imposition of strict measures against prostitutes who remained unaffiliated with any brothel. Since only 'official' *yūjo* could engage in relationships with foreigners, it was officially impossible for an ordinary woman to have sexual relations with foreigners. Nevertheless, there were women who paid to register as *yūjo* with a brothel, called *nazuke-yūjo* ('nominal *yūjo*') or *shikiri-yūjo* ('*yūjo* for one client'), and in this way were able to visit foreigners. They were not apprenticed to any brothel, however, and only had relationships with specific foreigners, and thus could be termed concubines or mistresses. These relationships were often established in order to earn money without becoming a *yūjo*, and there were many families in Nagasaki which depended on such arrangements for their livelihood. Although the authorities strictly prohibited this loophole, it was difficult to combat it because the brothels cooperated with this subterfuge.

In addition to a fee for rendered service paid to the master of the brothel, *yūjo* received many gifts from their clients. Such gifts were mostly of sugar, along with textiles and jewellery. The sugar given was sold by the accounting office as imported merchandise, and the *yūjo* received the money through ward officials as income. Payments made by foreigners for *yūjo* were added to the *tsukai-sute*, or 'living costs', charged for daily goods and services they received during their stay. Of course, the Dutch East India Company and the Dutch Governor General never paid such costs for the entertainment of their personnel. In some cases in the nineteenth century, the cost was deducted from the private trade carried on by personnel, so that from the Japanese perspective, a portion of the cost of imports was paid for with the earnings of the *yūjo*.[39] Thus, we must conclude that relations between *yūjo* and foreigners not only involved procuring women for foreigners to entertain them, but that such interactions were also an indispensable factor in maintaining foreign trade and contributed to the prosperity of the city of Nagasaki.

The 'Emancipation' of Japanese Prostitutes

The Opening of Ports and New Licensed Quarters in the Foreign Settlement

In 1854, the Bakufu concluded the Treaty of Kanagawa, which opened two ports to US ships. These ports, in which foreigners were permitted to walk around and stay overnight within a restricted area, were soon also opened to the Netherlands, Russia, France and Britain. Moreover, after the conclusion of the commercial treaties of the Ansei era, new licensed quarters were established in the foreign settlements of Yokohama, Hakodate, Niigata, Edo, Osaka and Kobe.[40] The Bakufu still limited foreign visitors to the companionship of the *yūjo*, however, as it was feared that relationships between foreigners and ordinary Japanese women would cause disputes or arouse the anger of xenophobic factions. To defend the interests of the licensed brothels, the strict regulations preventing illegal prostitution already in place were maintained, while regulation of prostitution was also expanded at this time at the behest of the treaty countries to include testing for syphilis.

In Nagasaki, Dutch residents were permitted to leave Deshima without a sword-bearing escort according to the Japanese–Dutch peace treaty of 1856. They could rest and drink in the brothels of the licensed quarter just as before and, what is more, they could make occasional visits to the tea house on the city's outskirts. The United States, Britain and Russia followed. Sailors when on shore enjoying entertainment sometimes caused troubles with their heavy drinking.

Like the Dutch residents who had vested interests there, the Russian Navy considered Nagasaki to be important. Nagasaki was one of the most important ports of the Russian fleet because of its geographical position, and the Russians had received permission in 1858 to use Inasa, on the opposite side of the bay from the city, as their embarkation point. As syphilis was spreading rapidly through intercourse between Russian sailors and Japanese prostitutes,[41] the Russian Navy demanded that the women who entertained their sailors be tested for syphilis and that brothels exclusively reserved for their crewmen be established in Inasa. The Bakufu fulfilled these demands, and a new establishment called the 'Rest House for Russian *matroos*' (from the Dutch word for 'sailor'), built with Russian funds opened in 1860. Officially, the women sent to this establishment were *yūjo* from the brothels of Maruyama-machi and Yoriai-machi, but in reality they were girls recruited from poor families around Inasa to work under the name of *yūjo* to entertain the sailors only as long as a Russian warship stayed in port.[42] While this establishment served Russian sailors, the naval officers of the Russian Navy rented houses around Inasa and were able to call on the real *yūjo*,[43] either visiting the licensed quarter or calling the *yūjo* to their houses in the settlement.

Although the Bakufu attempted to prevent ordinary Japanese women and men, save a limited number of officials, from having any contact with foreigners, it was gradually forced to allow foreigners to hire some Japanese as servants. That is why the once prohibited institution of the *nazuke-yūjo* was adopted as an expedient measure wherever there were newly established licensed quarters for foreigners. Foreigners could hire Japanese women as house servants or concubines once they registered as prostitutes at a brothel. In this way, the prostitution system of the Edo period still survived, although it was slowly eroding.

The Emancipation Decree for Prostitutes

After the Bakufu was overthrown in 1867, the new Meiji government immediately began to draft a new legal system, in which human trafficking, especially the sale of women into prostitution, was ostensibly prohibited. This arose from an effort to modernize the nation, which led some higher officials of the Meiji government to discuss the abolition of outcast status designations.[44] It has been pointed out that the contemporary emancipation movement in the United States may have had some influence on their thought.[45]

During this period of transition, on 4 June 1872, a Peruvian cargo vessel, the *Maria Luz*, transporting Chinese coolies from Qing China to the west coast of South America called at the port of Yokohama for some repairs.[46] One of the 'passengers', a Chinese coolie, ran away from the ship but was eventually returned, bringing the ill-treatment of the coolies on the ship to light. Following the advice of the British Consul, the Meiji government ordered an investigation. As a result, the Japanese authorities decreed that the coolies could leave the ship as they wished. The captain of the ship, however, initiated a lawsuit to force the coolies to fulfil their contracts. During the course of this trial, the English barrister of the captain produced a Japanese contract for the sale of a woman into prostitution in a licensed quarter, insisting that contracts selling individuals into a level of servitude equally deplorable to that faced by coolies were tolerated in Japan. The case was decided against the captain, but the revelation of the fact that similar forms of servitude existed in Japan severely damaged the Meiji government's plans to negotiate to revise unequal treaties. This became a stimulus for the Japanese to speed up the process of the 'emancipation' of prostitutes.

On 2 October 1872, the Meiji government issued an edict, the so-called 'Emancipation Decree for Female Performers and Prostitutes', which reiterated the old bans on human trafficking and established new rules for apprenticeships and the employment of servants. It declared that all prostitutes and others bound by similar kinds of contracts were to be set free, and that the government would reject any suits for the repayment of loans connected with emancipation. Just after this, an additional circular concerning the debt of the prostitutes was produced which declared, 'These prostitutes and other performers are being denied their right as human beings and treated just as if they are horses or oxen. It is not reasonable to claim payment from horses or oxen, and so no one should claim repayment of the debts of these women'.

The edict reached Nagasaki in the same month and was announced immediately, prompting the brothels to submit written pledges with their seals affixed that they would obey its strictures. Within a week, new rules, such as the 'regulations for prostitutes' and 'regulations for female performers', were issued. Thenceforth, the basic rule that sexual relations between Japanese women and foreigners were only allowed if the former were prostitutes belonging to licensed brothels was abolished.

The above-mentioned Emancipation Decree for Female Performers and Prostitutes banned brothels from using apprenticeships with advance payments to obtain prostitutes. This did not mean, however, the abolition of the prostitution business, but rather the establishment of a new system of licensed prostitution. The brothels continued their business by renting rooms to prostitutes, while prostitutes 'of their own free will' would apply for a license and attend to their clients in the rooms they rented. The authorities permitted such rooms only in a certain area to which prostitutes were restricted when carrying out their business. The authorities maintained control of prostitution through the imposition of a business tax and mandatory syphilis testing. Under this 'modern' system of licensed prostitution, the business of the prostitute was legally separated from her debt, though in reality many prostitutes were still forced to repay debts with their earnings.[47] The licensed prostitution system was entirely abolished in 1946, by order of the General Headquarter of the Allied Powers, but it was not until the enactment of the Anti-Prostitution Law in 1956 that the prohibition of contracts with advanced payments and brothels were written into law.

Conclusion

Although human trafficking was prohibited and there were no slaves of different ethnic groups in Japanese society of the Edo period, many women sold by their families into prostitution were locked into a situation like debt slavery, a situation which persisted even into the 'modernization' era. The existence of indentured prostitutes especially characterized gender relations with foreigners and played an indispensable role in the continued existence of the trading city of Nagasaki.

This analysis has demonstrated that prostitution was widespread and part of the structure of society. This societal form has been called a 'prostitution society',[48] because the authorities recognized the prostitution business and utilized the brothels for their own purposes, while prostitution attracted people to big cities and drove growth in them. There were plenty of families poor enough to be willing to sell their daughters, an 'act of sacrifice' on the daughter's part which, under the patriarchal family system, was considered among a woman's virtue.

Acknowledgements

This work was supported by JSPS KAKENHI Grant Numbers 21222001 and 19320095. I am grateful to Professor Dr Reinier H. Hesselink for his help in correcting the English translation of this paper, and to Ms Isabel Tanaka-van Daalen for her valuable comments.

NOTES

Campbell and Stanziani, 'Introduction'

1. J. Goody, 'Slavery in Time and Space', in J. L. Watson (ed.), *Asian and African Systems of Slavery* (Berkeley, CA: University of California Press, 1980), pp. 16–42, on p. 18; A. Wink, *Al-Hind. The Making of the Indo-Islamic World* (Leiden: Brill, 1996), pp. 30–1; A. Schottenhammer, 'Slaves and Forms of Slavery in Late Imperial China (Seventeenth to Early Twentieth Centuries)', in G. Campbell (ed.), *The Structure of Slavery in Indian Ocean Africa and Asia* (London: Frank Cass, 2004), pp. 143–54.
2. G. Campbell, 'Introduction: Slavery and Other Forms of Unfree Labour in the Indian Ocean World', in Campbell (ed.), *The Structure of Slavery*, pp. vii–xxxii.
3. Goody, 'Slavery in Time and Space', pp. 32–4; G. Campbell, 'The State and Pre-Colonial Demographic History: The Case of Nineteenth Century Madagascar', *Journal of African History*, 31:3 (1991), pp. 415–45.
4. See, for example, M. A. Dandamaev, *Slavery in Babylonia* (DeKalb, IL: Northern Illinois University Press, 2009), p. 560; C. M. Wilbur, *Slavery in China during the Former Han Dynasty, 206 BC–AD 25* (New York: Russell & Russell, 1943), p. 115.
5. See, for example, Chapter 11 by Bok-rae Kim in this volume.
6. Goody, 'Slavery in Time and Space', p. 18.
7. G. Lerner, 'Women and Slavery', *Slavery & Abolition*, 4:3 (1983), p. 179.
8. Dandamaev, *Slavery in Babylonia*, p. 560.
9. Campbell, 'Introduction'.
10. J. F. Warren, 'The Structure of Slavery in the Sulu Zone in the Late Eighteenth and Nineteenth Centuries', in Campbell (ed.), *Structure of Slavery*, pp. 111–28.
11. See Chapters 1 and 3 in this volume by W. G. Clarence-Smith and G. Campbell, respectively.
12. G. Campbell, *An Economic History of Imperial Madagascar, 1750–1895: The Rise and Fall of an Island Empire* (Cambridge: Cambridge University Press, 2005), pp. 295–6.
13. B. Lasker, *Human Bondage in Southeast Asia* (Chapel Hill, NC: University of North Carolina Press, 1950), pp. 147, 150.
14. See, for example, Kim's Chapter 11.
15. Ibid.
16. A. Reid, 'Introduction', in A. Reid (ed.), *Slavery, Bondage and Dependency in Southeast Asia* (St Lucia: University of Queensland Press, 1983), pp. 1–33, on p. 10.

17. J. F. Warren, *The Sulu Zone 1768–1898. The Dynamics of External Trade, Slavery, and Ethnicity in the Transformation of a Southeast Asian Maritime State* (Singapore: Singapore University Press, 1981), p. 216.

18. See Kim's Chapter 11 in this volume; see also P. E. Lovejoy, 'Pawnship and Seizure for Debt in the Process of Enslavement in West Africa', in G. Campbell and A. Stanziani (eds), *Debt and Slavery in the Mediterranean and Atlantic Worlds* (London: Pickering & Chatto, 2013), pp. 63–75.

19. See Chapters 3 and 11 of this volume.

20. Reid, 'Introduction', p. 10; P. Boomgaard, 'Human Capital, Slavery and Low Rates of Economic and Population Growth in Indonesia, 1600–1910', in Campbell (ed.), *The Structure of Slavery*, pp. 83–96.

21. Chapters 3 and 11 of this volume.

22. See Chapter 9 by Michael Salman in this volume.

23. Thus the Code of Hammurabi (1795–1750 BC) in Ancient Mesopotamia stated: 'If an obligation is outstanding against a man and he sells or gives into debt-service his wife, his son or his daughter, they shall perform service in the house of their buyer or of the one who holds them in debt-service for three years; their release shall be secured in the fourth year' (cited in E. M. Harris, 'Did Solon Abolish Debt-Bondage?', *Classical Quarterly*, 52:2 (2002), pp. 415–30, on p. 418). Different provisions applied to slaves: 'If he should give a male or female slave into debt-service, the merchant may extend the term (beyond three years), and he may sell him; there are no grounds for a claim' (Harris, 'Did Solon Abolish Debt-Bondage?', p. 418).

24. Schottenhammer, 'Slaves and Forms of Slavery', p. 145.

25. Boomgaard, 'Human Capital'; Delaye, 'Slavery and Colonial Representations'; Schottenhammer, 'Slaves and Forms of Slavery'; see also J. L. Watson, 'Transactions in People: The Chinese Market in Slaves, Servants, and Heirs', in J. L. Watson (ed.), *Asian and African Systems of Slavery* (Berkeley, CA: University of California Press, 1980), pp. 228–36.

26. M. A. Klein, 'Introduction: Modern European Expansion and Traditional Servitude in Africa and Asia', in M. A Klein (ed.), *Breaking the Chains. Slavery, Bondage and Emancipation in Modern Africa and Asia* (Madison, WI: University of Wisconsin Press, 1993), pp. 3–36, on p. 11; W. Patnaik and M. Dingwaney (eds), *Chains of Servitude, Bondage and Slavery in India* (Hyderabad: Sangam Books, 1985), pp. 25–6.

27. See Chapter 11 by Kim in this volume; Campbell, 'Introduction', p. 15.

28. Lasker, *Human Bondage in Southeast Asia*, p. 151.

29. Ibid., p. 138.

30. Boomgaard, 'Human Capital'.

31. See Chapter 7 by Matthew Hopper in this volume; Bok-rae Kim, '*Nobi*: A Korean System of Slavery', in Campbell (ed.), *The Structure of Slavery*, pp. 155–68; Reid, 'Introduction', p. 12.

32. Lasker, *Human Bondage in Southeast Asia*, p. 151; Reid, 'Introduction', p. 12.

33. Lerner, 'Women and Slavery', pp. 184–5.

34. T. Nelson, 'Slavery in Medieval Japan', *Monumenta Nipponica*, 59:4 (2004), pp. 463–92, on pp. 475–6.

35. Ibid., p. 485.

36. P. E. Lovejoy, *Transformations in Slavery. A History of Slavery in Africa* (Cambridge: Cambridge University Press, 2000), pp. 13–14; J.-G. Deutsch, 'Notes on the Rise of Slavery and Social Change in Unyamwezi, c. 1860–1900', in H. Médard and S. Doyle

(eds), *Slavery in the Great Lake Region of East Africa* (Oxford: James Currey, 2007), p. 89.

37. Chapter 2 by Edward A. Alpers in this volume.
38. Lovejoy, 'Pawnship and Seizure for Debt'.
39. Schottenhammer, 'Slaves and Forms of Slavery', pp. 145, 149.
40. Watson, 'Transactions in People', pp. 227–30; and Chapters 3 and 11 of this volume.
41. Boomgaard, 'Human Capital'.
42. John Foreman (1899), cited in Lasker, *Human Bondage in Southeast Asia*, p. 131.
43. Watson, 'Transactions in People', pp. 227–30; see also Chapter 11 of this volume.
44. See Chapter 1 by William Gervase Clarence-Smith in this volume.
45. See Matthew Hopper's and Alessandro Stanziani's chapters in this volume.
46. R. Brunschvig, ''Abd', in H. A. R. Gibb, *Encyclopedia of Islam,* 12 vols (Leiden: Brill, 1960), vol. 1, pp. 24–40.
47. Lovejoy, 'Pawnship and Seizure for Debt'.
48. See Chapter 1 by Clarence-Smith.
49. See, for example, J. Batou, 'Muhammad-'Ali's Egypt: A Command Economy in the 19th Century?', in *J. Batou (ed.), Between Development and Underdevelopment. The Precocious Attempts at Industrialization of the Periphery (1800–1870)* (Genève: Droz, 1991), pp. 181–218; Campbell, *An Economic History of Imperial Madagascar*; A. Feuerwerker, *China's Early Industrialization: Sheng Hsuan-huai (1844–1916) and Mandarin Enterprise* (Cambridge, MA: Harvard University Press, 1958).
50. G. Campbell, 'Servitude and the Changing Face of Demand for Labour in the Indian Ocean World, c. 1800–1900', paper given at the international conference on 'Slavery and the Slave Trades in the Indian Ocean and Arab Worlds: Global Connections and Disconnections', Yale University, 7–8 November 2008.
51. S. Guha, 'The Population History of South Asia from the Seventeenth to the Twentieth Centuries: An Exploration', in C. Liu, T.-j. Liu, J. Lee, D. S. Reher, O. Saito and W. Feng (eds), *Asian Population History* (Oxford: Oxford University Press, 2001), pp. 63–78, on p. 74.
52. D. D. Cordell and J. W. Gregory (eds), *African Population and Capitalism: Historical Perspectives* (Boulder, CO: Westview Press, 1987). For Madagascar, see Campbell, 'The State and Pre-Colonial Demographic History', pp. 415–45.
53. P. Manning, 'The Slave Trade: The Formal Demography of a Global System', *Social Science History*, 14:2 (1990), pp. 255–79; P. Manning, *Slavery and African Life: Occidental, Oriental and African Slave Trades* (Cambridge: Cambridge University Press, 1990); M. Klein, 'Simulating the African Slave Trade', *Canadian Journal of African Studies*, 28:2 (1994), pp. 296–9.
54. J. Chretien, 'Demography and Ecology in East Africa at the End of the Nineteenth Century: An Exceptional Crisis?', *Cahiers d'Etudes africaines*, 27 (1987), pp. 43–59, 225; Y.-G. Paillard, 'Les recherches démographiques sur Madagascar au début de l'époque coloniale et les documents de 'l'AMI'', *Cahiers d'Études Africaines*, 27 (1987), pp. 17–42; See also R. Austen, *African Economic History* (London: James Currey and Heinemann, 1987), p. 67.
55. Campbell, 'Servitude and the Changing Face of Demand for Labour'.
56. H. E. Landsberg, 'Past Climates from Unexploited Written Sources', in R. I. Rotberg and T. K. Rabb (eds), *Climate and History* (Princeton, NJ: Princeton University Press, 1981), pp. 61–2.

57. J. Gribben and H. H. Lamb, 'Climatic Change in Historical Times', in J. Gribben (ed.), *Climatic Change* (Cambridge: Cambridge University Press, 1978), p. 71.

58. W. S. Atwell, 'Volcanism and Short-term Climatic Change in East Asian and World History, c. 1200–1699', *Journal of World History*, 12:1 (2001), pp. 29–98, on pp. 31–40; C. Gudmundson, 'El Niño and Climate Prediction', in A. M. Babkina (ed.), *El Niño. Overview and Bibliography* (New York: Nova Science, 2003), pp. 5–28.

59. See Chapters 2, 10 and 11 in this volume; see also L. C. Hirata, 'Free, Indentured, Enslaved: Chinese Prostitutes in Nineteenth-Century. America', *Signs*, 5:1 (1979), p. 4; J. L. Dull (ed.), *Han Social Structure* (Seattle, WA: University of Washington Press, 1972), p. 110; F. Morton, 'Small Change. Children in the Nineteenth-Century East African Slave Trade', in G. Campbell, S. Miers and J. C. Miller (eds), *Children in Slavery Through the Ages* (Athens, OH: Ohio University Press, 2009), p. 59.

60. W. H. McNeill, *Plagues and Peoples* (New York: Anchor Books, 1976), pp. 231–4.

61. See, for example, Campbell, 'The State and Pre-Colonial Demographic History', pp. 415–45.

62. Campbell, 'Servitude and the Changing Face of Demand for Labour'.

63. N. Worden, 'Indian Ocean Slavery and its Demise in the Cape Colony', in G. Campbell (ed.), *Abolition and its Aftermath in Indian Ocean Africa and Asia* (London: Routledge, 2005), pp. 29–49.

64. W. G. Clarence-Smith (ed.), *The Economics of the Indian Ocean Slave Trade in the Nineteenth Century* (London: Frank Cass, 1989), pp. 4–5.

65. R. A. Austen, 'The 19th Century Islamic Slave Trade from East Africa (Swahili and Red Sea Coasts): A Tentative Census', in Clarence-Smith (ed.), *The Economics of the Indian Ocean Slave Trade*, pp. 29, 31, 33; A. Sheriff, *Slaves, Spices & Ivory in Zanzibar* (London: James Currey, 1987), p. 226; Campbell, *An Economic History of Imperial Madagascar*, pp. 55–6, 238; E. A. Alpers, *Ivory and Slaves in East Central Africa: Changing Patterns of International Trade to the Later 19th Century* (Berkeley, CA: University of California Press, 1975), pp. 151, 185–7.

66. See, for example, Campbell, 'Introduction: Abolition and Its Aftermath in the Indian Ocean World', in Campbell (ed.), *Abolition and its Aftermath*; and chapter by James Warren in this volume.

67. C. Anderson, 'The Bel Ombre Rebellion: Indian Convicts in Mauritius, 1815–53', in Campbell (ed.), *Abolition and its Aftermath*, pp. 50–65; see also S. P. Oliver, 'Sir Robert Townsend Farquhar and the Malagasy Slave Trade', *Antananarivo Annual and Madagascar Magazine*, 15 (1891), pp. 319–21.

68. E. Balfour, *The Cyclopædia of India and of Eastern and Southern Asia: Commercial, Industrial and Scientific, Products of the Mineral, Vegetable, and Animal Kingdoms, Useful Arts and Manufactures*, 3 vols (London: Bernard Quaritch, 1885), vol. 3, p. 674.

69. O. A. Eno, 'The Abolition of Slavery and the Aftermath Stigma: The Case of the Bantu/Jareer People on the Benadir Coast of Southern Somalia', in Campbell (ed.), *Abolition and its Aftermath*, pp. 83–9.

70. S. Miers, 'Slavery and the Slave Trade in Saudi Arabia and the Arab States on the Persian Gulf, 1921–63', in Campbell (ed.), *Abolition and its Aftermath*, pp. 120–36; see also I. Kopytoff and S. Miers, 'African "Slavery" as an Institution of Marginality', in I. Kopytoff and S. Miers (eds), *Slavery in Africa. Historical and Anthropological Perspectives* (Madison, WI: University of Wisconsin Press, 1977), p. 72; S. Miers and M. A. Klein, 'Introduction', in S. Miers and M. A. Klein (eds), *Slavery and Colonial Rule in Africa* (London: Frank Cass, 1999), pp. 1–2, 4–5.

71. Campbell, 'Servitude and the Changing Face of Demand for Labour'.
72. W. G. Clarence-Smith, 'Islam and the Abolition of the Slave Trade and Slavery in the Indian Ocean', in Campbell (ed.), *Abolition and its Aftermath*, pp. 137–49; M. Salman, 'The Meaning of Slavery: The Genealogy of "an Insult to the American Government and to the Filipino People"', in Campbell (ed.), *Abolition and its Aftermath*, pp. 180–97.
73. See Kim's Chapter 11.
74. M. Klein, 'The Emancipation of Slaves in the Indian Ocean', in Campbell (ed.), *Abolition and its Aftermath*, p. 206.
75. Robinson to Hunter, Tamatave, 28 June 1877, cited in G. Campbell, 'Unfree Labour and the Significance of Abolition in Madagascar, c. 1825–97', in Campbell (ed.), *Abolition and its Aftermath*, p. 75, and see also 65–82.
76. Chapter 3 by Campbell; Campbell, *An Economic History of Imperial Madagascar*; K. Fahmy, *All the Pasha's Men. Mehmed Ali, His Army and the Making of Modern Egypt* (Cambridge: Cambridge University Press, 1997); A. L. Al-Sayyid Marsot, *Egypt in the Reign of Muhammad Ali* (Cambridge: Cambridge University Press, 1990).
77. See, for example, Chapters 3 and 11 in this volume.
78. See Chapter 7 by Hopper in this volume; Boomgaard, 'Human Capital'; K. Delaye, 'Slavery and Colonial Representations in Indochina from the Second Half of the Nineteenth to the Early Twentieth Centuries', in G. Campbell (ed.), *The Structure of Slavery in Indian Ocean Africa and Asia* (London: Frank Cass, 2004), pp. 129–42; Schottenhammer, 'Slaves and Forms of Slavery'.
79. U. Patnaik, 'Introduction', in U. Patnaik and M. Dingwaney (eds), *Chains of Servitude, Bondage and Slavery in India* (Hyderabad: Sangam Books, 1985), pp. 29–31.
80. Chapter 4 by Susan Newton-King in this volume.
81. S. Evers, 'Solidarity and Antagonism in Migrant Societies on the Southern Highlands', in F. Rajaoson (ed.), *Fanandevozana ou Esclavage* (Antananarivo: Université d'Antananarivo, 1996), pp. 565–71; S. Evers, *Constructing History, Culture and Inequality: The Betsileo in the Extreme Southern Highlands of Madagascar* (Leiden: Brill, 2002).
82. See, for example, Chapter 6 by Warren; Campbell, *An Economic History of Imperial Madagascar*, pp. 42–3; R. C. Davis, *Christian Slaves, Muslim Masters: White Slavery in the Mediterranean, the Barbary Coast and Italy, 1500–1800* (Basingstoke: Palgrave Macmillan, 2003).
83. G. Campbell, 'Children and Slavery in the New World: A Review', *Slavery & Abolition*, 27:2 (2006), pp. 261–86.
84. See, for example, W. G. Clarence-Smith, 'The Redemption of Child Slaves by Christian Missionaries in Central Africa, 1878–1914', in G. Campbell, S. Miers and J. C. Miller (eds), *Child Slaves in the Modern World* (Athens, OH: Ohio University Press, 2011), pp. 173–90.
85. Lasker, *Human Bondage in Southeast Asia*, p. 38.
86. Warren's Chapter 6 in this volume.
87. N. Worden, E. van Heyningen and V. Bickford-Smith, *Cape Town. The Making of a City* (Cape Town: David Philip, 2004), p. 109.
88. Anderson, 'Bel Ombre Rebellion'.
89. C. Anderson, *Legible Bodies: Race, Criminality and Colonialism in South Asia* (Oxford: Berg Publishers, 2004).
90. N. Worden, 'Indian Ocean Slavery and its Demise'; P. Shirodkar, 'India and Mozambique: Centuries Old Interaction', *Purabhilekh-Puratatva*, 6:1 (1988), p. 51.
91. Anderson, 'Bel Ombre Rebellion'.

92. Campbell, 'Unfree Labour'.
93. See Alessandro Stanziani's Introduction to this collection.
94. Worden, 'Indian Ocean Slavery and its Demise'.
95. Ibid.; see also M. Carter, *Servants, Sidars and Settlers. Indians in Mauritius, 1834–1874* (Delhi: Oxford University Press, 1995).
96. Campbell, 'Servitude and the Changing Face of Demand for Labour'.
97. On Indian indentured labour, see S. B. Mookherrji, *The Indenture System in Mauritius, 1837–1915* (Calcutta: K.L. Mukhopadhyay, 1962); H. Tinker, *A New System of Slavery: The Export of Indian Labour Overseas, 1830–1920* (London, Oxford University Press, 1974); Carter, *Servants, Sirdars and Settlers*; H. Gerbeau, 'Engagés and Coolies on Réunion Island, Slavery's Masks and Freedom's Constraints', in P. C. Emmer (ed.), *Colonialism and Migration: Indentured Labour Before and After Slavery* (Dordrecht: Martinus Nijhoff, 1986), pp. 209–36; K. Dasgupta, 'Plantation Labour in the Brahmaputra Valley: Regional Enclaves in a Colonial Context', in Campbell (ed.), *Abolition and its Aftermath*, pp. 169–79.
98. A. D. Blue, 'Chinese Emigration and the Deck Passenger Trade', *Journal of the Hong Kong Branch of the Royal Asiatic Society*, 10 (1970), pp. 79–93, on pp. 80, 83.
99. A. McKeown, 'Global Chinese Migration, 1850–1940', paper presented at ISSCO V, Helsignor, Denmark, 10–13 May 2004. For the traditional view, see Blue, 'Chinese Emigration', pp. 79–93; P. Campbell, *Chinese Coolie Emigration to Countries within the British Empire: To Countries within the British Empire* (London: Routledge, 1971).
100. Chapter 10 by Ei Murakami, this volume.
101. M. Jaschok and S. Miers, 'Women in the Chinese Patriarchal System: Submission, Servitude, Escape and Collusion', in M. Jascok and S. Miers (eds), *Women and Chinese Patriarchy. Submission, Servitude and Escape* (London and New Jersey: Zed Books, 1994), pp. 19–20; J. F. Warren, 'Chinese Prostitution in Singapore: Recruitment and Brothel Organisation', in Jascok and Miers (eds), *Women and Chinese Patriarchy*, pp. 77–105.
102. I. Chatterjee, 'Abolition by Denial: The South Asian Example', in Campbell (ed.), *Abolition and its Aftermath*, pp. 150–68; Klein, 'Emancipation of Slaves'; Salman, 'Meaning of Slavery'.
103. Delaye, 'Slavery and Colonial Representations'; A. Turton, 'Violent Capture of People for Exchange on Karen-Thai Borders in the 1830s', in Campbell (ed.), *The Structure of Slavery in Indian Ocean Africa and Asia*, pp. 69–82; Klein, 'Introduction', p. 23.
104. Lovejoy, *Transformations in Slavery*, pp. 13–14; Miers and Klein, 'Introduction', p. 12.
105. S. Miers, *Slavery in the Twentieth Century* (Walnut Creek, CA: Altmira Press, 2003), p. 89.
106. J. Breman, *Labour Bondage in West India* (Oxford and New Delhi: Oxford University Press, 2007), p. 68.
107. A. Thorner and D. Thorner, *Land and Labour in India* (Bombay and London: Asia Publishing House, 1962), pp. 61–4.
108. Chapter 8 by Isabelle Guérin, this volume.
109. Miers, *Slavery in the Twentieth Century*, p. 423.

1 Clarence-Smith, 'Debt and the Coercion of Labour in the Islamic Legal Tradition'

1. W. G. Clarence-Smith, *Islam and the Abolition of Slavery* (London: Hurst, 2006).
2. F. Rosenthal, *The Muslim Conception of Freedom Prior to the Nineteenth Century* (Leiden: E. J. Brill, 1960), pp. 77–8.
3. Ibid., pp. 79–80; I. Lapidus, *Muslim Cities in the Later Middle Ages*, 2nd edn (Cambridge: Cambridge University Press, 1984), p. 64.
4. X. de Planhol, *L'Islam et la mer: la mosquée et le matelot, VIIe–XXe siècle* (Paris: Perrin, 2000), pp. 56–9, 220–1.
5. K. M. Cuno, *The Pasha's Peasants: Land, Society and Economy in Lower Egypt, 1740–1858* (Cambridge: Cambridge University Press, 1992), pp. 116, 122–5.
6. J. T. Chalcrat, *The Striking Cabbies of Cairo and Other Stories: Crafts and Guilds in Egypt, 1863–1914* (Albany, NY: State University of New York Press, 2004), pp. 85, 149.
7. A. Jaimoukha, *The Circassians: A Handbook* (New York: Palgrave, 2001), pp. 160, 163.
8. H.-G. Migeod, *Die persische Gesellschaft unter Nasiru'd-Din Sah, 1848–1896* (Berlin: Klaus Schwarz, 1990), p. 3404.
9. W. Adam, *The Law and Custom of Slavery in British India* (Boston, MA: Weeks, Jordan and Co., 1840), p. 171; B. Hjejle, *Slavery and Agricultural Bondage in South India in the Nineteenth Century* (Copenhagen: Scandinavian Institute of Asian Studies, 1967), p. 86.
10. V. Azarya, *Aristocrats Facing Change: The Fulbe in Guinea, Nigeria and Cameroon* (Chicago, IL: University of Chicago Press, 1978), p. 35; A. Bourgeot, 'Rapports esclavagistes et conditions d'affranchissement chez les Imuhag, Twarg Kel Ahaggar', in C. Meillassoux (ed.), *L'esclavage en Afrique précoloniale* (Paris: François Maspéro, 1975), pp. 92–3; J.-P. Olivier de Sardan, 'Captifs ruraux et esclaves impériaux du Songhay', in Meillassoux (ed.), *L'esclavage en Afrique précoloniale*, pp. 112–13, 119–22.
11. I. Schneider, *Kinderverkauf und Schuldknechtschaft: Untersuchungen zur frühen Phase des islamischen Rechts* (Stuttgart: Deutsche Morgenländische Gesellschaft, 1999) provides by far the most detailed treatment of this question. See also A. A. Elwahed, *Contribution à une théorie sociologique de l'esclavage* (Paris: Éditions Albert Mechelinck, 1931), pp. 120–2.
12. R. Brunschvig, ''Abd', in H. A. R. Gibb, *Encyclopedia of Islam*, 12 vols (Leiden: Brill, 1960), vol. 1, pp. 24–40; B. Lewis, *Race and Slavery in the Middle East, An Historical Enquiry* (New York: Oxford University Press, 1990), p. 6.
13. Schneider, *Kinderverkauf und Schuldknechtschaft*, pp. 13–14.
14. S. N. H. Naqvi, *Islam, Economics, and Society* (London: Kegan Paul, 1994), chs 9–11.
15. A. A. Batran, 'The *'ulama* of Fas, M. Isma'il and the Issue of the Haratin of Fas', in J. R. Willis (ed.), *Slaves and Slavery in Muslim Africa*, 2 vols (London: Frank Cass, 1985), vol. 2, pp. 13–14.
16. W. G. Clarence-Smith, 'Hadrami Entrepreneurs in the Malay World, c. 1750 to c. 1940', in U. Freitag and W. G. Clarence-Smith (eds), *Hadhrami Traders, Scholars and Statesmen in the Indian Ocean, 1750s–1960s* (Leiden: Brill, 1997), pp. 301–2.
17. M. G. S. Hodgson, *The Venture of Islam: Conscience and History in a World Civilization*, 3 vols (Chicago, IL: University of Chicago Press, 1974), vol. 2, pp. 135–9.
18. Schneider, *Kinderverkauf und Schuldknechtschaft*, pp. 52–3.
19. Clarence-Smith, *Islam and the Abolition of Slavery*, ch. 7.

20. M. Ennaji, *Serving the Master: Slavery and Society in Nineteenth Century Morocco* (Basingstoke: Macmillan, 1999), p. 121; J. Hunwick, 'Islamic Law and Polemics over Race and Slavery in North and West Africa, Sixteenth to Nineteenth Century', *Princeton Papers, Interdisciplinary Journal of Middle Eastern Studies*, 7 (1999), pp. 60–3; J. Hunwick and E. T. Powell, *The African Diaspora in the Mediterranean Lands of Islam* (Princeton, NJ: Markus Wiener, 2002), pp. 44–8; J. R. Willis, 'Islamic Africa: Reflections on the Servile Estate', *Studia Islamica*, 52 (1980), pp. 193–4, 196; J. R. Willis, 'Introduction: The Ideology of Enslavement in Islam', in J. R. Willis (ed.), *Slaves and Slavery in Muslim Africa*, 2 vols (London: Frank Cass, 1985), vol. 1, pp. 7–9.

21. Hodgson, *The Venture of Islam*, vol. 1, p. 57; vol. 2, p. 10; A. Christelow, *Thus Ruled Emir Abbas: Selected Cases from the Records of the Emir of Kano's Judicial Council* (East Lansing, MI: Michigan State University, 1994), pp. 8–9.

22. M. B. Olcott, *The Kazakhs* (Stanford, CA: Stanford University Press, 1987), p. 19.

23. A. M. Ali, *Alam pikiran Islam modern di Indonesia* (Modern Islamic Thought in Indonesia) (Jogjakarta: Jajasan Nida, 1969), p. 29.

24. C. Snouck Hurgronje, *The Achehnese*, 2 vols (Leiden: E. J. Brill, 1906), vol. 1, pp. 153, 168.

25. Hodgson, *The Venture of Islam*, vol. 2, p. 10.

26. Lewis, *Race and Slavery in the Middle East, An Historical Enquiry*, p. 6.

27. D. R. Chanana, *Slavery in Ancient India, As Depicted in Pali and Sanskrit Texts* (New Delhi: Peoples Publishing House, 1960); Y. Bongert, 'Réflexions sur le problème de l'esclavage dans l'Inde ancienne, à propos de quelques ouvrages récents', *Bulletin de l'École Française d'Extrême-Orient*, 51:1 (1963), pp. 143–94; A. K. K. Ramachandran Nair, *Slavery in Kerala* (Delhi: Mittal Publications, 1986).

28. I. Mabbett, 'Buddhism and Freedom', in D. Kelly and A. Reid (eds), *Asian Freedoms: The Idea of Freedom in East and Southeast Asia* (Cambridge: Cambridge University Press, 1998), pp. 27, 29.

29. A. Turton, 'Thai Institutions of Slavery', in J. L. Watson (ed.), *Asian and African Systems of Slavery* (Oxford: Basil Blackwell, 1980), pp. 251–92; D. Feeny, 'The Demise of Corvée and Slavery in Thailand, 1782–1913', in M. Klein (ed.), *Breaking the Chains: Slavery, Bondage and Emancipation in Modern Africa and Asia* (Madison, WI: University of Wisconsin Press, 1993), pp. 88–90.

30. A. Reid, '"Closed" and "Open" Slave Systems in Pre-Colonial Southeast Asia', in A. Reid (ed.), *Slavery, Bondage and Dependency in Southeast Asia* (Saint Lucia: University of Queensland Press, 1983), pp. 160–1.

31. L. F. F. R. Thomaz, 'A escravatura em Malaca no século XVI', *Studia*, 53 (1994), pp. 261, 285–6, 292; V. Matheson and M. B. Hooker, 'Slavery in the Malay Texts: Categories of Dependency and Compensation', in Reid (ed.), *Slavery, Bondage and Dependency in Southeast Asia*, pp. 184–6.

32. J. F. Warren, *The Sulu Zone, 1768–1898: The Dynamics of External Trade, Slavery and Ethnicity in the Transformation of a Southeast Asian Maritime State* (Singapore: Singapore University Press, 1981), pp. 215–17.

33. Reid, '"Closed" and "Open" Slave Systems in Pre-Colonial Southeast Asia', pp. 160–1.

34. W. E. Maxwell, 'The Law Relating to Slavery Among the Malays', *Journal of the Straits Branch of the Royal Asiatic Society*, 22 (1890), pp. 247–8; M. bin Mat, 'The Passing of Slavery in East Pahang', *Malayan Historical Journal*, 1:1 (1954), pp. 8–10; J. M. Gullick, *Indigenous Political Systems of Western Malaya* (London: Athlone, 1958), pp. 101–5; H. C. Clifford, *Malayan Monochromes* (London: John Murray, 1913), pp. 121–5; W. Line-

han, *A History of Pahang* (Kuala Lumpur: Malaysian Branch of the Royal Asiatic Society, 1973), pp. 128–9; A. Thosibo, *Historiografi perbudakan; sejarah perbudakan di Sulawesi Selatan abad XIX* (Magelang: Indonesiatera, 2002), p. 97; D. C. Worcester, *Slavery and Peonage in the Philippine Islands* (Manila: Bureau of Printing, 1913), p. 5.

35. G. Loyré-de-Hauteclocque, *À la recherche de l'Islam philippin; la communauté maranao* (Paris: L'Harmattan, 1989), pp. 145–6, 151.

36. I. L. Bird, *The Golden Chersonese and the Way Thither* (London: John Murray, 1883), pp. 370–5.

37. H. Djajadiningrat, 'Toepassing van het Mohammedaanischen slavenrecht in de Lampoengs', in *Feestbundel uitgegeven door het Koninklijk Bataviaasch Genootschap van Kunsten en Wetenschappen*, 2 vols (Weltevreden: G. Kolff, 1929), vol. 1, pp. 87–92.

38. T. Bigalke, 'Dynamics of the Torajan Slave Trade in South Sulawesi', in Reid (ed.), *Slavery, Bondage and Dependency in Southeast Asia*, p. 347.

39. R. Winstedt, *The Malays, A Cultural History* (Singapore: Tham Seong Chee, 1981), pp. 54–5.

40. P. F. S. Loh, *The Malay States, 1877–1895, Political Change and Social Policy* (Kuala Lumpur: Oxford University Press, 1969), pp. 189–90.

41. A. Reid, 'The Decline of Slavery in Nineteenth Century Indonesia', in M. A. Klein (ed.), *Breaking the Chains: Slavery, Bondage and Emancipation in Modern Africa and Asia* (Madison, WI: University of Wisconsin Press, 1993), pp. 64–82.

42. M. Yegar, 'The Abolition of Servitude in British Malaya: An Historical Analysis', *Israel Yearbook on Human Rights*, 5 (1975), pp. 202–13; Loh, *The Malay States, 1877–1895, Political Change and Social Policy*, pp. 184–6; K. Endicott, 'The Effects of Slave Raiding on the Aborigines of the Malay Peninsula', in Reid (ed.), *Slavery, Bondage and Dependency in Southeast Asia*, p. 236; B. Lasker, *Human Bondage in Southeast Asia* (Chapel Hill, NC: University of North Carolina Press, 1950), pp. 49–50, 55–6.

43. M. Hoadley, 'Slavery, Bondage and Dependency in Pre-Colonial Java: The Cirebon-Priangan Region, 1700', in Reid (ed.), *Slavery, Bondage and Dependency in Southeast Asia*, p. 99.

44. M. C. Hoadley and M. B. Hooker, *An Introduction to Javanese Law: A Translation of and Commentary on the Agama* (Tucson, AZ: University of Arizona Press, 1981).

45. W. G. Clarence-Smith, 'Southeast Asia and China, c. 1800 to c. 1910', in F. Robinson (ed.), *The New Cambridge History of Islam*, 6 vols (Cambridge: Cambridge University Press, 2010), vol. 5: The Islamic World in the Age of Western Dominance, p. 240.

46. D. H. Burger, *Sociologisch-economische geschiedenis van Indonesia*, 2 vols (Amsterdam: Koninklijk Instituut voor de Tropen, 1975), vol. 1, p. 58.

47. J. S. Trimingham, *Islam in West Africa* (Oxford: Clarendon Press, 1959), pp. 30, 134–5, 147.

48. H. J. Fisher, *Slavery in the History of Muslim Black Africa* (London: Hurst, 2001), p. 32.

49. J. Richardson, *Narrative of a Mission to Central Africa*, 2 vols (London: Chapman and Hall, 1853), vol. 2, p. 223.

50. P. E. Lovejoy, *Transformations in Slavery, A History of Slavery in Africa* (Cambridge: Cambridge University Press, 1983), pp. 13–14, 279; Trimingham, *Islam in West Africa*, pp. 134–5.

51. L. Harries, *Swahili Prose Texts: A Selection from the Material Collected by Carl Velten from 1893 to 1896* (London: Oxford University Press, 1965), pp. 206–7; S. Mirza and M. Strobel, *Three Swahili Women: Life Histories from Mombasa, Kenya* (Bloomington, IN: Indiana University Press, 1989), pp. 24, 39.

52. Harries, *Swahili Prose Texts,* p. 206.
53. W. Rodney, 'Jihad and Social Revolution in Futa Djalon in the Eighteenth Century', *Journal of the Historical Society of Nigeria,* 4:2 (1968), pp. 281–2; Fisher, *Slavery in the History of Muslim Black Africa,* p. 117.
54. S. Becker, *Russia's Protectorates in Central Asia: Bukhara and Khiva, 1865–1924* (Cambridge, MA: Harvard University Press, 1968), p. 200; S. Khan, 'The Development of Muslim Reformist (Jadid) Political Thought in the Emirate of Bukhara, 1870–1924, with Particular Reference to the Writings of Ahmad Donish and Abdal Rauf Fitrat' (PhD dissertation, University of London, 1998), p. 254.
55. Khan, 'The Development of Muslim Reformist (Jadid) Political Thought in the Emirate of Bukhara, 1870–1924', p. 57.
56. S.-s. H Tsai, *The Eunuchs in the Ming Dynasty* (Albany, NY: State University of New York Press, 1996), pp. 27–8; S. Mazumdar, *Sugar and Society in China: Peasants, Technology and the World Market* (Cambridge, MA: Harvard University Press, 1998), pp. 197–201; Lasker, *Human Bondage in Southeast Asia,* pp. 52–3.
57. M. Broomhall, *Islam in China, A Neglected Problem,* 2nd edn (London: Darf, 1987), p. 57; J. Anderson, *Mandalay to Momien: A Narrative of Two Expeditions to Western China, of 1868 and 1875* (London: Macmillan, 1876), pp. 228–9; M. Hartmann, *Zur Geschichte des Islams in China* (Leipzig: Wilhelm Heims, 1921), pp. 99–100.
58. M. b. A. Ibn Battuta, *Travels in Asia and Africa, 1325–1354: Selections* (London: Routledge and Kegan Paul, 1983), p. 244.
59. S. Kidwai, 'Sultans, Eunuchs and Domestics: New Forms of Bondage in Medieval India', in U. Patnaik and M. Dingwaney (eds), *Chains of   Servitude: Bondage and Slavery in India* (Madras: Sangam, 1985), pp. 188–9.
60. W. Adam, *The Law and Custom of Slavery in British India* (Boston, MA: Weeks, Jordan and Co., 1840), p. 48.
61. S. C. Levi, 'Hindus Beyond the Hindu Kush: Indians in the Central Asian Slave Trade', *Journal of the Royal Asiatic Society,* 12:3 (2002), pp. 277–88, on p. 282.
62. K. A. Nizami, *Akbar and Religion* (Delhi: Idarah-i-Adabiyat-i-Delli, 1989), pp. 106–7; K. S. Lal, *Muslim Slave System in Medieval India* (New Delhi: Aditya Prakashan, 1994), p. 73.
63. W. Knighton, *The Private Life of an Eastern King, Together with Elihu Jan's Story, or the Life of an Eastern Queen,* ed. S. B. Smith (London: Oxford University Press, 1921), p. 229; S. Moosvi, 'Domestic Service in Pre-Colonial India: Bondage, Caste and Market', in A. Fauve-Chamoux (ed.), *Domestic Service and the Formation of European Identity: Understanding the Globalization of Domestic Work, 16th–21st Centuries* (Bern and New York: Peter Lang, 2004), pp. 543–76.
64. V. Gregorian, *The Emergence of Modern Afghanistan: Politics of Reform and Modernization, 1880–1946* (Stanford, CA: Stanford University Press, 1969), pp. 34–5.
65. 'Correspondence Respecting Sir Bartle Frere's Mission to the East Coast of Africa, 1872–73', *Parliamentary Papers,* 61, C-820 (1873), p. 14.
66. Adam, *The Law and Custom of Slavery in British India,* pp. 23, 48, 67–8, 246; N. B. E. Baillie, *A Digest of Moohummudan Law,* 2nd edn (Lahore, 1957), pp. 365–6. I have been unable to find out when the *Mohit-u-Surakhsi* dates to, or who the author was. It may simply have been a translation of the Surraq Hadith, perhaps with annotations.
67. Adam, *The Law and Custom of Slavery in British India,* pp. 64–7; A. K. Chattopadhyay, *Slavery in the Bengal Presidency, 1772–1843* (London: Golden Eagle Publishing House,

1977), pp. 170–7; D. R. Banaji, *Slavery in British India* (Bombay: D. B. Taraporevala Sons & Co., 1933), pp. 243–53.

68. I. Chatterjee, *Gender, Slavery and Law in Colonial India* (New Delhi: Oxford University Press, 1999), p. 213.

69. S. Miers, *Slavery in the Twentieth Century: The Evolution of a Global Problem* (Walnut Creek, CA: AltaMira, 2003), pp. 306–7.

70. Chattopadhyay, *Slavery in the Bengal Presidency*, p. 253; Chatterjee, *Gender, Slavery and Law in Colonial India*, pp. 219–24; M. Dingwaney, 'Unredeemed Promises: The Law and Servitude', in U. Patnaik and M. Dingwaney (eds), *Chains of Servitude: Bondage and Slavery in India* (Madras: Sangam, 1985), p. 313.

71. Miers, *Slavery in the Twentieth Century: The Evolution of a Global Problem*, p. 224.

72. Dingwaney, 'Unredeemed Promises: The Law and Servitude', p. 324.

73. M. Winter, *Egyptian Society under Ottoman Rule, 1517–1798* (London: Routledge, 1992), p. 69.

74. A. Najmabadi, *The Story of the Daughters of Quchan: Gender and National Memory in Iranian History* (Syracuse, NY: Syracuse University Press, 1998).

75. J. E. Polak, *Persien, das Land und seine Bewohner*, 2 vols (Leipzig: F. A. Brockhaus, 1865), vol. 1, p. 249; Migeod, *Die persische Gesellschaft unter Nasiru'd-Din Sah*, p. 333.

76. J. Zdanowski, *Slavery in the Gulf in the First Half of the Twentieth Century: A Study Based on Records from the British Archives* (Warsaw: ASKON, 2008), pp. 152–5; M. Hopper, 'Imperialism and the Dilemma of Slavery in Eastern Arabia and the Gulf, 1873–1939', *Itinerario*, 30:3 (2006), pp. 76–94.

77. J. G. Lorimer, *Gazetteer of the Persian Gulf, Oman and Central Arabia*, 2 vols (Calcutta: Superintendent Government Printing, India, 1908–15), vol. II–2, pp. 2220, 2228, 2233.

78. Miers, *Slavery in the Twentieth Century*, pp. 266, 274 n. 61.

2 Alpers, 'Debt, Pawnship and Slavery in Nineteenth-Century East Africa'

1. Quoted in E. A. Alpers, 'The Story of Swema: Female Vulnerability in Nineteenth-Century East Africa', in C. C. Robertson and M. A. Klein (eds), *Women and Slavery in Africa* (Madison, WI: University of Wisconsin Press, 1983), p. 191.

2. Quoted in Alpers, 'The Story of Swema', p. 192.

3. M. Douglas, 'Matriliny and Pawnship in Central Africa', *Africa: Journal of the International African Institute*, 34:4 (1964), pp. 301–13.

4. Ibid., p. 302. See M. Douglas, 'Blood-Debts and Clientship among the Lele', *Journal of the Royal Anthropological Institute of Great Britain and Ireland*, 90:1 (1960), pp. 1–28.

5. Douglas, 'Matriliny and Pawnship in Central Africa', p. 303.

6. Ibid., p. 304.

7. M. Wright, *Strategies of Slaves & Women: Life-Stories from East/Central Africa* (New York and London: Lilian Barber Press and James Currey, 1993), p. 175, n. 2.

8. R. Coupland, *East Africa and Its Invaders from the Earliest Times to the Death of Seyyid Said in 1856* (Oxford: Clarendon Press, 1938), p. 17. For an extended examination of Coupland's argument, see E. A. Alpers, 'Image and Reality of Arabs in East Africa', *Journal of African Development*, 12:1 (2010), pp. 31–40.

9. A. Sheriff, *Ivory, Slaves & Spices in Zanzibar: Integration of an East African Commercial Empire into the World Economy, 1770–1873* (London: James Currey, 1987), pp. 224–31.

10. F. Cooper, *Plantation Slavery on the East Coast of Africa* (New Haven, CT and London: Yale University Press, 1977), pp. 221–3; for sex ratios in the Mascarene trade, see R. B. Allen, 'The Constant Demand of the French: The Mascarene Slave Trade and the Worlds of the Indian Ocean and Atlantic during the Eighteenth and Nineteenth Centuries', *Journal of African History*, 49:1 (2008), pp. 55–6; for those in the Gulf slave trade, see M. S. Hopper, 'The African Presence in Arabia: Slavery, the World Economy, and the African Diaspora in Eastern Arabia, 1860–1940' (PhD dissertation, UCLA, 2006).

11. J. Vansina, *Antecedents to Modern Rwanda: The Nyiginya Kingdom* (Madison, WI: University of Wisconsin Press, 2004), pp. 32, 47.

12. Vansina, *Antecedents to Modern Rwanda*, pp. 96, 158, 175, 182. The last years of Rwabugiri's reign were also marked by a series of natural calamities that stimulated the slave trade, for which see J.-P. Chrétien, 'The Slave Trade in Burundi & Rwanda at the Beginning of German Colonialism 1890–1906', in H. Médard and S. Doyle (eds), *Slavery in the Great Lakes Region of East Africa* (Oxford: James Currey, 2007), p. 223.

13. F. Morton, 'Pawning and Slavery on the Kenya Coast: The Miji Kenda Case', in P. E. Lovejoy and T. Falola (eds), *Pawnship, Slavery, and Colonialism in Africa* (Trenton, NJ and Asmara: Africa World Press, 2003), p. 239. The original publication appeared in the editors' *Pawnship in Africa: Debt Bondage in Historical Perspective* (Boulder, CO, San Francisco, CA and Oxford: Westview Press, 1994).

14. Morton, 'Pawning and Slavery on the Kenya Coast', p. 239.

15. J. Willis, *Mombasa, the Swahili, and the Making of the Mijikenda* (Oxford: Clarendon Press, 1993), p. 8, and for the complex networks of debt at the coast, pp. 68–9.

16. Morton, 'Pawning and Slavery on the Kenya Coast', pp. 240–2.

17. Willis, *Mombasa, the Swahili, and the Making of the Mijikenda*, pp. 52–3.

18. S. Mirza and M. Strobel (eds and trans.), *Three Swahili Women: Life Histories from Mombasa, Kenya* (Bloomington and Indianapolis, IN: Indiana University Press, 1989), p. 39.

19. Ibid., pp. 21, 24, quoted on p. 34.

20. J. W. T. Allen (ed. and trans.), *The Customs of the Swahili People. The Desturi za Waswahili of Mtoro bin Mwinyi Bakari and Other Swahili Persons* (Berkeley, Los Angeles, CA and London: University of California Press, 1981), pp. 169–70.

21. C. Velten, *Desturi za Wasuaheli na khabari za desturi za sheri'a za Wasuaheli* (Göttingen: Vandenhoef & Ruprecht, 1905), pp. 253–4. See also C. Sacleux, *Dictionnarie Swahili-Français* (Paris: Institut d'Ethnologie, 1939), p. 770. For modern uses of the verb *–weka* (keep, store up, set, put, place) and the noun *rahani* (pawn, pledge, debt, security, mortgage), see the Kamusi Project, online at http://www.kamusi.org [accessed 15 February 2012].

22. Wright, *Strategies of Slaves & Women*, p. 133; L. W. Swantz, *The Zaramo of Tanzania: An Ethnographic Study* (Dar es Salaam: Nordic Tanganyika Project, 1965), p. 21; interview with Mzee Idi Chadoma, Morogoro, 16 September 1972; A. T. Culwick and G. M. Culwick, *Ubena of the Rivers* (London: George Allen & Unwin, 1935), pp. 133, 209–10.

23. Allen, *The Customs of the Swahili People*, p. 176.

24. J. Glassman, *Feasts and Riot: Revelry, Rebellion and Popular Consciousness on the Swahili Coast, 1856–1888* (Portsmouth, NH: Heinemann, 1995), p. 73.

25. W. H. Whiteley (trans.), *Maisha ya Hamed bin Muhammad el Murjebi yaani Tippu Tip kwa meneno yake mwenyewe* (Kampala, Nairobi and Dar es Salaam: East African Literaturee Bureau, 1966), p. 47, §66.

26. Glassman, *Feasts and Riot*, pp. 87, 89; see also Cooper, *Plantation Slavery on the East Coast of Africa*, p. 188.

27. For Zaramo relations with Bagamoyo, see W. T. Brown, 'A Pre-Colonial History of Bagamoyo: Aspects of the Growth of an East African Coastal Town' (PhD dissertation, Boston University, 1971); for Wabagamoyo, see S. Fabian, 'Wabagamoyo: Redefining Identity in a Swahili Town, 1860s–1960s' (PhD dissertation, Dalhousie University, 2007).

28. For Zaramo famines, see R. Mwaruka, *Masimulizi Juu ya Uzaramo* (London: Macmillan, 1965), pp. 107–14. The first of these that Mwaruka records occurred during the era of Arab domination (*katika enzi ya Waarabu*) and was called Golola or Msuweni (p. 107).

29. Allen, *The Customs of the Swahili People*, p. 170.

30. A. C. Madan (ed. and trans.), *Kiungani; or, Story and History from Central Africa. Written by Boys in the Schools of the Universities' Mission to Central Africa* (London: George Bell and Sons, 1887), pp. 60–1.

31. Ibid., pp. 61–2.

32. See, i.a., interviews with Mzee Ali Selimani Meronge, Morogoro, 28 September 1972; Elders of Mtamba wa Kinole, 18 October 1972; Mzee Salezi b. Lusogo (Umbeumbe III), Dinilo, Mgeta, 19 October 1972; Mzee Shabani Kampen, Mlali, 9 November 1972; Mzee Mbrisho Kipindula and Mzee Ramadhani Mberwa, Wami Station, 14 November 1972; Elders of Mdaula, 19 November 1972; Mzee Anatoli Chamlungu and Mzee Geuza Kibungo, Chalinze, 21 November 1972; Elders of Kolero, 2 December 1972.

33. Zanzibar National Archive, AA 3/11.

34. C. H. Ambler, *Kenyan Communities in the Age of Imperialism: The Central Region in the Late Nineteenth Century* (New Haven, CT and London: Yale University Press, 1988), pp. 61–2, 70–1.

35. Ambler, *Kenyan Communities in the Age of Imperialism*, pp. 100, 132–4.

36. H. S. K. Mwaniki, *Embu Historical Texts* (Kampala, Nairobi and Dar es Salaam: East African Literature Bureau, 1974), pp. 12, 29, 53, 139, 167, 238, 304.

37. S. J. Rockel, *Carriers of Culture: Labor on the Road in Nineteenth-Century East Africa* (Portsmouth, NH: Heinemann, 2006).

38. J.-G. Deutsch, 'Notes on the Rise of Slavery & Social Change in Unyamwezi c. 1860–1900', in Médard and Doyle (eds), *Slavery in the Great Lakes Region of East Africa* (Oxford: James Currey, 2007), p. 89.

39. Deutsch, 'Notes on the Rise of Slavery & Social Change in Unyamwezi', p. 90, and 106–7, n. 122.

40. Madan, *Kiungani*, pp. 36–7.

41. Ibid., pp. 37–8.

42. Ibid., pp. 39–40.

43. Wright, *Strategies of Slaves & Women*, pp. 30, 52–4, also 139, 141.

44. N. Q. King, K. Fiedler and G. White (eds), *Robin Lamburn – From a Missionary's Notebook: The Yao of Tunduru and other Essays* (Saarbrückem and Fort Lauderdale, FL: Verlag Breitenbach Publishers, 1991), pp. 129–30; see H. Waller, *The Last Journals of David Livingstone in Central Africa* (New York: Harper & Brothers, 1875), pp. 66–8.

45. King, Fiedler and White, *Robin Lamburn – From a Missionary's Notebook*, p. 127, n. 1.

46. Ibid., pp. 128–9.

47. J. L. Giblin, 'Pawning, Politics and Matriliny in Northeastern Tanzania', in P. E. Lovejoy and T. Falola (eds), *Pawnship, Slavery and Colonialism in Africa* (Trenton, NJ and Asmara: Africa World Press, 2003), p. 265.

48. Giblin, 'Pawning, Politics and Matriliny in Northeastern Tanzania', p. 168.

49. Médard and Doyle (eds), *Slavery in the Great Lakes Region of East Africa*.
50. D. Schoenbrun, 'Violence, Marginality, Scorn & Honour: Language Evidence of Slavery to the Eighteenth Century', in Médard and Doyle (eds), *Slavery in the Great Lakes Region of East Africa*, pp. 38–75, especially 52, 54, 61 n. 4.2, 74 n. 84.
51. H. Médard, *Le royaume du Buganda au XIXᵉ siècle* (Paris, Karthala and Nairobi: IFRA, 2007), p. 402.
52. M. W. Tuck, 'Women's Experience of Enslavement & Slavery in Late Nineteenth- & Early Twentieth-Century Uganda', in Médard and Doyle (eds), *Slavery in the Great Lakes Region of East Africa*, pp. 174–88, on pp. 175–6, 183. See also H. Médard, 'Introduction', in Médard and Doyle (eds), *Slavery in the Great Lakes Region of East Africa*, p. 30. For Bunyoro, see S. Doyle, 'Bunyoro & the Demography of Slavery Debate: Fertility, Kinship & Assimilation', in Médard and Doyle (eds), *Slavery in the Great Lakes Region of East Africa*, p. 239; for the kingdom of Nkore in south-western Uganda, see E. A. Steinhart, 'Slavery & Other Forms of Social Oppression in Ankole 1890–1940', in Médard and Doyle (eds), *Slavery in the Great Lakes Region of East Africa*, p. 196.
53. Madan, *Kiungani*, p. 105.

3 Campbell, 'Debt and Slavery in Imperial Madagascar, 1790–1861'

1. R. P. Callet, *Histoire des Rois* (Tananarive: Imprimerie Nationale, 1974) (hereafter HdR), pp. 778–9, 884.
2. Le Sage, 'Mission to Madagascar', 1816, Public Record Office (Colonial Office), Kew, London (hereafter PRO.CO) 167/34; Raombana, 'Histoires', 1853, pp. 19, 24, Académie Malgache, Tsimbazaza, Antananarivo (hereafter AAM); S. P. Oliver, *Madagascar. An Historical and Descriptive Account of the Island and its Former Dependencies*, 2 vols (London: Macmillan, 1886), vol. 2, pp. 205, 209; L. Dahle, 'The Influence of the Arabs on the Malagasy Language: As a Test of Their Contribution to Malagasy Civilisation and Superstition', *Antananarivo Annual and Madagascar Magazine*, 2 (1876), pp. 84, 105–13; P. Taix, 'Extrait du diaire de Tamatave', 14 January 1885, in P. Taix, 'Tamatave: notes historiques', 1908, Archives historiques de la Vice-Province Société de Jésus de Madagascar, Antananariv; J. Chauvicourt and S. Chauvicourt, 'Les premières monnaies de Madagascar', *Bulletin de Madagascar*, 261 (1968), pp. 146–52; E. A. Alpers, *The French Slave Trade* (Dar es Salaam: Historical Association of Tanzania, 1967), pp. 87, 101–4; L. Sundström, *The Exchange Economy of Pre-Colonial Tropical Africa* (London: C. Hurst, 1974), pp. 96–8; M. Rasoamiaramanana, 'Aspects économiques et sociaux de la vie à Majunga entre 1862 et 1881' (PhD dissertation, Université de Madagascar, 1973), p. 55; G. Campbell, 'The Role of the London Missionary Society in the Rise of the Merina Empire, 1810–1861' (PhD dissertation, University of Wales, 1985), pp. 66–7; for an Ethiopian comparison, see R. Pankhurst, *Economic History of Ethiopia, 1800–1935* (Addis Ababa: Haile Selassie I University Press, 1968), pp. 460–8.
3. James Hastie, 'Diary', 1817, pp. 157, 188, PRO.CO 167/34; James Hastie, 'Diary', 1824–5, PRO.CO 167/78; S. Copland, *A History of the Island of Madagascar, Comprising a Political Account of the Island, The Religion, Manners and Customs of Its Inhabitants, and Its Natural Productions* ... (London: Burton & Smith, 1822), pp. 12–18; Oliver, *Madagascar*, vol. 2, pp. 16–17; A. Horn, *The Waters of Africa* (London: Jonathan Cape, 1932), p. 97; Nicolas Mayeur, 'Voyage dans le nord de Madagascar', 1775, British Library (hereafter BL) Add. 1812886; Nicolas Mayeur, 'Voyage au pays d'ancove, par le pays d'ancaye autrement dit des Baizangouzangoux', related by Dumaine, 1785, p. 227, BL

Add. 18128; Anonymous, 'Mémoire historique et politique sur l'Isle de Madagascar', 1790, p. 55, BL Add. 18126; Dumaine, 'Voyage à la côte de l'ouest, autrement dite pays des Séclaves', 1793, pp. 294–7, BL Add. 18128; L. A. Chapelier, 'Lettres adressées au citoyen préfet de l'ile de France, de décembre 1803 en mai 1805', *Bulletin de l'Académie Malgache*, 4 (1905–6), pp. 1–45, on p. 34.

4.   Chapelier, 'Lettres adressées au citoyen préfet de l'ile de France, de décembre 1803 en mai 1805', p. 34; Chazal, 'Notes', 1816, p. 24, BL Add. 18135; Chardenoux, 'Journal du voyage fait dans l'intérieure', 1816, p. 163, BL Add. 18129; N. Leminier, 'Notes sur une excursion faite dans l'intérieur de l'Île de Madagascar en 1825', *Bulletin de Madagascar*, 292 (1970), pp. 794–8, on p. 797; James Hastie, 'Diary', 1817, pp. 137, 147, 157, 164, 170, 177, 188–9, 197, 211, PRO.CO 167/34; James Hastie, 'Diary', 1820, p. 489, PRO.CO 167/50; Raombana, 'Histoires', pp. 21, 67, 82, 93–4; Raombana, 'Texts', in S. Ayache (ed.), *Raombana l'historien, 1809–1855: Introduction a l'edition critique de son œuvre*, 2 vols (Fianarantsoa: Ambozontany, 1976), vol. 2, p. 13; W. Ellis, *History of Madagascar*, 2 vols (London: Fisher, Son, 1838), vol. 2, pp. 16, 198; G. S. Chapus and G. Mondain, 'Un chapitre inconnu. Des rapports de Maurice et de Madagascar', *Bulletin de l'Académie Malgache*, 30 (1951–2), pp. 111–30, on p. 117; HdR, pp. 120, 441–2, 658; G. S. Chapus, 'Le soin du bien-être du peuple sous le règne d'Andrianampoinimerina', *Bulletin de l'Académie Malgache*, 30 (1951–2), pp. 1–11, on p. 1; J. Valette, *Études sur le règne de Radama Ier* (Antananarivo: Imprimerie Nationale, 1962), p. 19; Oliver, *Madagascar*, vol. 1, pp. 221–2, 227–9, 252–3; S. P. Oliver, 'General Hall and the Export Slave Trade from Madagascar. A Statement and a Vindication', *Antananarivo Annual and Madagascar Magazine*, 12 (1888), p. 678; G. Campbell, 'Madagascar and the Slave Trade, 1810–1895', *Journal of African History*, 22:2 (1981), pp. 202–8; Campbell, 'The Role of the London Missionary Society in the Rise of the Merina Empire', pp. 32–87 ; Le Sage, 'Mission', 1816, pp. 121–2; James Hastie, 'Diary', 1817, p. 150; A. Toussaint, *La route des Îles – contribution à l'histoire maritime des Mascareignes* (Paris: S.E.V.P.N., 1967); J. M. Filliot, *La traite des esclaves vers les Mascareignes au XVIIIe siècle* (Paris: ORSTOM, 1974).

5.   Nicolas Mayeur, 'Voyage au pays d'ancove', 1777, pp. 176–7, BL Add. 18128.

6.   This probably underpinned the 1822 female protest against the pro-British policies of the Merina crown. See G. Campbell, 'Review Article: Larceny in the Highlands of Madagascar', *Slavery and Abolition*, 23:1 (2002), pp. 137–46.

7.   Campbell, 'Role of the London Missionary Society in the Rise of the Merina Empire', pp. 172–7; A. B. Duhaut-Cilly, 'Notices sur le royaume d'Emirne, sur la capitale de Tananarivou et sur le gouvernement de Rhadama', in J. Valette (ed.), 'Deux documents français sur Madagascar en 1825; les rapports Duhaut-Cilly et Frère', *Bulletin de l'Académie Malgache*, 16:1–2 (1968), pp. 238–9.

8.   L. Munthe, C. Ravoajanahary and S. Ayache, '*Radama I et les anglais: les* négociations de 1817 d'après *les* sources malgaches', *Omaly sy Anio*, 3–4 (1976), pp. 9–104, on p. 56; Leminier, 'Notes sur une excursion faite dans l'intérieur de l'Île de Madagascar en 1825', p. 797; Canham to Burder, Ifenoarivo, 3 October 1827, London Missionary Society/Council for World Mission Archives, Madagascar – Incoming Letters (hereafter SOAS/LMS MIL), B2.F4.JC; Robert Lyall, 'Journal, 1828–29', in G. S. Chapus and G. Mondain, *Le Journal de Robert Lyall* (Tananarive: Imprimerie Officielle, 1954), pp. 11–13, 33; Jones and Griffiths to LMS, Antananarivo, 9 November 1826, SOAS/LMS MIL, B2.F3.JD; Campbell, 'Role of the London Missionary Society in the Rise of the Merina Empire', pp. 189–91, 319; G. M. Razi, 'Sources d'histoire malgache aux Etats-Unis,

1792–1882', paper presented at the 'Colloque des Historiens et Juristes lors du 75ème anniversaire de l'Académie malgache', Antanarivo, Madagascar, 6 September 1977, p.13.

9. Raombana, 'Manuscrit écrit à Tananarive (1853–1854)', trans. J. F. Radley, *Bulletin de l'Académie Malgache*, 13 (1930), pp. 1–26, on pp. 4, 16.

10. G. Campbell, 'An Industrial Experiment in Pre-colonial Madagascar, 1825–1861', *Journal of Southern African Studies*, 17:3 (1991), pp. 525–59.

11. G. Campbell, 'The History of Nineteenth Century Madagascar: 'le royaume' or 'l'empire'?', *Omaly sy Anio*, 33–36 (1994), pp. 331–79.

12. D. Griffiths, *Hanes Madagascar* (Machynlleth: Richard Jones, 1843), p. 29; Oliver, *Madagascar*, vol. 2, p. 194.

13. HdR, pp. 496, 719.

14. G. Campbell, *An Economic History of Imperial Madagascar, 1750–1895. The Rise and Fall of an Island Empire* (Cambridge: Cambridge University Press, 2005), p. 121.

15. HdR, pp. 719, 728 fn 729.

16. HdR, pp. 154, 496.

17. HdR, p. 155.

18. HdR, pp. 166–7.

19. HdR, p. 728 fn; Oliver, *Madagascar*, vol. 2, p. 194; Campbell, *An Economic History of Imperial Madagascar*, p. 76.

20. HdR, pp. 166, 496.

21. HdR, p. 719.

22. Jones and Griffiths to LMS, Antananarivo, 2 June 1824, SOAS/LMS MIL, B2.F1.JA; James Hastie, 'Diary', 1817, pp. 143, 148, 188; James Hastie, 'Diary', 1820, pp. 484, 493, 496; James Hastie, 'Diary', 1822; Hastie to Barry, Antananarivo, 22 April 1824, p. 43, PRO.CO.167/78, pt I; Nicolas Mayeur, 'Voyage au pays d'ancove', 1777, pp. 177–80, Add. 18128; Duhaut-Cilly, 'Notice sur le royaume d'Emirne', pp. 238–9; A. Grandidier, 'Property and Wealth among the Malagasy', *Antananarivo Annual and Madagascar Magazine*, 22:6 (1898), pp. 224–33, on pp. 228, 230.

23. Campbell, *An Economic History of Imperial Madagascar*, p. 202.

24. Finkelmeier to Hunter, 1 October 1878, Despatches of United States Consuls in Tamatave, 1853–1906, United States National Archives, Washington, DC; Wills to Mullens, Antananarivo, 7 November 1878 (LMS) Imerina District Committee Letterbook (1875–97), p. 174, Archives of the Fiangonana Jesosy Kristy aty Madagascar, Antananarivo.

25. Campbell, *An Economic History of Imperial Madagascar*, p. 277.

26. Campbell, 'Role of the London Missionary Society in the Rise of the Merina Empire', p. 244.

27. Oliver, *Madagascar*, vol. 2, pp. 75–8; Grandidier, 'Property and Wealth among the Malagasy', p. 247; Campbell, 'Role of the London Missionary Society in the Rise of the Merina Empire', p. 244.

28. HdR, p. 718.

29. HdR, p. 496.

30. HdR, p. 496.

31. HdR, p. 719.

32. Griffiths, *Hanes Madagascar*, pp. 52–3.

33. Campbell, *An Economic History of Imperial Madagascar*, p. 91.

34. HdR, p. 728 fn.

35. Oliver, *Madagascar*, vol. 2, p.194.

36. HdR, p. 718.
37. HdR, pp. 9, 49, 303, 489, 252–4, 256, 260, 262–3, 307, 313–34, 596, 632, 737, 812, 885, 1109; Campbell, 'Role of the London Missionary Society in the Rise of the Merina Empire', p. 28.
38. HdR, pp. 238–9, 275–6, 279–80, 282, 297–8; Raombana, 'Histoires', p. 247; A. Grandidier, *Souvenirs de voyages, 1865–1870 (d'après son manuscrit inédit de 1916. Documents anciens sur Madagascar 6* (Tananarive: Association malgache d'archéologie, 1971), p. 33; C. Keller, *Madagascar, Mauritius and the Other East African Islands* (London: Swan Sonnenschein & Co, 1901), p. 123; J. Dez, 'Éléments pour une étude de l'économie agro-sylvo-pastorale de l'Imerina ancienne', Université de Madagascar: École nationale supérieure agronomique, 8 (1970), pp. 39, 41.
39. Campbell, *An Economic History of Imperial Madagascar*, p. 121.
40. HdR, p. 304.
41. H.-M. Dubois, *Monographie des Betsileo* (Paris: Institut d'Ethnologie, 1938), p. 429.
42. HdR, pp. 1109, 1111–12, 1114, 1123; Raombana, 'Histoires', p. 96; James Hastie, 'Diary', 1817, p. 241, PRO.CO 167/34; E. Baker, *Madagascar, Past and Present: with Considerations as to the Political and Commercial Interests of Great Britain and France: and as to the Progress of Christian Civilisation* (London: R. Bentley, 1847), p. 57; Canham to Burder, Antananarivo, 30 June 1822, SOAS/LMS MIL, B1.F2.JB; Freeman to Hankey, Antananarivo, 10 Feb 1829, SOAS/LMS MIL, B3.F1.JA; Baker to Arundel, Antananarivo, 29 March 1829, SOAS/LMS MIL, B3.F1.JB; 'Expenses from November 1st 1831 to April 30th 1832', SOAS/LMS MIL, B4.F3.JB; L. Munthe, *La bible à Madagascar. Les deux premières traductions du Nouveau Testament malgache* (Oslo: Egede instituttet, 1969), pp. 84, 112–13; Campbell, 'Role of the London Missionary Society in the Rise of the Merina Empire', pp. 171–234.
43. James Hastie, 'Diary', 1822.
44. G. Campbell, 'Slavery and Fanompoana: The Structure of Forced Labour in Imerina (Madagascar), 1790–1861', *Journal of African History*, 29:3 (1988), pp. 463–86.
45. Baker to Arundel, Antananarivo, 5 April 1831, SOAS/LMS MIL, B4.F1.JB; Freeman to Ellis, Antananarivo, 15 February 1834, SOAS/LMS MIL, B5.F1.JA.
46. Campbell, *An Economic History of Imperial Madagascar*, p. 127.
47. Hastie, 'Diary', 1820; Hastie to Barry, Antananarivo, 22 April 1824, PRO.CO 167/77; Oliver, *Madagascar*, vol. 2, p. 160; Bojer, 'Journal', in J. Valette (ed.), 'L'Imerina en 1822–1825 d'après les journaux de Bojer et d'Hilsenburg', *Bulletin de Madagascar*, 3 (1965), p. 23; Ellis, *History of Madagascar*, vol. 1, p. 119; J. Cameron, *Recollections of Mission Life in Madagascar in the Early Days of the LMS Mission* (Antananarivo: A. Kingdon, 1874), pp. 24–6.
48. Freeman to Hankey, Antananarivo, 12 March 1829, SOAS/LMS MIL, B3.F5; HdR, p. 1075.
49. Campbell, *An Economic History of Imperial Madagascar*, p. 87.
50. Ellis, *History of Madagascar*, vol. 2, pp. 234, 258; 'Religion in Madagascar', *Church Quarterly Review*, 6 (1878), pp. 385–418, on p. 381; Griffiths, *Hanes Madagascar*, p. 87; Freeman to Orme, Antananarivo, 9 January 1829 and Freeman to Hankey, Antananarivo, 10 February 1829, SOAS/LMS MIL, B3 F1 JA; 'Extracts of the Minutes of the Madagascar Mission', 27 May 1829, SOAS/LMS MIL, B3 F2 JA; 'Report of the Madagascar Missionary School Society', March 1828–December 1829, and 'Minute Book of the Mission', March 1829, SOAS/LMS MIL, B3 F2 JC; Freeman and Philips, 'Memorial' to the French government, Cape Town, 24 November 1830, SOAS/LMS MIL,

B3 F4 JB; Johns to Hankey, Antananarivo, 23 June 1830, SOAS/LMS MIL, B3 F3 JB; Freeman to Orme, Port Louis, 2 August 1830, SOAS/LMS MIL, B3 F3 JC; Freeman to Hankey, 'Pero', 6 September 1830, SOAS/LMS MIL, B3 F5; 'Minutes of the Mission in Madagascar', Antananarivo, 23 August 1832, SOAS/LMS MIL, B4 F3 JB; Griffiths to Clayton, Antananarivo, 25 October 1832; Freeman to Philip, Antananarivo, 25 September and 10 October 1832, SOAS/LMS MIL, B4 F4 JC; Johns, Freeman and Canham to Ellis, Antananarivo, 18 November 1833, SOAS/LMS MIL, B4 F4 JC; Freeman to Ellis, Antananarivo, 18 May 1835, SOAS/LMS MIL, B5 F2 JA; Campbell, 'Slavery and Fanompoana', fn 23; Raombana, ms. VIII B1, pp. 11–12, AAM.

51. Campbell, 'Slavery and Fanompoana', pp. 468–9.
52. Campbell, *An Economic History of Imperial Madagascar*, p. 163.
53. Bojer, 'Journal', p. 14.
54. Ellis, *History of Madagascar*, vol. 2, p. 304.
55. Ibid., vol. 2, p. 305.
56. Oliver, *Madagascar*, vol. 2, p. 196.
57. Campbell, *An Economic History of Imperial Madagascar*, p. 91; Oliver, *Madagascar*, vol. 2, p. 196.
58. Oliver, *Madagascar*, vol. 2, p. 284.
59. G. Rantoandro, 'Le gouvernement de Tamatave de 1845 à 1865; développement économique' (PhD dissertation, Université de Madagascar, 1973), pp. 83–6; Campbell, 'Slavery and Fanompoana', pp. 472–4.
60. Raombana, 'Livre' 12 C1, p. 489, AAM; Ellis, *History of Madagascar*, vol. 2, p. 367.
61. See James Hastie, 'Report on the Examination of the Schools', Antananarivo, 17 March 1825, SOAS/LMS MIL, B2 F2 JA; Griffiths to Arundel, Antananarivo, 20 December 1825, SOAS/LMS MIL, B2 F2 JC.
62. T. T. Matthews, *Thirty Years in Madagascar* (London: Religious Tract Society, 1904), p. 257.
63. Campbell, *An Economic History of Imperial Madagascar*, chs 9 and 11.
64. James Hastie, 'Diary', 1822; Griffiths to Arundel, Antananarivo, 20 December 1825, SOAS/LMS MIL, B2.F2.JC; L. Molet, 'Les monnaies à Madagascar', *Cahiers de l'institut de science économique appliquée*, 129 (1962), pp. 7–48, on pp. 4, 9–12, 26–7, 30, 33–4; M. Bloch, *Placing the Dead: Tombs, Ancestral Villages, and Kinship Organization in Madagascar* (Cambridge: Cambridge University Press, 1971), pp. 114–21; J. Dez, 'Monnaie et structure traditionnelle à Madagascar', *Cahiers Vilfredo Pareto – Revue européene des sciences sociales*, 8:21 (1970), pp. 175–202; Campbell, 'Madagascar and the Slave Trade'; Campbell, 'Role of the London Missionary Society in the Rise of the Merina Empire', pp. 176, 293; Oliver, *Madagascar*, vol. 2, pp. 206–7, 217; Grandidier, 'Property among the Malagasy', p. 226; see also Sundström, *The Exchange Economy of Pre-Colonial Tropical Africa*, pp. 34–5, 37.
65. James Hastie, 'Diary', 1817, p. 186; HdR, p. 919.
66. K. Evers, 'Das Hamburger Zanzibarhandelshaus Wm. O'Swald & Co. 1847–1890. Zur Geschichte des Hamburger Handels mit Ostafrika' (PhD dissertation, University of Hamburg, 1986), p. 16.
67. HdR, p. 919.
68. Ellis, *History of Madagascar*, vol. 2, pp. 148–9; Chauvicourt, 'premières monnaies', p. 150; Valette, *Études sur le règne de Radama Ier*, p. 45.
69. HdR, pp. 778–9; Ellis, *History of Madagascar*, vol. 2, p. 149.
70. James Hastie, quoted in Ellis, *History of Madagascar*, vol. 2, p. 242.

71. James Hastie, 'Report on the Schools Superintended by the Missionaries at Tananarive', 19 April 1824, PRO.CO 167/78, pt. II.
72. Ellis, *History of Madagascar*, vol. 2, p. 149.
73. Ibid.; Chauvicourt, 'premières monnaies', p. 150; Valette, *Études sur le règne de Radama Ier*, p. 45.
74. G. Rantoandro, 'Le gouvernement de Tamatave de 1845 à 1865; développement économique' (PhD dissertation, Université de Madagascar, 1973), pp. 83–6; Campbell, 'Slavery and Fanompoana', pp. 472–4.
75. A. Martineau, *Madagascar en 1894* (Paris: Ernest Flammarion, 1894), p. 409.
76. Campbell, 'Slavery and the Slave Trade'.
77. Martineau, *Madagascar en 1894*, p. 467.
78. Ibid., p. 468.
79. G. Campbell, 'Missionaries, Fanompoana and the Menalamba Revolt in Late Nineteenth Century Madagascar', *Journal of Southern African Studies*, 15:1 (1988), pp. 54–73; G. Campbell, 'Currency Crisis, Missionaries, and the French Takeover in Madagascar, 1861–1895', *International Journal of African Historical Studies*, 21:2 (1988), pp. 273–89; Campbell, *An Economic History of Imperial Madagascar*, pp. 229–42, 276–304, 332–8.

4 Newton-King, 'Credit and Debt in the Lives of Freed Slaves at the Cape of Good Hope: The Case of Arnoldus Koevoet, 1697–1735'

1. I understand 'debt bondage' to refer to a relationship between a borrower and a lender in which the services of the borrower, or those of a person under his or her control, are pledged to the lender in repayment of the debt. In cases where the nature and duration of the services required to repay the debt are undefined and the debt is passed from one generation to the next, one may speak of debt bondage
2. It is possible that historians have overlooked the potential for permanent and irreversible bondage inherent in such relationships. Cf. R. Elphick, *Kraal and Castle: Khoikhoi and the Founding of White South Africa* (New Haven, CT: Yale University Press, 1977), pp. 33–5 and J. B. Peires, *The House of Phalo: A History of the Xhosa in the Days of Their Independence* (Johannesburg: Ravan Press, 1981), p. 40.
3. The Orphan Chamber lent large sums of money at interest, as did the Church Poor Fund. Money-lending was also widely practised by senior Company officials, rich widows, retired farmers and wealthy merchants in Cape Town, such as those who held special licences to market meat, wine or brandy.
4. See, for example, Transfers, vol. 24, 1715, Deeds Office, Cape Town (hereafter DO), no. 136; *Custingbrieven*, no. 69, 28 July 1718, Western Cape Archives and Records Service, Cape Town (hereafter WCARS), MOOC 11/1.
5. Company employees might begin their contracts indebted to a *volkhouder* or *zielverkoper* in a Dutch port, but such debts were finite and were paid in installments by deductions from the employee's salary. S. Newton-King, *Masters and Servants on the Cape Eastern Frontier* (Cambridge: Cambridge University Press, 1999), pp. 14–15.
6. W. Frijhoff and M. Spies, *1650: Bevochten eendracht: Nederlandse cultuur in Europese context* (Den Haag: Sdu Uitgevers, 1999), p. 186. For an in-depth discussion of the importance of credit-worthiness at the Cape, see G. Groenewald, 'Kinship, Entrepreneurship and Social Capital: Alcohol *pachters* and the Making of a Free-Burgher Society in Cape Town, 1652–1795' (PhD dissertation, University of Cape Town, 2009).

7. It seems that, on rare occasions, a sentence of imprisonment in the *gijselkamer* in the Castle was imposed upon defaulting debtors (G. Groenewald, personal communication, 12 March 2009).

8. G. Groenewald, personal communication, 3 August 2011.

9. The project was led by Professor N. Worden of the University of Cape Town and funded by the South African National Research Foundation.

10. Destitute freed slaves apparently received a smaller grant from the Church Poor Fund than did destitute free burghers. See N. Worden, E. van Heyningen and V. Bickford-Smith, *Cape Town: The Making of a City* (Cape Town: David Philip Publishers, 1998), p. 68.

11. S. Newton-King, 'Sodomy, Race and Respectability in Stellenbosch and Drakenstein, 1689–1762: The Story of a Family, Loosely Defined', *Kronos*, 33 (2007), pp. 30–1. See also L. Hattingh, *Die Eerste Vryswartes van Stellenbosch, 1679–1720* (Bellville: University of the Western Cape, 1981), pp. 20–31.

12. 'Free black' or '*vrijswart*' was the term used by the authorities at the Cape to denote persons who had been born in slavery and later freed, either by their owners, themselves or a third party. Such persons often preferred to refer to themselves as 'free burghers', which put them on a par with the other free inhabitants of the colony, but this latter term was generally reserved by the authorities for those born free. H. Heese correctly criticizes R. Elphick and R. Shell for using the term 'free black' too loosely in *The Shaping of South African Society, 1652–1840* (Cape Town: Maskew Miller Longman, 1989). See H. Heese, *Groep Sonder Grense: Die Rol en Status van die Gemengde Bevolking aan die Kaap, 1652–1795* (Bellville: University of the Western Cape, 1984), p. 21.

13. Resolutions of the Council of Policy, 17 May 1731, TANAP Project, WCARS, C 88.

14. Resolutions of the Council of Policy, 17 May 1731, TANAP Project, WCARS, C 88. It seems that the Company baptized the majority of its slave children (R. Elphick and R. Shell, 'Intergroup Relations: Khoikhoi, Settlers, Slaves and Free Blacks, 1652–1795', in R. Elphick and H. Giliomee (eds), *The Shaping of South African Society, 1652–1840* (Cape Town: Maskew Miller Longman, 1989), pp. 184–239, on p. 189. For a brief explanation of the Company's approach to the manumission of its slaves, see Elphick and Shell, 'Intergroup Relations', pp. 188–90, 211. A 'reasonable' command of the Dutch language had been a requirement for manumission since 1642 (J. A. van der Chijs (ed.), *Nederlandsch-Indisch Plakaatboek, 1602–1811*, 17 vols (Batavia: Landsdrukkerij's Hage: M. Nijhoff, 1885), p. 575).

15. Inventory of the *vrijswart* Arnoldus Koevoet, 4 January 1736, WCARS, MOOC 10/4; Annexures to Liquidation Account of the *vrijswart* Arnoldus Koevoet, 1738, WCARS, MOOC 14/8, Part 1.

16. Resolutions of the Council of Policy, 17 May 1731, TANAP Project, WCARS, C 88.

17. Annexures to Liquidation Account of the *vrijswart* Arnoldus Koevoet, 1738, WCARS, MOOC 14/8, Part 1.

18. Minutes of Proceedings in Civil Cases, 1737, p. 52, WCARS, CJ 831.

19. M. Cairns, 'Freeblack Landowners in the Southern Suburbs of the Cape Peninsula during the Eighteenth Century', *Kronos*, 10 (1985), pp. 23–31.

20. Annexures to the Liquidation Account of the *vrijswart* Arnoldus Koevoet, 1738, WCARS, MOOC 14/8.

21. Resolutions of the Council of Policy, 23 September 1727, TANAP Project, WCARS, C 77. See below for an explanation of the relationship between Arnoldus Koevoet and Johannes Morgh.

22. See references to 'Broer Pieter' in the letters of Anna Maria van Thiel.

23. Annexures to the Liquidation Account of the *vrijswart* Arnoldus Koevoet, 1738, Maria Magadalena Langenberg to Arnoldus Koevoet, 25 December 1731, WCARS, MOOC 14/8, Part 1. Pieter Kalden served as a Dutch Reformed minister in Cape Town from 1695 to 1708, but 'between 1696 and the end of 1699, he also visited Stellenbosch to perform the sacraments there' (G. Groenewald, personal communication, 9 September 2010). Barend van den Brink was a farmer and free burgher in Stellenbosch in the 1690s. He was also a member of the Stellenbosch Church Council. It is just possible that Maria Langenberg was the '*halfslag*' (half-breed) child Marija born to Christine van de Kaap and christened by Kalden in Stellenbosch on 12 July 1699 (*Doopregister*, NG Kerk Kaapstad, 173, WCARS, VC 632). If so, she had a brother or half-brother named Willem, christened in Stellenbosch in 1694.

24. Annexures to the Liquidation Account of the *vrijswart* Arnoldus Koevoet, Maria Langenberg to Arnoldus Koevoet, Batavia, 19 March 1732, WCARS, MOOC 14/8, Part 1.

25. *Doopregister*, NG Kerk Kaapstad, p. 63, 3 March 1697, WCARS, VC 604.

26. I am deeply indebted to R. Shell, whose CD-ROM, *From Diaspora to Diorama: The Old Slave Lodge in Cape Town* (Cape Town: Ancestry24, 2009) has allowed me to identify Koevoet as the child of Christijn Pietersz and to trace his siblings.

27. H. C. V. Leibbrandt, *Precis of the Archives of the Cape of Good Hope: Requesten (Memorials), 1715–1806*, 5 vols (Cape Town: Government Printers, 1905), vol. 1, p. 1.

28. Leibbrandt, *Precis of the Archives of the Cape of Good Hope*, vol. 1, p. 1.

29. I cannot be absolutely sure that the Anna of the Cape who married Jan Jans van Böllen in 1719 was the same person as Anna van Christijn Pietersz, but I think it very likely, for reasons explained below. For the marriage, see J. Hoge, *Personalia of the Germans at the Cape, 1652–1806. Archive Year Book for South African History* (Cape Town: Government Printer, 1946), p. 38.

30. Hoge, *Personalia of the Germans at the Cape*, p. 38.

31. Leibbrandt, *Precis of the Archives of the Cape of Good Hope*, vol. 1, p. 2.

32. Ibid., vol. 1, p. 2 and Resolutions of the Council of Policy, 5 December 1724, TANAP Project, WCARS, C 71.

33. L. Hattingh, 'Slawevrystellings aan die Kaap tussen 1700 en 1720', *Kronos*, 4 (1981), p. 29; Elphick and Shell, 'Intergroup Relations', p. 211.

34. A. Böeseken, *Slaves and Free Blacks at the Cape, 1658–1700* (Cape Town: Tafelberg Publishers, 1977), p. 46.

35. Resolutions of the Council of Policy, 17 May 1731, TANAP Project, WCARS, C 88.

36. *Obligatien, transporten van slaven en schuldbrieven*, 1715–1731, WCARS, CJ 3074 to CJ 3081.

37. J. R. Bruijn, F. S. Gaastra and I. Schöffer, *Dutch-Asiatic Shipping in the 17th and 18th Centuries* (The Hague: Martinus Nijhoff, 1987), pp. 210–11.

38. *Doopregister*, NG Kerk Kaapstad, 3 March 1697, p. 63, VC 604: '*een kint van Christijn van de Caap, Arnoldus*'.

39. *Doopregister*, NG Kerk Kaapstad, 4 November 1703, p. 68, WCARS, VC 604: '*een kind van Christina Pieterz van de Caab, gent Johannes halfslag*'.

40. She was forty-four years old. 'Index to Personalia of Lodge Slaves', in Shell (ed.), *From Diaspora to Diorama*, p. 3344.

41. 'Index to Personalia of Lodge Slaves', in Shell (ed.), *From Diaspora to Diorama*, p. 3344.

42. Annexures to Liquidation Account of the *vrijswart* Arnoldus Koevoet, 1738, WCARS, MOOC 14/8, Part 1; *Vendurol* of Arnoldus Koevoet, 4 January 1736, WCARS, MOOC 10/4.

43. *Verklaaringen*, 13 January 1727–28 February 1727, No. 62, WCARS, C 2449: '*Monster Rolle van soodanige slaaven, banditen en slavinnen als in weesen bevonden sijn, onder ult. Feb.y 1727*. According to R. Shell, the word 'mandoor' was a 'corrupted form of the Portuguese *mandador*, which means foreman, overseer, or driver' (R. Shell, *Children of Bondage: A Social History of the Slave Society at the Cape of Good Hope, 1652–1838* (Hanover, NH: Wesleyan University Press, 1994), p. 180).

44. Shell, *Children of Bondage*, pp. 183–5.

45. K. Schoeman, *Armosyn van die Kaap: Armosyn van die Kaap: die Wêreld van 'n Slavin, 1652–1733* (Cape Town: Human and Rousseau, 2001), p. 553.

46. 'Index to Personalia of Lodge Slaves', in Shell (ed.), *From Diaspora to Diorama*.

47. 'Extracts of Instructions for the Commander Simon van der Stell', in D. Moodie (ed.), *The Record: or A Series of Official Papers Relative to the Condition and Treatment of the Native Tribes of South Africa* (Cape Town: Balkema, 1960), p. 397, cited in Shell (ed.), *From Diaspora to Diorama*, p. 1010. See also Böeseken, *Slaves and Free Blacks at the Cape*, p. 48 and Shell, *Children of Bondage*, ch. 6.

48. *Doopregister*, NG Kerk Kaapstad, 3 March 1697, WCARS, VC 604.

49. Shell, *Children of Bondage*, p. 187.

50. Ibid., p. 375. I do believe that Shell has under-counted the number of Company slaves who were freed; nonetheless, his point stands.

51. Shell, *Children of Bondage*, p. 376.

52. For contemporary descriptions of the lodge, see Shell (ed.), *From Diaspora to Diorama*. For secondary accounts, see Shell, *Children of Bondage*, ch. 6 and Schoeman, *Armosyn van die Kaap*, ch. 16.

53. Annexures to Liquidation Account of the *vrijswart* Arnoldus Koevoet, Maria Magdalena Langeberg to Arnoldus Koevoet, Batavia, 25 December 1731, WCARS, MOOC 14/8, Part 1.

54. Annexures to Liquidation Account of the *vrijswart* Arnoldus Koevoet, Johannes Morgh to *Mons:r* Arnoldus Koevoet and *juff:r* Anna Rebecca, Batavia, 10 February 1732, WCARS, MOOC 14/8, Part 1.

55. Annexures to Liquidation Account of the *vrijswart* Arnoldus Koevoet, Johannes Morgh *van de Caap* to Arnoldus Koevoet, Batavia, 1729, WCARS, MOOC 14/8, Part 1.

56. Annexures to Liquidation Account of the *vrijswart* Arnoldus Koevoet, Johannes Morgh van de Caap de Goede Hoope to Arnoldus Koevoet, Batavia, 29 September 1729, WCARS, MOOC 14/8, Part 1.

57. Johannes was freed on 23 September 1727 (Resolutions of the Council of Policy, 23 September 1727, TANAP Project, WCARS, C 77). The *Elisabeth* was in Table Bay from October to December 1727 (Resolutions of the Council of Policy, 7 October 1727 and 11 December 1727, TANAP Project, WCARS, C 77 and 78).

58. Resolutions of the Council of Policy, 17 May 1731, TANAP Project, WCARS, C 88.

59. Marriage Register and Church Membership, NG Kerk Kaapstad, p. 23, VC 621. The church was adjacent to the slave lodge.

60. *Attestatien*, 11 May 1731, C 2464 ('Index to Personalia of Lodge Slaves', in Shell (ed.), *From Diaspora to Diorama*). Christina was killed in an accident on 11 May 1731, just six days before the Council met to consider her father's petition for freedom, among other items. Arnoldus was also involved in the accident.

61. Annexures to Liquidation Account of the *vrijswart* Arnoldus Koevoet, Maria Langenberg to Arnoldus Koevoet, Batavia, 6 October 1731, WCARS, MOOC 14/8, Part 1.

62. Annexures to Liquidation Account of the *vrijswart* Arnoldus Koevoet, Johannes Morgh to Arnoldus Koevoet, Batavia, 8 October 1731, WCARS, MOOC 14/8, Part 1.

63. Annexures to Liquidation Account of the *vrijswart* Arnoldus Koevoet, Maria Langenberg to Arnoldus Koevoet, Batavia, 19 March 1732, WCARS, MOOC 14/8, Part 1.

64. For a vivid description of the importunate behaviour of such well-connected visitors to Cape Town, with their large retinues of servants and hangers-on, see K. Schoeman, *Burgers en Amptenare: die Vroeë Ontwikkeling van die Kolonie aan die Kaap, 1662–1679* (Pretoria: Protea Boekhuis, 2011), pp. 136–40.

65. Annexures to Liquidation Account of the *vrijswart* Arnoldus Koevoet, Johannes Morgh to Arnoldus Coefoet, n.d. but presumed late 1729, WCARS, MOOC 14/8, Part 1.

66. *Testament boek*, 21 September 1722 – 27 June 1725, WCARS, CJ 2602, will of the free black woman Anna Rebecca van Bengalen, 26 June 1724.

67. In 1722, Hendricksz was appointed captain of the militia regiment created in that year to accommodate free blacks separately from free burghers. In 1723 he was granted an *erf* (plot of land) in Waalstraat, near the Company's slave lodge. With his wife, Christina de Canarie, a former slave of Simon van der Stel, he was also the owner of the farm Stellenburgh (Cairns, 'Freeblack Landowners in the Southern Suburbs of the Cape Peninsula during the Eighteenth Century', p. 25).

68. *Testament boek*, 21 September 1722 – 27 June 1725, WCARS, CJ 2602, will of the free black woman Anna Rebecca van Bengalen, 26 June 1724.

69. Marriage Register and Church Membership, NG Kerk Kaapstad, VC 621. There may be further details in the minutes of the Church Council, which I have not yet had the opportunity to read.

70. Annexures to the Liquidation Account of the *vrijswart* Arnoldus Koevoet, 1738, Jan Tercks to Anna Rebecca of Bengal, Amsterdam, 28 October 1731, WCARS, MOOC 14/8, Part 1.

71. See S. Newton-King, 'Family, Friendship and Survival among Freed Slaves', in N. Worden (ed.), *Cape Town between East and West: Social Identities in a Dutch Colonial Town* (Cape Town: Jacana and Hilversum, Uijtgeverij Verloren, 2012), pp. 153–75.

72. Annexures to Liquidation Account of the *vrijswart* Arnoldus Koevoet, Anna Maria van Thiel to Rabecka, Amsterdam, 26 June 1733, WCARS, MOOC 14/8, Part 1.

73. Annexures to Liquidation Account of the *vrijswart* Arnoldus Koevoet, Anna Maria van Thiel to Rabecka, Amsterdam, 1 November 1731, WCARS, MOOC 14/8, Part 1.

74. Wills, no. 159, 13 August 1731, WCARS, MOOC 7/1/4; Marriage Register and Church Membership, 24 June 1720, NG Kerk Kaapstad, VC 621.

75. *Testament boek*, 21 September 1722 – 27 June 1725, no. 1, WCARS, CJ 2602.

76. Annexures to Liquidation Account of the *vrijswart* Arnoldus Koevoet, Anna Maria van Thiel to Rabecka, Amsterdam, 4 June 1732, WCARS, MOOC 14/8, Part 1.

77. Resolutions of the Council of Policy, 4 May 1735, TANAP Project, WCARS, C 98. Koevoet purchased Salamat van Java from the *oudburgerraad* Johannes Cruijwagen for 100 rix dollars, to be repaid in six months' time (Annexures to Liquidation Account of the *vrijswart* Arnoldus Koevoet, 1738, WCARS, MOOC 14/8, Part 1).

78. Annexures to Liquidation Account of the *vrijswart* Arnoldus Koevoet, 1738, WCARS, MOOC 14/8, Part 1.

79. *Transporten en scheepenkennissen*, 14 December 1731, DO, T 2045.

80. One Cape guilder was equal to 16 stuivers, whereas one Dutch guilder was equal to 20 stuivers. There were 48 stuivers to one Cape rix dollar.

81. Annexures to Liquidation Account of the *vrijswart* Arnoldus Koevoet, 1738, WCARS, MOOC 14/8, Part 1.
82. Annexures to Liquidation Account of the *vrijswart* Arnoldus Koevoet, 1738, WCARS, MOOC 14/8, Part 1. Appolonia Bergh was the granddaughter of the freed slave Angela of Bengal.
83. Annexures to Liquidation Account of the *vrijswart* Arnoldus Koevoet, 1738, WCARS, MOOC 14/8, Part 1.
84. Leibbrandt, *Precis of the Archives of the Cape of Good Hope*, vol. 1, p. 58.
85. Ibid., vol. 1, p. 66.
86. Annexures to Liquidation Account of the *vrijswart* Arnoldus Koevoet, 1738, WCARS, MOOC 14/8, Part 1.
87. Annexures to Liquidation Account of the *vrijswart* Arnoldus Koevoet, 1738, WCARS, MOOC 14/8, Part 1.
88. *Doop Boek van Christen kinderen van Januarij 1713 tot 1742 en van slaven kinderen van den E Compagnie Januarij 1713 tot 16 September 1742*, WCARS, VC 605.
89. Van Graan was married to Rebecca van de Kaap, daughter of Moses of Macassar (Heese, *Groep Sonder Grense*, p. 71).
90. B Liquidation Account of Arnoldus Koevoet, 1738, WCARS, MOOC 13/1/3, no. 7.
91. Annexures to Liquidation Account of the *vrijswart* Arnoldus Koevoet, Johannes Morgh to Arnoldus Koevoet, 13 October 1733, WCARS, MOOC 14/8, Part 1.
92. *Vendurol* of Arnoldus Koevoet, 4 January 1736, WCARS, MOOC 10/4, no. 143.
93. Liquidation Account of Arnoldus Koevoet, 1738, WCARS, MOOC 13/1/3, no. 7.
94. Diana Koevoet married Pieter van Heemert on 26 August 1736: Liquidation Account of Arnoldus Koevoet, 1738, MOOC 13/1/3, no. 7.
95. Minutes of Proceedings in Civil Cases, 1737, pp. 52 and 110, CJ 831.

5 Stanziani, 'Debt, Labour and Bondage: English Servants versus Indentured Immigrants in Mauritius, from the Late Eighteenth to Early Twentieth Century'

1. H. Tinker, *A New System of Slavery: The Export of Indian Labour Overseas, 1830–1920* (Hansib and London, 1974); U. Patnaik and M. Dingwaney (eds), *Chains of Servitude: Bondage and Slavery in India* (Madras: Sargam books, 1985); G. Prakash, *Bonded Histories: Genealogies of Labour Servitude in Colonial India* (Cambridge: Cambridge University Press, 1990); H. H. Quang, *Histoire économique de l'île de la Réunion, 1849–1881: engagisme, croissance et crise* (Paris: Lavoisier, 2004); S. Fuma, *De l'Inde du sud à la Réunion* (Port-Louis: Graphica, 1999); S.-S. Govindin, *Les engagés indiens* (Saint-Denis la Réunion: Azalées, 1994); M. Marimoutou, *Les engagés du sucre* (Saint-Denis la Réunion: Editions du tramail, 1999); E. Wong-Hee-Kam, *La diaspora chinoise aux Mascareignes: le cas de la Réunion* (Paris: L'Harmattan, 1996).
2. D. Northrup, *Indentured Labor in the Age of Imperialism. 1834–1922*. (Cambridge: Cambridge University Press, 1995); M. Carter, *Servants, Sirdars and Settlers. Indians in Mauritius, 1834–1874* (Delhi: Oxford University Press, 1995); E. Maestri, *Esclavage et abolition dans l'Océan Indien, 1723–1860* (Paris: L'Harmattan, 2002).
3. Useful bibliographies are: R. Scott, T. Holt, F. Cooper and A. McGuinness, *Societies After Slavery. A Selected Annotated Bibliography of Printed Sources on Cuba, Brazil, British Colonial Africa, South Africa and the British West India* (Pittsburgh: University of Pitts-

burgh Press, 2004); J. C. Miller, *Slavery and Slaving in World History: A Bibliography, 1900–1996* (Armonk, NY: M. E. Sharpe, 1999); S. Drescher and S. Engerman (eds), *A Historical Guide to World Slavery* (New York: Oxford, 1998); O. Pétré-Grenouilleau, *Les traites négrières.* (Paris: Gallimard, 2004); M. Dorigny and B. Gainot, *Atlas des esclavages* (Paris: Editions autrement, 2006).

4. R. Steinfeld, *The Invention of Free Labour: The Employment Relation in English and American law and Culture, 1350–1870* (Chapel Hill, NC: University of North Carolina Press, 1991). On the mobile boundary between 'free' and 'unfree' labour: S. Engerman (ed.), *Terms of Labour: Slavery, Serfdom and Free Labour* (Stanford, CA: Stanford University Press, 1999); M. L. Bush, *Servitude in Modern Times* (Cambridge: Polity Press, 2000). F. Cooper, T. Holt and R. Scott, *Beyond Slavery: Explorations of Race, Labour and Citizenship on Post-Emancipation Societies* (Chapel Hill, NC: North Carolina Press, 2000); T. Brass and M. van der Linden (eds), *Free and Unfree Labour. The Debate Continues* (Bern: Peter Lang, 1997).

5. J. Lucassen and L. Lucassen (eds), *Migration, Migration History, History. Old Paradigms and New Perspectives* (Berne: Peter Lang, 1997); D. Eltis, *Coerced and Free Migration: Global Perspectives* (Stanford, CA: Stanford University Press, 2002).

6. D. Galenson, *White Servitude in Colonial America: An Economic Analysis* (Cambridge: Cambridge University Press, 1981); F. Grubb, 'The Incidence of Servitude in Trans-Atlantic Migration, 1771–1804', *Explorations in Economic History*, 22:3 (1985), pp. 316–39; G. P. Barth, *Bitter Strength: A History of the Chinese in the United States, 1850–1870* (Cambridge, MA: Harvard University Press, 1964); C. Wanquet, *La France et la première abolition de l'esclavage (1794–1802)* (Paris: Karthala, 1998); C. Schnakenbourg, *Histoire de l'industrie sucrière en Guadeloupe aux XIXe et XXe siècles* (Paris: L'Harmattan, 2007); C. Flory, 'Le Noir: permanence des représentations et travail libre (1848–1860)', in M. L. Fouck and J. Zonzon (eds), *L'histoire de la Guyane depuis les civilisations amérindiennes* (Matoury: Ibis Rouge Editions, 2006), pp. 393–406.

7. See M. Klein, *Breaking the Chains. Slavery, Bondage and Emancipation in Modern Africa and Asia* (Madison, WI: University of Wisconsin Press, 1993).

8. P. Lovejoy, and T. Fayola (ed), *Pawnship, Slavery and Colonialism in Africa* (Asmara: Africa World Press, 2003).

9. J. M. Filliot, *La traite des esclaves vers les Mascareignes au XVIIIe siecle* (Paris: ORSTOM, 1974).

10. R. Allen, 'Licentious and Unbridled Proceedings: The Illegal Slave Trade to Mauritius and the Seychelles during the Early Nineteenth Century', *Journal of African History*, 42:1 (2001), pp. 91–116, in particular table 2, p. 100.

11. Northrup, *Indentured Labour*, appendix A.

12. K. N. Chaudhuri, *Trade and Civilisation in the Indian Ocean. An Economic History from the Rise of Islam to 1750* (Cambridge: Cambridge University Press, 1985); K. N. Chaudhuri, *Asia before Europe: Economy and Civilisation of the Indian Ocean from the Rise of Islam to 1750* (Cambridge: Cambridge University Press, 1992); C. Markovitz, *The Global World of Indian Merchants* (Cambridge: Cambridge University Press, 2000).

13. W. G. Clarence-Smith, *The Economics of the Indian Ocean Slave Trade* (London: Frank Cass, 1989); G. Campbell (ed.), *The Structure of Slavery in Indian Ocean, Africa and Asia* (London: Frank Cass, 2004); F. Cooper, *Plantation Slavery on the East Coast of Africa* (New Haven, CT: Yale University Press, 1977).

14. J. Watson (ed.), *Asian and African Systems of Slavery* (Berkeley and Los Angeles, CA: University of California Press, 1980); D. Scarr, *Slaving and Slavery in the Indian Ocean*

(London and New York: Longman 1998); L. Benton, *Law and Colonial Culture* (Cambridge: Cambridge University Press, 2002); M. Craton, *Empire, Enslavement and Freedom in the Caribbean* (Kingston: Randle publishers, 1997); M. Galanter, *Law and Society in Modern India* (Delhi: Oxford University Press, 1989); D. Hay and P. Craven, *Masters, Servants and Magistrates in Britain and the Empire, 1562–1955* (Chapel Hill, NC and London: University of North Carolina Press, 2004); A. Watson, *Slave Law in the Americas* (Athens, GA: University of Georgia Press, 1989).

15. Steinfeld, *The Invention of Free Labour*, p. 30; A. Kussmaul, *Servants in Husbandry in Early Modern England* (Cambridge: Cambridge University Press, 1981).

16. D. C. Woods, 'The Operation of the Masters and Servants Act in the Black Country, 1858–1875', *Midland history*, 7 (1982), pp. 93–115; M. R. Freedland, *The Contract of Employment* (Oxford: Oxford University Press, 1976); D. Galenson, 'The Rise of Free Labour: Economic Change and the Enforcement of Service Contract in England, 1361–1875', in J. James and M. Thomas (eds), *Capitalism in Context: Essays on Economic Development and Cultural Change in Honour of R.M. Hartwell* (Chicago, IL: Chicago University Press, 1994), pp. 114–37.

17. F. Slyder and D. Hay (eds), 'Introduction', in *Labour, Law, and Crime* (London: Tavistock, 1987), p. 15.

18. S. Deakin and F. Wilkinson, *The Law of the Labour Market: Industrialization, Employment and Legal Evolution* (Oxford: Oxford University Press, 2005).

19. Woods, 'The Operation of the Masters and Servants Act'; G. Barnsby, *Social Conditions in the Black Country* (Wolverhamptom: Integrated Publishers, 1980).

20. D. Hay, Nick Rogers, *English Society in the Eighteenth Century: Shuttles and Swords* (Oxford: Oxford University Press, 1997); D. Hay, 'Masters and Servants in England: Using the Law in the Eighteenth and Nineteenth Century', in W. Steinmetz (ed.), *Private Law and Social Inequality in the Industrial Age* (New York: Oxford University Press, 2000), pp. 227–64.

21. J. Innes, 'Prisons for the Poor: English Bridewells, 1555–1800', in F. Snyder and D. Hay (eds), *Labour, Law and Crime: An Historical Perspective* (London: Tavistock Publications, 1987), pp. 92–122.

22. R. H. Tawney, *The Agrarian Problem in the Sixteenth Century* (New York: Harper and Row, 1967), p. 47.

23. J. Lane, *Apprenticeship in England, 1600–1914* (London: UCL Press, 1996).

24. Kussmaul, *Servants in Husbandry*.

25. A. L. Beier, *Masterless Men: The Vagrancy Problem in England, 1560–1640*, (London: Meuthen, 1985), pp. 147–54.

26. Hay, 'Masters'; P. Craven and D. Hay, 'The Criminalization of Free Labour: Masters and Servants in Comparative Perspective', *Slavery and Abolition*, 15:2 (1994), pp. 71–101.

27. *Judicial Statistics, England and Wales, 1857–1875*, 19 vols (London, 1858–76). Also, R. Steinfeld, *Coercion, Contract and Free Labour in the Nineteenth Century* (Cambridge: Cambridge University Press, 2001), pp. 73–8.

28. D. Hay, 'England 1562–1875: The Law and its Uses', in Hay and Craven, *Masters, Servants and Magistrates*, p. 67.

29. Ibid.

30. Woods, 'The Operation of the Masters and Servants Act', p. 102.

31. Ibid., pp. 93–4.

32. Hay and Craven, *Masters, Servants and Magistrates*, introduction.

33. R. Burn, *The Justice of Peace and Parish Officer* (1755), 15th edn, 4 vol (London, 1785), vol. 1, p. 98.

34. J. Taylor, *Elements of the Civil Law*, 3rd edn (London, 1767), p. 413.

35. J. Murray and R. Wallis Herndon, 'Markets for Children in Early America: A Political Economy of Pauper Apprenticeship', *Journal of Economic History*, 62:2 (2002), pp. 356–82; F. Grubb, 'The Auction of Redemptioner Servants, Philadelphia, 1771–1804', *Journal of Economic History*, 48:3 (1988), pp. 583–603. B. Llebaner, 'Pauper Auctions: The New England Method or Public Poor Relief', *Essex Institute Historical Collection*, 91 (1955), pp. 195–210.

36. Ibid.

37. S. Drescher, 'Paradigms Tossed: Capitalism and the Political Sources of Abolition', in S. Engerman and B. Solow (eds), *British Capitalism and British Slavery* (Cambridge: Cambridge University Press, 1987), pp. 191–208. D. B. Davis, *The Problem of Slavery in the Age of Revolution, 1770–1823* (New York: Oxford University Press, 1999).

38. House of Commons, Papers in explanation of the condition of the slave population, 5 November 1831, *Parliamentary Papers*, 1830–1 (230), 16.1, pp. 59–88.

39. M. Turner, 'The British Caribbean, 1823–1838. The Transition from Slave to Free Legal Status', in Hay and Craven, *Masters, Servants and Magistrates*, pp. 303–22; J. R. Ward, *British West India Slavery, 1750–1834: The Process of Amelioration* (Oxford: Oxford University Press, 1988).

40. Emmer, 1986; on apprentices in Réunion: S. Fuma, *Esclaves et citoyens, le destin de 62000 réunionnais; histoire de l'insertion des affranchis de 1848 dans la société réunionnaise* (Saint-Denis: Fondation pour la Recerche et le Développement dans l'océan Indien, 1979) For a comparison: S. Engerman, 'Economic Change and Contract Labour in the British Caribbean: The End of Slavery and the Adjustment to Emancipation', *Explorations in Economic History*, 21 (1984), pp. 133–50. T. Holt, *The Problem of Slavery: Race, Labour and Politics in Jamaica and Britain, 1832–1938* (Baltimore, MD and London, 1992).

41. Galenson, *White Servitude*.

42. Northrup, *Indentured Labour*; M. L. Bush, *Servitude in Modern Times* (Polity Press: Cambridge, 2001); Tinker, *A New System*.

43. R. Allen, *Slaves, Freedmen, and Indentured Labourers in Colonial Mauritius* (Cambridge: Cambridge University Press, 1999), p. 84. C. Wanquet, 'Violences individuelles et violence institutionnalisée: le régime servile de l'Ile de France à la fin du XVIIIe siècle à la lumière des dossiers de procédure criminelle', in Maestri, *Esclavage et abolition*, pp. 203–26.

H. Gerbeau, 'Les indiens des Mascaraignes. Simples jalons pour l'histoire d'une réussite (XVIIe-XXe siècle)', *Annuaire des pays de Indian Ocean*, 12 (1990–1991), pp. 15–45, Éditions du CNRS / Presses universitaires d'Aix-Marseilles, 1992.

44. M. Jumeer, 'Les affranchissements et les libres à l'ile de France à la fin de l'Ancien Régime, 1768–1789' (PhD dissertation, University of Poitiers, 1979), pp. 24, 54, 105, 212–14.

45. H. Gerbeau, 'Engagés and Coolies on Réunion Island, Slavery's Masks and Freedom's Constraints', in P. C. Emmer (ed.), *Colonialism and Migration: Indentured Labour Before and After Slavery* (Dordrecht, MA: Martinus Nijhoff, 1986), pp. 209–36; Carter, *Servants, Sirdars and Settlers*.

46. V. Teelock, *Bitter Sugar: Sugar and Slavery in Nineteenth Century Mauritius* (Moka: Mahatma Gandhi Institute, 1998).

47. Correspondence concerning the Indian immigration to Mauritius in: *Parliamentary Papers*, 1840: XXXVII (331), 1842: XXX (26), 1844: XXXV (356 and 530), 1846: XXVIII (691 II); also, London, India office library, Bengal Public proceedings, in particular: 13/57 (col. Secy to Secy gov. India, 16 December 1845; 13/44 Chief Magistrate to Secy gov. Bengal, 21 October 1843; 13/44 deposition of R. Das, 6 November 1843. TNA CO 167/245, Stanley, 26 July 1843.

P. P. Mohapatra, 'Regulated Informality: Legal Construction of Labour Relations in Colonial India', in S. Bhattacharya and J. Lucassen (ed.), *Workers in the Informal Sector: Studies in Labour History, 1800–2000* (Delhi: Macmillan, 2005), pp. 65–95.

48. Colony of Mauritius, Annual report, 1854, *British Parliamentary Sessional Papers* XLII, 2050. See also: Allen, *Slaves*, p. 56; J. Breman, *Timing the Coolie Beast* (Delhi: Oxford University Press, 1989); U. Patnaik and M. Dingwaney (eds), *Chains of Servitude: Bondage and Slavery in India* (Madras: Sangam Books, 1985).

49. Allen, *Slaves*, pp. 16–17. Also A. Toussaint, *Histoire de l'ile Maurice* (Paris: PUF, 1974).

50. *Parliamentary Papers*, 1841 xvi (45), Petition of the inhabitants of Calcutta.

51. Carter, *Servants, Sirdars and Settlers*, p. 3.

52. S. Peerthum, 'Le système d'apprentissage à Mauritius 1835–1839: plus esclave mais pas encore libre', in Maestri, *Esclavage et abolition*, pp. 285–94; J. Chan-Low, 'Aux origines du malaise créole? Les ex-apprentis dans la société mauricienne, 1839–1860', in Maestri, *Esclavage et abolition*, pp. 267–84.

53. *Parliamentary Papers*, 1842: xxxx (26), 25.

54. Carter, *Servants, Sirdars and Settlers*.

55. Allen, *Slaves*, p. 60.

56. Colony of Mauritius, *Protector of Immigrants*.

57. 'Report of the Royal Commissioners Appointed to Enquire into the Treatment of Immigrants in Mauritius', in *British Parliament Sessional Papers*, 1875: XXXIV, parag. 704, and appendix A and B. Colony of Mauritius, Printed documents, *Annual Report of the Protector of Immigrants*, 1860–85.

58. Ibid.

59. Allen, *Slaves*, pp. 69–71.

60. *Parliamentary Papers*, 1836: XLIX (166); 1837–8: LII (180); 1840: XXXVII (58); 1847–8: XLVI (250); TNA CO 167/201.

61. Allen, *Slaves*, p. 72.

62. *Parliamentary Papers*, 1837–8: LII (180).

63. *Parliamentary Papers*, 1837–8: LII (180), 1849: XXXVII (280). Also Carter, *Servants, Sirdars and Settlers*, pp. 162–3.

64. TNA CO 167/263. Labour committee evidence, appendix A, 22 October 1845. *Parliamentary Papers*, 1847: XXXIX (325).

65. TNA CO 167/213, 202, 266.

66. CAOM, FM/SG REU 380/3228, minute 6 March 1876.

67. CAOM, FM/SG REU 380/3228, minute 6 March 1876.

68. CAOM, FM/SG REU 380/3228, minute of council, n. 7, 19 March 1877.

69. CAOM, FM/SG REU 380/3228, minute 6 March 1876, p. 13.

70. CAOM, FM/SG REU 380/3228, minute of council, n. 7, 19 March 1877.

71. Carter, *Servants, Sirdars and Settlers*, p. 179.

72. CAOM, FM/SG REU 380/3228, minute 6 March 1876.

73. CAOM, FM/SG REU 380/3228, minute 6 March 1876.

74. CAOM, FM/SG REU 380/3228, several minutes, 1877–82.

75. Allen, *Slaves*.

76. Ibid., introduction and ch. 6.
77. Mauritius National Archives (hereafter MA NA) 80, 83, 84.
78. *Parliamentary Papers*, 1901: CVI: 78–81.
79. MA NA 80, 83, 84. For loans by Indian merchants in Mauritius: MA NA 102, several files.
80. Mauritius Blue Book, 1900–8.
81. Allen, *Slaves*, p. 160.
82. *Parliamentary Papers*, 1910: XLII (Cd 5194), section 70.
83. *Parliamentary Papers*, 1924: XXIV: 99–102.
84. Allen, *Slaves*, p. 169.
85. Ibid., p. 170.
86. M. K. Banton, 'The Colonial Office, 1820–1955: Constantly the Subject of Small Struggles', in Hay and Craven (eds), *Magistrates*, pp. 251–302; F. Cooper, 'From Free Labour to Family Allowances: Labour and African Society in Colonial Discourse', *American Ethnologist*, 16:4 (1989), pp. 745–65. B. Fall, *Le travail forcé en Afrique occidentale française, 1900–1946* (Paris: Karthala, 1993).

6 Warren, 'Ransom, Escape and Debt Repayment in the Sulu Zone, 1750–1898'

1. J. Warren, *The Sulu Zone 1768–1898: The Dynamics of External Trade, Slavery, and Ethnicity in the Transformation of a Southeast Asian Maritime State* (Singapore: Singapore University Press, 2007), p. xviii.
2. Ibid., p. xiv.
3. For population calculations, see ibid., pp. 67–102, 198–211; T. Kiefer, 'The Taosug Polity and the Sultanaate of Sulu: A Segmentary State in the Southern Philippines', *Sulu Studies*, 1 (1972), pp. 19–64.
4. Statements of Manuel de los Santos and Juan Salvador, 4 October 1836, Philippine National Archive (hereafter PNA), Mindanao/Sulu, 1803–90, Declaraciones de todos los cautivos fugados de Jolo y acogidos a los buques de la expresada division, con objeto de averiguar los puntos de donde salen los pancos piratas, la clase de gente que los tripulan, la forma en que se hacen los armamentos y otros particulares que arrojan las mismas declaraciones, exp. 12.
5. El Obispo de Zebu a Senor Don Joseph Galvez, 22 May 1779, Archivo General de Indias, Seville, Filipinas (hereafter AGI), 687.
6. *GCG a Senor Secretario de Estado*, June 1806, AGI, 510, 27, No. 7, 4. Extracts from *Singapore Free Press*, 6 April 1847, Public Records Office, London (hereafter PRO), Admiralty, 125/133.
7. R. P. Robinson (Pursers Clerk), Entries for 31 January 1842 and 4 February 1842, Journal kept aboard the *Vincennes*, 6 April 1841–15 May 1842, United States National Archive, Washington, DC (hereafter USNA).
8. Memoir of Sooloo, – India Office Library, London, Orme Collection (hereafter IOL), 67, 128.
9. *El Gobernador de Zamboanga a Gobernador Captain General*, 12 April 1769, PNA, Varias Provinces, Zamboanga; No. 226, II, AGI Filipinas, 492.
10. R. P. Robinson (Pursers Clerk), Entries for 31 January 1842 and 4 February 1842, Journal kept aboard the *Vincennes*, 6 April 1841–15 May 1842, USNA.

11. J. M. y Vidal, Historia General de Filipinas desde el descrubrimiento de dichas Islas hasta nuestras dias, 3 vols (Madrid: M. Tello, 1894–1895), vol. 2, p. 482.
12. *Sultan Muyamad Alimudin a Gobernador D. Juan de Mir*, 13 May 1781, PNA, Mindanao/Sulu 1769–1898; J. B. Barrantes, *Guerras Piraticas de Filipinas contra Mindanaos y Joloanos* (Madrid: Imprenta de Manuel H. Hernandez, 1878), p. 162.
13. V. Hurley, *Swish of the Kris* (New York: E.P. Dutton, 1936), p. 122.
14. F. Gainza, *Memoria y antecedents sobre las expediciones de Balangingi y Jolo* (Manila: Establecimiento tipografico de Colegio de Santo Tomas, 1851), pp. 39–40; C. Z. Pieters, 'Adventures of C. Z. Pieters among the Pirates of Maguindanao', *Journal of the Indian Archipelago and Eastern Asia* (1858), pp. 301–12.
15. J. M. de Zuniga, *Estadismo de las Filipinas: a mis viajez por este pais*, 2 vols (Madrid: M. Minuesa de los Rios, 1893), vol. 1, pp. 118–20.
16. Vidal, *Historia de los Filipinas*, vol. 2, p. 482.
17. 'The Illanoon', extract from the *Singapore Free Press*, 6 April 1874, PRO, Admiralty, 125/133.
18. Pieters, 'Adventures of C.Z. Pieters', p. 310.
19. Ibid., pp. 309–10.
20. Ibid., pp. 310–11.
21. Ibid., p. 311.
22. Ibid., p. 311.
23. Ibid., pp. 311–12.
24. Hurley, *Swish of the Kris*, p. 147.
25. H. Keppel, *A Visit to the Indian Archipelago in H.M.S. Maeander, with Portions of the Private Journal of Sir James Brooke K.C.B.* (London: Richard Bentley, 1853), p. 59.
26. Statement of Eulalio Camposano, Relacion jurada de los cuarenta y cinco cautivos venidos de jolo sobre el Bergantin Espanol Cometa, PNA, Piratas, 1824–77.
27. Juan Bautista Barrera, *Diario de Los Pancos Piratas que han entrado mi residencia en al Puerto de Jolo*, 25 September 1845, Archivo-Museo Don Alvaro de Bazan, Legajo, 1176.262.
28. Barrera, Diario de Los Pancos Piratas que han entrado mi residencia en al Puerto de Jolo, pp. 1–2.
29. See the statements in *Relacion jurada de los individuos cautivos venidos en las Fragata de guerra Inglesia Samarang*, 15 March 1845, PNA, Piratas, p. 3; J. Hunt, 'Some Particulars Relating to Sulo in the Archipelago of Felicia', in J. H. Moor (ed.), *Notices of the Indian Archipelago and Adjacent Countries* (London: Cass, 1967), p. 50.
30. A. J .F. Jansen, 'Aanteekeningen omtrent Sollok en de Solloksche Zeerovers', Tijdscrift voor Indische Taal-, Land -en Volkenkunde, 7 (1858), pp. 212–39, 225.
31. Statement of Francisco Augustino in Relacion jurada de los individuos cautivos venidos en las Fragata de Guerra Inglesia Samarang, 15 March 1845, PNA, Piratas, p. 3.
32. O. J. W. Scott and I. C. Brown, 'Ethnography of the Magandanaos of Parang', Library of Congress, Beyer-Holleman Philippine Collection Customary Law (hereafter BH-PC), VI, paper 163, no. 34, p. 187; M. Mednick, 'Some Problems of Moro History and Political Organization', *Philippine Sociological Review*, 5:1 (1957), pp. 39–52, on p. 48; S. Elkins, 'Slavery and its Aftermath in the Western World', in A. de Reuck and J. Knight (eds), *Caste and Race: Comparative Approaches* (London: J. and A. Churchill, 1967), pp. 192–203, on p. 200; Hunt, 'Some Particulars Relating to Sulo', p. 50.

33. *GCG a Presidente del Consejo de Ministro*, 9 December 1858, Archivo Historico Nacional (hereafter AHN), Madrid, Ultramar 5184; Hunt, 'Some Particulars Relating to Sulo', p. 50.

34. Statements of Pedro Flores and Pedro Isidoro in *Relacion jurada de los cuaranta y cinco cautivos venidos de Jolo sobre el Bergantin Espanol* Cometa, 19 March 1847, PNA, Piratas, p. 3; statements of Francisco Anastacio and Jacinto Pedro in *Relacion jurada de los individuos cautivos venidos en las Fragata de guerra Inglesia Samarang*, 15 March 1845, Piratas, p. 3; 'Berigten omtrent de Zeeroof in den Nederlandsch-Indischeb Archipel, 1857', pp. 440, 445; 'Berigten omtrent de Zeeroof in den Nederlandsch-Indischeb Archipel, 1858', p. 304.

35. Keppel, *A Visit to the Indian Archipelago in H.M.S. Maeander*, p. 69.

36. See log kept aboard the brig *Leonides*, entry for 31 August 1836, Peabody Museum, Salem, 656/1835A.

37. Statement of Juan Santiago in exp. 12, 4 October 1836, PNA, Mindanao/Sulu, 1803–1890, p. 22.

38. Keppel, *A Visit to the Indian Archipelago in H.M.S. Maeander*, p. 69; T. J. Jacobs, *Scenes, Incidents and Adventures in the Pacific Ocean, or the Islands of the Australasian Seas, during the Cruise of the Clipper Margaret Oakley under the Captain Benjamin Morrell* (New York: Harper and Bros, 1844), p. 340.

39. See log kept aboard the brig *Leonides*, entry for 31 August 1836, Peabody Museum, Salem, 656/1835A.

40. Jacob, *Scenes, Incidents and Adventures in the Pacific Ocean*, p. 340.

41. The War Department to the Governor General, exp. 15, 23 June 1842, PNA, Guerra, 1834–48.

42. The Consul of Spain in Singapore to the Governor Captain General, exp. 354, 15 April 1864, PNA, Piratas 1828–91.

43. The Consul of Spain in Singapore to the Governor Captain General, 29 March 1864, PNA, Piratas 1828–91.

44. The War Department to the Governor Captain General, exp. 15, 23 June 1842, PNA, Guerra, 1834–48.

45. Statement of Mariano Francisco, exp. 13, 5 October 1849, PNA, Ereccion de Pueblos, Cebu, 1818–77.

46. Statement of Mariano Francisco, 916, February 1850, PNA, Ereccion de Pueblos, Cebu, 1818–77.

47. Captaincy of the Port of Manila and Cavite, Manuel Paes, to His Excellency and Governor General of these Islands, Narciso Clavería y Zaldua, 14 April 1848, PNA, Marina, 1847–98, Legajo 26, ff. 661–2.

48. 13 March 1839, PNA, Marina 1836–40, Exp. 363, ff. 525b–526.

49. Statement of Ignacio Solas, exp. 13, 13 October 1849, PNA, Ereccion de Pueblos, Cebu, 1818–77.

50. Statements of Dionicio Domingo and Juan Fernando, 23 November 1850, PNA, Piratas, 1824–77.

51. Governor Captain General to the Alcalde Mayor of Camarines Norte, exp. 191, 12 December 1864, PNA, Piratas, 1824–77.

52. Warren, *The Sulu Zone*, p. 190.

53. 'Advantages and Disadvantages of the Territory in Zamboanga', PNA, Memorias – Zamboanga, 1845–90, p. 3.

54. Jose Maria Halcon to Governor Captain General, Pedro Antonio Salazar, exp. 22, 27 December 1836, PNA, Cedularios/Cartas, 1836–7.

55. Statements of Feliciano Maria and Jose Clemencia, exp. 13, June 1849, PNA, Ereccion de Pueblos Cebu, 1817–77.

56. General Command of Mindanao, Basilan and the Samal Islands to Governor Captain General, exp. 15, 10 March 1860, PNA Varias Provincias, Zamboanga, 1868–99.

57. *Gobierno Militar y Politico de Zamboanga a GCG*, 6 February 1860, PNA Varias Provincias, Zamboanga, no. 15.

58. *Jose Maria Halcon a GCG*, 31 December 1837, Archive of the University of Santo Tomas (hereafter AUST), Manila, seccion folletos, tomo 117.

59. *Mariano de Goecoecha a GCG*, 24 April 1838, PNA, unclassified Mindanao/Sulu bundle.

60. General Command of Mindanao, Basilan and the Samal Islands to Governor Captain General; *Jose Maria Halcon a GCG*, 31 December 1837, AUST, 'Memoria sobre Mindanao y demas puntas del Sur', Seccion Folletos, Tomo 117.

7 Hopper, 'Debt and Slavery among Arabian Gulf Pearl Divers'

1. Statement of slave Marzuq bin Mubarak, aged about twenty-two years, recorded at the Political Agency, Bahrain, 20 July 1928, India Office Records, British Library, London (hereafter IOR), R/15/1/204.

2. Shaikh Sultan bin Saqar, Chief of Sharjah to Residency Agent, Sharjah, 19 September 1928, IOR, R/15/1/204.

3. Shaikh Sultan bin Saqar, Chief of Sharjah to Residency Agent, Sharjah, 19 September 1928, IOR, R/15/1/204.

4. Shaikh Sultan bin Saqar, Chief of Sharjah to Residency Agent, Sharjah, 19 September 1928, IOR, R/15/1/204.

5. Agency Bahrain [presumably Cyril Charles Johnson Barrett] to H. R. P. Dickson, Secretary to Political Resident in the Persian Gulf, Bushire, 16 November 1928, IOR, R/15/1/204.

6. W. G. Palgrave, *Personal Narrative of a Year's Journey through Central and Eastern Arabia, 1862–63* (London: Macmillan & Co., 1883), p. 387.

7. See for example: P. E. Lovejoy and J. S. Hogendorn, *Slow Death for Slavery: The Course of Abolition in Northern Nigeria, 1897–1936* (New York: Cambridge University Press, 1993); S. Miers, 'Slavery to Freedom in Sub-Saharan Africa: Expectations and Reality', in H. Temperley (ed.), *After Slavery: Emancipation and Its Discontents* (Portland, OR: Frank Cass, 2000), pp. 237–64; S. Miers and R. Roberts, *The End of Slavery in Africa* (Madison, WI: University of Wisconsin Press, 1988), pp. 1–68; S. L. Engerman, 'Slavery, Serfdom and Other Forms of Coerced Labour: Similarities and Differences', in M. L. Bush (ed.), *Serfdom and Slavery: Studies in Legal Bondage* (New York: Longman, 1996), pp. 18–67.

8. E. L. Durand, *Administration Report of the Persian Gulf Political Residency and Muscat Political Agent for the Year 1877–78*, 32, the National Archives (UK), Kew, London (hereafter TNA), Foreign Office, 78/5108. The term *sidi* (also rendered variously as 'seedee' and 'seedie') originated in northern India and was used to describe people of African descent, many of whom were employed in maritime trade. In the wider Indian Ocean context, British officials applied the term to descendants of East Africans, both enslaved and free, outside of East Africa. See J. J. Ewald, 'Crossers of the Sea: Slaves, Freedmen,

and Other Migrants in the Northwestern Indian Ocean, c. 1750–1914', *American Historical Review*, 105:1 (2000), pp. 69–91, on p. 83.

9. J. G. Lorimer, *Gazetteer of the Persian Gulf, Oman and Central Arabia*, 2 vols (Calcutta: Government Printing, 1915), vol. 1, p. 2228.

10. P. W. Harrison, *The Arab at Home* (New York: Thomas Y. Crowell Company, 1924), p. 88.

11. C. Belgrave, *Personal Column* (London: Hutchinson, 1960), p. 44.

12. Senior Naval Officer, Persian Gulf Division, HMS *Triad*, to Commander in Chief, East Indies Station, 12 September 1929, No. 27G/56/1, IOR, L/PS/12/4091.

13. 'Notes on the Slave Trade by Wazir Thomas, August 1929', P. 7418/29, IOR, L/PS/12/4091.

14. Lorimer, *Gazetteer of the Persian Gulf, Oman and Central Arabia*, vol. 1, p. 2227.

15. A. Villiers, *Sons of Sinbad: An Account of Sailing with the Arabs in their Dhows in the Red Sea, around the Coasts of Arabia, and to Zanzibar and Tanganyika: Pearling in the Persian Gulf: and the Life of the Shipmasters, the Mariners and Merchants of Kuwait* (New York: Charles Schribner's Sons, 1940), pp. 393–6.

16. E. L. Durand, *Administration Report of the Persian Gulf Political Residency and Muscat Political Agent for the Year 1877–78*, 32, TNA, Foreign Office, 78/5108; Lorimer, *Gazetteer of the Persian Gulf, Oman and Central Arabia*, vol. 1, and Villiers, *Sons of Sinbad*.

17. Belgrave, *Personal Column*, p. 43.

18. Statement of account showing the debts of Bashir bin Umran bin Abdullah as copied from the Account Book of Matar bin Matar resident of Dubai, attachment to Bashir bin Umran bin Abdullah to Family of Bin Ali, 7 October 1925, IOR, R/15/1/208.

19. Statement of account showing the debts of Ismail bin Sanqah to Rashid bin Abdullah, 26 May 1924, IOR, R/15/1/208.

20. Case of Jumah bin Sanqur, known as Jumah Kanaidish, aged forty years, 27 October 1936, IOR, R/15/1/219.

21. M. S. Hopper, 'The African Presence in Arabia: Slavery, the World Economy, and the African Diaspora in Eastern Arabia, 1840–1940' (PhD dissertation, UCLA, 2006), Appendix A: Slave Prices in Eastern Arabia, 1895–1940, p. 308.

22. M. S. Hopper, 'Imperialism and the Dilemma of Slavery in Eastern Arabia and the Gulf, 1873–1939', *Itinerario*, 30:3 (2006), pp. 76–94.

23. Percy Cox, for example, once wrote that 'The Government of India will understand that the fact that a negro only has to run over to Bunder Abbas or Bahrain to get a Manumission Certificate on his own ex-parte statement is almost as much calculated to cause resentment in the Shaikh's mind as the manumission of slaves by our Political Agent in Kuwait itself without reference to him. Our ultimate object in pursuing the philanthropic policy which we do in regard to the manumission of slaves is to secure the greatest good for the greatest number and this end can best be served by gradually bringing the Shaikhs of Kuweit under our civilizing influence in this as well as other directions': Maj. P. Z. Cox, Political Resident in the Persian Gulf to S. H. Butler, Secretary to Government of India, Foreign Department, 22 March 1908, IOR, R/15/1/213.

24. M. S. Hopper, '"Slaves of One Master": Globalization and the African Diaspora in Arabia in the Age of Empire', in R. Harms and B. Freamon (eds), *Slavery and the Slave Trades in the Indian Ocean and Arab Worlds: Global Connections and Disconnections* (New Haven, CT: Yale University Press, forthcoming).

25. G. F. Kunz and C. H. Stevenson, *The Book of the Pearl* (New York: Century Co., 1908), p. 80; L. Rosenthal, *The Pearl Hunter, an Autobiography* (New York: H. Schuman, 1952), p. 66.

26. Senior Naval Officer in Persian Gulf (and Commander HMS *Vulture*) to Rear Admiral Arthur Cumming, Commander in Chief, East Indies, 10 September 1872, TNA, ADM, 1/6230; Lt. C. M. Gilbert Cooper, 'Capture of a Slave Dhow: Or the Vulture and Its Prey', not dated, Lt. C. M. Gilbert-Cooper Papers, National Maritime Museum (UK), Greenwich, London (hereafter NMM), BGY/G/5.

27. Commander HMS *Philomel* to Commander in Chief, East Indies, 15 October 1884, TNA, ADM, 1/6714.

28. Herbert W. Dowding, Commander HMS *Osprey*, to Rear Admiral Frederick W. Richards, Commander in Chief, East Indies, 19 September 1885, TNA, ADM, 1/6758.

29. See, for example, the following from Bahrain: 'I did not like to go to Isa bin Abdul Latif, as he takes money from slave traders and men like my master and would burden me with heavy debts or he would create some other excuses for the retention of slaves like me with their masters'. Statement of Marooq bin Saad, aged about thirty-five years, appears to be Abyssinian, 3 May 1927, IOR, R/15/1/204.

30. For more on the role of native agents and residency agents, see J. Onley, *The Arabian Frontier of the British Raj: Merchants, Rulers, and the British in the Nineteenth-Century Gulf* (Oxford: Oxford University Press, 2007). For more on the life of 'Isa bin 'Abd al-Latīf, see R. S. Zahlan, *The Origins of the United Arab Emirates: A Political and Social History of the Trucial States* (New York: St Martin's Press, 1978).

31. Sheikh Sultan bin Salem bin Sultan, Chief of Ras Ul-Khaimah to Lt. Col. C. G. Crosthwaite, Political Resident in the Persian Gulf, 25th Muharram 1344 (16 August 1925), IOR, R/15/1/208.

32. Sheikh Sultan bin Salem bin Sultan, Chief of Ras Ul-Khaimah to Lt. Col. C. G. Crosthwaite, Political Resident in the Persian Gulf, 25th Muharram 1344 (16 August 1925), IOR, R/15/1/208.

33. Shaikh Sultan bin Saqar to Residency Agent, Sharjah, 12 December 1925, IOR, R/15/1/208.

34. Political Agent Bahrain to PRPG, No. 35, 23 January 1926, IOR, R/15/1/208.

35. Political Resident, notes on letter: Residency Agent, Sharjah to Political Resident in the Persian Gulf, 19 January 1927, IOR, R/15/1/216.

36. Secretary to PRPG, 27 September 1925, IOR, R/15/1/208.

37. Secretary's notes, Office of Political Resident in the Persian Gulf, 5 August 1931, IOR, R/15/1/205.

38. Debt records of Marzuq bin Mubarak in file containing Statement of slave Marzuq bin Mubarak, aged about twenty-two years, recorded at the Political Agency, Bahrain, 20 July 1928, IOR, R/15/1/204.

39. Debt records of Marzuq bin Mubarak in file containing Statement of slave Marzuq bin Mubarak, aged about twenty-two years, recorded at the Political Agency, Bahrain, 20 July 1928, IOR, R/15/1/204.

40. Debt records of Marzuq bin Mubarak in file containing Statement of slave Marzuq bin Mubarak, aged about twenty-two, recorded at the Political Agency, Bahrain, 20 July 1928, IOR, R/15/1/204.

41. Debt records of Marzuq bin Mubarak in file containing Statement of slave Marzuq bin Mubarak, aged about twenty-two years, recorded at the Political Agency, Bahrain, 20 July 1928, IOR, R/15/1/204.

42. See for example: F. Cooper, 'Conditions Analogous to Slavery: Imperialism and Free Labor Ideology in Africa', in F. Cooper, T. C. Holt and R. J. Scott (eds), *Beyond Slavery: Explorations of Race, Labor, and Citizenship in Postemancipation Societies* (Chapel Hill, NC: University of North Carolina Press, 2000), pp. 107–50; E. Allina, *Slavery By Any Other Name: African Life Under Company Rule in Colonial Mozambique* (Charlottesville, VA: University of Virginia Press, 2012); A. A. Sikainga, *Slaves Into Workers: Emancipation and Labor in Colonial Sudan* (Austin, TX: University of Texas Press, 1996); K. Grant, *A Civilised Savagery: Britain and the New Slaveries in Africa, 1884–1926* (New York: Routledge, 2005); G. Campbell, 'Introduction: Abolition and Its Aftermath in the Indian Ocean', in G. Campbell (ed.), *Abolition and Its Aftermath in Indian Ocean Africa and Asia* (London: Routledge, 2005), pp. 1–28.
43. D. Brook, 'Usury Country: Welcome to the Birthplace of Payday Lending', *Harper's Magazine*, 318:1907 (2009), pp. 41–8.

8 Guérin, 'The Political Economy of Debt Bondage in Contemporary South India'

1. J. Breman, *Labour Bondage in West India. From Past to Present* (Oxford: Oxford University Press, 2007); K Sankaran, 'Bonded Labour and the Courts', in J. Breman, I. Guérin and A. Prakash (eds), *India's Unfree Workforce. Old and New Practices of Labour Bondage* (New Delhi: Oxford University Press, 2009), pp. 335–51.
2. C. Malamoud (ed.), *Lien de vie, nœud mortel. Les représentations de la dette en Chine, au Japon et dans le monde indien* (Paris: Editions EHESS, 1988).
3. Fieldwork was conducted by the author and by G. Venkatasubramanian, S. Ponnarasu and Marc Roesch. We thank them here for their involvement. The three studies were conducted in partnership with the International Labour Organisation.
4. As suggested by J. Banaji, 'The Fictions of Free Labour: Contract, Coercion, and So-Called Unfree Labour', *Historical Materialism*, 11 (2003), pp. 69–95.
5. See for instance P. Bardhan, 'The Economist's Approach to Agrarian Structure', in J. Parry and R. Guha (eds), *Institutions and Inequalities: Essays in Honour of Andre Béteille* (New Delhi and Oxford: University Press, 2001), pp. 88–99.
6. The most representative and prolific author is Tom Brass. See for example T. Brass, 'Class Struggle and Deproletarianisation of Agricultural Labour in Haryana (India)', *Journal of Peasant Studies*, 18:1 (1990), pp. 36–67; T. Brass, *Towards a Comparative Political Economy of Unfree Labour. Case Studies and Debates* (London: Frank Cass, 1999).
7. See for instance J. M. Rao, 'Freedom, Equality, Property and Bentham: The Debate over Unfree Labour', *Journal of Peasant Studies*, 27:1 (1999), pp. 97–127.
8. We can mention here the pioneering work of J. Breman (*Patronage and Exploitation: Changing Agrarian Relations in South Gujarat, India* (Berkeley, CA: University of California Press, 1974)) till its most recent developments (Breman, *Labour Bondage in West India*); collected essays (T. K. Byres, K. Kapadia and J. Lerche (eds), *Rural Labour Relations in India* (New Delhi: India Research Press, 1999); Breman, Guérin and Prakash (eds), *India's Unfree Workforce*); monographs (S. S. Jodhka, 'Agrarian Changes and Attached Labour: Emerging Patterns in Haryana Agriculture', *Economic and Political Weekly*, 29 (1994), A102–6; K. Kapadia, *Siva and her Sisters. Gender, Caste and Class in Rural India* (Delhi: Oxford University Press, 1996); G. de Neve, *The Everyday Politics of Labour. Working Lives in India's Informal Economy* (New Delhi: Social Sciences Press,

2005); J. Lerche, 'Is Bonded Labour a Bound Category? Reconceptualising Agrarian Conflict in India', *Journal of Peasant Studies*, 22 (1995), pp. 484–515; D. Picherit, 'Entre villages et chantiers: circulation des travailleurs, clientélisme et politisation des basses castes en Andhra Pradesh, Inde' (PhD dissertation, Université Paris 10 Nanterre, 2009)); and reviews and essays (J. Harriss, 'Does the "Depressor" Still Work? Agrarian Structure and Development in India: A Review of Evidences and Arguments', *Journal of Peasant Studies*, 19:2 (1992), pp. 189–227; S. S. Jodhka, 'Unfree Labour and "Postmodern Myths": Towards a Critical Examination', *Historical Materialism*, 12:4 (2004), pp. 463–72; J. Lerche, 'A Global Alliance against Forced Labour? Unfree Labour, Neo-liberal Globalization and the International Labour Organization', *Journal of Agrarian Change*, 7:4 (2007), pp. 424–52; R. Srivastava, *Bonded Labour in India: Its Incidence and Pattern*. Special Action Programme to Combat Forced Labour, Declaration/WP/43/2005 (ILO: Geneva, 2005), at http:// www.ilo.org/sapfl/Informationresources/ILOPublications/lang--en/docName--WCMS_081967/index.htm [accessed 12 May 2012]; R. Srivastava, 'Conceptualising Continuity and Change in Emerging Forms of Labour Bondage', in Breman, Guérin and Prakash (eds), *India's Unfree Workforce*, pp. 129–46).

9.   Srivastava, 'Conceptualising Continuity and Change in Emerging Forms of Labour Bondage', p. 133.

10. I. Guérin, A. Bhukhut, K. Marius-Gnanou and J.-M. Servet, *Indebtedness, Vulnerability to Bondage and Microfinance, Report for the ILO (Social Finance Unit)* (Puducherry: French Institute of Pondicherry, 2004); see also Lerche, 'A Global Alliance Against Forced Labour?'; G. de Neve and G. Carswell, 'From Field to Factory: Tracing Transformations in Bonded Labour in the Tiruppur Region, South India', *Economy and Society* (forthcoming, 2013); V. Rawal, 'The Labour Process in Rural Haryana (India): A Field Report from Two Villages', *Journal of Agrarian Change*, 6:4 (2006), pp. 538–83.

11. A. Prakash, 'Towards Understanding the Nature of Labour Markets in Brick Kilns', in Breman, Guérin and Prakash (eds), *India's Unfree Workforce*, pp. 199–232.

12. Ibid.

13. F. Landy, *Un milliard à nourrir. Grain, territoire et politique en Inde* (Paris: Belin, 2006), p. 80.

14. In 2004, 1 US$ = 45 INR. The official threshold of poverty in India in 2004 was put at about 15,000 Rs per family (for a family with five members), knowing that this amount is clearly underevaluated; a decent living standard would actually be an income of 50,000 Rs. In this area of research, obtaining reliable data is also a challenge.

15. By comparison, in 2006 daily wages in agriculture were around 80 INR for around six hours of labour, which translates into around 13.3 INR per hour.

16. I. Guérin, 'Corridors of Migration and Chains of Dependence: Brick Kiln Moulders in Tamil Nadu', in Breman, Guérin and Prakash (eds), *India's Unfree Workforce*, pp. 170–97.

17. On this point see Picherit, 'Entre villages et chantiers: circulation des travailleurs, clientélisme et politisation des basses castes en Andhra Pradesh, Inde'.

18. See for instance G. Cederlof, *The Origins of Industrial Capitalism: Business Strategies and the Working Classes in Bombay, 1900–1940* (Cambridge: Cambridge University Press, 1994) for a historical analysis in Tamil Nadu. See also K. T. Rammohan, 'Modern Bondage: Atiyyayma in Post-Abolition Malabar', in Breman, Guérin and Prakash (eds), *India's Unfree Workforce*, pp. 69–96 for Kerala.

19. For other examples, see N. Gooptu, *The Politics of the Urban Poor in Early Twentieth-Century India* (Cambridge: Cambridge University Press, 2001), p. 55; J. Breman, *Footloose Labour: Working in the Indian Informal Economy* (Cambridge: Cambridge University

Press, 1996); K. Kapadia, 'The Profitability of Bonded Labour: The Gem Cutting Industry of Rural South India', *Journal of Peasant Studies*, 23:3 (April 1995), pp. 446–83.

20. This is not universal, however: bondage can also be a means of ensuring the loyalty of a qualified workforce, as found in weaving (De Neve, *The Everyday Politics of Labour*).

21. Breman, *Footloose Labour*; Breman, *Labour Bondage in West India*; Breman, Guérin and Prakash (eds), *India's Unfree Workforce*.

22. Landy, *Un milliard à nourrir*.

23. For a literature review, see Srivastava, *Bonded Labour in India*.

24. National Commission for Enterprises in the Unorganised Sector, *Report on Conditions of Work and Promotion of Livelihoods in the Unorganised Sector* (New Delhi: NCEUS, 2007).

25. J.-M. Servet, 'Entre protection et surexploitation: l'ambiguïté de la rémunération par avance en Inde', *Autrepart*, 43 (2007), pp. 103–19.

26. Most of the brick kiln owners do not respect legislation like the Prohibition of Child Labour in Hazardous Industries Act (1970); the Employment Provident Fund and Miscellaneous Provisions Act (1971); the Factory Act (1948), which regulates working hours and provides compensation for overtime; and the Inter-State Migrant Workmen Act (1979), which provides for specific measures (housing, medical coverage, etc.) when more than 50 per cent of a company's work force are migrants.

27. Naidus and Beri Chettiars are natives of Andhra Pradesh and speak Telugu, though they have settled in Tamil Nadu for several generations.

28. See, for instance, merchants' communities such as Beeri Chettiyar in Chennai (M. Mines, *Public Faces, Private Voices. Community and Individuality in South-India* (Delhi: Oxford University Press, 1996, pp. 49ff)) or corporatist communities, such as the weavers in Coimbatore (De Neve, *The Everyday Politics of Labour*, pp. 269ff).

29. Guérin, 'Corridors of Migration and Chains of Dependence: Brick Kiln Moulders in Tamil Nadu'.

30. R. Deliège, 'Job Mobility among the Brickmakers of South India', *Man in India*, 69 (March 1989), pp. 43–63.

31. K. S. Singh, *People of India: The Scheduled Tribes* (Delhi: Oxford University Press, 1994); E. Thurston and K. Rangachari, *Castes and Tribes of Southern India* (Delhi: Cosmo, 1975).

32. For a review, see B. Harriss-White, *India Working: Essays on Society and Economy* (Cambridge: Cambridge University Press, 2003).

33. Harriss-White, *India Working*, p. 208.

34. This has already been highlighted by the work of Breman, *Footloose Labour*; Byres, Kapadia and Lerche (eds), *Rural Labour Relations in India*; Kapadia, *Siva and her Sisters*; Harriss, 'Does the "Depressor" Still Work?'; Harriss-White, *India Working*; Srivastava, *Bonded Labour in India*.

35. V. Dupont and F. Landy (eds), *Circulation et territoires dans le monde indien contemporain* (Paris: Editions de l'EHESS, Collection Purushartha vol. 28, 2010); Srivastava, 'Conceptualising Continuity and Change in Emerging Forms of Labour Bondage'; National Commission for Enterprises in the Unorganised Sector, *Report on Conditions of Work and Promotion of Livelihoods in the Unorganised Sector*.

36. D. Heuzé, 'Bondage in India: Representing the Past or the Present? The Case of the Dhanbad Coal Belt During the Eighties', in Breman, Guérin and Prakash (eds), *India's Unfree Workforce*, pp. 146–7.

37. K. Kapadia, 'Translocal Modernities and Transformations of Gender and Caste', in K. Karin (ed), *The Violence of Development. The Politics of Identity, Gender and Social Inequalities in India* (New Delhi: Kali for Women, 2002), pp. 142–82.

38. Guérin, 'Corridors of Migration and Chains of Dependence: Brick Kiln Moulders in Tamil Nadu'.

39. Breman, *Labour Bondage in West India*; Srivastava, 'Conceptualising Continuity and Change in Emerging Forms of Labour Bondage'.

9 Salman, 'The Name of the Slave and the Quality of the Debt: When Slaves Are Not Debtors and Debtors Are Not Slaves in the Family Narrative of a Filipina Comfort Woman'

1. M. I. Finley, *Economy and Society in Ancient Greece* (New York: Viking Press, 1981), p. 152.

2. G. Prakash, *Bonded Histories: Genealogies of Labor Servitude in Colonial India* (Cambridge: Cambridge University Press, 1990), pp. 2–11.

3. 'Introduction', in A. Reid and J. Brewster (eds), *Slavery, Bondage and Dependency in Southeast Asia* (New York: St. Martin's Press, 1983), pp. 1–43, on pp. 8, 11, 22.

4. Ibid., p. 8.

5. Ibid., p. 7.

6. M. R. Henson, *Comfort Woman: A Filipina's Story of Prostitution and Slavery under the Japanese Military* (Lanham, MD: Rowman & Littlefield, 1999).

7. Ibid., p. 25.

8. Ibid., pp. 24–34; B. J. T. Kervliet, *The Huk Rebellion: A Study of Peasant Revolt in the Philippines* (Berkeley, CA: University of California Press, 1982).

9. Henson, *Comfort Woman*, pp. 27–8, 34.

10. Ibid., p. 34.

11. M. Salman, *The Embarrassment of Slavery* (Berkeley, CA: University of California Press, 2001).

12. Henson, *Comfort Woman*, pp. 35–7.

13. Ibid., pp. 38–41.

14. Ibid., p. 41.

15. Ibid., pp. 41–2.

16. Ibid., p. 42.

17. Ibid., p. 43.

18. Ibid., pp. 43–4.

19. Ibid., p. 44, emphasis mine.

20. F. Cannell, *Power and Intimacy in the Christian Philippines* (Cambridge: Cambridge University Press, 1999), pp. 29–76.

21. R. C. Ileto, *Pasyon and Revolution: Popular Movements in the Philippines, 1840–1910* (Quezon City: Ateneo de Manila University Press, 1979).

22. Henson, *Comfort Woman*, p. 44.

23. Ibid., p. 48.

24. Ibid., pp. 2–3.

25. Ibid., p. 3.

26. Ibid., pp. 5–6.

27. Ibid., p. 6.

28. Ibid., p. 6.
29. Ibid., pp. 7–8.
30. Ibid., p. 8.
31. Ibid., pp. 8–9.
32. V. L. Rafael, *Contracting Colonialism* (Durham, NC: Duke University Press, 1993).
33. Henson, *Comfort Woman*, p. 9.
34. Rafael, *Contracting Colonialism*.
35. Cannell, *Power and Intimacy in the Christian Philippines*, pp. 103–4.
36. Henson, *Comfort Woman*, p. 9.
37. 'Introduction', p. 7.
38. Henson, *Comfort Woman*, p. 13.
39. Ibid., p. 17.
40. Ibid., p. 19.
41. Ibid., p. 22.
42. I. Chatterjee, *Gender, Slavery and Law in Colonial India* (New Delhi: Oxford University Press, 1999), p. 17.

10 Murakami, 'Two Bonded Labour Emigration Patterns in Mid-Nineteenth-Century Southern China: The Coolie Trade and Emigration to Southeast Asia'

1. R. L. Irick, *Ch'ing Policy toward the Coolie Trade 1847–1878* (Taipei: Chinese Materials Centre, 1982); C.-h. Yen, *Coolies and Mandarins: China's Protection of Overseas Chinese during the Late Ch'ing Period (1851–1911)* (Singapore: Singapore University Press, 1985); G. Zhuang, *Zhongguo Fengjian Zhengfu de Huaqiao Zhengce* (The Chinese Feudal Government's Policies towards Overseas Chinese) (Xiamen: Xiamen Daxue Chubanshe, 1989)
2. S.-w. Wang, *The Organization of Chinese Emigration 1848–1888: With Special Reference to Chinese Emigration to Australia* (San Francisco, CA: Chinese Materials Centre, Inc., 1978).
3. For the Amoy riot, see J. Ozawa, '1852 nen Amoi Bōdō nit suite' ('The Amoy Riot of 1852'), *Shiron (Tōkyō Joshi daigaku)*, 38 (1985), pp. 47–67 and C.-k. Ng, 'The Amoy Riot of 1852: Coolie Emigration and Sino-British Relations', in K. S. Matthew (ed.), *Marines, Merchants and Oceans Studies in Maritime History* (New Delhi: Manohar Publishers & Distributors, 1995), pp. 419–46. For the attack on foreigners in Shanghai, see H. Kani, 'Kanpo Kyū nen Shanhai ni okeru Gaikokujin shugeki jiken ni tsuite' ('On the Anti-Foreign Incident in Shanghai in 1859') *Tōyōshi kenkyū*, 43:3 (1984), pp. 486–507. Y. Nishisato, *Shinmatsu Chūryūnich Kankeishi no Kenkyū* (The Relationship between China, Ryūkyu and Japan during the Late Qing Period) (Kyoto: Kyōto Daigaku Gakujyutsu Shuppankai, 2005) examines the riot aboard the *Robert Bowne*, a coolie transport ship, in the context of the history of Ryūkyū.
4. H. Kani, *Kindai Chūgoku no Kūrī to 'Choka'* (Coolies and 'Slave Girls' of Modern China) (Tokyo: Iwanami Shoten, 1979).
5. W. Stewart, *Chinese Bondage in Peru: A History of the Chinese Coolie in Peru, 1849–1874* (Westport, CT: Greenwood Press, 1970); S. Sonoda, *Nanboku Amerika kamin to Kindai Chūgoku: Jyūkyū seiki Transnashonaru maigrēshon* (Overseas Chinese in the Americas

and Modern China: Transnational Migration in the Nineteenth Century) (Tokyo: Tokyo Daigaku Shuppankai, 2009)

6. Robertson to Bonham, 15 April 1853, no. 28, Great Britain Foreign Office, Embassy, and Consular Archives, China: Amoy, National Archives of United Kingdom, Kew, London (hereafter NAUK, FO 663), 663/10.

7. P. C. Campbell, *Chinese Coolie Emigration to Countries within the British Empire* (London: Frank Cass & Co. Ltd, 1923), pp. 27–9.

8. 'Correspondence with the Superintendent of British Trade in China, upon the Subject of Emigration from that Country', 25 August 1852, Encl. no. 1 in no. 8, Elmslie to Bowring, *Area Studies Series, British Parliamentary Papers, China*, 42 vols (Shannon: Irish University Press, 1972) (hereafter *BPP*), vol. 3, p. 8 (18).

9. Note by Dr Winchester, 26 August 1852, Encl. no. 3 in no. 127, NAUK, FO 663/9.

10. Ozawa, '1852 nen Amoi Bōdō nit suite', p. 54.

11. Yen, *Coolies and Mandarins*, pp. 41–7.

12. Wang, *The Organization of Chinese Emigration 1848–1888*, pp. 5–6, 119–20.

13. 'Memorial of Wu Wenrong on September 21st in the Nineteenth Year of the Daoguang Era', in Zhongguo diyi lishi danganguan (ed.), *Yapian zhanzheng dangan shiliao*, 7 vols (The Collection of the Archives on the Opium War) (Tianjin: Tianjin guji chubanshe, 1992), vol. 1, pp. 714–5.

14. Note by Dr Winchester, 26 August 1852, Encl. no. 3 in no. 127, NAUK, FO 663/9.

15. E. C. Arensmeyer, 'British Merchant Enterprise and the Chinese Coolie Labour Trade 1850–1874' (PhD dissertation, University of Hawaii, 1979), pp. 83, 98.

16. Yen, *Coolies and Mandarins*, pp. 37–41.

17. E. Murakami, *Umi no Kindai Chūgoku: Fukkenjin no katsud to Igirisu/Shinchō* (Maritime History of Modern China: Local Fujian Actors and British and Chinese Empires) (Nagoya: Nagoya Daigaku Shuppankai, 2013), pp. 44–9.

18. Murakami, *Umi no Kindai Chūgoku*, pp. 61–88, 103–34.

19. J. K. Fairbank, *Trade and Diplomacy on the China Coast: The Opening of the Treaty Ports, 1842–1854* (Cambridge, MA: Harvard University Press, 1953); F. Wakeman, Jr, *Strangers at the Gate: Social Disorder in South China, 1839–1861* (Berkeley and Los Angeles, CA: University of California Press, 1966); T. Okamoto, *Kindai Chūgoku to Kaikan* (China and the Maritime Customs System in Modern Times) (Nagoya: Nagoya Daigaku Shuppankai, 1999); Murakami, *Umi no Kindai Chūgoku*, pp. 137–41.

20. M. H. Lin, *China Upside Down: Currency, Society, and Ideologies, 1808–1856* (Cambridge, MA: Harvard University Asia Centre, 2006), pp. 72–142.

21. Wang, *The Organization of Chinese Emigration 1848–1888*, p. 20; Yen, *Coolies and Mandarins*, p. 37.

22. According to the confessions of the twenty-five brokers arrested in Huangpu near Guangzhou in November 1859, all were poor, some were single, and most were between twenty-four and forty years of age. The occupations given were seamen, etc., and eight had already lost their fathers. Wang, *The Organization of Chinese Emigration 1848–1888*, pp. 53–4; Parkes to Hammond, 13 November 1859, *Correspondence Respecting Emigration from Canton*, Encl. 20 in no. 6, *BPP*, vol. 4, pp. 32–40 (136–43).

23. Morrison to Bruce, 22 June 1859, no. 14, Great Britain Foreign Office, Embassy, and Consular Archives, China: Correspondence Series I, National Archives of United Kingdom, Kew, London (hereafter NAUK, FO 228), 228/265.

24. Note by Dr Winchester, 26 August 1852, Encl. no. 3 in no. 127, NAUK, FO 663/9.

25. Kennedy, K. to Kimberley, 7 June 1872, Encl. in no. 1, *Measures Taken to Prevent the Fitting Out of the Ships at Hong Kong for the Macao Coolie Trade. A Correct Statement of the Wicked Practice of Decoying and Kidnapping, Respectfully Laid Before his Excellency, BPP*, vol. 4, pp. 1–2 (313–4).
26. Layton to Davis, 25 February 1847, Encl. 6 in no. 23, NAUK, FO 228/70.
27. Note by Dr Winchester, 26 August 1852, Encl. no. 3 in no. 127, NAUK, FO 663/9; Backhouse to Bowring, 23 September 1852, Encl. 2 in no. 48, NAUK, FO 228/141.
28. Note by Dr Winchester, 26 August1852, Encl. no. 3 in no. 127, NAUK, FO 663/9; Consul-General Crawford to Viscount Palmerston, Havana, 4 August 1847, *Correspondence on the Slave Trade with Foreign Powers*, 1847–8, *BPP*, Command Papers (976), p. 43.
29. *Emigration*, Encl. no. 8 in no.14, *Minutes of Evidence Taken at a Court of Inquiry Held at Amoy to Investigate the Causes of the Late Riots, and into the Manner in which Coolie Emigration Has Been Lately Carried on at That Port, BPP*, vol. 3, pp. 62–3 (74–5).
30. Lin, *China Upside Down*, pp. 86–7, 121–4.
31. Chinese Enclosure, proclamation issued by the gentries and merchants of Amoy, FO 228/903.
32. Swinhoe to Alcock, 19 May 1866, Encl. 2 in no. 4, NAUK, FO 228/405.
33. Swinhoe to Alcock, 19 May 1866, Encl. 2 in no. 4, NAUK, FO 228/405.
34. This is inconsistent with the traditional Chinese principle of 'live together and share property' (*tongju gongcai*). Under this principle, the income as a migrant worker was to be paid to the household (S. Shiga, *Chūgoku Kazokuhō no Genri* (Principles of Chinese Family Law) (Tokyo: Sōbunsha, 1967), pp. 68–73).
35. Layton to Bonham, 19 November 1849, no. 37, NAUK, FO 228/98.
36. Layton to Davis, 25 February 1847, no. 23, NAUK, FO 228/70.
37. Consul-General Crawford to Viscount Palmerston, Havana, 4 August 1847, *Correspondence on the Slave Trade with Foreign Powers*, 1847–1848, *BPP*, Command Papers (976), p. 43.
38. R. L. Irick, *Ch'ing Policy toward the Coolie Trade 1847–1878* (Taipei: Chinese Materials Centre, 1982), pp. 27–8.
39. Kennedy, K., to Kimberley, 7 June 1872, Encl. in no. 1, *Measures Taken to Prevent the Fitting out of the Ships at Hong Kong for the Macao Coolie Trade, BPP*, vol. 4, p. 3 (315).
40. Wang, *The Organization of Chinese Emigration 1848–1888*, pp. 56–64.
41. Morrison to Bowring, June 2, 1858, Encl. 2 in no. 46, NAUK, FO 228/251.
42. In the case of those who were kidnapped by brokers around Guangzhou, most were manual laborers who moved to the city from agricultural villages (M. June, 'Socioeconomic Origin of Emigration: Guangdong to California, 1850–1882', *Modern China*, 5:4 (1979), pp. 479–81).
43. Letter from Chen, the magistrate of Tongan county to the British consul in June in the ninth year of the Xianfeng era, NAUK, FO 663/65.
44. Sub-prefect Tao to British consul, 21 August 1859, NAUK, FO 663/65.
45. Sub-prefect Li to British consul, 26 April 1857, NAUK, FO 663/65.
46. Chinese Enclosure, proclamation issued by the gentries and merchants of Amoy, NAUK, FO 228/903.
47. Harvey to Bowring, Encl. no. 7 in no. 14, *Emigration, BPP*, vol. 3, p. 41 (53).
48. Petition of Chen Sha, NAUK, FO 228/903.
49. Ozawa, '1852 nen Amoi Bōdō nit suite'; Ng, 'The Amoy Riot of 1852', pp. 423–40.
50. Murakami, *Umi no Kindai Chūgoku*, pp. 275–82.

51. Campbell, *Chinese Coolie Emigration to Countries within the British Empire*, pp. 117–8.
52. Irick, *Ch'ing Policy toward the Coolie Trade*, pp. 89–140.
53. Note by Dr Winchester, 26 August 1852, Encl. no. 3 in no. 127, NAUK, FO 663/9.
54. W. L. Blyth, 'Historical Sketch of Chinese Labour in Malaya', *Journal of the Malayan Branch of the Royal Asiatic Society*, 20 (1947), pp. 71–2.
55. Minutes of a meeting held on board the US Ship *Levant* on 5 July 1856, *American Diplomatic and Public Papers: The United States and China Series 1. The Treaty System and the Taiping Rebellion, 1842–1860* (Wilmington, DE: Scholarly Resources Inc., 1973), vol. 17, p. 42.
56. Morrison to Bowring, 2 June 1858, no. 46, NAUK, FO 228/251.
57. Gingell to Bruce, 4 December 1860, no. 87, NAUK, FO 228/285.
58. Wang, *The Organization of Chinese Emigration 1848–1888*, p. 58.
59. Backhouse to Bowring, 11 January 1853, no. 5, NAUK, FO 228/155.
60. Gingell to Bruce, 4 December 1860, no. 87, NAUK, FO 228/285.
61. Note by Dr Winchester, 26 August 1852, Encl. no. 3 in no. 127, NAUK, FO 663/9.
62. Drawing on Maritime Customs statistics of the number of emigrants: see K. Fujimura, 'Kanryū teki rōdō ijū no shakai teki jōken' ('The Social Condition of the Circumfluent Migration of Laborers'), in M. Tomioka and H. Nakamura (eds), *Kindai sekai no rekishizō* (Historical Image of the Modern World) (Tokyo: Sekai shoin, 1995), pp. 129–72 and K. Sugihara, *Ajialan bōeki no kēsē to kōzō* (Patterns and Development of Intra-Asian Trade) (Tokyo: Mineruva Shobō, 1996).
63. Layton to Davis, 1847, no. 87, NAUK, FO 228/71; *China Mail*, 7 January 1847.
64. Gingell to Bruce, 4 December 1860, no. 87, NAUK, FO 228/285.
65. Swinhoe to Alcock, 1 August 1867, no. 24, NAUK, FO 228/427.
66. Arensmeyer, 'British Merchant Enterprise and the Chinese Coolie Labour Trade', pp. 54–5.
67. Encl. in Alcock to Swinhoe, 10 August 1867, no. 26, NAUK, FO 228/427.
68. For example, in 1877, there were 19,840 emigrants from Amoy, of whom British ships carried 16,266. Alabaster to Fraser, 2 April 1878, Encl. no. 2 in no. 17, NAUK, FO 228/606.
69. Gile to Wade, 12 March 1881, no. 10, NAUK, FO 228/671; Alabaster to Wade, 18 April 1879, Encl. in no. 13, NAUK, FO 228/623.
70. The conditions of Chinese laborers in Southeast Asia improved after the 1930s (Sugihara, *Ajialan bōeki no kēsē to kōzō*, pp. 311–2).

11 Bok-rae, 'Debt Slaves in Old Korea'

1. 'The family in historical perspective', *Magnus Hirschfeld Archive for Sexology*, at http://www2.huberlin.de/sexology/ATLAS_EN/html/the_family_in_historical_persp.html [accessed 13 August 2011].
2. Jung Y.-s., *Chosun Story* [in Korean], 2 vols (Seoul: Chongnyon-sa Publishing Co., 2001), vol. 2, p. 21.
3. A Korean name consists of a family name followed by a given name. Thus, his family name is Jong and his given name is Il-jae.
4. Korean tradition dictated that the eldest son must live with and support his parents: Jung, *Chosun Story*, vol. 2, pp. 21–2.
5. Koguryo was an ancient Korean kingdom located in the northern and central parts of the Korean Peninsula, southern Manchuria and southern Russian Maritime province.

Koguryo was one of the Three Kingdoms of Korea which flourished for much of the first millennium AD, along with Baekje and Silla.

6. 'Koguryo History', *Northern History 94* [in Chinese].

7. 'Silla History', *New Tang History* [in Chinese].

8. J. B. Palais, *Confucian Statecraft and Korean Institutions* (Seattle, WA: Washington University Press, 1996), p. 41.

9. Yi Y.-h. and Yang D.-h., 'A Comparison between the *Nobi* System in Chosun Korea and Black Slavery in Antebellum U.S.' [in Korean], *Kyongjenonjip*, 37:2 (1998), pp. 293–336.

10. Chi S.-j., *A Study of the* Nobi *in Fifeenth- to Sixteenth-Century Korea* [in Korean] (Seoul: Ilchokak, 1995), pp. 1–2.

11. *Annals of King Tae-jo* 2, November, the first year of King Tae-jo, Gapojo.

12. *Annals of King Jong-jo* 1, June, the first year of King Jong-jo, Gapinjo.

13. *Annals of King Sung-jong* 57, July, the sixth year of King Sung-jong, Shinhaejo.

14. A key figure of the Neo-Confucian literati, he established the Yeongnam School and set up the Dosan Seowon, a private Confucian academy.

15. Jung, *Chosun Story*, vol. 2, p. 41.

16. Keryong was his given name; as a *nobi*, he could not have a family name.

17. Jung, *Chosun Story*, vol. 2, p. 23.

18. *Contubernium* means literally 'dwelling together', often used to refer to, for instance, soldiers or animals, but especially to refer to quasi-marital unions between slaves or between slaves and free persons. Since a slave lacked most legal rights, a *contubernium* was not a legal marriage.

19. An G.-j., *The History of Daily Life in the Chosun Period* [in Korean], 2 vols (Seoul: Sakyejol Publishing Co. 2000), vol. 2, pp. 140–1.

20. Palais, *Confucian Statecraft and Korean Institutions*, p. 225.

21. Yi U-y and Cha M.-s., 'The Structure of *Nobi* Price and its Level in the Late Chosun Period 1678–1889' [in Korean], *Economics Research*, 58:4 (2010), p. 110.

22. Jung, *Chosun Story*, vol. 2, p. 42.

23. These slaves were called *seiko* (living mouths).

24. Korea, Japan and Korea all used the same Chinese characters, '奴婢', to designate their quasi-indigenous slavery systems: the *nobi* system in Korean, the *nuhi* system in Japanese and the *nubi* system in Chinese.

25. *Hwang-sung Newspaper*, 22 May 1905.

26. An, *The History of Daily Life in the Chosun Period*, vol. 2, p. 185.

27. *Daehan Daily Newspaper*, 27 September, 1898.

28. An, *The History of Daily Life in the Chosun Period*, vol. 2, pp. 184–5. See also F. C. Ridel, *Relation de la captivité & de la délivrance de Mgr Ridel* (Paris and Lyon: Librairie Victor Lecoffre, 1879).

12 Matsui, 'The Debt-Servitude of Prostitutes in Japan during the Edo Period, 1600–1868'

1. A comprehensive study of human trafficking in Japan is H. Maki, *Kinsei Nihon no jinshin baibai no keifu* (Studies on Human Trafficking in Early Modern Japan) (Tokyo: Soubunsha, 1970), as well as the popular version of this work, H. Maki, *Jinshin Baibai* (Human Trafficking) (Tokyo: Iwanami shoten, 1971). This paper is greatly indebted to his work.

2. Maki, *Kinsei Nihon no jinshin baibai no keifu*, pp. 23–4.

3. Ibid., p. 26.
4. Isogai F., *Nihon chūsei doreisei ron* (Studies on Slavery in Medieval Japan) (Tokyo: Aze-kura shobō, 2007), section 3.
5. Ibid., p. 562.
6. Ibid., pp. 542–9, K. Takahashi, 'Iminzoku no jinshin baibai –hito no ryūtsū' ('The Human Trafficking of Foreigners: The Circulation of Human Beings'), in *Ajia no nakano nihonshi. 2, Kaijō no michi* (A New History of Japan in Asia 2: Sea Routes in Premodern History) (Tokyo: Tōkyō daigaku shuppankai, 1992), pp. 225–44, 233–9.
7. Isogai, *Nihon chūsei doreisei ron*, pp. 542–3
8. K. Shimojū, 'Miuri houkou to josei' ('Women and Human Trafficking Disguised as Indentured Servitude'), in Y. Yabuta and K. Yanagiya (eds), *Edo no hito to mibun. 4, Mibun no naka no josei* (People and the Status System in the Edo Period 4: Women in the Status System) (Tokyo: Yoshikawa kōbunkan, 2010), pp. 103–6.
9. The concept of 'selling' in the pre-modern period was not the same as that of the present day. In the medieval period, the authorities could declare any change in ownership in the past null and void. In the Edo period, the custom of fixed-term sales was used for both human beings and land (see Maki, *Kinsei Nihon no jinshin baibai no keifu*, pp. 47–54).
10. Ibid., p. 91–3.
11. There was little stigma against prostitutes in Japanese society. When a prostitute finished the term of her apprenticeship, it would not be difficult for her to marry an ordinary man; moreover, she could leave the brothel within her term if a man paid her debt.
12. H. Sone, *Shōfu to Kinsei shakai* (Prostitutes in the Society of Early Modern Japan) (Tokyo: Yoshikawa kōbunkan, 2003), pp. 14–17, termed this situation the 'popularized stage' of prostitution in Japan..
13. There were different terms for the prostitutes of licensed districts, such as *keisei, oiran* and *tayū*, which differed with place, period and rank. In this paper, I use the word *yūjo* only for the prostitutes of the licensed quarters and 'prostitutes' as a general term including other 'non-licensed' women. I have to stress that the famous word *geisha* did not origi-nally denote a prostitute; *geisha* literally means 'performer', and they made money from their singing, dancing and playing the *shamisen*.
14. On these prostitutes who worked near major routes, see M. Usami, *Shukuba to meshi-mori onna* (Rice-Serving Girls in the Post-Station Towns) (Tokyo: Dōseisha, 2000).
15. There are a number of studies dealing with the licensed quarters, especially the Yoshi-wara, mainly concerned with popular customs and literature. For an account in English, see C. Segawa Seigle, *Yoshiwara: The Glittering World of the Japanese Courtesan* (Hono-lulu, HI: University of Hawaii Press, 1993).
16. Maki, *Kinsei Nihon no jinshin baibai no keifu*, pp. 295–6.
17. Ibid., pp. 405–6.
18. Ibid., pp. 288–93
19. There are quite a few studies on Japanese foreign relations in the Edo period. For an account in English, see R. P. Toby, *State and Diplomacy in Early Modern Japan: Asia in the Development of the Tokugawa Bakufu* (Princeton, NJ: Princeton University Press, 1984), M. Kanai and E. Katō (eds), *Foreign Relations of Tokugawa Japan: Sakoku Recon-sidered* (Acta Asiatica 67) (Tokyo: Toho Gakkai, 1994) and L. Blussé, W. Remmelink and I. Smits (eds), *Bridging the Divide: 1600–2000, 400 Years, the Netherlands–Japan* (Leiden and Utrecht: Hotei and Teleac/NOT, 2000).
20. Nagasaki kenshi hensan iinkai (ed.), *Nagasaki kenshi: Taigai koushou hen* (The History of the Nagasaki Prefecture: Its Relationship with the Outside World) (Tokyo: Yoshi-kawa kōbunkan, 1986), pp. 380–2.

21. A comprehensive study of the prostitutes in Nagasaki is J. Koga, *Maruyama yūjo to tōkōmōjin* (Prostitutes and Foreigners in Maruyama) (Nagasaki: Nagasaki bunkensha, 1969). See also Y. Miyamoto, 'Maruyama yūjo no seikatsu –'Nagasaki bugyōsho hanketsu kiroku *Hanka chō*' wo chūshin to shite' ('The Lives of Consorts in Maruyama from the Criminal Judgment Book of the Magistrate Office in Nagasaki'), *Komazawa Shigaku*, 31 (1984), pp. 19–46 and Y. Miyamoto, 'Maruyama yūjo *Hanka chō* –Tōkōmōjin tono kakawari wo chushin to shite' ('Legal Reports on Prostitutes in Maruyama: With a Focus on their Relationships with Foreigners'), in Nishiyama Matsunosuke sensei koki kinennkai (ed.), *Edo no geinou to bunka* (Culture and Entertainment in Edo) (Tokyo: Yoshikawa kōbunkan, 1985), pp. 209–44. For complete references, see R. H. Hesselink, 'The Two Faces of Nagasaki: The World of the Suwa Festival Screen', *Monumenta Nipponica*, 59:2 (2004), pp. 170–222.

22. *Nagasaki shichū meisaichō* (A Detailed Guidebook of the City of Nagasaki of the 18th Century), Nagasaki Museum of History and Culture, Nagasaki, no. 13-82-2-1.

23. For figures see Koga, *Maruyama yūjo to tōkōmōjin*, p. 116. See also Hesselink, 'The Two Faces of Nagasaki', pp. 202–10.

24. 'Yoriai-machi shoji kakiage hikaechō' ('Documents of Yoriai-machi'), in Harada T. et al. (ed.), *Nihon toshi seikatsu siryō shūsei: Minato-machi hen I & II* (A Compilation of the Documents on City Life in Early Modern Japan: The Port City vols I & II), 2 vols (Tokyo: Gakushū kenkyūsha, 1975–6), vol. 1, pp. 286, 288–9

25. It is said that there were more than ten ranks from *tayū* to the lowest ranked *tsubone-jorō* in the Yoshiwara (T. Ono, *Yoshiwara to Shimabara* (Famous Licensed Quarters Yoshiwara and Shimabara) (Tokyo: Kyōiku sha, 1987)). See also Segawa Seigle, *Yoshiwara*.

26. Miyamoto, 'Maruyama yūjo *Hanka chō* –Tōkōmōjin tono kakawari wo chushin to shite', pp. 236–40.

27. See Toby, *State and Diplomacy in Early Modern Japan* and Blussé, Remmelink and Smits, *Bridging the Divide*.

28. Y. Matsui, 'The Legal Position of Foreigners in Nagasaki during the Edo Period', in M. Haneda (ed.), *Asian Port Cities 1600–1800: Local and Foreign Cultural Interactions* (Singapore and Kyoto: NUS Press and Kyoto University Press, 2009), pp. 26–7. This was because they led an existence apart from that of normal households. Women in Japanese society of the Edo period were conceptualized in terms of their relationship to the male head of their household: as his wife, his concubine with the position of servant, or his daughter. To have a relationship with a male without a household, i.e. a foreigner, was only possible for prostitutes who did not belong to any specific man, or who belonged to a provisional household, namely her brothel.

29. Daghregister des Comptoirs Nangasacky, Nederlandse Factorij Japan/Deshima Archive, Nationaal Archief, the Hague, NFJ no. 62 (Historiographical Institute University of Tokyo (ed.), *Nihon kankei kaigai shiryō Oranda shōkanchō nikki* (Diaries of the Heads of the Dutch Factory in Hirado and Deshima) (Tokyo: Tōkyō daigaku shuppankai, 2007), vol. 11, p. 166.

30. Matsui, 'The Legal Position of Foreigners in Nagasaki during the Edo Period', pp. 33–5.

31. Miyamoto, 'Maruyama yūjo *Hanka chō* –Tōkōmōjin tono kakawari wo chushin to shite', pp. 234–40.

32. Q. Tang, *Umi wo koeta tsuyagoto –Nicchū bunka kouryū shi* (Romances Across the Sea: Cultural Intercourse between Japan and China) (Tokyo: Shinyōsha, 2005), pp. 35–6.

33. Y. Matsui, 'Jendā kara miru kinsei nihon no taigai kankei' ('The Foreign Relations of Early Modern Japan, from the Perspective of Gender'), in Y. Arano, M. Ishii and S. Murai (eds), *Nihon no taigai kannkei 6: Kinsei teki sekai no seijuku* (Japanese Foreign Relations

6: The Maturity of the Early Modern Japanese System) (Tokyo: Yoshikawa kōbunkan, 2010), p. 110.

34. *Ai sadame mousu kakimono no koto* (A Sample of the Indenture Contract of Yūjo in the Eighteenth Century), Nagasaki Museum of History and Culture, Nagasaki, Documents of the Fuji Family, no. 14–1065.

35. This statement was intended to prove that the young woman was not a hidden Christian.

36. Maki, *Kinsei Nihon no jinshin baibai no keifu*, pp. 472–7.

37. Ibid., pp. 466–87, S. Honma, *Boueki toshi Nagasaki no kenkyū* (Studies on the Trading City of Nagasaki) (Fukuoka: Kyūshū daigaku shuppankai, 2009), pp. 58–9.

38. Honma, *Boueki toshi Nagasaki no kenkyū*, pp. 51–103.

39. Matsui, 'Jendā kara miru kinsei nihon no taigai kankei', pp. 68–71.

40. About the new licensed quarters, see T. Yoshida, 'Bakumatsu gaikou shi jou ni okeru gaijin kyūsoku jo oyobi baijo settai no mondai' ('A Study on Rest Houses for Foreigners and Prostitutions in the Last Days of the *Bakufu* Regime'), *Kokushigaku*, 32 (1937), pp. 41–71; 35 (1938), pp. 19–37; 36 (1939), pp. 9–42; 37 (1939), pp. 15–46.

41. About the Russian establishment and syphilis, see C. Miyazaki, 'Nihon saisho no baidoku kensa to roshia kantai –bakumatsu no Nagasaki kou ni okeru roshia mura keisei no tancho' ('The First Tests of Syphilis in Japan and the Russian Fleet: The Establishment of the 'Russian Village' in the Last Days of the *Bakufu* Regime'), in M. Fukuda and N. Suzuki (eds), *Nihon baidokushi no kenkyu: Iryou, Shakai, kokka* (Historical Studies on Syphilis in Japan: The Medical, Social and National Perspective) (Kyoto: Shibunkaku shuppan, 2005), pp. 177–85.

42. Koga, *Maruyama yūjo to tōkōmōjin*, pp. 244–50

43. Ibid., p. 266.

44. Y. Abe, 'Meiji 5nen Inoue Kaoru no yūjo kaihou kengi no kousatsu – Kindai koushousei eno shikou' ('A Study of Kaoru Inoue's Proposal for the Emancipation of "Yūjo" in 1872'), *Shiryū*, 36 (1996), p. 76.

45. D. Botsman, 'Freedom without Slavery? The Case of the Maria Luz, and the Question of Emancipation in Nineteenth Century Japan', in Urban-Culture Research Center (ed.), *Searching for a Comparative Urban Theory: Compilation of Papers and Seminar Proceedings* (Osaka: Osaka City University, 2007), p. 137.

46. There are many accounts of the incident of the Maria Luz, such as Maki, *Kinsei Nihon no jinshin baibai no keifu*. For recent important studies, see S. Obinata, *Nihon kindai kokka no seiritsu to keisatsu* (The Establishment of the Modern Nation and the Police Force in Japan) (Tokyo: Azekura shobō, 1992), pp. 279–305; Abe, 'Meiji 5nen Inoue Kaoru no yūjo kaihou kengi no kousatsu – Kindai koushousei eno shikou'; Y. Abe, 'Meiji 5nen Yokohama ni okeru kashizashiki sei –Kindai koushousei no seiritsu' ('The Formation of the *Kashizashiki* System of Yokohama in 1872'), *Shiryū*, 37 (1997), pp. 15–40; T. Morita, *Kaikoku to chigai houken: Ryouji saiban ken no unyō to maria rusu gou jiken* (The Opening Up of Japan and Extraterritoriality: Consular Jurisdiction in the Case of the Ship Maria Luz) (Tokyo: Yoshikawa kōbunkan, 2005). For an English study, see Botsman, 'Freedom without Slavery?'

47. A. Onosawa, *Kindai nihon shakai to koushou seido –Minshū shi to kokusai kankei shi no shiten kara* (The Licensed Prostitution System in Modern Japanese Society: From the Perspective of the Populace and International Relations) (Tokyo: Yoshikawa kōbunkan, 2010), pp. 1–6.

48. Sone, *Shōfu to Kinsei shakai*, pp. 36–9

INDEX

For Product Safety Concerns and Information please contact our EU
representative GPSR@taylorandfrancis.com
Taylor & Francis Verlag GmbH, Kaufingerstraße 24, 80331 München, Germany

www.ingramcontent.com/pod-product-compliance
Ingram Content Group UK Ltd.
Pitfield, Milton Keynes, MK11 3LW, UK
UKHW021615240425
457818UK00018B/575